THE
MAMMALS OF INDIA

THE MAMMALS OF INDIA;

A

Natural History

OF ALL

THE ANIMALS KNOWN TO INHABIT CONTINENTAL INDIA.

BY

T. C. JERDON

GYAN

Published by

Gyan Publishing House
5, Ansari Road
Daryaganj, New Delhi-110002
Phone: 011-47034999, 9811692060
E-mail: books@gyanbooks.com

Distribution Network
gyanbooks.com
India, USA, Canada, UK, Australia, France

ISBN: 978-81-212-8324-3 (PB)
First Published, 1867

2nd Impression 2023

Printed at: Gyan Press, Delhi.

THE MAMMALS OF INDIA
Author: T. C. JERDON

THE
MAMMALS OF INDIA;

A

Natural History

OF ALL

THE ANIMALS KNOWN TO INHABIT CONTINENTAL INDIA.

BY

T. C. JERDON,

SURGEON MAJOR, MADRAS ARMY; "AUTHOR OF THE BIRDS OF INDIA," ETC.

In One Volume.

ROORKEE:

PRINTED FOR THE AUTHOR BY THE THOMASON COLLEGE PRESS.

1867.

PREFACE.

THE present work is the second of the series of Manuals of the Vertebrata of India. The greater portion of it has been printed for above a twelvemonth, but the publication was delayed in the hopes of getting some additional information to be inserted in the Appendix.

The author trusts that the present Manual will be found equally useful as that on the Birds of India, and he knows that many sportsmen and observers have been anxiously awaiting its appearance. He has been able to give considerable information on the habitat and geographical distribution of many of the animals which was previously but little known. The portion of the work on the Micro-Mammalia of India is still confessedly very imperfect, and contributions of good specimens (in spirits) of Bats, Shrews, Rats and Mice, from all parts of the country, but especially from the hills, sent either to the Museum at Calcutta, or to the British Museum, will be highly acceptable.

The author trusts that the imperfections of the present publication will be overlooked in consideration of the undoubted value of the work to future observers, who it is hoped will be numerous, and by whose means a more complete natural history of the Mammals of India may hereafter be compiled.

The Volume on Reptiles will, the author trusts, appear very shortly.

LIST OF CONTENTS.

INTRODUCTION.

THE Animal Kingdom was divided by Cuvier into four great divisions or sub-kingdoms—Vertebrata, Mollusca, Articulata and Radiata. The last of these has been greatly divided of late, and the limits of two of the others been slightly altered. Vertebrata are essentially distinguished from the others by the possession of an internal osseous frame or skeleton, enclosing a distinct brain and spinal cord. They never have more than four limbs; the mouth consists of two jaws placed vertically, the blood is red, and they have distinct organs of vision, hearing, taste and smell.

Vertebrate animals comprise four distinct classes, some of which are cold blooded, *i. e.*, with blood nearly the temperature of the surrounding medium, Fishes and Reptiles; whilst the others are warm blooded, Birds and Mammals. The former have been already treated of in this series.

Mammals are warm-blooded viviparous animals, and are distinguished from Birds, as well as from the other vertebrated animals, by the possession of mammary glands, secreting a nutritious fluid called milk, for the nourishment of their young, and terminating outwardly in all (except one or two) by teats. They are also distinguished by a covering of hair, entire or partial. Whales appear to be exceptional; but even in these the fœtus has some tufts of hair.

The lungs are free and are separated from the abdominal viscera by a muscular partition called the Diaphragm, which is also one of the chief agents for inspiration. Most animals have four limbs, hence the old term Quadruped, which, on account of its non-applicability to the Cetaceæ, has properly been allowed to become obsolete.

Mammals, says Cuvier, require to be placed first, because they enjoy the most numerous faculties, the most delicate sensations, the most varied powers of motion. Their organization is more differentiated than in any other Vertebrates, and they have a more perfect combination of powers. They are inferior to Birds in muscular movement, their respiration being less in amount, and the circulation less rapid, on which account their demand for food is not so constant.

The generality of them are terrestrial, some inhabit trees, others burrow in the ground, whilst a few can fly, and some are perfectly aquatic. With such differences in habit we of course find corresponding differences in external structure. The anterior extremities in Bats are lengthened to support the flying membrane, whilst in Whales they are shortened and fin-like, and the terminal points of the phalanges vary from sharp raptorial claws, to the solid hoof of the Horse, or the flat pad of the Camel and Elephant. On these characters, combined with those of teeth, are founded the different orders of Mammals.

The form of the body varies, but we can generally distinguish the head, neck and trunk, and most have caudal appendages. The head varies greatly in its form and proportions, as does the ear, and from these also characters of more or less importance are drawn; but the teeth, in form, number, differences, and relative position, afford the most varied, prominent, and decisive characters, as well for the Orders of Mammals as for genera, and even sometimes species, and require more lengthened notice than any other point in the external anatomy of Mammals.

Teeth being used by Mammals both to seize and collect food, and to reduce it to a fit state for swallowing, their form furnishes a clue to the instincts and habits of the animal. They are placed in a single series along the edge of the upper and lower jaw bones, so as to oppose each other, and are always fixed in cavities called sockets or alveoli, an arrangement which elsewhere is only found in the Crocodiles among Reptiles.

Ivory or Dentine, forms the sole material of some simple teeth, as in some Cetacea, and in the tusk of the Elephant; but in most teeth another substance of crystalline texture and extremely hard, called *enamel*, coats the tooth, and penetrates into it in some; whilst in a few a third substance is added, called *crusta petrosa*, or cement.

A tooth consists of two parts, a *crown*, or external portion, and a root, which is fixed in the socket. The root is either real or fictitious, in the latter case being merely a continuation of the crown, and continuing to grow for an indefinite period, as in the tusk of the Elephant, and the quasi-incisors of Rodents. Certain teeth are deciduous, and fall or are pushed out (after a longer or shorter period) by their successors. Others are permanent, and from their first appearance are never succeeded by others. The first are often called milk-teeth, but in some animals they are shed before birth, and in others not till a late period of life. They are never (or very rarely) renewed more than once, in this differing essentially from the teeth of Reptiles and Fishes, which are being continually shed and renewed.

Teeth vary much in number among Mammals, and are entirely wanting in a very few. In the more perfect animals they are of four kinds, viz., Incisors, Canines, Præmolars or false molars, and Molars. Incisors are situated in the front of each jaw, in the intermaxillary bones, and corresponding portion of the lower jaw. They never exceed six above and six below, except in Marsupial animals. They are sometimes wanting in the upper jaw, as in Ruminating animals, and entirely in Ant-eaters and Armadillos. They vary much in form and size, and in many Bats are unequal in number in the upper and lower jaws.

The Canine teeth are one on each side of the incisors, both above and below, and are also fixed in the intermaxillary bone. They usually, except in Man and one or two others, succeed the incisors after more or less interval. They are absent in several animals, especially among the Ruminants, but are present in some of that order. In some they occur only in the males, in others they are larger in that sex, and in a few are very largely developed. The præmolars are those next the canines, and like them and the incisors, are deciduous, and succeeded by others. They vary greatly in form and size, being unicuspid in some, bicuspid in others. They are not found amongst Rodents, but in these animals they are present in the fœtal state, and are either shed before birth, or very shortly after. The last of the præmolars is called the flesh-tooth, or carnassier, or scissor-tooth, as the upper one acts on the lower one like a pair of scissors. It is greatly developed in the Cat tribe.

The true molars never exceed three in number on each side, above and below, and always end in two, three, or even four roots or fangs, sometimes considerably divergent from each other. They vary much in form and size, and are present in all Mammals except a few Ant-eaters, Whales, and the curious Duck-billed *Platypus*. They have four tubercles in most Monkeys, two sharp-pointed tubercles in Shrews and other Insectivorous animals; are three-pointed in some, and conical or flat in others. They are more or less numerous according to the herbivorous or carnivorous nature of the animal, there being only one on each side in the Feline tribe.

In the Elephant there is only one molar on each side, above and below, and this forms a seeming exception to the non-renewal of of these teeth, for as it gets worn away another is developed posteriorly, and gradually pushes the other out, so that there are sometimes two on one side at a time, but never more. The typical number of teeth is considered to be 44, and this number is never exceeded except in the fish-like Cetacea, and a few others of reptilian affinities. These teeth are arranged thus: Incisors $\frac{3-3}{3-3}$ = 12; Canines $\frac{1-1}{1-1}$ = 4; Præmolars $\frac{4-4}{4-4}$ = 16; Molars $\frac{3-3}{3-3}$ = 12.

The mouth of Mammals is surrounded by fleshy lips, more or less protusile, and the cheeks in some form pouches for the reception of food taken hurriedly.

The extremities vary more than in Birds, in length, form and structure, as noticed previously. The nails or claws are useful guides to assist in classifying Mammals. In some they are blunt and terminal as in Monkeys; in others sharp as in Shrews; much curved, powerful, sharp and retractile in Cats; long and strong, and well adopted for digging (fossorial), as in the Scaly Ant-eaters and Bears. In the herbivorous animals they are solid as in the Horse, hoofed or ending in two blunt horny toes, as in Ruminants, and some Pachyderms, or blunt and almost entirely enclosed, as in the Elephant and Camel.

The temperature of Mammals being lower than that of Birds, less effectual means are required of preserving the internal heat, and, accordingly, we find them provided with a covering more or less dense of hair, or fur. In Monkeys and Bats there is only one kind of hair, in most other animals there are both hair and wool, and these vary in amount in different animals. Wool differs from hair in having a serrated edge as seen under the microscope, and on this depends the quality of felting. It is generally more abundant in animals living in cold countries, and is highly developed in all the Himalayan Mammals. Hairs are of two kinds as regards their growth. One kind grows continually and is never shed, as the mane of the Horse. The second kind, of which is the fur of most animals, grows to its full extent, and is shed and renewed periodically. This causes a very considerable change in the general hue of many animals, as well as in the amount of fur, so that the winter and summer vestures are exceedingly dissimilar.

A few animals have some of the hairs thick and strong (bristles), and others have them flat and somewhat rigid, as in certain Rats. Spines are found on Hedgehogs and Porcupines; and a very few Mammals are clad with scales or horny plates, as the Scaly Anteaters and Armadillos. These spines and scales are all made up of agglutinated hairs. Many Ruminants are adorned with horny appendages on their heads, some of which are of the nature of a horny sheath covering an internal bony cone; others have no internal nucleus and are renewed yearly. The former kind of horn is, like the spines mentioned above, formed of agglutinated hairs. The latter kind of horns partakes more of the nature of bone.

In many animals the hairs are not uniformly colored, but are colored differently at the base and the tip, and in some tribes are ringed with different colors. The wearing down of these hairs causes a difference in the external hue of such animals.

In the Cetacea, which have no hair, the warmth of the body is retained by a thick coating of fat or blubber.

The bones of Mammals are distinguished from those of Birds by the absence of air-cells, except in some of the cranial bones, and these do not communicate with the lungs. Most of them are solid, or if hollow are filled with a fatty or oily matter, termed marrow.

The cervical vertebræ are always seven in number, without exception, for in the Sloths, generally considered to have nine, it has been lately demonstrated by Bell that the two posterior vertebræ (called cervical) have rudiments of ribs attached to them, and are therefore in reality modified dorsal vertebræ. The occipital bone articulates with the atlas, or first vertebra, by two lateral condyles.

The head is made up of numerous bones, which are divided into the cranial, or those inclosing the brain, and the facial. The normal number of facial bones is seventeen, viz., 2 nasal bones, 2 upper maxillary, 2 intermaxillary, 2 lachrymal bones, 2 inferior turbinated bones, 2 palatal bones, 2 jugal or malar bones, 2 lower-jaw bones, and 1 vomer. Of these the nasal, upper and intermaxillary, and the palatal bones bound the nasal cavity, and constitute the bony palate. The cranial bones are eleven in number, viz., 2 frontal, 2 parietal, 2 squamous, and 2 tympano-petrous bones (which together make up the two temporal bones), 1 occipital, 1 sphenoid, and 1 ethmoid.

The orbit is bounded anteriorly by the molar and lachrymal bones, and its posterior boundary is generally absent. The orbital cavity is formed by processes from the frontal bones, the lachrymal, the molar, and sphenoid bones; the ethmoid and palatine bones occasionally assisting. The ethmoid, the turbinated bones, and the vomer are internal, connecting the nasal bones with the base of the skull.

The lower maxillary bones, united at the chin, are moveably articulated with the temporal bone by a convex condyle, in this differing from Birds and Reptiles, in which the articulation takes place through a separate piece, the tympanic bone. In Man and many Mammals several of these bones are united, viz., the frontals, the parietals in some Mammals, and the temporal bones.

The number of dorsal vertebræ depend on that of the ribs, and varies from eleven to twenty; and the lumbar, sacral, and coccygeal vertebræ also vary from four to forty-five.

The thorax is inclosed by ribs, some of which, called the true ribs, are attached to the sternum by a cartilage, the representative of the sternal ribs of other Vertebrata. The posterior ribs are called the false or floating ribs. The sternum is composed of several pieces, and gives attachment to the clavicles when present. The ribs are capable of considerable motion of elevation and depression, aiding the diaphragm in respiration.

The anterior extremity is fixed to a broad scapula, generally only connected by muscles to the trunk. A clavicle is present in those mammals that use the arm as an instrument of prehension or flight, and the coracoid bone, so conspicuous in other vertebrata, is reduced to an appendage. The rest of the limb is composed of the humerous,, two bones of the forearm, the radius and ulna, the carpus, metacarpus and phalanges. These last vary much in number.

The posterior extremity consists of the pelvis, comprising the iliac, ischial and pubic bones, the femur or thigh bone articulated to the iliac bones, the tibia and fibula, tarsus, metatarsus, and phalanges. Modifications of some of these bones and reductions of many of them occur among various Mammals, and will be pointed out in the proper place.

Considered generally, the muscular system of Mammals varies little from that of Man. The cutaneous muscle is much developed in some, especially in the Porcupine and Hedgehog, by means of which the spines can be suddenly raised. The same is noticeable to a less degree in Dogs and Cats, when they, as it is popularly called, "get their backs up."

Among Mammals the demand for food is less constant, and the digestive process less rapidly accomplished than in Birds. There is a considerable amount of uniformity in the structure of their digestive organs. The tongue varies much, and is free in most, being only fixed in the Whales. In some it is capable of great extension as in the Ant-eaters and is used to procure food, as it is also, to a certain extent, by some Ruminants. The surface of the tongue is usually covered with papillæ, which in some of the Carnivora, the Cat tribe notably, are developed into sharp, recurved horny spines, used to scrape the last fragments of flesh off bones.

The tongue is supported by a bone called the Hyoid bone, the anterior horns of which, small in Man, are greatly developed in most Mammals. The *velum palati*, which protects the communication between the mouth and posterior nasal cavity is only found in this class; and the trachea, which lies in front of the œsophagus, is protected by the epiglottis. The œsophagus leads straight to the stomach from the end of the pharynx, and is of moderate width, but dilatable. The stomach presents great varieties of form. In most it is a simple bag of varied shape and size, in some divided into compartments by constrictions, but without any apparent difference of structure. In one tribe, however, the Ruminants, it is a truly compound structure, consisting of several distinct cavities differing both in size, structure and functions. The small intestines vary little, but the large intestines are very variable in size, and the division between them is in many marked by an appendage called the *cœcum*, sometimes double, and in certain animals of great size. In some, especially the Plantigrade Carnivora and Cetacea, it is entirely absent.

The liver is generally of large size, and is usually divided into several lobes. In most it is furnished with a gall-bladder. The pancreas and spleen are always present.

The inferior muscular energy of Mammals compared with that of Birds is accompanied by an inferior amount of respiration, and on this account the heat of animals is much less, rarely exceeding 100° of Fahrenheit. The organs of respiration and circulation differ little throughout the class from those of Man. The heart consists of four cavities; and the lungs, which are always in pairs, are completely enclosed, and have no communication with air-cells as in Birds. These viscera are separated from those of the abdomen by the diaphragm, a muscular partition, which is one of the chief agents in respiration. The lungs are more porous and spongy in texture than in Birds. Variations in the structure of the heart and circulating system are only met with in Cetaceous animals, which have some interesting peculiarities dependent on their remaining long immersed in water, some arteries appearing to be intended as reservoirs of arterial blood, and dilatations of some of the veins prevent too great distension while the respiration is stopped.

The brain is larger than in any other class of animals, owing chiefly to the increased size of the cerebral hemispheres, which are united in most by a fibrous band called the *corpus callosum.* The cerebellum too has lateral lobes which are united by the *pons varolii*, and the hemispheres are usually convoluted externally. The Marsupial animals however do not possess the great commissures, and the cerebrum is smooth externally, thus more resembling Birds. The olefactory tubercles, and the optic lobes, are greatly reduced in size.

The organs of the senses are highly specialized, and in a great state of perfection in Mammals. The sense of touch is very delicate, and is usually concentrated in various parts, *e. g.*, in the whiskers of the Seals, of some Insectivora and Carnivora, in the lips of the Horse, the trunk of the Elephant; and this sense is greatly developed and extended among Bats in every part of the body, but especially in the naked wings, the ears and facial appendages.

The sense of smell is very acute in most animals, and many have a mobility of the outer nostrils to aid it, never found in the other Vertebrata. The olefactory tubercles are so diminished in size as barely to be recognized. We are all familiar with the power of the scent in the Dog, as well as in most of the Carnivora, which enables them to discover and hunt down their prey. Antelope, Deer and other timid animals have likewise very acute sense of smell, to enable them to avoid approaching danger. The nasal plates of the ethmoid bone, and the convolutions of the turbinated bones are coated with a delicate membrane, which forms a large surface, amply supplied with minute branches of the olefactory nerves, and the air inhaled passing to the lungs over this membrane imparts the impression.

The structure of the eye is in all Mammals almost identical with that in Man. In some the pupil is round, in others oblong or linear.

In Bats, and some nocturnal Insectivora, the external eye is very minute, but the sense of sight appears to be compensated for by an increase of that of touch. Many of the Ruminants have the eye large and full, and several of the Carnivora have a very keen sight, though not so acute perhaps as that of many raptorial birds. The eyelids in most are double as in Man, but in some of the lower forms a remnant of the nyctitating membrane is also met with. A lachrymal apparatus exists in most animals except the Cetacea.

The sense of hearing attains its greatest perfection in Mammals, and an external ear is present in most, generally mobile, to assist in conveying the sound from every direction, and concentrating it. The internal ear is imbedded in the petrous portion of the temporal bone, and is remarkable for the development and complexity of the cochlea. The tympanic cavity is large, and communicates with the pharynx by the eustachian tube. The communication between the membrane of the tympanum and the inner ear, which in the other vertebrates takes place by one ossicle, here consists of four.

Owing to the fleshy nature and mobility of the tongue, the sense of taste is much greater than in any other animals.

The leading peculiarity of the class of Mammals, viz., the nourishing of the new born young with milk has been already alluded to. The milk is secreted by the mammary glands, and these vary in number and position, being most numerous in the more prolific races. In most animals they are ventral, inguinal in many, and pectoral in a few. They vary in number from two to twelve. The yelk of the ovum which suffices for the nourishment of the young of Reptiles and Fishes, only affords a very small amount of nutriment to the Mammalian ovum, when expelled from the ovary, and the fœtus is supported in the uterus by the blood of the mother, conveyed by means of a vascular connection, called the placenta, the shape and situation of which, within the uterus, varies considerably. In one tribe of animals, however, the Marsupials, the young are expelled from the uterus at a very early period of development, and receive no nourishment beyond that derived from the yelk, no placenta being formed.

The young of several animals are born blind, others with their eyes open. Most are helpless at first, whilst a few are able to run about very shortly after birth; some attain their full size in a few months, others take several years.

In the majority of Mammals there is little to mark the signs of sex, except superior size and strength, and a different color in a few; but in certain tribes there are other external marks. The Lion, and a few others have a shaggy mane, and the males of many Ruminants are adorned with fine horns, either altogether absent in the females, or much smaller. In a few, the canine teeth are greatly superior in size in the males, or only found in them.

The male generative organs differ much in size and shape, and some are provided with the succenturiate glands of large size, whilst others are wholly without them. The males of some animals have a seasonal development, and at such times only have the power to procreate, whilst others are able at all seasons. Most animals perhaps are monogamous, a few are polygamous.

The females of most Mammals have certain periods of heat or *œstrum* coincident with a catamenial discharge, and will in general only receive the males at these times. The uterus is single in most Mammals, but double in a few, as in the Rabbit, and they open by separate orifices into the vagina. In many of the lower animals, and especially in such as are remarkable for their fecundity, the horns of the uterus are more developed in pregnancy than the body of the uterus, and the fœtus lie there, but as we ascend in the scale the body of the uterus becomes larger.

The urine is contained in the bladder, which is large, and it is evacuated by a distinct opening in the generative organs, except in the Monotremata, the lowest organized Mammals, where there is only one passage for fœces and urine. The excretory canal in the female is quite separate from the vagina.

Mammals are silent compared with Birds, and their voice is not generally musical or capable of harmony. It is chiefly employed to call one another, or to express anger, fear or hunger.

The skin contains numerous glands and follicles, secreting a lubricating fluid, to maintain it in a moist and supple state.

In many animals there are special glands in various parts of the body. Some of the Carnivora have special anal glands, which usually secrete a fetid fluid. The Elephant has a temporal gland; and many Ruminants have both large hollow glands below the eyes, secreting a waxy fluid, and inguinal, and foot-glands as well. A few, as the Musk-deer, have a preputial gland, secreting a most powerfully scented substance, musk; and the kindred substance, *castor*, is secreted by a Rodent animal. Many of these secretions appear to be connected with sexual purposes.

In cold climates several animals pass the winter in a state of torpidity, and even in India certain Bats and Hedgehogs, and perhaps some Rats, are more less torpid during the cold season. In Southern India I do not think that Bats usually becomes torpid, but they certainly do in the Northern Provinces. The two species of Bears found in the Himalayas both retire to their caves during winter, and are rarely or never seen from December till the end of March.

Most animals are habitually solitary or live in pairs; but many are gregarious. Some live chiefly on animal food, *e. g.*, Bats, Shrews, Moles, &c., on insects and worms; the Carnivora on Birds, Reptiles, and Mammals; and the Otter and the Seal on fish. Some of the Carnivora, however, have a mixed diet, as Bears, which eat insects, honey and fruit, as do several of the smaller Plantigrades; whilst a few partake of carrion. Many live solely on vegetable food. Some graze, others browse, and few dig up roots or plunder grain.

Wanting the great powers of locomotion of Birds, no extensive migrations can take place among Mammals; but partial migrations have been observed among certain Rodents, as the Lemming; and the Coffee-rat of Ceylon is stated to migrate at times from place to place in countless thousands.

There are not many constructive habits in this class compared with that of Birds. The Beaver is one of the most noted exceptions, and Squirrels and certain Rats and Mice build nests.

Most animals content themselves with holes excavated in the ground, or bring forth their young under rocks, in caves, or in thickets, or like many Ruminants, on the bare ground.

Man has brought under his dominion various animals either for food, carriage, or the chase, many of these have been domesticated for ages, and numerous varieties occur among them, the result of long domestication in varied climes, and perhaps partly of different origin.

The previous remarks (page x) will have prepared the reader for the first step in the arrangement of Mammals, viz., their division into those in which the young are nourished in the maternal uterus by means of a placenta,—PLACENTAL MAMMALS,—and those in which the young fœtus is expelled at a very early period, and maintained in a pouch firmly attached to a nipple, IMPLACENTAL, or Marsupial animals. None of these last occur in the Asiatic province, being chiefly developed in the Australian region, and a few in America. They have, moreover, very anomalous forms of dentition.

Having separated the Marsupial animals, the great mass of the Mammals still remains. Taking the teeth as our guide, we find a large number of animals possessed of all four kinds of teeth (*vide* page iv) though in varying number and proportion. These are called by Blyth, TYPODONTIA, *i. e.*, animals with the typical forms of teeth developed, and include Man,* Monkeys, Bats, Carnivorous animals and Shrews, &c., in fact all the most perfect forms of Mammals. We next find a large and still more varied association of animals, of inferior and more specialized organization, in which the teeth vary much from the typical formation, and have rarely more than two kinds of teeth developed. This group is called by Blyth, DIPLODONTIA, and includes Rats and Squirrels, Deer, Sheep and Cattle, the Elephant, Pig and Horse, and the almost toothless Ant-eaters. They chiefly live on vegetable matter, as the majority of the Typodontia do on animal food.

A third small division, comprising the Whales and Porpoises, &c., were called ISODONTIA by Blyth, because the teeth when present are all of one kind.

Having thus divided Placental Mammals into three great groups, which can in most cases be recognized by a glance at the teeth, the next step is to divide them into orders; and first the typically toothed Mammals. On examining the hairy covering of a Monkey and a Bat, it will be seen that there is only one kind of hair, no underhair or wool being present. In both these animals too, the penis is pendent, and not sheathed as in all other animals. As Man belongs to this division, it was called PRIMATES by Linnæus.

* Man is excluded from the scope of the present work.

It is composed of two very distinct orders, that of QUADRUMANA, *i. e.*, the four-handed, comprising Monkeys and Lemurs, in most of which there is a thumb or opposable finger on the foot; and CHEIROPTERA, *i. e.*, hand-winged, the Bats, which have the forearm and hand extended into an organ of flight. The remaining groups of perfect-toothed animals have two kinds of hair, in variable amount, and were named SECUNDATES by Blainville. They are likewise divisible into two orders. The first is the CARNIVORA, or beast of prey, the most typical of the two, and distinguished by powerful canines and trenchant molars, which are never studded with sharp points, and the clavicle is generally imperfect. The other order is that of INSECTIVORA, a group of small Mammals, having their molar teeth studded with sharp points to bruise their insect prey, and they usually have a greater number of teeth than the Carnivora. They all possess clavicles.

The Diplodontia present much greater differences of aspect and structure than the more perfect group, and it is only as a matter of convenience that they are grouped together. One order, which like the preceding orders, has claws, or is unguiculate, possesses two chisel-shaped teeth in front of each jaw, no apparent canines, and a small number of flattened molars. This is the RODENTIA, or Gnawers, comprising Rats and Squirrels, &c. Another order, likewise with claws, which are large and fossorial, or capable of digging, but partially enclosing the toes and somewhat hoof-like, is distinguished by the total absence of incisors and canine teeth, and in some of all teeth whatsover, are called EDENTATA, or Toothless, and they include the Ant-eaters and Armadillos.

All the remaining animals of this group have the toes more or less joined together, and ending in a hoof, which is single and solid in the Horse, double or bisulcate in the Deer and Pig, with three divisions as in the Rhinoceros, four unsymmetrical in the Hippopotamus, and with five hoof-like nails terminating the pad of the Elephant. These form the UNGULATA of some writers, and are usually divided into the RUMINANTIA, or Ruminants, and the PACHYDERMATA, or thick-skinned Mammals. The former is a very natural group, and comprises all that chew the cud—Deer, Cattle,

Sheep, &c. They have two hoofs, and two upper supplemental ones, no upper incisors (except in the Camel) and flattened molars. A canine is present in a few.

The PACHYDERMATA is a more varied and artificial group than the Ruminants, comprising the Elephant, Rhinoceros, Hippopotamus, Pig, Horse and Tapir. They differ much in their dentition and only agree in the negative character of not ruminating, and perhaps it would be more scientific to divide them into separate orders as some have done, viz., CHŒRODIA for the Hippopotamus and Pig; PROBOSCIDEA for the Elephant; and BELLURA for the others.

The herbivorous Cetaceans, sometimes classed with Pachydermata, are generally separated as a distinct order, called SIRENIA, and are distinguished from the other Diplodonts by the absence of limbs.

The ISODONTIA, comprising the Whales, Dolphins and Porpoises, are generally called Cetacea, and have no posterior extremities, whilst their anterior limbs are changed into fins.

Such is the Classification adopted in the present work, of which the accompanying synopsis may be found useful.

A. PLACENTAL MAMMALS.

(Fœtus nourished in the uterus through a placenta.)

I. TYPODONTIA.—Teeth of all four kinds.

1st Group, PRIMATES.—Hair of one kind only.

Ord. *Quadrumana.*—With thumb on the feet.

„ *Cheiroptera.*—Winged.

2nd Group, SECUNDATES.—Hair of two kinds.

Ord. *Carnivora.*—Molars trenchant mixed with tubercular ones.

„ *Insectivora.*—Molars studded with cusps.

II. DIPLODONTIA.—Teeth generally of two kinds only, abnormal.

Ord. *Rodentia.*—Front teeth long and chisel-like.

„ *Pachydermata.*—Teeth varied—skin thick—do not ruminate.

Ruminantia.—Upper incisors generally absent—chew the cud.

„ *Sirenia.*—Want posterior extremities.

„ *Edentata.*—Incisors absent.

III. Isodontia.—Teeth when present of one kind and often very numerous.

Ord. *Cetacea.*—Post-extremities wanting.

B. IMPLACENTAL OR MARSUPIAL MAMMALS.

In the body of the work the orders do not follow exactly as in this synopsis. I have made the Insectivora follow the Bats, and the Cetacea the Carnivora.

This classification is nearly that of Cuvier, but he classed Bats, *Insectivora* and *Carnivora* in one group, Carnaria, and placed the *Sirens* with the true *Cetacea*.

The following is the classification adopted by Linnæus.

I. Unguiculata.—With nails.

Ord. *Primates.*—Monkeys and Bats.

,, *Feræ.*—Insectivora and Carnivora.

,, *Glires.*—Are Rodentia.

,, *Bruta.*—The Ant-eaters, Elephant and Rhinoceros.

II. Ungulata.—Hoofed.

Ord. *Pecora.*—Ruminantia.

Bellua.—Pachydermata, except the order *Bruta* above.

III. Mutica.—Wanting the posterior extremities, Cetacea.

This it will be seen is, with the exception of his separating the Elephant and Rhinoceros from the other *Pachydermata*, essentially the same as Cuvier's, and the system adopted here.

Professor Owen classifies Mammals according to the structure of the brain alone, and, excluding Man, whom he places by himself, as the type of his *Archencephala,* he divides the Mammal class into three great groups—*Lyencephala, Lissencephala,* and *Gyrencephala.* The first comprises the Implacental or Marsupial animals, and is quite natural. In this group the olefactory lobes, part of the optic lobes, as well as the cerebellum, are all exposed, and the lobes of of the cerebrum are not connected by a corpus callosum.

The Lissencephalla, or smooth-brained Mammals, have the carpus callosum, but the cerebrum is smooth in most and of small bulk. This group is composed of the *Cheiroptera, Insectivora, Rodentia* and

Edentata; and the separation of the perfect-teethed Bats and Shrews from the Monkeys and *Carnivora,* does not appear to be felicitous, or so natural as the system of Linnæus. The Gyrencephala have more or less convolutions on the surface of the brain, and are divided into three groups—MUTILATA, the *Cetacea* and *Sirenia;* UNGULATA, the *Pachydermata* and *Ruminantia;* and UNGUICULATA, the *Carnivora* and *Quadrumana.*

But few naturalists in India have recorded their observations on the class of Mammals. Colonel Sykes was the first who published a list of the animals observed by him in the Deccan, in which he described several of the common animals of the country. Sir Walter Elliot followed in 1839, with a Catalogue of the Mammalia of the Southern Mahratta country, and this excellent observer was the first to distinguish many of the smaller mammals, of which he has given an admirable account. He has not published since, but has continued his researches, and discovered several novelties, amongst others the *Tupaia* of Southern India. That indefatigable observer and collector, Mr. Hodgson, has published several lists of the Mammals of Nepal, and has described many species, giving detailed accounts of the habits and structure of a few. Colonel Tickell has published a detailed history of a few animals in such a full and interesting manner, as to lead one to wish he had written much more. Major Hutton has also recorded some interesting facts on the Mammals of Afghanistan, and has largely collected, especially the Bats and smaller animals of the Himalayas. I understand that he is at present engaged on a popular natural history of the Himalayan animals, and I can only express my regret that it had not been published previously to the appearance of this work. Other scattered notices will be referred to in their proper place.

It only remains to make a few observations on the geographical distribution of the Mammals of India.

The Lungoors (Gen. *Presbytis*) form a well-marked group of Monkeys in India, and are still further developed in the Indo-Chinese provinces and Malayana. Out of five species found on the continent, there is only one spread through all the plains of Central and Northern India, and one through the Himalayas, whilst there are three well-marked species in the extreme south of the peninsula. Whilst *Macacus radiatus* of Southern India replaces *Inuus rhesus* of all Northern and Central India, a well-marked form of this group, *Inuus silenus* is peculiar to the south-west corner of the peninsula.

The Lemurs are only outliers of the Madagascar Fauna, and whilst one species is very abundant in the extreme south, another Malayan species extends sparingly through Burmah into the north-eastern corner of Bengal.

Of the Frugivorous Bats, two species are spread throughout the whole of India, and one additional species occurs in the south only. Among Insectivorous Bats, the *Rhinolophus* group is much more developed on the Himalayas than in all the rest of India; seven species being recorded as Himalayan, whilst only two occur in southern India; but the *Hipposideros* section, which is more Malayan, is about equally represented in the north and south of India. A peculiar form, *Cælops* of Blyth, has hitherto only been found in the Bengal Sunderbuns. The yellow-bellied *Nycticeji* occur pretty generally throughout India, but the largest species is from the south; whilst a peculiar type, *N. ornatus*, is only found in the Himalayas. Most of the other Bats are generally distributed through the continent, except a few European forms, which only occur on the Himalayas.

Moles are only found in India in the south-east portion of the Himalayas, being apparently an offshoot from the Indo-Chinese region; and the Shrews are more numerously developed in the same portion of the Himalayas than in other parts of India. One species of the peculiar Insectivorous genus, *Tupaia*, a Malayan form, occurs in southern India, and another spreads from Burmah into the south-eastern Himalayas.

India abounds in Carnivora. Two species of Bears are Himalayan, and one of a somewhat different type extends throughout the whole plains of India. A very remarkable form of Ursidæ, *Ailurus fulgens*, is peculiar to the Eastern Himalayas. One Marten is found both on the Himalayas and Neelgherries, but Weasels, in India, only occur on the former range. There is only one species of Otter found in the South of India, but two are found in Bengal, and more on the Himalayas. Out of the fifteen Feline animals found in India, five are common to India and Africa; seven are found in India and the Indo-Chinese region, but of these there are three that only occur, in India, in the south-east Himalayas; one (the *Ounce*) is Himalayan, extending there from Central Asia, and three (and these are the smallest of the family) are peculiar to the plains of India, two of them occurring in the extreme south of the peninsula, and the other in the north-west. The genus *Paradoxurus* is strictly Asiatic, and more Malayan than Indian. One species only is common in most parts of India, and there are two in the Himalayas and adjoining Terai. Out of seven species of *Herpestes*, a genus common to India and Africa, five are only found in the southern portion of the peninsula, and four of these in the extreme south. Of the Civet Cats, one small species is found throughout India, common also to Malayana; and there is a large species in Northern India, replaced in the extreme south by a different race. Several peculiar forms of Carnivora, viz., *Arctongx, Arctictis, Helictis, Urva,* and *Prionodon,* are found in the South-east Himalayas, but they all extend there from the Indo-Chinese region.

Of the Canidæ, the Wolf, Jackal, and Wild Dog are found throughout India, and two small desert Foxes are found throughout the plains, whilst a Fox of the European type occurs in the Himalayas.

Of the large Squirrels, three species or races occur in Southern India, and one in the Eastern Himalayas, extending from the Indo-Chinese district, and in the same region two closely allied races of Squirrel are found of a type immensely developed in Assam, Burmah, and Malayana. Three species of ground Squirrel are found in Southern India, one of which extends to the foot of the Himalayas, and another to Central India; and one small species is found in the eastern Himalayas spreading to Assam. Only two species of Flying Squirrel are met with in Southern India, one of them limited to the extreme south of the peninsula, the other extending through Central India; but several species are found in the Himalayas. Marmots only occur on the same range, being outliers from Central Asia.

There is not much remarkable in the distribution of the numerous *Muridæ* of India. A few are peculiar to the South of India, and these are somewhat more distinct in type, viz., *Golunda,* three species of *Leggada,* and the curious *Platacanthomys. Arvicola* only occurs in the Himalayas; and *Rhizomys,* an Indo-Chinese type, in the most eastern Himalayas.

One species of Hare is found in the south of the peninsula, and another in Northern and Central India; whilst a very curious form, the *Hispid Hare,* inhabits the north-eastern portion of Bengal. *Lagomys,* a northern type, is only found on the Himalayas.

One Elephant is found throughout India, and two species of Rhinoceros occur in the north-eastern parts of Bengal, one of them extending to the extreme south of the Malayan peninsula. One Wild Pig, with some slight differences of race, occurs throughout all India, and a peculiar dwarf species is found sparingly in the Terai adjoining the south-eastern Himalayas. A Wild Ass is found in the north-western deserts, an extension from Persia and Western Asia.

True Deer, of the type of the Red Deer, only occur, in India, within the Himalayas beyond the outer snowy range, in Kashmir and Sikim, and these two species extend over great part of Asia; but four Rusine Deer, all peculiar to the Indian region, are found throughout India, one of them that most approaches the Elaphine group *(Rucervus)*, only occurring in Northern and Central India, but extending into Assam. The little Mouse-deer, *Memimna,* a Malayan form, occurs throughout India; but the northern Musk-deer only in the Himalayas.

Four species of Antelope are found throughout India, two of them, the Nylgai and the four-horned Antelope, being distinct in type from any African form; whilst the Gazelles occur both in Africa and Asia. Two goat-like Antelope *(Nemorhædus)* are found on the Himalayas, the form being peculiar to eastern Asia from Japan to Burmah. Of the true Goats, one type, *Hemitragus,* has a representative on the Himalayas, and another on the Neelgherries. The Siberian Ibex extends to the Himalayas, and a splendid wild goat, the Markhor, quite of the type of the domestic goat, is found on the north-west Himalayas and adjoining hilly districts. Two species of Wild Sheep occur, one in the Punjab Salt Range, the other in the Himalayas. The occurrence of the former at such a low altitude, and in such a hot summer climate, is very remarkable.

The magnificent Gaur, the Bison of sportsmen, abounds in the forests of Southern India, and extends more sparingly into Central India, as well as to Burmah and the Malay peninsula; and the wild Buffalo is found in the eastern portions of both Northern and Central India.

Two species of Scaly Ant-eater, *Manis*, occur in India, one common throughout all India; the other a Chinese species, just reaching our north-east limit at Darjeeling.

Little is known of the distribution of the marine Cetacea and Sirenia. The Dugong occurs sparingly in the southern coasts of India, and various species of *Delphinus*, one *Globicephalus*, and one *Balænoptera* are occasionally captured off the coasts or stranded. The Ganges and the Indus abound with a fresh water Porpoise of a peculiar type, *Platanista*.

To conclude, Southern India, more particularly the richly wooded Malabar coast, possesses more species peculiar to it than all Central and Northern India, except the Himalayan range; and of the animals only found in this latter region, several equally belong to the Indo-Chinese Fauna, of which they appear to be the western extension, and a few others to Central Asia, whilst a moderate number of species appear to be peculiar to this mountainous region.

THE MAMMALS OF INDIA.

Ord. PRIMATES.

Fam. Simiadæ, Monkeys.

Syn. *Quadrumana* in part, Auct. *Heopitheci,* Van-Hoeven—*Catarrhinæ,* Geoffroy.

Incisors, $\frac{4}{4}$; canines, $\frac{1-1}{1-1}$; molars, $\frac{5-5}{5-5}$; total, 32 teeth; as in man. Nails flat or somewhat rounded, blunt; fore-feet usually with 5 toes; hind feet always pentadactylous, thumb remote; nostrils separated by a small and narrow septum. Tail never prehensile, sometimes wanting; the region of the tuberosity of the ischium usually destitute of hair and callous. Peculiar to the old world.

In their anatomical characters monkeys generally closely resemble man, differing chiefly in the relative proportions of parts. The incisors are approximate in both jaws; the canines are conic, larger than the incisors, and the upper ones remote from them; the molars are nearly cubical in form with short tubercles, and equally enamelled. The face and hands are devoid of hair, and the fore-feet are often larger than the hind-feet. Some have cheek-pouches, others have none. Some have laryngeal pouches, or membranous expansions, sending prolongations into the muscles; these are receptacles of air, and communicate with the cavity of the larynx by an aperture at the base of the epiglottis. Their probable use is to diminish the specific gravity of their body in the action of climbing. The cheek-pouches enable them to eat with rapidity; their callosities enable them to assume the sitting posture readily; and the long tails of some enable them to balance themselves in their surprising leaps.

Their dentition resembles that of man very closely, differing in the incisors, and especially in the canines being larger; this necessitates a larger space between the incisors and the false molars. The other points in which even the nearest allied species differ from man are the conspicuously longer fore-arms, the long flexible toes, and the thumb on the hind-feet. The pelvis is narrow and does not assist the equilibrium in the erect position, and when they stand erect they cannot do so on the soles of their feet, but rest on the outer edge of the foot. In the young of some, the form of the skull approaches that of man, but with age it differs much, the jaws lengthening. The skeleton generally may be said to deviate from man towards some of the larger carnivora. The mass of the brain is smaller comparatively than in man, usually broader than long, and the central convolutions are less numerous and deep, the corpus callosum of less extent, and the nerves thicker in proportion to the size of the brain.*

The intestines of monkeys generally are similar to those of man. The penis is free and pendent, and they possess vesicular prostrate glands. The mammæ are pectoral. The uterus is simple, and they menstruate. The placenta is usually discoid, sometimes double.

As a general rule monkeys are herbivorous, but some live on a mixed diet. Most live in societies, and they are chiefly arboreal in habit. They seldom give birth to more than two young at a time, frequently only one; and they carry their young about with them. The liberty of their arms and the make of their hands permit many actions and gestures similar to those of man. Many are capable of domestication, and their intelligence and docility are familiar to all.

The monkeys of the old world may be divided into 1st, Apes, without a tail, to which division belong the Orangs and Gibbons; 2nd, Monkeys properly, so called; and 3rd, Baboons.

The Apes, sub-fam. SIMIANÆ comprise the Chimpanzee, *Troglodytes niger*; the Gorilla, *T. Gorilla*; and perhaps a third species, all from Africa; and the Orangs, *Simia Satyrus* and *S. Morio*, from Borneo and Sumatra.

The Gibbons are separated by some as a sub-family, HYLOBATINÆ. They are peculiar to the Indo-Chinese countries and Malayana. One of the best known is *Hylobates hoolook*, found in the forests and hill ranges of Assam, Sylhet, Cachar, &c., whose extraordinary howlings I have heard in the Khasia hills and in Cachar; *Hylobates lar* occurs in Tenasserim, and *H. agilis* in the Malayan peninsula, and there are several other

* Owen's separation of man from the monkeys, under the title of *Archencephala*, founded on the supposed greater extent of the hemispheres posteriorly, and some other points, is opposed by Huxley and others.

species from the Malayan islands. They are of small size, gentle in disposition, and progress on the ground on their hind legs in a series of hops or jumps sideways, with their arms raised erect.

Monkeys.

The Entellus group of monkeys are placed by Mr. Blyth in a sub-family, Colobinæ, along with an African genus, *Colobus*. They are distinguished from the other monkeys and baboons by wanting the cheek-pouches, and having a peculiar sacculated stomach.

Gen. Presbytis, Illiger.

Syn. *Semnopithecus*, F. Cuvier—*Langur*, H. *Hunumán*, of Hindus.

Char.—Cheek-pouches rudimentary or wanting; head round, the face but little produced, having a high facial angle. The last molar tooth of the lower jaw, with a fifth or accessory tubercle behind; canines much longer than the incisors; extremities and feet long; fore-feet with the thumb short, and the third and fourth fingers long and sub-equal. Tail very long, slender and straight. Callosities present. Peculiar to the Indian region.

The body of these monkeys is comparatively slender, and the Germans call them slim-apes. Their long and slender limbs, long tail, and the black face with an eye-brow of long stiff black hairs, pointing forwards, distinguish the *Langurs* from all other monkeys. The absence of the cheek-pouch appears to be in some measure compensated by a peculiar sacculated stomach, described fully by Owen, in the 1st Vol. "Transactions of the Zoological Society;" several distinct sacs or pouches being added to and communicating with the stomach. In a specimen of *P. entellus*, 20 inches long to the root of the tail, the small intestines were 13½ feet long, the large ones 2 feet 10 inches, and the cœcum 4 inches. The distended stomach measured 31 inches along the greater curve, and was 1 foot in circumference. It consisted firstly, of a simple cardiac pouch; secondly, of a wide and sacculated middle portion; and thirdly, of a narrow lengthened canal, sacculated at first, and simple afterwards, vascular, and the true digestive stomach. Owen in this paper, asks if they feed on young shoots or leaves, from the quasi-ruminant character of the stomach; and it has since been ascertained beyond a doubt that they constantly do partake of leaves. Bezoars have been found in the stomach of a Malayan *Presbytis*, thus affording a curious analogy to the ruminants, in whom alone they otherwise occur.

The species of this genus abound in most of the forests of India, and their loud calls resound to vast distances through the jungles. They leap with surprising agility and precision from branch to branch, and when pressed take most astonishing jumps. I have seen them cross from tree to tree, a space of 20 to 30 feet wide, with perhaps 40 or 50 feet in descent, and alight in safety on the branch they sought. They can run on all fours with considerable rapidity, taking long strides or rather bounds. The tail of these monkeys of course is not prehensile; yet I have heard several men whom I considered persons of observation, and whose testimony I would willingly take on other subjects, assert most positively that they had seen *Langurs* holding on by their tails and thus swinging themselves from tree to tree. Such is the force of a pre-conceived idea, that it prevails over actual observation of the senses.

Several species of *Presbytis* have been described of late years, which were formerly confounded under the old name of *Entellus*, and there are five undoubted species of the genus inhabiting India proper.

1. Presbytis entellus.

Simia apud Dufresnoy—fig. F. Cuvier, Mamm. I., 3, and III., 6.—*Hunumán* of Hindus.—*Langur* H.—*Wanur*, and *Makur*, Mahr.—*Musya*, Can.—Blyth, Cat. 27.—Elliot, Cat. 2.—Horsfield, Cat. 4.—*P. anshises*, Elliot?

The Bengal Langur.

Descr.—The general hue of this species is a pale dirty or ashy stramineous, darker (in some) on the shoulders, rump, and sides of the limbs, and paler on the head and lower parts; entire hands and feet conspicuously black; no trace of a crest of hairs on the vertex.

Length of a male, 30 inches to root of tail, which was 43 inches; but it attains a still larger size.

This is the common *Langur* or *Hunumán* of Bengal and Central India. Buchanan Hamilton says, that it is not found north of the Ganges, and that even south of that river it is rare in certain parts that would appear suitable for it, as at Rajmahal. Mr. Blyth states that, he has never seen it wild east of the Hoogly, but that it extends up the right bank of that river and the Ganges, and thence to Cuttack and Central India. It is uncertain how far it extends southwards and westwards, and one variety or race from the south was named as distinct by Elliot. My impression of the *Langur* found in the Deccan is, that it had less black on the hands and feet, and was of a decidedly more ashy hue than the Bengal monkey, thus corresponding with part of Horsfield's description of *entellus*; and it is still a desideratum to define the geographic boundaries of *Presbytis entellus* and *P. priamus*.

This monkey, like all others of the genus, abounds most in forests and highly wooded districts, but it not unfrequently takes up its abode in large groves near towns and villages, and occasionally enters towns and plunders the shops of the grain-dealers with impunity; for Hindoos, in the North of India especially, deem it sacrilege to kill one. In some parts of the country indeed it would hardly be safe to do so, though Mr. Blyth records that some villagers along the Hoogly are not at all sorry to see one shot by a European.

The Entellus feeds on grain, fruit, pods of various trees, especially of leguminosæ, and also of leaves and young shoots. It is said* that, the males live apart from the females, who have only one or two old males with each colony. These are said to drive away or kill, if they can, the younger males, whom however the females protect, all assisting. At a particular season all the males sally forth to the nearest colony of females and a regular fight ensues, at the end of which the vanquished males receive charge of the young ones of that sex from the females, and retire to some neighbouring jungle. This account was partly confirmed by Blyth, who found in one locality males alone, of all ages; and in another, chiefly females. The female has usually only one young one, occasionally it is said, twins.

Hunumán, the meaning of which is long-jaw, was one of the monkeys of the monkey kingdom of Southern India, who aided Rama in his conquest of Ceylon, by forming a bridge of rocks opposite Manár, and greatly distinguished himself. His figure is often found in Hindoo temples in the guise of a man, with a black monkey face, and a long tail: he is not worshipped, only greatly reverenced. In some temples in the West of India, this monkey is regularly fed by the priests.

In confinement the Entellus monkey is quiet, sedate, and indolent.

* "Bengal Sporting Magazine," August, 1836.

Messrs. Elliot and Blyth, at one time separated from *P. entellus* a race or variety, under the name of *P. anchises*, Elliot. It nearly corresponds in color with *P. entellus*, but has the hands and feet much less black than that species, and the hair of greater length, that of the toes particularly being remarkably long; and the hairs moreover are straight, not wavy, as in *Entellus*. This race was founded, I believe, on a single skin from the table-land of Southern India, and further specimens are required to establish it satisfactorily as a distinct species. Mr. Blyth, indeed, in his Catalogue, now puts it as a variety of *Entellus*. As before stated, however, I think it by no means impossible that another race does take the place of *Entellus* in the Southern portion of Central India.

2. Presbytis schistaceus.

Hodgson, J. A. S., IX., 1212.—Blyth, Cat. 28.—Horsfield, Cat. 5.—*Langur*, H.—*Kamba suhú*, Lepch.—*Kubúp*, Bhot.

The Himalayan Langur.

Descr.—Dark slaty above; head and lower parts, pale yellowish; hands concolorous with body, or only a little darker; tail slightly tufted; hair on the crown of the head, short and radiated, on the cheeks long, directed backwards and covering the ears. In old individuals the general color is gray, inclining to hoary, and the head yellowish-white. Grows to a larger size than *Entellus*. A moderately sized one measured, head and body 30 inches, tail 36.

This fine species has only of late been fully recognised in Europe as distinct from *Entellus*, much to the surprise of observers in India. It is found along the whole range of the Himalayas, from Nepal to far beyond Simla, but has not to my knowledge been actually procured in the Sikim Himalayas. Mr. Hodgson says, that it inhabits the Terraie and lower hills of Nepal, being rare in the Cachar, or upper range. Further west, however, it ascends to nearly 12,000 feet, at which elevation I saw it in Kumaon, in summer; whilst Captain Hutton states, that he has seen them leaping and playing about at an elevation of 11,000 feet, while the fir-trees among which they sported were loaded with snow-wreaths. It is common about the stations of Nynee Tal, Mussoorie, and Simla, and extends much further West. Its reputed absence in Sikim is only founded on negative evidence, and I heard of some *Langurs* having been seen near Punkabari, about 1,600 feet of elevation, and that some of this herd actually used to seize fruit and vegetables from some of the women and children who passed that way. On one occasion, two or three huge fellows attempted to take a bottle from the servant of a friend of mine who was following his master, and it was not till the gentleman rode close up to them that these bold Turpins gave up their felonious attempts. I cannot say whether these individuals were of this species or *Entellus*, but most probably the former.

Hodgson in a copy of a new edition of his Catalogue of Nepal Mammalia, gives a *Presbytis thermophilus*. This is probably *Entellus*.

3. Presbytis priamus.

ELLIOT, apud BLYTH, J. A. S. XII.—BLYTH, Cat. 30.—HORSFIELD, Cat. 6.—*Gandangi*, Tel.

THE MADRAS LANGUR.

Descr.—Ashy gray color with a pale reddish or "chocolate au lait" tint overlaying the whole back and head; sides of the head, chin, throat and beneath, pale yellowish; hands and feet, whitish; face, palms and fingers, and soles of the feet and toes, black; a high compressed vertical crest of hairs on the top of the head; hairs long and straight, not wavy; tail of the color of the darker portion of the back, ending in a whitish tuft.

Much of the same size as *Entellus*.

This species inhabits the Eastern Ghâts and Southern portion of the table-land of Southern India, not extending however to the Malabar Coast. It also occurs in the Northern part of Ceylon. We have no authentic information recorded of its extension to the Deccan and Southern Mahratta country, and we cannot be certain whether the species recorded by Mr. W. Elliot* and Colonel Sykes, are *Entellus* or *Priamus* or *Anchises?* I have seen this monkey on the Eastern Ghâts near Nellore, at Bangalore, where it is exceedingly numerous; near Trichinopoly, and elsewhere. It is found both in forests and large groves of trees, and has the usual habits and call of its tribe. It is often domesticated at Madras and other places.

4. Presbytis Johnii.

Simia apud FISHER.—*Semnopithecus Dussumierii*, SCHINZ.—*S. Johnii*, var., MARTIN.—*S. cucullatus*, IS. GEOFF.—*S. hypoleucos*, BLYTH.—BLYTH, Cat. 29.—HORSFIELD, Cat 9.

* Catalogue of the Mammalia of the Southern Mahratta country.

THE MALABAR LANGUR.

Descr.—Above, dusky brown, slightly paling on the sides; crown, occiput, sides of head and beard, fulvous, darkest on the crown; limbs and tail, dark brown, almost black; beneath, yellowish white. Not quite so large as *Entellus*.

This monkey is found on the Malabar Coast, from about N. L. 14 or 15 to Cape Cormorin, that is to say in the provinces of South Canara, Malabar, Cochin, and Travancore. Horsfield, in his Catalogue, states, it to have been found "near Madras, and also in the interior of the peninsula." This is certainly erroneous, and I do not believe that it extends beyond the limit of the forests of Malabar. It does not ascend the mountains to any great height above the sea, and I never saw it above 1,200 or 1,300 feet on the various passes that I have traversed. It certainly does not occur on the wooded table-land of the Wynaad. It is not confined to the forests, but frequents gardens and the belt of cultivated wooded land that extends all along the sea coast of Malabar.

Like others of this genus, it generally by a noisy and alarmed chatter, gives notice of the presence of tigers, leopards, and other animals of prey. A pair that frequented my garden at Tellicherry pointed out the situation of a tiger that had come during the night. Its food is similar to that of its congeners—fruit, seeds, and leaves—and it has the usual loud cry as it leaps from branch to branch. Though frequenting high trees in garden land it is not at all familiar, like *Entellus* in similar spots, and rather shuns observation. It is frequently taken when young and tamed, as is mentioned by Belanger.

Blyth, in his Catalogue, considers that *cucullatus* of Is. Geoffroy in Belanger's voyage, belongs to the next species, which he formerly looked upon as *Johnii*; but I am convinced that Geoffroy described our monkey, which indeed he procured at Mahi, only 5 miles from Tellicherry, where, as I know, it abounds. It varies a good deal in the intensity of its color, and especially in the blackness of its limbs and tail, and the young are throughout of a sooty brown.

5. Presbytis jubatus.

Semnopithecus apud WAGNER.—*S. Johnii* apud MARTIN, and BLYTH (olim).—BLYTH, Cat. 35 (syn. exc.)

The Neelgherry Langur.

Descr.—Of a dark glossy black throughout, except the head and nape, which are reddish-brown, the hair very long; in old individuals, a grayish patch on the rump. Length of one, head and body, 26 inches; tail, 30; but larger individuals are seen, though it does not attain the size of *Entellus*.

This handsome monkey is found on the Neelgherry hills, the Animallies, Pulneys, the Wynaad, and all the higher parts of the range of Ghâts as low as Travancore. It does not, as far as I have observed it, descend lower than from 2,500 to 3,000 feet. It is shy and wary, and does not affect the neighbourhood of man. It is, or used to be, very abundant in the dense woods of the Neelgherries, and when they were beaten for game, these black monkeys would make their way rapidly and with loud cries to the lowest part of the shola, and thence to some neighbouring wood at a lower level. The fur is fine and glossy, and is much prized.

Presbytis pileatus, Blyth, inhabits the hilly regions of Sylhet, Cachar and Chittagong; *P. Barbei*, Blyth, the interior of the Tippera hills; *P. obscurus*, Reid, Mergui; *P. Phayrei*, Blyth, Arrakan; and *P. albocinereus*, the Malayan peninsula. Several others inhabit various of the Malayan isles; and Ceylon possesses *P. cephalopterus*, and *P. ursinus*, Blyth, peculiar to that island.

The genus *Colobus* contains several species from Africa, most of them black, and some with fine white manes. These monkeys differ from *Presbytis* in wanting the thumb of the fore-hands.

Papioninæ, Baboons.

This sub-family comprises the true baboons of Africa and the monkey-like baboons of India. They have the stomach simple, and cheek-pouches are always present.

Gen. Inuus, Geoffroy.

Macacus in part, Auct.

Char.—Face, somewhat produced, but rounded; callosities, present; the last molar tooth of the lower jaw has five tubercles, the other two true molars with four tubercles; tail, short.

The monkeys of this genus have a somewhat prominent muzzle, and protruded superciliary ridge; the nostrils open obliquely at some distance above the end of the muzzle; their canines are very strong, and the first molars are inclined backwards to make room for the large upper canine. The limbs are strong and compact, and they are as much terrestrial as arboreal. They eat frogs, crabs, lizards and insects, as readily as vegetable food. Their callosities are large, as are their cheek-pouches, and they have also laryngeal expansions. Their tails are short. They are quiet and intelligent in youth, but become ferocious and untameable in old age.

6. Inuus silenus.

Simia apud LINNÆUS.—*S. leonina*, SHAW.—*Silenus veter*, GRAY.—BLYTH, Cat. 12.—HORSFIELD, Cat. 23.—*Nil bandar*, Beng.—*Shia bandar*, H.—*Nella manthi*, Mal.

THE LION MONKEY.

Descr.—Black, with a reddish-white hood or beard surrounding the face and neck; tail, with a tuft of hair at the tip.

Length of one, about 2 feet; tail, 10 inches.

This well known monkey has been bandied about in several genera, some making him a *Papio*, others a *Cynocephalus*, and many a *Macacus;* whilst Lesson, followed by Gray, places him as a distinct genus. It certainly has the baboon-like characters, viz., the stronger teeth, more lengthened face, and the tufted tail more strongly marked than others. Till lately it has been looked upon in Europe as a native of Ceylon as well as of the Southern parts of India, and the name *Wanderoo,* applied to it by Buffon, is properly the Ceylonese name of the Langurs; but Templeton and Layard pointed out that it was never found on that island. It is a native of the more elevated forests of the Western Ghâts of India, from N. L. 14° to the extreme South, but most abundant in Cochin and Travancore. It is said to occur still further North up to *Goa*, N. L. 15½, but I have no authentic information of its occurrence so high. It frequents the most dense and unfrequented parts of the forests, always as far as I have observed it, at a considerable elevation, and I had often traversed the Malabar forests before I first fell in with it. This was at the top of the Cotiaddy pass, leading from Malabar into the Wynaad. I since have met with it in several other localities, but always near the crest of the Ghâts. It occurs in troops of from twelve to twenty or more, and those I observed were exceedingly shy and wary. It is not, to my knowledge, often caught in the Wynaad, and most of the individuals seen in captivity appear to be taken in Travancore. In its nature it is more sulky and savage than the next species, and is with difficulty taught to perform any feats of agility or mimicry.

7. Inuus rhesus.

Macacus apud DESMAREST.—*In. erythræus*, SCHREBER.—*Pithex oinops*, HODGSON.—HORSFIELD, Cat. 20.—BLYTH, Cat. 15.—*Bandar*, H.—*Mor-kot*, Beng; also *Banur* or *Marcut banur*.—*Suhu*, Lepch.—*Piyu*, Bhot.—Figd. F. CUVIER, Mamm., II. 9 and 10, and III. 14.

THE BENGAL MONKEY.

Descr.—Above brownish-ochrey or rufous; in old individuals more rufous, or rusty on the lower back and rump; limbs and beneath, ashy-brown; callosities and regions in their vicinity, red; face of adult males, red; tail, about half the length of the body; hairs on the crown not radiating.

Length of one, about 22 inches (head and body); tail, 11 inches.

This is the common monkey of all Northern India, extending South to about N. L. 18° or 19°. I have observed it in Goomsoor and near Nagpore, but not further South. It extends into the Himalayas up to at least 4,000 or 5,000 feet of elevation. It frequents alike forest and groves in the open country, and may be seen in abundance in many large towns and villages in Northern India. It is very commonly tamed, and made to exhibit various feats of agility. When old, the males especially become somewhat savage, and less tractable than younger individuals.

8. Inuus pelops.

Macacus apud HODGSON.—*M. assamensis*, MCLELLAND?—HORSFIELD, Cat. 21.—BLYTH, Cat. 16.

THE HILL MONKEY.

Descr.—Brownish-gray, somewhat mixed with slaty, and rusty-brownish on the shoulders in some; beneath, light ashy-brown; fur, fuller and more wavy than in the last; canine teeth, long; of stout habit. Length of one specimen, 20 inches; tail, 9½; face and callosities less red than in *rhesus*.

There is still some doubt about the distinctness of this monkey from *rhesus*; as well as its identity with the Assam one, and the materials in the museum of the Asiatic Society are insufficient to form a decided opinion. Major Hutton, however, considers that he has obtained this monkey in the interior of the Mussoorie hills, where it replaces *rhesus* at a high elevation; and he had one or two young individuals alive which showed the wavy fur noted by Hodgson.

Hodgson in the last edition of his Catalogue has, in addition to *rhesus* and *pelops*, another species which he names in MSS. *Macacus sikimensis.* If this be distinct from the other two, it may be *assamensis*; and it is perhaps the monkey, not rare near Darjeeling at from 4,000 to 5,000 feet high, which I considered to be *rhesus*, and which is very destructive to the fields of Indian corn.

Other species of *Inuus* are *I. nemestrinus*, from the Tenasserim provinces and Malayana; and *I. leoninus*, Blyth, from Arrakan, perhaps the same as *I. arctoides* of Is. Geoffroy.

Gen. Macacus.

Tail longer than in *Inuus*, and face not so lengthened; otherwise as in that genus.

9. Macacus radiatus.

Cercopethecus apud Kuhl.—*Simia sinica*, Lin. (in part).—Elliot, Cat. 1.—Blyth, Cat. 18.—Horsfield, Cat. 22—*Bandar* H.—*Makadu*, Mahr.—or *Wanur* (Sykes).—*Kerda*, Mahr. of the Ghâts.—*Múnga*, Can. —*Koti*, Tel.—*Vella munthi*, Mal.—Figd. F. Cuvier, Mamm. I. 13.

The Madras Monkey.

Descr.—Of a dusky olive-brown color, paler and albescent on the belly, and somewhat ashy on the outer sides of the limbs; hairs on the crown of the head, radiated; tail, dusky-brown above, whitish beneath. Length of one, head and body, 20 inches; tail, 15.

This monkey is found over all the Southern parts of India, extending North to N. L. 18°, or thereabouts, where it is replaced by *Inuus rhesus.* "It abounds," says Mr. Elliot, "over all this portion of country, sometimes inhabiting the wildest jungles, and at others living in populous towns, and carrying off fruit and grain from the shops of the dealers with the greatest coolness and address."

It is the monkey most commonly found in Menageries, and led about to show various tricks and feats of agility. It is certainly the most inquisitive and mischievous of its tribe, and its powers of mimicry are surpassed by none. With age it becomes more sullen and less amenable to discipline.

A variety, with an apparently longer tail, was brought to me at Nellore from the Eastern Ghâts, and the shikarees called it the *Konda koti*, or hill monkey, to distinguish it from the common one, but I had not an opportunity at the time of comparing it with a specimen of the common one; and must therefore, in the absence of specimens, consider it only as an individual variety.

Ceylon possesses a representative of *M. radiatus* in *M. pileatus*, Shaw, (*sinica* of Linnæus); and *M. cynomolgos*, L., and *M. carbonarius*, F. Cuvier, are both found in Burmah.

The African monkeys of this sub-family belong to *Cynocephalus* and *Papio*, true short-tailed baboons, of savage disposition and carnivorous habits; whilst the species of *Cercopithecus*, with their long tails and sombre colors, externally more resemble *Presbytis*.

The family Cebidæ or Platyrhinæ, with the nostrils far apart, are all American. They are divided into 1st, Hapalinæ, or Marmosets, of very small size, the ears tufted, the tail bushy but not prehensile, the teeth as in the last family, but the tubercles of the molars sharp: they feed both on insects and fruit. 2nd, Cebinæ, with 36 teeth, viz., incisors, $\frac{4}{4}$; canines, $\frac{1-1}{1-1}$; molars, $\frac{6-6}{6-6}$; a prehensile tail; small, or of moderate size; the face often naked. They are mild and tractable in their disposition, and feed both on insects and fruit.

Fam. Lemuridæ.

Upper incisors, 4, usually in pairs; lower ones 4 or 2; molars, $\frac{6-6}{5-5}$. Nostrils terminal; first finger of the hind feet with recurved claw; other nails flat; thumbs of both extremities opposable; molars with pointed and alternating tubercles.

This highly interesting family, classed by some under the name of *Strepsirhini*, has been lately separated into the sub-families *Indrisinæ*, *Lemurinæ*, *Nycticebinæ*, and *Galaginæ*.

The great majority are natives of Madagascar; one genus from Africa; and two or three species from India, including Malayana. They are distinguished from monkeys by the two-horned uterus, by the lower jaw remaining permanently divided in the middle, and by the bony orbits being open behind, but with a bony ring separating them from the temporal fossæ. The Indian members of this family belong to the sub-family named *Nycticebinæ*.

Gen. Nycticebus, Geoffroy.

Char.—Head, round; muzzle, short and triangular; ears, short, hairy; extremities, strong and robust; thumb, widely separated from the fingers in both limbs; tail, short; teeth, incisors, $\frac{2 \text{ or } 4}{4}$; canines, $\frac{1-1}{1-1}$; molars, $\frac{6-6}{6-6} = 34$ or 36. Eyes, large, approximate; index finger of hand, short; nostrils, projecting beyond the mouth; body, slender.

The first molar of the lower jaw is acuminated and incurved, resembling a canine tooth. The tongue is long, narrow and rough, and is supported by a cartilaginous plate. The stomach is almost globular with the cardiac and pyloric orifices very close. The cœcum and colon are both large. The uterus is long, and there is a large perforated clitoris through which the urethra passes. The base of the arteries of the limbs are divided into small branches as in the Sloths.

10. Nycticebus tardigradus.

Lemur apud Geoffroy.—*Stenops javanicus*, Auct.—*N. bengalensis*, Geoffroy.—Horsfield, Cat. 25.—Blyth, Cat. 47.—*Lajja banar*, or *Lajjawoti-banar*, Beng., *i. e.*, the bashful monkey.—*Sharmindi billi*, H., *i. e.*, the bashful cat.

The Slow-paced Lemur.

Descr.—Dark ashy-gray with a darker band down the middle of the back; beneath, lighter gray; forehead in some dark, with a narrow white stripe between the eyes, disappearing above them; ears and round the eye, dark; tail, very short. Length of one, 14½ inches; tail, ⅝ths of an inch; another was 16 inches long.

This species is joined to *N. javanicus* by Blyth as a local variety. It has only two upper incisors. The Javanese race has also only in general 2 upper incisors, but it has five well marked dark stripes on the forehead and head. The race from the Malay peninsula has usually 4 upper incisors, and the fur much darker in hue.

The slow-faced Lemur is only found, within our limits, in the most eastern portion of Bengal, Rungpore, Dacca, &c. It keeps to the forests, and is quite nocturnal in its habits, sleeping in the day time in holes of trees, and coming forth at night to feed on leaves and shoots of trees, fruit; and also, it is said, insects and small birds.

Sir W. Jones, in 4th Vol. Asiatic Researches, gives an interesting account of one kept in captivity by him. It is stated to sleep with its head downwards, suspended by the hooked claw of the thumb of the hind feet. It closes its eyelids diagonally, the lower one having most motion. The intestines of one examined were 64 inches long; and the cœcum 3½ inches.

Gen. Loris, Schreber.

Body and limbs slender; no tail; eyes very large, almost contiguous; nose, acute, slightly ascending; otherwise as in *Nycticebus*.

11. Loris gracilis.

Lemur apud Shaw.—*L. ceylonicus*, Fischer.—Blyth, Cat. 48.—*Tevangar*, Tam.—*Dewantsi-pilli*, Tel. Sloth of Europeans in Madras, &c.

The Slender Lemur.

Descr.—Above of a grayish rufescent color; beneath, the same but paler; a white triangular spot on the forehead extending down the nose; fur, short, dense and soft; ears, thin, rounded.

Length of one, about 8 inches; arm, 5; leg, 5½.

I believe that this curious little animal is found in most of the forests of Southern India, but it is difficult to find owing to its small size and nocturnal habits, and it generally escapes the observation of travellers. It does not appear to be common, or at all events well known in the Malabar Coast, yet I have heard of it near there. It is, however, very abundant in the forests of the Eastern Ghâts, and large numbers are brought alive at times to the Madras market, their eyes being a highly esteemed remedy for certain diseases of the eyes among the Tamul doctors.

This lemur is of course quite nocturnal, and it is said to eat fruit, young leaves, insects, eggs, and young birds. In confinement it will eat boiled rice, plantains, honey or syrup; and also it is stated, raw meat. Though slow in its motions in general, it can make its way along a branch with considerable activity, and its grasp is very tenacious. Several made their escape one night from my house in Fort St. George in 1845, and found their way along windows, balconies, and roofs, to some of the public offices in the neighbourhood, considerably alarming some of the native writers by clambering in at the open windows.

The slender Lemur occurs also in Ceylon. Kelaart mentions that the intestines of one examined by him were 35 inches long, and the cœcum 2 inches. A black variety is mentioned by Tennent as found in Ceylon.*

Tarsium, with one species, from Java, is the only other Asiatic member of this family. *Lemur*, *Indris*, and *Lichanotus* are Madagascar forms, and *Galago* is African. *Cheiromys*, a very singular form from Madagascar, having teeth allied to those of the Rodents, is generally placed in this family.

The genus *Galeopithecus* is usually made the type of a distinct family, GALEOPITHECIDÆ. They are the flying lemurs of English authors, having a membrane connecting their limbs. They have not the power of sustaining flight, are nocturnal and insectivorous, with pectoral mammæ, and sleep with their heads downwards. They are natives of Malayana, and may be said to form a link to the frugivorous bats.

Sub-order. CHEIROPTERA, Bats.

Incisors, various in number; canines, distinct; molars uniformly enamelled, with many points, or with a flat depressed crown. Feet, pendactylous; bones of the anterior extremities and especially of the fingers (except the pollux which is always unguiculate) elongated, sustaining a large naked membrane serving for flight; posterior toes all unguiculate. Two pectoral mammæ.

Bats, as is well known, are nocturnal animals of usually small size, with very small eyes and large ears, capable of sustaining a rapid and continuous flight for some hours. Most are insectivorous, a few frugivorous. They produce one or at most two young ones at a birth, which are of a very large size compared to the parent, and are carried about by her. Their sense of hearing and smell is very acute. They roost in the day-time in trees, in the hollows of trees, in caves, old buildings, under roofs, &c., hanging head downwards by their hind claws. They may be said to resemble *Insectivora* with the addition of wings.

The skull is thin, the temporal bone, especially its acoustic portion and the cochlea, much developed. The ribs are extraordinarily long, and the

* May not this be the last species?

sternum greatly developed, the manubrium or anterior portion being much extended laterally to afford a strong attachment for the clavicles which are always present and very robust. The ulna is almost rudimentary and firmly joined to the radius, and the forearm is quite incapable of any rotation. The metacarpal bones are greatly elongated. The pelvis is straight and long, and the coccygeal bones are lengthened in some to support the membrane, and assist them in turning rapidly. The organ of hearing is greatly developed in the insectivorous species, especially the tragus. The foliaceous appendages to the organs of smell in some (*Rhinolophinæ*) may be perhaps intended to give increased power and delicacy to this organ. Their wings form an enormously expanded organ of touch, by means of which they can direct their flight even when their eyes are extirpated, and their hearing blunted, as was proved by some experiments by Spallanzani.

Bats do not possess a cœcum. The penis is pendulous and has a small bone in it. The testes only descend during the breeding season. The uterus has two short horns. The supposed additional inguinal teats of the *Rhinolophi* are probably only cutaneous glands. The females of many bats have nursing pouches. Many become periodically torpid, hybernating in cold countries.

The hairs of bats generally appear under the microscope as serrated and jointed, in some almost annulated, mostly so at the tip. Many are infested by insects of the genus *Nycteribia*. Bats are found throughout the whole world. They are divided into the families *Pteropodidæ*, *Vampyridæ*, *Noctilionidæ* and *Vespertilionidæ*.

Fam. Pteropodidæ.

Frugivorous Bats.

Molars with the crown flat with a median longitudinal groove. Ears small without a tragus. Index with three phalanges, generally unguiculate. Tail very short, or none. Interfemoral membrane small, deeply excised posteriorly. Face lengthened. Gape moderate.

The frugivorous bats, differing so much in their dentition from the insectivorous species, seem to lead through the flying Lemurs directly to the *Quadrumana*. They comprise the largest species in the order, and are chiefly found in the tropical regions of the East, being very numerous in the Malayan islands as far as Australia. Their molars have rounded eminences; the stomach is complex, long and twisted on itself, has two dilatations and some deep longitudinal rugæ or folds. The pyloric orifice is very small, whilst the œsophageal is dilated widely. The intestinal canal is long, being about seven times the length of the body. The females of some are provided with nursing pouches. It is possible that the fabulous Harpy of the ancients was one of these large bats.

Gen. PTEROPUS, Geoffroy.

Char.—Incisors, $\frac{4}{4}$; canines, $\frac{1-1}{1-1}$; molars, $\frac{5-5}{6-6}$. Index finger unguiculate. Snout lengthened. No tail in some; a short one in others. The tongue is covered with large papillæ, pointing backwards, each terminating in a brush.

12. Pteropus Edwardsi.

GEOFFROY.—*P. medius*, TEMMINCK.—*P. leucocephalus*, HODGSON.—*P. assamensis*, McLELLAND.—ELLIOT, Cat. 3—BLYTH, Cat. 51.—*Gadal*, or *Barbagal*, H. in the South.—*Bádún* and *Pata debli*, H. in the North.—*Badúl*, *Beng.*—*Warbagúl* Mahar.—*Toggul bawali*, Can.—*Sikat-yelli*, of *Wuddurs.*—*Sikurayi*, Tel—Flying-fox of Europeans in India.

THE LARGE FOX BAT.

Descr.—Head and nape rufous-black; neck and shoulders golden-yellow; back, dark-brown; chin, dark; rest of body beneath, fulvous or rusty brown; interfemoral membrane, brownish-black.

Length, 12 to 14½ inches; extent of wings, 46 to 52 inches.

This large bat, the flying fox of Europeans, is found throughout all India, Ceylon, and Burmah. Specimens vary considerably in shade and coloration.

During the day they roost on trees, generally in large colonies, many hundred often occupying a single tree to which they invariably resort if not driven away. Towards sunset they begin to get restless, move about along the branches, and by ones and twos fly off for their nightly rounds. If water is at hand, a tank, or a river, or the sea, they fly cautiously down and touch the water, but I could not ascertain if they took a sip, or merely dipped part of their bodies in.* They fly vast distances occasionally to

* A recent writer on observing this has jumped to the conclusion that they do this for the purpose of fishing, and a note on the fishing propensities of the *Pteropus* is to be found in a late number of the Proceedings of the Zoological Society.

such trees as happen to be in fruit. They are fond of most garden fruit (except oranges, &c.); also, the neem, jamoon, bér, and various figs. About the early dawn they return from their hunting grounds, and the scene that then daily takes place is well described by Tickell, in an excellent memoir published in the Calcutta Journal of Natural History, from which I extract the following:—

"From the arrival of the first comer, until the sun is high above the horizon, a scene of incessant wrangling and contention is enacted among them, as each endeavours to secure a higher and better place, or to eject a neighbour from too close vicinage. In these struggles the bats hook themselves along the branches, scrambling about hand over hand with some speed, biting each other severely, striking out with the long claw of the thumb, shrieking and cackling without intermission. Each new arrival is compelled to fly several times round the tree being threatened from all points, and when he eventually hooks on, has to go through a series of combats, and be probably ejected two or three times before he makes good his tenure."

The female brings forth only one young one, which adheres firmly to the breast, retaining its position whether the dam be flying or at rest. The flesh is esteemed good eating by some. Colonel Sykes calls it delicate, and with no bad flavour, and states that it is eaten by the native Portuguese. Many classes in the Madras presidency also eat it.

Whilst on service with my regiment in the Ghazeepore district during the mutiny in 1858, the force was encamped in a grove of trees, on one of which was a rather small colony of these *Pteropi*. The wind which had hitherto been from the east and moist, suddenly changed to a fierce hot, dry, westerly blast, and this so affected the bats, that one by one they descended to lower branches, being blown to leeward of course at the same time, and eventually fell to the ground, and many were picked up, panting and all but lifeless, others quite dead, by our followers, Madras grooms and grass-cutters. Several birds and numerous flies also perished from the same cause.

13. Pteropus Leschenaultii.

DESMAREST—*P. seminudus*, KELAART.—BLYTH, Cat. 54.

THE FULVOUS FOX-BAT.

Descr.—Fur, of a fulvous ashy, or dull light ashy brown color, paler beneath, the hairs whitish at the base; membranes, dark brown; fur, short and downy.

Length, head and body, 5 to $5\frac{1}{2}$ inches; extent, 18 inches. Of another, length, 6 inches; extent, 20 inches; forearm, $3\frac{1}{10}$; tibia, $1\frac{1}{2}$; ear, $\frac{7}{10}$ths.

I have only procured this species in the Carnatic, at Madras, and Trichinopoly, and know nothing of its habits. It is stated to have been procured at Pondicherry and Calcutta. One specimem from the Coromandel coast is stated to have the fur browner, a white collar with the hairs on the sides of the neck longer and directed forwards. Could this have been a specimen of *P. Dussumierii*, Is. Geoffroy, stated to occur on the continent of India, but of which little is known. It is described as being fulvous-rufescent of different shades, lighter beneath, and on the sides of the neck, sometimes brown with a white collar. Length, 7 inches; exterior, 27. A specimen is stated to exist in the British Museum from Saharunpore.

The membrane of *P. Leschenaultii* is described as occasionally marked with white spots in rows. Kelaart met with such in Ceylon.

Many *Pteropi* are found throughout Malayana; one of large size, *P. edulis*, in Java and Malacca; one species at least occurs in Africa; and and some in Australia.

Gen. CYNOPTERUS, F. Cuvier.

Syn. *Pachysoma.*

Char.—Incisors, $\frac{4}{4}$; canines, $\frac{1-1}{1-1}$; molars, $\frac{4-4}{5-5}$.

Two rudimentary false molars in each jaw, but they want the last molars. Snout, short; tail, very short, or none.

14. Cynopterus marginatus.

Vespertilio apud HAMILTON.—*Pteropus pyrivorus*, HODGSON.—*P. tittæcheilus*, TEMMINCK.—ELLIOT, Cat. 4.—BLYTH, Cat. 58—HORSFIELD, Cat. 35.—*Cham-gadili*, Beng.

THE SMALL FOX-BAT.

Descr.—General color fulvous olivaceous, paler beneath and with an ashy tinge; ears, with a narrow margin of white.

Length, 4 to $4\frac{1}{2}$ inches. Of one, $4\frac{1}{2}$, the extent of wing, $17\frac{1}{2}$; forearm, $2\frac{6}{10}$; tail, $\frac{4}{10}$ths, Kelaart gives larger dimensions; one measured $5\frac{1}{2}$ inches; extent, $20\frac{1}{2}$; forearm, $2\frac{3}{4}$; tibia; tail, $\frac{5}{8}$ths.

In some the neck and sides are deeply ferruginous, and fresh specimens are often deeply tinged with dark ferruginous throughout, but fade quickly on drying.

This bat is found throughout all India, from the Himalayas to Cape Comorin and Ceylon. It roosts during the day in clusters on the folded leaves of the plantain, Palmyra palm, and other trees. It is exclusively frugivorous in habit.

Several species are recorded, apparently very closely allied, and some of them perhaps not distinct. *C. affinis*, Gray, from the Himalayas, is usually considered the same. It may, however, be distinct, and is perhaps Hodgson's *P. pyrivorus* in part, described as "wholly earthy brown, nude skin of lips, of joints, and the toes fleshy gray, length, 6 inches; expanse, 24; weight, 5 oz."*

Of this family, other genera are *Xantharpyia* and *Epomophorus* from Africa; and *Macroglossus*, the type of which is *Pt. minimus*, from Tenasserim and Malayana.

The rest of this sub-order are all insectivorous. They have true molars, $\frac{3-3}{3-3}$, beset with pointed tubercles adapted for crushing the hard cases of beetles, &c. The canines are often of large size. The gape is large. The fore feet have the thumb clawed, the hind feet without a claw. Index with one or two bony phalanges. The stomach is small and simple, and the intestinal canal short, being only about twice the length of the body, or less. They are found all over the world. They are called *Gadal*, *Chamgidar* in Hindustani; *Chamgúddri*, Beng.; *Chidgu* at Bhagulpore; *Gabbelay* and *Jiburai* in Telugu; *Kanka-pati* in Canarese; *Phiyu longtá*, Bhotia; and *Brin*, Lepcha.

Fam. VAMPYRIDÆ.

A nose leaf, either simple or complicated.

Sub-fam. MEGADERMATINÆ.

Nose leaf complicated. Index finger of two joints.

Gen. MEGADERMA. Geoffroy.

Char.—Incisors, $\frac{0}{4}$; molars, $\frac{4-4}{5-5}$. Nose furnished with a complicated

* I see that in the last edition of Hodgson's Catalogue by Mr. Gray, *P. pyrivorus* is given, in addition to *Cynopterus marginatus*, from the Sikim Terai. This, if really distinct, may be *C. affinis*, as noted above; or *Pteropus dussamierii*.

membranous apparatus; ears very large, connate at the base, with a small tragus. No tail. Interfemoral membrane cut square. Peculiar to the Eastern hemisphere.

15. Megaderma lyra.

GEOFFROY.—*M. carnatica,* ELLIOT, Cat. 5.—*M. schistacea,* HODGSON.—BLYTH, Cat. 59—HORSFIELD, Cat 73.

THE LARGE-EARED VAMPIRE BAT.

Descr.—Of a slaty blue or pale mouse color, albescent or yellowish-ashy beneath. Nasal appendage, large, oblong, free at the tip, reaching to the base of the ears with a fold down the centre; tragus cordate, two-lobed, anterior lobe pointed, twice as high as the posterior, which is rounded; muzzle, truncated; under lip, cleft.

Length of one, head and body, $3\frac{1}{2}$ inches; extent, $19\frac{1}{2}$; forearm, $2\frac{3}{4}$; tibia, $1\frac{3}{10}$.

The molar teeth above are occasionally only three on each side, as found by Mr. Elliot, but Hodgson and others have observed four on each side.

This curious looking bat is found over all India, from the foot of the Himalayas to the extreme South, frequenting old buildings, pagodas, caves, roofs of houses, &c. It is very abundant in the innermost compartments of the cave temples of Ellora and Ajunta. Hodgson considered those he procured (which were under the roof of the Dâk bungalow at Silligoree, at the foot of the Sikim Himalayas) distinct; but I got specimens from the very same locality, and found them apparently quite identical with those from Southern India. Horsfield, indeed, when noticing Hodgson's new Mammals, &c., stated that dry specimens could not be distinguished from *M. lyra.*

Mr. Blyth has fully ascertained that this bat at times sucks the blood from other bats, fixing on them behind the ear, sucking the blood during flight, and then devouring the body. It has also been known to eat frogs and fish. Hodgson found insects only in those he examined.

16. Megaderma spectrum.

WAGNER.—In Hügel's Kaschmir, IV. p. 569, with figure.

THE KASHMIR VAMPIRE BAT.

Descr.—Above slaty cinereous, whitish beneath; the vertical nose leaf of moderate size, oval; inner lobe of tragus ovate.

Length, head and body, $2\frac{3}{4}$ inches; ear, $1\frac{8}{12}$ths. Wagner, in his supplemental volume to Schreber, makes Hodgson's species *schistacea*, as synonymous with this one; and as part of his description is apparently taken from Hodgson, I can give no other characters than those above. I have not seen a specimen. It is stated to have been found in Kashmir by Baron Hügel.

Two other species are recorded from the East, *M. Horsfieldii*, Blyth, from Tenaserim; and *M. spasma*, L. from Malayana and Ceylon. Dr. Cantor states that in the latter species he found a small cœcum, $\frac{1}{16}$th of an inch long.

One species, *M. frons*, is from Egypt.

Sub-fam. Rhinolophinæ.

Nasal leaf, complicated, membranous. Forefinger of a single joint; wings, largely developed. Females with pubic warts simulating mammæ.

This family is greatly developed in India and Malayana.

Gen. Rhinolophus, Geoffroy.

Char.—Incisors, $\frac{0}{4}$, or $\frac{2}{4}$; the upper ones small and distant; molars, $\frac{4-4}{5-5}$ or $\frac{5-5}{5-5}$ or $\frac{5-5}{6-6}$; nose furnished with a complicated apparatus, consisting of a cordate or semi-orbicular leaf, bilobed in front of the nostrils; a longitudinal crest along the nose, and an erect frontal leaf posteriorly, more or less lanceolate. Ears, large, not joined at the base, without a tragus, but often with a lobe at the base of the outer margin. Tail long, connate with the membrane. Wings, long, ample.

These bats are said to hang with their body rolled up in their wings as in a mantle.

17. Rhinolophus perniger.

Hodgson, J. A. S. XII. 414.—Blyth, Cat. 62.—*R. luctus*, Temminck?

The Large Leaf-bat.

Descr.—Ears, very large, much longer than the head, broad, acutely pointed; nasal apparatus, very complicated, the lower leaf very large, concealing the upper lip like a door-knocker; the upper leaf like a graduated spire; ears, transversely striate; a rather large semi-circular lobe at base of ear; lower lip with two warts; molars, $\frac{5-5}{6-6}$. Fur, long, dense, soft, and lax, slightly curled or woolly, black, with a silvery grizzle, or grayish-black, or rich chesnut-brown.

Length of one, head and body, 3¼ inches; tail, 1¾; expanse, 17; fore-arm, 2½; tibia, 1¼; ear, 1¼ by ¾-inch wide. Hodgson gives one, head and body, 3¼; tail, 2⅛; expanse, 17; forearm 2⅝; leg, 1⅜.

This fine bat has been usually considered the same as Temminck's *R. luctus* from Java, &c.; but latterly, Blyth considered it distinct, stating that its facial membranes are less complicated than in *luctus*. Hodgson procured it in Nepal, and I got it at Darjeeling in warm valleys. I procured one specimen at Tellicherry, which I forwarded to Mr. Elliot, who pronounced it to be *R. luctus*. It was of a reddish-brown color, and a rufescent variety of *luctus* has been described by Eydoux. It is impossible now to decide if the Malabar bat be the same as the Himalayan one, but if not, it will probably turn out to be true *luctus*.

R. perniger occurs also on the Khasia hills.

18. Rhinolophus mitratus.

Blyth, J. A. S. XIII. 483.—Cat. 63.

The Mitred Leaf-bat.

Descr.—Ears, large, anti-helix moderately developed; upper leaf, triangular, acute; tail, extending beyond the tibia; above light-brown, paler beneath. Length, head and body, 2½ inches; tail, 1½; forearm, 2¼; tibia, 1; ear, 1. Expanse "probably 12," according to Blyth, but from its size I should judge considerably larger, probably 14 at least.

This species has only been hitherto recorded from Chybassa, Central India, whence sent by Colonel Tickell. Hutton, however, considers that he obtained it at Mussoorie.

19. Rhinolophus tragatus.

Hodgson, J. A. S. IV. 699.—Blyth, Cat. 66.

The Dark-brown Leaf-bat.

Descr.—Upper process like a barred spear-head; central one small and narrow, a little expanded at the summit; anti-tragus less developed than usual; lips, simple; color an uniform deep brown, with the tips of the hairs paler and somewhat rusty.

Length, head and body, 2⅝ inches; tail, 1⅞; expanse, 15½; forearm, 2¼; tibia, 1$\frac{1}{16}$.

This bat has been found in the central region of Nepal, and also at Mussoorie. It conceals itself in cavities of rocks, and issues forth soon after dusk, earlier, says Hodgson, than the species of *Vespertilio*. Blyth remarks on the inappropriate name, for, says he, the anti-helix is less developed than usual.

20. Rhinolophus Pearsoni.

HORSFIELD, Cat. 43.—BLYTH, Cat. 64.

PEARSON'S LEAF-BAT.

Descr.—"Color above, dark-brown, with a slight shade of chesnut; underneath, brown with a sooty cast; fur, very long, dense and soft; ears distinct, with an additional rounded lobe below, measuring anteriorly three-fourths of an inch; point of facial crest moderately developed. Length to root of tail, 3 inches; tail, $\frac{1}{2}$ inch; forearm, 2; expanse, 11 inches. Although allied to *tragatus* possesses distinct characters."

This bat has been found at Darjeeling, and Capt. Hutton informs me is common about Mussoorie.

21. Rhinolophus affinis.

HORSFIELD.—BLYTH, Cat. 67.—*R. rubidus* and *R. cinerascens*, KELAART.

THE ALLIED LEAF-BAT.

Descr.—Ears, large, pointed, emarginate externally, anti-helix well developed; upper leaf triangular, emarginate at the tip, reaching above the base of the ears; incisors, $\frac{2}{4}$. Varies much in color—above, bright rufous, or ferruginous brown, or brown; paler beneath. Length, about 3 inches, of which the tail is 1; forearm, $1\frac{10}{12}$; extent, 11 to 12. Kelaart gives head and body, $2\frac{3}{10}$; tail, $\frac{9}{10}$ths; expanse, 12; forearm, $1\frac{9}{10}$; tibia, $\frac{9}{10}$ths; ears, $\frac{7}{10}$ths.

This variable bat is most abundant in Ceylon, Burmah, and Malayana; but it is said to have been taken on the Malabar coast. It appears to be very closely allied to the next species, but is stated to differ in having 2 upper incisors, 6 lower molars, in the tail being longer than the tibia, and in the fur being long. It is possible that the specimens stated to be from Malabar belonged to the next species.

22. Rhinolophus rouxi.

TEMMINCK.—BLYTH, Cat. 68—*R. lepidus*, BLYTH.

THE RUFOUS LEAF-BAT.

Descr.—Ears, large, pointed, externally notched; tragus, broad; tip of upper nose-leaf triangular, with its sides well emarginate, reaching above the base of the ears; no upper incisors; lower molars only five; canines very large; fur, short, crisp; color above, smoky brown in some, red-brown in others, and golden rufous in some; beneath, paler.

Length of one, $3\frac{1}{2}$ inches, of which the tail is $1\frac{1}{8}$; expanse, 13; forearm, $1\frac{7}{8}$; tibia, $\frac{7}{8}$ths; ear, $\frac{7}{10}$ths. Blyth gives much smaller dimensions to his *lepidus*, which, however, he identifies with *Rouxi*, viz., head and body, $1\frac{3}{4}$ inches; tail, $\frac{1}{2}$; expanse, 9; forearm, $1\frac{5}{8}$. Wagner gives total length, $3\frac{5}{12}$; tail, $\frac{10}{12}$ths; forearm, $1\frac{10}{12}$.

I procured specimens of this beautiful bat in a covered drain near Tellicherry on the Malabar coast, and Blyth has procured specimens from the neigbourhood of Calcutta, from a cave near Colgong, and also from Mussoorie, where Hutton tells me it is rare.

23. Rhinolophus macrotis.

HODGSON, J. A. S. XIII. 485—BLYTH, Cat. 70.

THE LARGE-EARED LEAF-BAT.

Descr.—Ears, very large, broad, oval, with pointed recurved tip, and a large obtuse tragus; anterior central crest of nose leaf produced in front over the top of the flat transverse front edge; hinder leaf lanceolate, triangular; above, sooty-brown, or light earthy olive brown; paler below; some with a rufous or isabelline tint. No pubic teats.

Length, head and body, $1\frac{3}{4}$ inches; tail, $\frac{3}{4}$ths; forearm, $1\frac{7}{12}$; expanse, $9\frac{3}{4}$.

This species occurs in the Himalayas, having been sent from Nepal and Mussoorie, where stated to be rare.

24. Rhinolophus sub-badius.

HODGSON, J. A. S. XIII. 486—BLYTH, Cat. 69.

THE BAY LEAF-BAT.

Descr.—Ears not larger than the head, obtusely pointed, and ovoid; nasal appendage quadrate, with a transverse bar nearly surmounting it, upper leaf triangular with slightly emarginate sides; above clear brown; paler below and on the head and face.

Length, head and body, $1\frac{1}{2}$ inches; tail, $1\frac{1}{4}$; expanse, $7\frac{1}{2}$; forearm, $1\frac{1}{4}$; ears, $\frac{5}{8}$ths.

From the Himalayas. Has been sent from Nepal only. Blyth has a RHINOLOPHUS BREVITARSUS from Darjeeling—not described.

One or two *Rhinolophi* are European, a few from Africa, and there are several others from the Malayan islands, China, and Japan.

Gen. HIPPOSIDEROS, Gray.

Char.—Nasal leaf, broad, depressed, transverse; ears, with transverse wrinkles; incisors $\frac{2}{4}$; molars $\frac{4-4}{5-5}$; the upper incisors near the canines, the lower ones close, crenelate, tricuspid; interfemoral membrane large.

Most of the species of this genus have a remarkable peculiarity, viz., a circular cavity or sac behind the nasal crest, which the animal can turn out at pleasure like the finger of a glove; it is lined by a pencil of stiff hairs, and is probably a glandular organ, as it contains a peculiar waxy matter. The ears are very tremulous. Most of the species are from India and Malayana, a few African.

25. Hipposideros armiger.

HODGSON, J. A. S. IV. 699.—BLYTH, Cat. 74.—*H. nobilis*, var. BLYTH, olim.

THE LARGE HORSE-SHOE BAT.

Descr.—Nasal leaf large, quadrate; lips, with a triple fold of skin on each side; "tragus, vaguely developed, and wavily emarginate." Of an uniform light-brown color with maronne tips to the hairs of the upper parts; membranes, black.

Length, head and body $4\frac{1}{2}$ inches; tail $2\frac{1}{4}$; expanse 22; forearm $3\frac{5}{8}$; tibia $1\frac{1}{2}$.

This fine bat was first procured by Hodgson in Nepal; and Hutton found it at Mussoorie at 5,000 feet of elevation. I obtained specimens at Darjeeling. This species is represented in Ceylon by *H. lankadiva*, Kelaart, and in Burmah and the Malay countries, by *H. nobilis*.

26. Hipposideros speoris.

Rhinolophus apud SCHNEIDER.—BLYTH, Cat. 78.—ELLIOT, Cat. 7.—*H. apiculatus* and *H. penicillatus*, GRAY.—*R. dukhunensis*, SYKES.

THE INDIAN HORSE-SHOE BAT.

Descr.—Ears, large, erect, acuminate, rounded at the base, emarginate on the outer margin; facial membrane complicated; muzzle short; interfemoral membrane, narrow, square, enclosing the tail, the half of the last joint alone free; body short, thick, of variable color; sometimes light mouse color, paler beneath; at times, fulvous-brown; at other times, bright rufo-ferruginous or golden fulvous.

Length of a male about $3\frac{3}{10}$ inches, of which the tail is 1; forearm 2; tibia $\frac{9}{10}$ths; expanse 13; ear $\frac{6}{10}$ths. The females are a little smaller.

Sykes' species has generally been considered the same as *speoris*, but I see that Wagner separates it, and Blyth states that "the races from different localities may yet prove to be distinct however closely affined."

It inhabits India, Ceylon, Malayana, as far as Timor, &c.; and is far from rare in Southern India, inhabiting old buildings, wells, &c. It has been sent from Deyra Doon. I procured it at Madras, Nellore, and in the Deccan.

27. Hipposideros murinus.

Rhinolophus apud Elliot, Cat. 8.—*R. fulgens*, Elliot, Cat. 9.—Blyth, Cat. 80.

The Little Horse-shoe Bat.

Descr.—Ears, large, erect, rounded; muzzle, short; a transverse frontal leaf and sac; in front a simple membrane round the nostrils; interfemoral membrane, large, including the tail all but the extreme tip; body short and thick; color, dusky-brown or mouse color, sometimes light fawn or ferruginous; wing membranes blackish.

Length to end of tail, $3\frac{1}{10}$ inches, of which the tail is $1\frac{2}{10}$; expanse $10\frac{1}{2}$; forearm $1\frac{6}{10}$; tibia $\frac{8}{10}$ths; ear $\frac{7}{10}$ths.

This small bat has only been obtained, in our limits, in Southern India; but it also occurs in Ceylon, in Burmah, Malayana, and the Nicobar islands.

The mouse-colored race is common in the Carnatic, but I have only seen the light rufous race on the Neelgherries, at Kaitee, and Rallia. Mr. Elliot obtained both races in the Southern Mahratta country. Blyth considers that a dark race of this bat was named *Rhinolopus ater* by Templeton, and *H. atratus* by Kelaart.

28. Hipposideros cineraceus.

Blyth, J. A. S. XXII. 410, and Cat. 79.

The Ashy Horse-shoe Bat.

Descr.—Similar to *H. murinus* in structure, but larger; above, ashy gray, the hairs whitish at the base, dusky gray at the tip; beneath whitish.

Length of forearm, $1\frac{3}{16}$; ears posteriorly, $\frac{5}{8}$ths of an inch.

Blyth states, that this is larger than *murinus*, but the forearm as given is much shorter. It may prove to be a local race of *H. murinus*, and has only been found in the Punjab salt range.

H. larvatus, Horsfield, is common in Sylhet, Burmah, and Malayana; and Cantor gives *H. nobilis*, *insignis*, *diadema*, and *galeritus*, from the Malay peninsula. Gould has one species from Australia.

Gen. Cœlops, Blyth.

Char.—General characters of *Rhinolophus*, but the tail and calcanea wanting entirely, the intercrural membrane acutely emarginate to the depth of a line even with the knees. Ears, large, broad, rounded; the summit of the facial membranes rising abruptly, obtusely bifid, bent forward; fur, long, delicately fine.

29. Cœlops Frithii.

Blyth, J. A. S. XVII. 251.—Cat. 81.

The Tailless Bat.

Descr.—Color dusky or blackish; the fur tipped with dull ashy-brown above, paler and somewhat ashy beneath; membranes fuscous. Length to rump, $1\frac{7}{8}$ inch; membrane beyond, $\frac{3}{4}$ths; forearm, $1\frac{3}{4}$.

Mr. Blyth obtained one specimen only of this curious bat, which was procured by Mr. Frith in the Soonderbuns.

Gen. Rhinopoma, Geoffroy.

Char.—Incisors, $\frac{2}{4}$; canines, $\frac{1-1}{1-1}$ molars, $\frac{4-4}{5-5}$. Ears, moderate, connate; auricle, small, erect; forehead, excavated; nostrils, operculate by a small lamina; tail, connate by its base with the intercrural membrane, but produced beyond it.

The genus by its connate ears approaches *Megaderma*, near which it is classed by some.

30. Rhinopoma Hardwickii.

Gray.—Blyth, Cat. 83.

The Long-tailed Leaf-bat.

Descr.—Muzzle, long, thick, truncated, and surmounted by a small leaf; tragus, oblong, bi-acuminate; forehead, concave, with a fossa or channel down the centre; fur, soft and very fine; dull brown throughout; face, rump, and part of the abdominal region, naked.

Length, $5\frac{1}{10}$ inches, of which the tail is $2\frac{1}{2}$ inches; expanse, 13; forearm, $2\frac{4}{10}$; tibia, $1\frac{1}{2}$; ear in front, $\frac{7}{8}$ths.

This bat is found over almost all India, in Burmah and Malayana. It frequents old ruins, caves, clefts in rocks, &c. In 1848, many were captured in Madras by Mr. Elliot and myself in a house for three successive nights, this bat being not of common occurrence there in general. They had probably been blown there by the strong westerly winds which had just set in from the rocky hills to the westward of Madras.

This species is very closely allied to *R. microphylla*, from Egypt, on which the genus was founded, the only other species known.

Nycteris is another allied form, mostly African, but with one species, *Nycteris javanica*, Geoffroy, from Java and Malacca.

The remaining animals of this family are American, and comprise the sub-families *Phyllostomatinæ* and *Desmodinæ* of some. The former, which represent the *Rhinolophinæ* in the new world, have a nose leaf, usually 4 incisors in each jaw, ear with a distinct tragus, and the tongue long and extensile. The Vampire of authors, *Vampyrus spectrum*, L., is one of the largest of the group, but it does not appear certain that this bat and its allies are so sanguivorous as those of the next sub-family. The tongue, however, is furnished with a suctorial disc. One genus, *Glossophaga*, has the tongue very long and narrow, furnished at the tip with a brush of hair-like papillæ; another genus, *Stenoderma*, is stated to be frugivorous. The *Desmodinæ* are furnished with most formidable lancet-shaped incisors and canines, evidently adapted for blood letting.

Fam. NOCTILIONIDÆ.

No facial membrane; head, short and obtuse; lips, large; wings, long; tail usually free at the tip.

Sub-fam. TAPHOZOINÆ.

Ears, distant; tail, much shorter than the membrane, free at the tip.

Gen. TAPHOZOUS, Geoffroy.

Char.—Two small incisors above in young individuals only, none in adults.

Molars, $\frac{5-5}{5-5}$. Snout, conical, with the nostrils approximate. Forehead, with a rounded cavity. Ears, moderate, apart. Tail, short, emerging by a free tip above the intercrural membrane.

The face is flat, and the nostrils can be closed at pleasure. There is a large gular sac in the males, which is glandular; a longitudinal fold on each side leads to this sac. The fur is close, soft, and velvety. The wing is long and narrow, and collapses with a double flexure outwards. From the warmer regions of the old world and Australia.

31. Taphozous longimanus.

HARDWICKE, Lin. Trans. XIV. pl. 17.—BLYTH, Cat. 85.—*T. brevimanus, cantori,* and *fulvidus,* BLYTH (olim).

THE LONG-ARMED BAT.

Descr.—Ears oval, with many distinct folds, naked except at the base; tragus, securiform; fur, thick, close, fuscous-black or dark fuscous brown above; beneath paler, except on the throat, the hairs being conspicuously tipped with gray; the upper hairs all white at their base; face nude; it and the membranes, dark brownish black.

A fulvescent variety was named *T. fulvidus* by Blyth, who subsequently stated that young individuals are fulvescent and become gradually blacker with age.

Length about 5 inches; expanse 15 to 16 inches; tail 1, capable of being protruded for $\frac{3}{4}$ inch; forearm $2\frac{5}{8}$; tibia 1; ear $\frac{9}{10}$ths internally.

The long-armed bat is very common about large towns, as at Madras and Calcutta, and is found generally throughout India. It frequents dark out-houses, cellars, stabling, old temples, and the like. Blyth noticed that it had the faculty of creeping about on a vertical board (of a cage) in a most surprising manner, hitching its claws into the minute pores of the wood.

32. Taphozous melanopogon.

TEMMINCK.—HORSFIELD, Cat. 69.

THE BLACK-BEARDED BAT.

Descr.—Ears, moderate, oval, with the outer margin extending under the eyes, dilated into a large rounded lobe; the tragus, leaf-shaped; the head, muzzle, and chin covered with short hairs. Above brown or reddish-brown; beneath brownish-white, with a long black collar or beard round the throat of the male, surrounded by a light brown band. Many males, however, it is stated, want this collar. The females are brownish mouse, gray above, lighter beneath.

Length $3\frac{3}{4}$ to 4 inches, of which the tail is $\frac{8}{12}$ths; expanse 14 to 15 inches.

This bat is stated in Horsfield's Catalogue to have been sent from some caves in Canara by Dr. Wight, but no other record of its occurrence in our province is known to me. It is common in various parts of Malayana.

33. Taphozous saccolaimus.

Temminck.—Blyth, Cat. 84.—*T. crassus*, Blyth.—*T. pulcher*, Elliot.

The White-bellied Bat.

Descr.—Muzzle, angular, naked, very acute; nostrils, small, close; ears, distant, shorter than the head, large inner margin recurved, outer ditto, dilated, reaching to the conmissure of the mouth; tragus, wide, securiform; fur, short, smooth, blackish on the head, chesnut-brown on the back; beneath, dirty white; or black-brown above with white pencillings; pure white below.

Length, nearly 5 inches; expanse 17; tail $\frac{9}{12}$ths. One obtained by Mr. Elliot at Madras, was $4\frac{6}{10}$ inches long; expanse 17; forearm $2\frac{7}{10}$. Malayan examples appear to be smaller.

This fine *Taphozous* has been procured occasionally in various parts of the peninsula, and it also inhabits Burmah and Malayana.

Taphozous bicolor, Temminck, is said to be from the East Indies, and Wagner states that M. Roux brought four examples from Calcutta. As it was never obtained by Blyth, I imagine there must be some mistake, and that the specimens if of a distinct species from those recorded above, were not obtained at Calcutta; *T. bicoler* is described as having the ears, oval, long, nude; the tragus, short and securiform; the hairs white at the base, and dusky black at the tip. Length $3\frac{6}{12}$ inches; expanse 13.

There are one or two more Asiatic species of *Taphozous*, several from Africa, and one from Australia.

Most of the remaining groups of this sub-family are from America; one, *Emballonura*, having a representative in Java.

Sub-fam. Noctilioninæ.

Tail longer than the membrane, free at the tip for some length in several.

Gen. Nyctinomus, Geoffroy.

Syn. *Dysopes* in part, Illiger.

Char.—Incisors, in the young $\frac{2}{6}$; in adults $\frac{2}{4}$ or $\frac{2}{2}$ or $\frac{2}{0}$; molars,

$\frac{4-4}{5-5}$ or $\frac{5-5}{5-5}$. Ears broad, short, approximate or connate, with the outer margin terminating in an erect lobe beyond the conch; tragus small, concealed; wings narrow, folded as in *Taphozous;* intercrural membrane short, truncate; tail free at the tip; feet short, thick, with strong toes; muzzle thick; lips tumid, lax; upper lip with coarse wrinkles.

34. Nyctinomus plicatus.

Vespertilio apud BUCHANAN, Linn. Trans. V. 11-18. with figure.—BLYTH, Cat. 88.—*N. bengalensis*, GEOFFROY.—*N. dilatatus* and *tenuis*, HORSFIELD.

THE WRINKLED-LIPPED BAT.

Descr.—Ears large; incisors $\frac{2}{2}$; tail thick; above smoky or snuff-brown; paler and somewhat ashy beneath.

Length, $4\frac{1}{4}$ to $4\frac{7}{10}$ inches; expanse $13\frac{1}{2}$; tail $1\frac{3}{4}$.

This curious looking bat is generally distributed throughout the country. It is tolerably common about Calcutta, and I have taken it near Madras. It frequents ruins, dark buildings, and occasionally, it is said, the hollows of trees. Several species are found in Africa.

Cheiromeles torquatus, a very curious bat found in Java, has the thumb of the hind feet separate from the toes, and capable of separate motion.

Most of the other species of this family of bats are American; and some of them have a very remarkable physiognomy.

Fam. VESPERTILIONIDÆ.

No facial leaf; ears usually separated; upper incisors four or two, the two middle ones apart; five or six lower incisors, sharp and somewhat notched; molars with very pointed tubercles; lips simple; tail long, included in the membrane; wings wide; a single phalanx in the index fingers.

This family comprises the ordinary bats, and is divided into two groups, differing in the number of teeth. They are of general distribution.

Sub-fam. SCOTOPHILINÆ.

Molars $\frac{4-4}{5-5}$ or $\frac{5-5}{5-5}$; ears of medium size; upper incisors in adults 4 or 2, widely separated, and close to the canines.

The species of this sub-family have the muzzle somewhat more abbreviated and blunt than those of the next group. They are the most numerous and diffused of all Indian bats.

Gen. SCOTOPHILUS, Leach.

Char.—Upper incisors usually 4; molars $\frac{4-4}{5-5}$ or $\frac{5-5}{5-5}$; membranes attached to the foot close to the base of the toes; ears small, ovoid, rounded at the tip; tragus short, rounded.

35. Scotophilus serotinus.

Vespertilio apud SCHREBER.—*V. noctula*, GEOFFROY, Ann. Mus. VIII. t. 17 and 18.—BLYTH, Cat. 100.

THE SILKY BAT.

Descr.—Ears distant, ovately triangular, much shorter than the head; tragus short, semicordate; muzzle somewhat denuded; fur deep bay or chesnut-brown above, somewhat fulvous-gray beneath; hairs of the back long and silky. Molars, $\frac{4-4}{5-5}$.

Length, head and body, $2\frac{1}{2}$ to $2\frac{3}{4}$ inches; extent 13; tail 2; forearm nearly 2; ears $\frac{3}{4}$ths.

This European bat has been killed in the Himalayas. Hutton tells me that he procured it on the Tyne range beyond Mussoorie—rare.

36. Scotophilus leisleri.

Vespertilio apud KUHL.—*V. dasycarpus*, LEISLER.—BLYTH, Cat. 102.

THE HAIRY-ARMED BAT.

Descr.—Ears short, oval, triangular; tragus short, rounded at the tip; membrane attached to the base of the outer toe; all toes short; membrane over the arm very hairy; some cross lines of hairs on the interfemoral membrane; molars, $\frac{4-4}{5-5}$ in adults; fur long, deep fuscous-brown at base, chesnut at the tip; beneath, grayish-brown.

Length, head and body, $2\frac{1}{4}$ inches; tail $1\frac{3}{4}$; extent $11\frac{1}{2}$; forearm $1\frac{1}{2}$.

This bat is said by Hutton to be common in valleys of the Tyne range.

37. Scotophilus pachyomus.

TOMES, P. Z. S. 1857. 50.

THE THICK-MUZZLED BAT.

Descr.—Muzzle rounded, obtuse; ears ovoid; tragus short, of nearly uniform breadth, rounded at the end; wing membranes extending to the base of the toes, which exceed the rest of the foot in length; fur bicolored; above, dark brown, with whitish-brown tips; beneath, brown at the base, the tip yellowish-brown.

Length, head and body, $2\frac{1}{2}$ inches; tail $1\frac{10}{12}$; expanse $13\frac{1}{2}$; forearm $2\frac{1}{12}$; tibia $\frac{10}{12}$ths.

This species of bat was brought from some part of India by Captain Boys.

38. Scotophilus coromandelianus.

Vespertilio apud F. Cuvier.—Blyth, Cat. 105.—*Kerivoula Sykesii*, Gray.—No. 12, Elliot, Cat.

The Coromandel Bat.

Descr.—Ears rather large, broad; tragus lunate, or slightly curved forwards, and obtuse and rounded at the tip; a minute præmolar above, situated laterally internally, not visible from without; two lower præmolars; two pair of upper incisors about equal in size; fur short; above, dingy fulvous-brown, beneath grayish fulvous; in some dark-brown both above and below.

Total length, $2\frac{5}{8}$ inches, of which the tail is $1\frac{1}{8}$; expanse $7\frac{1}{2}$ to $7\frac{3}{4}$; forearm $1\frac{1}{10}$. Elliot gives total length $2\frac{8}{10}$; forearm 1.

This minute bat is found in every part of India, and usually conceals itself in the roofs of dwelling-houses, in holes in the thatch, under tiles, &c.

39. Scotophilus lobatus.

Vespertilio apud Gray.—Hardwicke, Ill. Ind. Zool.—*V. abramus*, Temminck?

The Lobe-eared Bat.

Descr.—Ears small, ovoid, ends rounded, scarcely emarginate, with a lobe at the base; tragus short, of nearly uniform breadth, curved inwards and rounded at the end; muzzle very short, pointed. Fur above blackish-yellow, ashy beneath. Some cross lines of hairs on the interfemoral membrane.

Length, $2\frac{5}{12}$ inches, of which the tail is $1\frac{1}{4}$; extent $7\frac{8}{12}$; forearm $1\frac{2}{12}$.

This bat, figured in Hardwicke's Illustrations, is considered by Tomes to be very close to, if not identical with the Japanese bat, named *V. abramus* by Temminck. It is not certain from what part of India it was procured.

40. Scotophilus fuliginosus.

HODGSON, J. A. S. IV. 700.

THE SMOKY BAT.

Descr.—" Feet very small, included in the wing-membrane, nearly to the ends of the toes; ears acutely pointed, shorter than the head; muzzle grooved, nudish; face sharp; rostrum somewhat recurved. Wholly sooty-brown. A little smaller than *Vesp. formosa.*" Such is Hodgson's description of this bat, which does not seem to have been recognized of late. I see it stated to have six lower molars, and it is perhaps not a *Scotophilus.* Blyth at one time considered it to be his *Nycticejus atratus.* Hodgson procured it from the central region of Nepal.

Blyth describes a *Scotophilus fulvidus* from Tenasserim, and Tomes has *S. pumiloides* from China. Gray, in his Catalogue of British Museum, has enumerated, but not described, *S. Hodgsoni* from Calcutta, *S. falcatus,* from India, and *S. fulvus* from Madras and Java, the latter probably Blyth's *fulvidus.*

Gen. NOCTULINIA, Gray.

Feet quite free from the membrane, which is attached to the ankle only; otherwise as in *Scotophilus.* Incisors $\frac{4}{6}$; molars $\frac{5-5}{5-5}$; by age $\frac{4-4}{4-4}$, with a very small false molar.

41. Noctulinia noctula.

Vespertilio apud SCHREBER.—*V. lasiopterus,* SCHREBER.—*V. altivolans,* WHITE.—*V. labiata,* HODGSON.—BLYTH, Cat. 89.

THE NOCTULE BAT.

Descr.—Ears remote, oval-triangular, or rounded, wide, extending nearly to the angle of the mouth; tragus short, broad, curved, ending in a broad rounded head; muzzle short, blunt, nude; lips somewhat tumid; fur dark reddish-brown, both above and below.

Length, $4\frac{1}{2}$ to 5 inches, of which, the tail is nearly 2; expanse 14 to 15 inches; forearm $1\frac{10}{12}$.

This fine bat has been sent from Nepal by Hodgson, who states that it is found in the central hills of Nepal. It is not uncommon in England, and its flight is lofty.

Gen. NYCTICEJUS, Horsfield.

Char.—Incisors in the young $\frac{4}{6}$; in adults $\frac{2}{6}$; molars $\frac{4-4}{5-5}$; upper incisors resembling canine teeth; ears short and broad, distant, and stand out from the head; muzzle, broad.

The bats of this group are more brightly colored than any of the tribe, most of them being yellow beneath, of different shades; this, added to their peculiar physiognomy caused by the short muzzle and the ears standing out laterally, causes them to be easily recognized. There are several species in India, and they are mostly numerous in individuals.

42. Nycticejus Heathii.

HORSFIELD, P. Z. S. 1831. 113.—BLYTH, Cat. 91.

THE LARGE YELLOW BAT.

Descr.—Ears shorter than the head, straight, oblong, with rounded tip, sub-emarginate posteriorly, lobed; tragus linear, slightly curved; fur short, soft, shining; above, bright olivaceous with a tinge of ferruginous or golden-brown; beneath pale and slightly greenish-yellow.

Length, 6 to 6½ inches, of which the tail is 2¼; expanse 18; forearm 2½ to 2¾.

This handsome bat is by no means rare in Southern India, in the Carnatic, and the Malabar coast; and it is also met with, though rarely, in some parts of Central India. It roosts both in houses and trees.

43. Nycticejus luteus.

BLYTH, J. A. S. XX. 157, and Cat. 92.—*N. flaveolus* apud HORSFIELD, Cat.

THE BENGAL YELLOW BAT.

Descr.—Similar to the last species but smaller; above, rich yellow-brown, or bright golden rufous, or dark olive-brown; beneath pale buff, or dark buff, or yellow, or yellowish-gray.

Length, 5¼ inches, of which the tail is 2¼; expanse 14¾; forearm 2½. Others are smaller.

This bat is found over all the continent of India. I have seen it in the Carnatic, also in the N. W. Provinces, and it is very common about Calcutta. It also occurs all over Burmah to Assam. The colors of this, and the allied species, fade much on exposure to light.

44. Nycticejus Temminckii.

Vespertilio apud HORSFIELD.—BLYTH, Cat. 93.—*V. belangeri*, IS. GEOFFROY; also *V. noctulinus*.

THE COMMON YELLOW BAT.

Descr.—Ears short, rounded; tragus moderate curved inwards; above, castaneous-olive, or rufous, or rufo-fulvous; beneath flavescent, or fulvous.

Length, 4½ inches, of which the tail is 1½; expanse 13; forearm 2.

This bat is found over all India, also Burmah and Malayana. *V. noctulinus*, Is. Geoffroy, is confidently stated to be the young of this, but it is described as having an elongated muzzle, triangular ears, and a long straight tragus.

45. Nycticejus castaneus.

GRAY, apud HORSFIELD, Cat.—BLYTH, Cat. 94.

THE CHESNUT BAT.

Descr.—Very similar to the last, but slightly smaller, and the colors much darker; chestnut or tawny rufous, or dark ferruginous above, the under parts scarcely paler.

This species or race is chiefly found in the countries to the eastward, Burmah and Malayana, but it extends into Eastern Bengal. Tytler sent it from Dacca.

46. Nycticejus atratus.

BLYTH, Cat. 96.—*Sc. fuliginosus*, apud BLYTH, olim.

THE SOMBRE BAT.

Descr.—Fur rich dark brown above, a little paler beneath. Size nearly of *Scotophilus fuliginosus*; forearm 1¾ inches.

This bat was procured at Darjeeling by Major Sherwill.

47. Nycticejus canus.

BLYTH, Cat. 99.—*Vespertilio*, No. XI. ELLIOT, Cat.—*Scot. maderaspatanus*, GRAY?

THE HOARY BAT.

Descr.—Light dusky above, with the tips of the hairs pale grayish or fulvous; lighter beneath; sometimes variegated with bright ferruginous.

Length, $3\frac{4}{10}$ inches, of which the tail is $1\frac{3}{10}$; extent $9\frac{1}{2}$; forearm $1\frac{4}{10}$.

This bat is exceedingly common in most parts of India. Mr. Blyth mentions in a note to this species (Cat. p. 32), that there is another and very similar species common about Calcutta, which has permanently the two small pairs of upper incisors characteristic of *Scotophilus*, instead of the one larger pair of adult *Nycticejus*.

The next species differ considerably in coloration, and are typical of another section.

48. Nycticejus ornatus.

Blyth, J. A. S. XX. 517, and Cat 90.

The Harlequin Bat.

Descr.—Ear-conch elongate, oval, erect; tragus rather narrow, semilunate, curved towards the front; above pale rusty isabelline color, somewhat paler below; a pure silky-white spot on the centre of the forehead; others on each shoulder, and on the axillæ above; and a narrow stripe of the same along the middle of the back; face and chin deep brown; a broad white demi-collar from ear to ear, succeeded by a dark-brown one, and below this again, a narrow white one; membranes black; interfemoral membrane tawny red; limbs and digits, the same.

Length of a female, $4\frac{3}{4}$ inches, of which the tail was $1\frac{7}{8}$; expanse, $14\frac{1}{2}$; forearm, $2\frac{1}{4}$; tibia, $\frac{7}{8}$ths; another was $4\frac{1}{2}$ inches; tail, $2\frac{1}{10}$; forearm, $2\frac{3}{8}$; tibia, $\frac{7}{8}$ths.

This remarkably colored bat was sent from Darjeeling. I obtained one specimen from the same place, which was said to have been taken from a folded plantain leaf, in the warm valley of the great Rungeet river.

49. Nycticejus nivicolus.

Hodgson, Ann. Mag. Nat. Hist. 1855.—Horsfield, Cat.

The Alpine Bat.

Descr.—Head and body above uniform light-brown, with a slight yellowish shade; underneath, from the throat to the vent, dark-gray with a brownish tint, lighter on the sides of the throat. Ears long, attenuated to an obtuse point.

Length, 5 inches, of which the tail is 2; expanse 19; forearm $2\frac{1}{2}$; tibia, $1\frac{1}{2}$; ears, $\frac{5}{8}$ths.

Horsfield states that this bat has the fur similar in character to *Lasiurus Pearsoni*, being delicate, soft, and silky; and I see that in the last edition of the Catalogue of Hodgson's specimens, it is classed as a *Lasiurus* and *N. ornatus* is considered to be the male. It is also stated to have some affinity to *Vesp. formosa*, Hodgson. This bat is stated to have been procured from near the snows in Sikim. If this be the case, its habitat is very different from that of *ornatus*, which frequents warm valleys; and as there are various other differences in the descriptions, without further evidence I shall keep them distinct.

Sub-fam. VESPERTILIONINÆ.

Lower molars usually six on each side; incisors $\frac{4}{6}$; tragus, long thin and narrow, more or less pointed. These bats are difficult to group in genera, and almost require a special cheiropterologist. Mr. Tomes, indeed, has undertaken the task partially, and it is to be hoped he will publish a complete history of *Cheiroptera*. Several groups have been generally recognized.

Gen. LASIURUS, Horsfield.

Char.—Head small; ears oval, short, pointed; tragus short, bent forwards; molars $\frac{4-4}{5-5}$ or $\frac{4-4}{6-6}$; with a minute præmolar close to the canines above; interformal membrane hairy above; wings hairy along the forearm.

This group is classed as a section only of *Vespertilio* by Tomes, but Blyth, in his Catalogue, places it separately from other species of *Vespertilio*, though classing it as a typical *Vespertilio* apud Tomes, which I do not think that naturalist intended; and as the bats referred "to, or near to this group," by him, viz., *suillus*, *Pearsoni*, *formosus*, and *emarginatus*, are certainly of a different type from various other species of *Vespertilio*. I shall class them here under the three sub-generic groups of *Lasiurus*, *Murina*, and *Kerivoula*.

50. Lasiurus Pearsoni.

HORSFIELD, Cat.—BLYTH, Cat. 106. *Noctulinia lasiura*, HODGSON (in part.)

THE HAIRY-WINGED BAT.

Descr.—Ears ovoid; tragus rather long, nearly straight, acute at the tip; muzzle somewhat thick; wing membranes extend to the base of the toes; fur, above very soft, silky and long, brownish-gray with a ferruginous cast, and variegated with whitish hairs on the head, neck, and shoulders; the rest of the body above, with the base of the membrane, thighs, and interfemoral membrane, deep bay, or reddish-brown, with a few hairs of the same tint scattered over the membrane, and projecting from its edge; body beneath gray, palest on the throat and breast; membranes brown; interfemoral membrane marked with transverse lines.

Length $4\frac{1}{2}$ inches, of which the tail is $1\frac{1}{2}$; expanse 14; forearm $2\frac{1}{4}$; ear $\frac{1}{2}$; tragus $\frac{4}{12}$ths.

Hodgson's description of *Noctulinia lasiura* is as follows:—"Entire legs and caudal membrane clad in fur like the body, which is thick and woolly; color bright rusty above, sooty below, the hairs tipped with hoary."

This handsome bat has only, I believe, been procured at Darjeeling, where Hodgson says he took it near his own house, and whence also specimens were sent by Mr. Theobald. Mr. Blyth states, that Hodgson sent specimens of the next species, *Murina suillus*, under the name of *N. lasiura;* and I see that this is included by Horsfield in the list of new species sent by Hodgson from Sikim, though not recorded in Gray's Catalogue of his collection.

Lasiurus has been considered chiefly an American group.

Gen. Murina, Gray.

Char.—Head and face somewhat lengthened, hairy; nostrils produced; ears large, with the outer margin folded; tragus long, filiform, acute; wing-membrane broad, united to the whole length of the outer toe; interfemoral membrane and toes hairy; canines small; molars, $\frac{5-5}{5-5}$.

51. Murina suillus.

Vespertilio apud Temminck.—Blyth, Cat. 107.—*N. lasiura,* in part, Hodgson, and *L. Pearsoni* apud Blyth.

The Pig Bat.

Descr.—Fur long, woolly, bright rufous, the hairs whitish at the base; abdomen isabelline.

Length, head and body, $1\frac{3}{4}$ to 2 inches; expanse 9-10; tail $1\frac{1}{2}$; forearm $1\frac{1}{4}$; tibia $\frac{5}{12}$ths.

This curious bat obtained its specific name from the lengthened snout. It is chiefly an inhabitant of the Malayan archipelago, but has been sent from Darjeeling, where I also procured several examples.

The next species has not usually been placed under this genus, being classed as a *Kerivoula* by Gray, and as a *Nycticejus* by Blyth, whilst Tomes considers it as belonging to that section of *Vespertilio* in which he also classes the last species. As, however, I have retained *Vespertilio* for another group of true bats, I have preferred retaining this species under the generic name of one of its nearest affines, which, indeed, with some extended characters, might include all belonging to this section as understood by Tomes.

52. Murina formosa.

Vespertilio apud HODGSON, J. A. S. IV. 700.—*Kerivoula* apud GRAY, Cat. HODGSON'S Collection.—*Nycticejus Tickelli*, BLYTH, Cat. 95.—*N. isabellinus* apud HORSFIELD, Cat.—Figd. P. Z. S. 1858, pl. XV.

THE BEAUTIFUL BAT.

Descr.—Head conic; face acute; ear moderate ovoid, emarginate, acute; incisors $\frac{4}{6}$; molars $\frac{6-6}{6-6}$; fur thick and cottony; above bright soft ruddy yellow, pale-yellowish beneath; membranes yellow along the fingers, the rest brownish-black.

Length, head and body, $2\frac{1}{2}$ inches; tail 2; expanse $12\frac{1}{2}$. Blyth gave the dimensions of *N. Tickelli* as total length $4\frac{3}{4}$ inches, of which the tail is $2\frac{1}{8}$; forearm, $2\frac{3}{8}$.

This beautiful bat has been found both in Nepal and Sikim, in the Himalayas, and also in Central India, if Blyth be right in referring his *N. Tickelli* to this species. Tickell procured his specimens at Chybassa. I got one or two examples at Darjeeling.

Gen. KERIVOULA, Gray.

Char.—Face short, hairy; chaffron concave; muzzle narrow; ears broad not very acute at tip; tragus very long, narrow, and pointed; two pair of upper incisors, the anterior the longest; feet hairy above, half attached; interfemoral membrane large, pointed, somewhat hairy beneath; tail long.

53. Kerivoula picta.

Vespertilio apud PALLAS.—BLYTH, Cat. 109—*V. kerivoula*, BODDAERT.

THE PAINTED BAT.

Descr.—Fur fine, woolly; above yellowish-red, or golden rufous; beneath less brilliant and more yellow; wing membranes inky-black with rich orange stripes along the fingers, extending in indentations into the membrane.

Length, $3\frac{8}{10}$ inches, of which the tail is $1\frac{4}{10}$; expanse 10; forearm $1\frac{3}{10}$; tibia $\frac{6}{10}$ths; ears $\frac{6}{10}$ths. One measured head and body $1\frac{9}{10}$ inches; tail $1\frac{1}{2}$; forearm $1\frac{4}{12}$; tibia $\frac{7}{12}$ths; expanse $10\frac{1}{2}$.

This very beautiful bat, which, when disturbed in the day-time, looks more like a butterfly or moth than a bat, has been found over a great part of India, though nowhere common. I first obtained it at Madras, and subsequently on the Malabar coast. It has also been found in Bengal, in Dacca, where said not to be rare, and called the "orange bat;" also in Ceylon, and in Burmah and Malayana. It conceals itself in the folded leaf of the plantain, and its Ceylonese name is properly, as Kelaart tells us, *Kehelvoulha*, meaning *plantain bat.*

54. Kerivoula pallida.

BLYTH, Cat. 108.

THE PALE PAINTED BAT.

Descr.—"Much larger than *K. picta*, with the woolly fur shorter, denser, and much paler in coloring; fulvous, with a slight ruddy or ferruginous cast, paler on the under parts; the orange portion of the wings broader and less defined; forearm 2; longest finger 3; expanse 11."

This bat was sent from Chybassa by Tickell.

55. Kerivoula papillosa.

Vespertilio apud TEMMINCK.—TOMES, P. Z. S. 1858.

THE PAPILLOSE BAT.

Descr.—Fur fine, woolly, long, bicolored; above dusky at the base, brown, with a rufous tinge at the tip; beneath, dusky at base, yellowish-brown at tip. Interfemoral membrane margined with minute papilli.

Length, head and body, 2 inches; tail 2; forearm $1\frac{1}{3}$; tibia $\frac{3}{4}$ths.

This bat, said to inhabit Java and Sumatra, has been sent to England both from Calcutta and Ceylon.

Vesp. tenuis and *V. Hardwickii*, both from Java and Sumatra, are considered by Tomes to belong to this group.

Gen. VESPERTILIO L. (as restricted.)

Char.—Feet more or less free from the membrane, the wings in some attached only as far as the ankles; face short, hairy; forehead somewhat convex; ears moderate; interfemoral membrane with only a few scattered hairs; molars usually $\frac{6-6}{6-6}$.

There are two groups indicated by Tomes, even in this limited generic division; the first typified by *V. mystacinus*, the other by *V. tralatitius*.

Group like *V. mystacinus*.

56. Vespertilio caliginosus.

TOMES, Ann. Mag. Nat. Hist. 1860. p. 60.

THE MUSTACHOED BAT.

Descr.—Muzzle pointed, short; two tufts of hair projecting laterally like whiskers from the upper lip; ear moderate, with a distinct round lobe at the base, narrow at the tip; tragus not quite half the length of the ear, with an angular lobe at its base, barely bent outwards, not very acute; feet small; wing membrane attached to the base of the outer toe; fur long, soft, rather silky; above, the hairs black at the base, yellowish chesnut at tip; beneath, dead black at base, with a grayish-brown tip.

Length, head and body, 1½ inch; tail 1; forearm $1\frac{2}{12}$; tibia ½; expanse 8½.

This bat was brought from some part of India by Captain Boys.

57. Vespertilio siligorensis.

HODGSON apud HORSFIELD, Ann. Mag. Nat. Hist. 1855. 102.

THE TERAI BAT.

Descr.—Muzzle pointed, with a moustache on the upper lip; ears oval, slightly emarginate, and somewhat pointed; tragus elongate, acute; wing membrane attached to the base of the toes; fur above uniform dark brown, paler below.

Forearm $1\frac{8}{12}$; tibia $\frac{6\frac{1}{2}}{12}$ths.

From Siligoree in the Sikim Terai.

58. Vespertilio darjelingensis.

HODGSON, Ann. Mag. Nat. Hist. 1855.

THE DARJEELING BAT.

Descr.—Very like the last, differs in the ears being more emarginate with a distinct lobe at their base; tibia somewhat shorter; upper fur darker color, tipped with chesnut, and glossed.

Tomes notices that this bat is exceedingly like *V. mystacinus* of Europe.

The next group has received from Gray the name of *Tralatitius.* It has the feet wholly disengaged from the wing membranes.

59. Vespertilio Blythii.

TOMES, P. Z. S. 1857. 53.

BLYTH'S BAT.

Descr.—Ears ovoid, somewhat pointed, the ends sloping outwards; tragus narrow, tapering to a sub-acute point; crown moderately elevated; feet large, wholly disengaged; tip of the tail free; membrane naked; fur long; above, dark brown at the root, the tip cinnamon-brown, brightest on the rump; beneath, dark at the base, the terminal half brownish-white.

Length, head and body, $2\frac{1}{4}$ inches; tail $1\frac{3}{4}$; expanse 15; forearm $2\frac{2}{12}$; tibia, $\frac{11}{12}$ths.

This bat was found by Captain Boys at Nusseerabad in Rajpootana.

60. Vespertilio adversus.

HORSFIELD, Zool. Res.—BLYTH, Cat. 110.

THE MALAYAN BAT.

Descr.—Ears straight, obtuse, curved backwards, with a small lobe at their base; tragus straight, linear, blunt, half the length of the ear; fur soft, silky, grayish-brown above, light-grayish beneath. Length, $3\frac{1}{4}$ inches, of which the tail is $1\frac{1}{2}$; expanse $10\frac{1}{2}$.

This Malayan species of bat has been taken at Calcutta. It is also found in Ceylon and Burmah.

Other eastern species of *Vespertilio* are *V. Horsfieldi*, T. (*V. tralatitius*, Horsfield) from the Malayan peninsula and Java, belonging to the last group; and *V. tralatitius*, Temminck, which belongs to the *mystacinus* group.

Gen Myotis, Gray.

Char.—Ears large, longer than the head, oval, distant; tragus moderately long, slender, sickle-shaped; face lengthened, somewhat denuded; nostrils elongate; upper lip pendulous on each side; feet partly free; interfemoral membrane with distinct hairy bands beneath; molars $\frac{6-6}{6-6}$.

61. Myotis murinus.

Vespertilio apud Geoffroy.—Blyth, Cat. 111.

The Mouse-like Bat.

Descr.—Fur long, smooth, reddish-brown above, dull or hoary white beneath.

Length head and body, 3 to $3\frac{1}{2}$ inches; expanse 15; tail 2; forearm $2\frac{4}{12}$.

This European bat has been sent from Mussoorie by Captain Hutton.

62. Myotis Theobaldi.

Blyth, J. A. S. XXIV. 363, olim *M. pallidiventris*, Hodgson apud Blyth.

Theobald's Mouse Bat.

Descr.—Very close to *M. pipistrellus* of Europe, but differs by the much greater length of the fore-thumb; above, dark dull brown, paler and more albescent beneath; feet very large; same size as *pipistrellus*, *i. e.*, about 3 inches long; tail, $1\frac{1}{2}$; expanse, 8.

This bat was sent by Mr. Theobald from Kashmir. He found it in some limestone caves near Islamabad.

63. Myotis parvipes.

Blyth, J. A. S. XXII. 360, olim *M. pipistrellus*.

The Small-footed Mouse Bat.

Descr.—Characterized by the diminutive size of the foot, which, with claws scarcely $\frac{3}{16}$ inch; much darker than the last, and than *pipistrellus*; dimensions much the same.

This bat, formerly considered by Blyth to be the same as the *M. pipistrellus* of Europe, was sent from Mussoorie by Captain Hutton.

Hodgson has a *M. pallidiventris*, not described, which may be either of the above species. Blyth describes another, *M. lepidus* from Kandahar, and *M. Berdmorei*, from Tenasserim.

It appears from Mr. Tomes' observations, that he looks on *M. pipistrellus* as a *Scotophilus*, of which it has, says he, the dentition, viz., 5 molars only on each side.

Gen. PLECOTUS, Geoffroy.

Char.—Ears very large, united at their base; tragus large, elongated; molars $\frac{5-5}{6-6}$ or $\frac{5-5}{5-5}$.

64. Plecotus auritus.

Vespertilio apud LINNÆUS.—BLYTH, Cat. 114.—*Pl. homochrous*, HODGSON.—*P. darjilingensis*, HODGSON.

THE LONG-EARED BAT.

Descr.—Fur silky, short, uniform dull brown; tail long, the tip alone free.

Length, head and body, $1\frac{7}{8}$; expanse 10; tail $1\frac{3}{4}$; forearm nearly $1\frac{1}{2}$; ear $1\frac{1}{2}$.

Hodgson considers that his *homochrous*, of which he gives a very ample description in the Journal of the Asiatic Society, is distinct from the European bat, but I see that it is considered identical. *Pl. darjilingensis*, also considered distinct by Hodgson, is probably the same, for Major Sherwill sent a specimen from Darjeeling, which Blyth considered identical with the European species.

Plec. timorensis, Geoffroy, from Timor, and *P. velatus* from S. America, are other recorded species.

Gen. BARBASTELLUS, Gray.

Char.—Ears large connate at the base in front, triangular, emarginate on the outer margin, broad, concealing the back of the head, hairy in the middle; tragus broad at the base, narrow at the tip, and curved outwardly; muzzle short, obtuse; incisors $\frac{4}{6}$; molars $\frac{5-5}{5-5}$; but the first one very minute and concealed by the gums.

65. Barbastellus communis.

GRAY.—BLYTH, Cat. 115.—*V. barbastellus*, SCHREBER.—*B. daubentoni*, BELL.

THE BARBASTELLE BAT.

Descr.—Fur above blackish-brown, the hairs fulvous at the tip; abdomen grayish-brown; hairs fine, silky.

Length, head and body, 2 inches; tail $1\frac{2}{12}$; expanse $10\frac{1}{2}$; forearm $1\frac{1}{2}$.

This bat has been found in the Himalayas, at Mussoorie by Hutton, and in Nepal by Hodgson.

V. leucomelus, Rüppell, from the coast of the Red Sea, and *V. macrotis*, Temminck, from Sumatra, are considered to belong to the present genus; and there are others from America.

The next bat has usually been placed among the *Noctilioninæ*, but erroneously so according to Blyth and others, who say that its affinities are with *Myotis* and *Plecotus*.

Gen. NYCTOPHILUS, Leach.

Char.—A simple transverse nose leaf; ears large, ovoid, united at their base as in *Plecotus*; tragus short and broad; wings as in *Vespertilio*; incisors $\frac{2}{6}$; molars $\frac{4-4}{5-5}$.

66. Nyctophilus Geoffroyi.

LEACH, Lin. Trans. XIII.—BLYTH, Cat. 116.

THE LARGE-EARED LEAF BAT.

Descr.—Over the eyes, at the hind corner, a tuft of black hairs; fur dark brown above, long, thick, and soft; throat and flanks brownish-white; all the rest of the lower parts with the fur black at the base, whitish at the tip.

Length, head and body, $1\frac{3}{4}$ to 2 inches; tail $1\frac{5}{12}$; expanse $9\frac{3}{4}$: forearm $1\frac{4}{12}$; ear $\frac{3}{4}$ths.

This bat, which has been found in Europe and Australia, was sent from Mussoorie by Hutton.

Ord. INSECTIVORA.

Incisor teeth various in number and almost always different in the two jaws; no distinct canines in most; molars with acuminated tubercles. Feet usually pentadactylous, plantigrade.

The insectivorous mammals are mostly of small size, with short limbs, and some of them superficially much resemble the Rodents. Many live under ground, and most are nocturnal. They feed chiefly on insects. Some are torpid in winter in cold countries. They are timid and unobtrusive in their habits, and rather slow in their motions. The tail is variously developed. In running they place the entire sole of the foot upon the ground.

The skull is of slight make and elongated form, the bones of the face and jaws being much produced, and the latter are weak. The distinct division of the teeth into sets is not apparent here, and it is sometimes difficult to say to which set particular teeth belong. There are usually eight teeth in front of each jaw, of which the outermost are regarded by some as the canines, though often smaller than the others, no placental mammal having more than six incisors in each jaw. The orbit and temporal fossa are confounded in one cavity, except in *Tupaia*. The molar teeth are studded with sharp cusps or tubercles, for the purpose of breaking down the hard elytra of beetles, on which they chiefly subsist. All have clavicles, and the number of ribs is large. The deciduous teeth of the moles and shrews are developed and disappear before birth. The stomach is perfectly simple; and, except *Tupaia*, they have no cœcum. The brain and organs of sense closely resemble those of the Rodents. The mammæ are ventral and generally numerous. The testes pass periodically from the abdomen into a temporary scrotum.

Insectivorous mammals are nearly confined to the old continent, none being found in South America, if we except the curious *Solenoden paradaxus* of St. Domingo; and only a few moles in North America. They are represented on that continent chiefly by small species of *Didelphys* or Opossum, a marsupial animal. There are likewise none in Australia, but several marsupials resemble them so closely that, were it not for their special anatomical structure, they would undoubtedly be classed with them.

Blainville looks on the Insectivora as being intermediate between Bats and the Edentata. Cuvier places them next the Bats, as do most systematists; Blyth removes them to the end of the Carnivora. This interrupts the series perhaps more than the generally adopted plan.

The Insectivorous mammals may be divided into *Talpidæ*, or Moles; *Sorecidæ*, Shrews; *Erinaceidæ*, Hedgehogs; and *Tupaiadæ*, or Tree Shrews; all of which have representatives in India.

Fam. TALPIDÆ, Moles.

Body, hairy. Fore feet, large, fossorial, with large claws. External ears, none. Eyes, very minute. Tail, short or none.

Moles are better known in Europe than in India, where they are only represented on the Eastern Himalayas, and the Khasia hills. The body is short and thick; the legs short and strong, and the muzzle lengthened. The shovel-like hand of the mole is furnished with a curved prolongation of one of the carpal bones, called the falciform bone, which gives additional strength to the hand. The structure of their fore-feet is beautifully adapted for burrowing, being broad and furnished with strong large claws, supplied by very powerful muscles. The hind feet are comparatively small and weak. The eyes are very minute, and in some cases not discernible, the skin over them not being pierced. The tympanum of the ear is large, but there is no external ear, though the sense of hearing is very acute. The hairs of their fur are set on vertically, and hence have no particular grain or direction, and can be smoothed down in any direction, so that in moving backwards in their runs, the hairs lie equally smooth as when advancing. Moles are quite subterraneous in their habits, being very rarely seen above ground. They live chiefly on worms and insects, to find which they burrow most extensively. They are found in Europe, Asia, North America, and a peculiar section in Africa.

Gen. TALPA, Linnæus.

Char.—Incisors, apparently $\frac{6}{6}$ or $\frac{6}{8}$; molars, $\frac{7-7}{7-7}$ or $\frac{8-8}{7-7}$; but of these the first false upper molars, and the outermost pair of lower incisors, represent the canine teeth. Nose, lengthened, truncated at the point. Eyes, very small, in some the integument not pierced. Tail, very short or wanting. Anterior feet turned outwards, with the toes connected or palmate, and with very strong claws.

True moles are found in Europe and Asia, and, in our province, are restricted to the South-east portion of the Himalayas.

67. Talpa micrura.

HODGSON. J. A. S. X. 910.—BLYTH, Cat.—*T. cryptura*, BLYTH.—Skull figd. J. A. S. XIX. 217.—*Pariam*, Lepch.—*Biyu-kantyem*, Bhot.

THE SHORT-TAILED MOLE.

Descr.—Uniform velvet black with a silvery-gray gloss, iridescent when moist; snout, nude; feet and tail fleshy-white, the last very minute.

Length, $4\frac{3}{4}$ to 5 inches; tail, $\frac{3}{16}$ths, sometimes less; head alone, $1\frac{3}{4}$; palm with claws, $\frac{7}{8}$ths.

There is no perforation of the integument over the eye. There are three small upper præmolars between the quasi-canine tooth and the large scissor-toothed præmolar, which is much developed. Blyth states that Darjeeling specimens almost want the tail, but that those from Nepal have it. Some I procured at Darjeeling, however, had the tail well marked.

This mole is not uncommon at Darjeeling, and many of the roads and pathways in the station are intersected by its runs, which often proceed from the base of some mighty oak-tree to that of another. If these runs be broken down or holes made in them, they are generally repaired during the night. The moles do not appear to form mole hills as in Europe. The Lepchas do not know how to set mole-traps, and the few specimens I procured at Darjeeling were picked up early in the morning on the ground or in ditches.

68. Talpa macrura.

HODGSON, J. A. S. XXVII. 176.—Cat. Hodgson's Coll. 82.

THE LONG-TAILED MOLE.

Descr.—Deep slaty-blue with canescent gloss, iridescent when wet. Tail cylindric, pretty well covered with soft hairs, which extend a little beyond the tip.

Length, 4 inches; tail (with the hair), $1\frac{1}{4}$; head, $1\frac{1}{8}$; palm, $\frac{3}{4}$ths. This species differs most conspicuously from the previous one by its long tail. It was procured in Sikim by Hodgson.

Blyth has described *Talpa leucura*, from Sylhet and Tenasserim, differing from *micrura* in only having two small præmolars between the upper canine and the scissor-tooth; and the short tail is clad and tufted with white hairs. A species from Japan, *T. mogura*, is described by Temminck, and there are two in Europe, *T. europæa*, and *T. cæca* of Italy and Greece.

A writer in the Bengal Sporting Review (the Rev. H. Baker), suspects the presence of moles on the Neelgherry hills, having found mutilated remains of what he took to be such. This conjecture has not to my knowledge been verified, and I much doubt their existence on those hills.

In *Condylura*, a North American genus of moles, there is a peculiar star of moveable cartilaginous filaments at the end of the snout, and the tail is longer than in *Talpa*. The shrew-moles, *Scalops*, also from North America, chiefly differ from true moles by their teeth. *Urotrichus talpoides* is a Japanese mole, with a moderate hairy tail; and a second species of this genus has been quite recently discovered in North America.

The African or Cape moles, have been by some classed as a distinct group, *Chrysochlorinæ*. They have two incisors above, and four below; and their fur has a peculiar metallic lustre, hence-called Golden Moles. They have no external ears nor eyes, and want the tail.

Fam. Sorecidæ, Shrews.

Body, covered with soft hair. Eyes, small but distinct. External ears in most, generally small. Muzzle, elongated. Fore feet, of ordinary form.

The Shrews comprise a large number of small animals, which, from their general appearance and nocturnal habits, are popularly confounded with rats and mice. The two middle incisors above are large and hooked, the lower ones are slanting and lengthened, and these are followed by several smaller ones. There is a tuberculous tooth in the upper jaw, and three cuspidated molars in each jaw. The feet are pentadactylous, the toes well cloven, and the tail of moderate length, more or less naked, or thinly clad with hairs. The snout is lengthened, pointed and very mobile. On each side of the body in certain species there is a gland under the skin surrounded by a circlet of short hairs, which secretes a fluid of the odour of musk. It exists in both sexes, and appears to be more developed at certain periods. During the day shrews remain concealed in drains or holes, dark outhouses, under boxes, mats, &c, and those that dwell in forests, under stones or in holes under trees. At nightfall they sally forth and hunt for their food, which is chiefly insects. Shrews are found over all the old continent. Several genera have been formed of late, founded on some peculiarities of dentition.

Gen. SOREX, Linnæus, as restricted.

Syn. *Pachyura*, DE SELYS LONGCHAMPHS.—*Crocidura*, WAGNER.

Char.—Upper front teeth large and strongly hooked, and much longer than their posterior spur; inferior incisors entire, or rarely so much as a trace of a serrated upper edge; following those in the upper jaw are four teeth anterior to the scissor-tooth, the first large, the next two much smaller, the third exceeding the second, aud the fourth diminutive. Teeth generally wholly white. Ear-conch very distinct. Tail thick and tapering, and furnished with a few long scattered hairs, which certain species likewise exhibit upon the body.

This genus includes the majority of those shrews that inhabit tropical countries. Some of them do not appear to be furnished with the musk-gland.

69. Sorex cærulescens.

SHAW.—BLYTH, Cat. 244.—*S. indicus*, *giganteus* and *Sonnerati*, GEOFFROY.—*S. myosurus*, GRAY, figd., HARDWICKE, Ill. Ind. Zool.—*Chachúndar*, H.—*Sondeli*, Can.—Musk-rat of Europeans.

THE COMMON MUSK SHREW.

Descr.—Of an uniform bluish-ash or pale gray color, very slightly tinged with ferruginous, and most so on the under parts; naked parts flesh-colored.

Length, head and body, 6 to 7½ inches; tail, 3½ to nearly 4. The skull of an adult male, according to Blyth, 1⅝; caudal vertebræ, 24 in number.

This appears to be the common musk-rat of almost all India, frequenting houses at night, and hunting round rooms for cock-roaches or any other insects, occasionally uttering a sharp, shrill cry. It will, however, not refuse meat, for it is sometimes taken in rat-traps baited with meat. It is popularly believed in India that the musky odour emitted by this shrew is so volatile and penetrating, that if it pass over a corked bottle of wine or beer, it will infect the fluid within; and certainly many bottles are met with in this country quite undrinkable from the musky odour. I much doubt, however, the possibility of infection in this way, and think it much more probable that the corks of such bottles were inpregnated previously to being used in bottling, and in support of this I may state that I have never found this odour in English bottled liquor. I notice that Kelaart also scouts the idea of the scent passing through the bottles, but thinks that it may pass through a bad cork in the bottle. I think that this is not so probable as the former supposition.

Horsfield, in his Catalogue, considers *S. indicus*, vel *Sonneratii*, Is. Geoffroy, as distinct from *cærulescens*. Is. Geoffroy states that his *S. sonneratii* is smaller than *cærulescens*, and with the tail always one quarter of the entire length; fur, ashy, washed with russet brown, pale ashy below. From the Corromandel coast. I have followed Blyth and Tomes in joining this to *cærulescens*.

70. Sorex murinus.

Linnæus.—Blyth, Cat. 246—*S. myosurus*, Pallas—*S. swinhæi*, and *S. viridescens*, Blyth (olim).

The Mouse-colored Shrew.

Descr.—Brownish, or dark brownish-gray above, grayish-brown beneath, the fur longer and coarser than in *cærulescens* ; ears, larger; tail nearly equal in length to the body, rounded thick at the base, nearly nude with a few longish hairs scattered over it; feet and tail, fleshy.

Length of one, head and body, 5 inches; tail, 3; but larger specimens are met with.

This is the common large musk-rat of China, Burmah, and the Malayan countries, extending into lower Bengal and Southern India, especially the Malabar coast, where it is said to be the common species, the bite of which is considered venemous by the natives. The musky odour of this shrew is much less powerful than in *cærulescens*.

71. Sorex nemorivagus.

Hodgson, Cal. Jour. Nat. Hist. IV. 288.—Ann. Mag. Nat. Hist. XV. 269.—*S. murinus* from Nepal, apud Horsfield ?

The Nepal Wood Shrew.

Descr.—Similar to *S. murinus*, but of stouter make, with smaller ears; legs, entirely nude; a longer and more tetragonal tail; color, sooty black, with a vague reddish smear, or shining rufescent-brown, paler beneath; nude parts, fleshy grey.

Length of one, head and body, $3\frac{5}{8}$ inches; tail, 2; foot, $\frac{11}{16}$ths.

This species was formerly considered by Blyth to be the same as *murinus*, but in his Catalogue he places them separately. There are no specimens, however, of this shrew in the Calcutta Museum. It inhabits Nepal, only in woods and coppices, says Hodgson, not entering houses. In the late edition of the Catalogue of his Collection, he also gives it from Sikim, and states that there are specimens in spirits in the India House Museum from the latter country.

Sorex Griffithii, Horsfield, is a nearly allied species to *S. murinus*, from the Khasia hills, distinguished, according to Tomes, by its large teeth, deep blackish-gray, glossy, and rather coarse fur, and by its small ears.

Length, head and body, $5\frac{3}{4}$ inches; tail, $2\frac{5}{12}$ths. This ought to be compared with Hodgson's species.

72. Sorex serpentarius.

IS. GEOFFROY.—BLYTH, Cat. 248—*S. kandianus*, KELAART.

THE RUFESCENT SHREW.

Descr.—Above, dusky-slate color with rufescent tips to the fur; beneath, paler with a faint rufous tinge about the breast; ears, moderately large; limbs, small; tail, slender; teeth, small.

Length of one, head and body, 4 inches; tail $2\frac{1}{12}$th. Another, head and body, $4\frac{1}{2}$; tail, $2\frac{1}{8}$; foot, $\frac{12}{16}$ths.

This musk-rat has been found, within our province, only in Southern India, but it is common in Ceylon, and extends into Southern Burmah, Mergui. It has been taken on the Malabar coast, but is said to be more common on the east coast of Southern India, at about Tinnevelly. Kelaart, who calls it the common godown musk-rat of Kandy, says that its odour is quite as offensive as that of *cærulescens*.

Blyth has described *Sorex heterodon* from the Khasia hills, like *serpentarius*, but smaller and with stouter limbs. He elsewhere likens it to *S. soccatus*.

73. Sorex saturatior.

HODGSON, Ann. Mag. Nat. Hist. 2nd series, XVI. 110.

THE DARK-BROWN SHREW.

Descr.—Color, uniform deep brown inclining to blackish, with a very slight rufescent shade; fur, short, with an admixture of a few lengthened piles, when adpressed to the body smooth, but reversed, somewhat harsh and rough; tail, cylindrical, long, gradually tapering; snout, elongate, regularly attenuated; ears, moderate, rounded.

Length, head and body, 5½ inches; tail, 3.

This shrew is said to be nearly allied in habits and dimensions to *S. Griffithii* from the Khasia hills, the more lengthened and cylindrical tail forming the chief distinction. It was procured by Hodgson at Darjeeling in his fowl-house.

74. Sorex Tytleri.

Blyth, J. A. S. XXVIII. 285.

The Dehra Shrew.

Descr.—Light rufescent sandy-brown, paler beneath; unusually well clad even on the feet and tail, this last being covered with a shortish fur, having numerous long hairs intermixed; form very robust; basal portion of tail very thick.

Length, head and body, 4½ inches; tail, 2¾; hind foot, ⅞ths.

This shrew is a native, according to Lieut.-Col. Tytler, of Dehra Doon.

75. Sorex niger.

Elliot, MSS.—Horsfield, Cat. 147.—Blyth, Cat. 251.

The Neelgherry Wood Shrew.

Descr.—Blackish-brown with a rufescent shade on the upper parts; abdomen, dusky-grayish; tail, equal in length to the body, gradually tapering to a point; snout, much attenuated.

Length, head and body, 3½ inches; tail, 2½.

This shrew is said to be quite a miniature of the Khasian *S. Griffithii*, but with a long and slender tail. It is tolerably common on the Neelgherry hills, frequenting woods and gardens, especially about Ootacamund, and dead specimens are often found on the roads. I have seen it turned out from the hollow of an old tree. It has a very faint musky odour.

76. Sorex leucops.

Hodgson, Ann. Mag. Nat. Hist. New series, XVI. III.

The Long-tailed Shrew.

Descr.—Of a uniform blackish-brown color; tail, very long, slender, exceeding in length the head and body, and terminating in a whitish tip of half an inch long.

Length, head and body 3 inches; tail $3\frac{1}{2}$.

This shrew is stated to be from Nepal. As a MSS. name, *nivicola*, was also given it by Hodgson, it is to be presumed that he obtained it at a great elevation.

77. Sorex soccatus.

Hodgson, Ann. Mag. Nat. Hist. XV. 270.—Not of Cal. J. N. H.—Blyth, J. A. S. XXIV. 30, Cat. 249.

The Hairy-footed Shrew.

Descr.—Distinguished, according to Hodgson, by its feet being clad with fur down to the nails, by its depressed head and tumid, bulging cheeks; ears large, exposed; color a uniform sordid or brownish-slaty hue.

Length, head and body $3\frac{1}{2}$ inches; tail $2\frac{1}{8}$; foot $\frac{1}{1}\frac{2}{6}$ths.

Blyth states that, it has a considerable resemblance to *S. serpentarius*, but is a good deal darker, with well clad feet and tail, head and limbs proportionally larger; tail compressed towards the tip, which is furnished with a pencil tuft of stiffish hairs. One measured, head and body 5 inches; tail 3.

This species has been found in Nepal, Sikim, and also at Mussoorie. I procured it at Darjeeling.

The remaining species of this section are of diminutive size.

78. Sorex Hodgsoni.

Blyth, J. A. S. XXIV. 334.—Cat. 257.—*S. pygmæus* apud Hodgson.

The Nepal Pigmy-shrew.

Descr.—Uniform brown with a slight tinge of chesnut, and scarcely paler below; feet and tail distinctly furred, besides the usual scattered long hairs in the latter; claws whitish and conspicuous; tail brown above, pale beneath, tapering evenly throughout.

Length, head and body $1\frac{1}{2}$ inch; tail 1; hind foot, $\frac{1}{3}\frac{1}{2}$. Hodgson gives larger dimensions—head and body nearly 2; tail $1\frac{3}{16}$; foot $\frac{3}{8}$ths.

This little shrew has been found in Nepal and Sikim. Hodgson states that it dwells in coppices and fields, rarely entering houses, and that it has no musky smell.

79. Sorex Perroteti.

DUVERNOY, Mag. Zool. 1842, pl. 47.

THE NEELGHERRY PIGMY-SHREW.

Descr.—Back deep blackish-brown; belly pale; limbs and feet brown; palms and plantæ clad with hairs; ears large conspicuous.

Length head and body, $1\frac{4}{12}$ inches; tail, $\frac{11}{12}$ths.

This minute shrew was first sent from the Neelgherries by M. Perrotet. I have taken it there myself; and have also seen what at the time I took for the same species in Mysore, at Madras, and at Jalna in the Deccan. Possibly other minute shrews occur in Southern India.

80. Sorex micronyx.

BLYTH, J. A. S. XXIV. 33.—Cat. 258.

THE SMALL-CLAWED PIGMY-SHREW.

Descr.—Claws very minute; feet and tail nearly nude; fur paler and more chesnut than any of the other small shrews, and more silvery beneath.

Length, head and body $1\frac{5}{8}$ inch; tail $1\frac{1}{8}$; hind foot $\frac{13}{32}$.

This species inhabits the Western Himalayas, having been procured in Kumaon and at Mussoorie, where many were picked up dead during a fall of snow.

The next species differs from all the previous ones in having the teeth black, and Wagner makes it the type of his section, *Paradoxodon* (Suppl. IV. 805).

81. Sorex melanodon.

BLYTH, J. A. S. XXIV. 33.—Cat. 255.

THE BLACK-TOOTHED PIGMY-SHREW.

Descr.—Allied to *S. Hodgsoni*; color an uniform fuscous, scarcely paler below; feet and tail nearly naked; ears, and snout livid; claws white; teeth, piceous, white-tipped.

Length, head and body $1\frac{7}{8}$; tail $1\frac{1}{16}$; hind foot $\frac{5}{16}$ths.

A single specimen of this remarkable little shrew was obtained by Blyth from a house in Calcutta. Blyth indicates two other Himalayan shrews, J. A. S. XXVIII. 255; and in the late edition of Hodgson's collection, are enumerated the following species not described:—

Sorex sikimensis, *S. homourus*, *S. oligurus*, *S. macrurus*, *S. holosericeus*, and another, No. 94, without a specific name, which, in the copy sent me by that gentleman, is marked on MSS. as *S. tenuicauda*. All these are from Darjeeling, but unfortunately skins of few of these appear to have been preserved. Besides those previously alluded to from Ceylon, *S. ferrugineus* and *S. montanus*, Kelaart; *S. Kelaarti*, Blyth; *S. purpurascens*, Templeton; and *S. Horsfieldii*, Tomes, are on record from Ceylon. Blyth has described *S. fuliginosus* and *S. nudipes* from Tenasserim, and *S atratus* from the Khasia hills, the two latter species being pigmy shrews. The same naturalist has described *S. albinus* from China. A shrew from Central Asia, *S. pulchellus*, has been described by Lichtenstein, which is said to have only two intermediate teeth, between the upper incisors and the scissor tooth, and has been made the type of *Diplomesodon*, Brandt. *Sorex araneus* of Europe belongs to this group, and there are many from Africa, some of which are said to have only three intermediate teeth in place of four.

Gen. Soriculus, Blyth.

Char.—Teeth white, tipped with ferruginous or pitch color; upper quasi-incisors much larger than their posterior spur (as in the last); the lower incisors with a single posterior spur, more or less rudimental; of the four lateral intermediate teeth what follow the incisors, the first two equal, the third somewhat smaller, and the fourth minute; tail, slender, tapering, mouse-like, with no scattered hairs on it; ears concealed amid the fur; hind feet of ordinary form.

One species only of this group occurs in the Himalayas.

82. Soriculus nigrescens.

Corsira apud Gray.—Blyth Cat.—*S. sikimensis*, Hodgson apud Horsfield. Cat.—*S. aterrimus*, Blyth.—*S. soccatus*, Hodgson, Cal. Jour. Nat. Hist. IV. 288.—*Tang-zhing*, Lepch.—*Ting-zhing*, Bhot.

The Mouse-tailed Shrew.

Descr.—Above dark-blackish, or blackish-brown, slightly tinged rufescent, and with a silvery cast in certain lights; beneath grayish-black; snout long, regularly attenuated, with few lateral hairs; body abruptly terminated behind; tail slender, rigidly straight, naked, half as long as the body; feet and claws pale; fur short, smooth, delicately soft, closely adpressed.

Length, head and body 3¼ inches; tail 1½; hind foot ⅝ths.

This shrew is very common in Sikim, and also occurs in Nepal. I found many dead on the roads at Darjeeling without any apparent injury. The same has been noticed of the common shrew of England, and no satisfactory explanation has been given. An allied species from Ceylon has been named *Corsira newera-ellia* by Kelaart, which ought perhaps to occur on the Neelgherries.

Gen. Crossopus, Wagner.

Syn. *Hydrosorex*, Duvernoy.

Char.—The hind feet large and ciliated; tail compressed and ciliated beneath towards its extremity; otherwise as in the last.

The water-shrew of Europe is the type of this division.

83. Crossopus himalaicus.

Gray, Ann. Mag. Nat. Hist. 1842, 261.—*Oong lagniyu*, Lepch.—*Choopitsi*, Bhot.

The Himalayan Water-shrew.

Descr.—Fur dark-brown, or blackish above, somewhat paler beneath, and rusty-brown on the lower part of the throat and the middle of the belly; fur rather long, with scattered long white-tipped hairs; a few on the sides, many on the rump and round the root of the tail; ears very small, hairy, concealed; tail long, slender, with a brush of hairs at the tip, and ciliated with rigid whitish hairs beneath; feet distinctly ciliated; claws very short; whiskers elongate, brown.

Length, head and body 5 inches; tail 3¼; hind foot nearly ¾ths.

Another measured 6 inches; tail 3½; hind foot $\frac{11}{12}$ths.

I procured this water-shrew at Darjeeling, from the little Rungeet river, where it is said not to be uncommon, and its aquatic habits are well known to the natives, who distinguish it by a distinct name signifying, water-shrew. It is said to kill small fish, tadpoles, water-insects, &c. It is not recorded among Hodgson's collections, though I imagine he must have procured it in Sikim, and probably one of his undescribed species may be referred to this.

Crossopus fodiens, Pallas, is the well known water-shrew of Europe; and there are other species from North America and Japan.

Gen. Corsira, Gray.

Syn. *Amphisorex*, Duvernoy.

Char.—Lower incisors distinctly serrated, with three or four points; anterior point of upper incisors not prolonged beyond a level with its posterior spur; the lateral small teeth following in the upper jaw are five, gradually diminishing in size from the first backwards; tail cylindrical, not tapering, furnished with a stiff brush at the tip; teeth tipped with ferruginous.

84. Corsira alpina.

Sorex apud Schinz.—*S. caudatus*, Hodgson.—Blyth, Cat. 261.

The Alpine Shrew.

Descr.—Deep blackish-brown, very slightly rufuscent in certain lights; tail slender, nearly naked, very slightly attenuated, equal in length to the head and body; compressed at the tip.

Length, head and body 2½ inches; tail 2½.

Mr. Tomes has identified this species with the Alpine shrew of Europe, to which indeed Blyth had previously noted its close affinity. It has only been procured, I believe, from the neighbourhood of Darjeeling.

Sorex vulgaris L., and *S. pygmæus*, Pallas, of Europe, belong to this group, and there are several American members of it, some of which, with a shorter tail, were named *Brachysorex* by Duvernoy, and others with prominent ears, *Otisorex*, by Dekay.

Sorex macropus, Blyth, from Ceylon, has been made the type of *Feroculus*, by Kelaart. It has a thick tapering tail, strong feet, and ears almost concealed. It is of large size.

The genus *Myogalea* (olim *Mygale*) or musk-rat, of which there are two species in Europe, is another genus of this family. They have long cartilaginous snouts, a long scaly tail, and are aquatic in their habits. *Solenodon paradoxus* of the West Indies, previously alluded to, has the habit of a large shrew, with a long naked tail, and is placed in the family by some naturalists.

Fam. Erinaceidæ, Hedgehogs.

Back protected by spines, or rigid bristles with setœ intermixed; feet pentadactylous, not fossorial; tail very short or none.

The body of the hedgehogs is short, thick, and stout, and the muzzle is less pointed than in the other groups of this order. The cranium is said to approach the form of that of some of the smaller Carnivora. They are only found in the old continent.

Gen. Erinaceus, Linnæus.

Char.—Dental formula, according to Owen, incisors $\frac{3-3}{3-3}$; præmolars $\frac{4-4}{2-2}$; molars $\frac{3-3}{3-3}$; total 36 teeth. Upper middle incisors distant; lower ones procumbent; no canines; molars with the crown square, tuberculate; snout lengthened; ears moderate; tail very short; body densely covered with spines on the back and sides, with hairs and bristles beneath.

The skin of the back is furnished with muscles which enable the animal to roll itself into a ball, so as to present spines on every side. Hedgehogs hybernate in cold countries, but do not burrow, concealing themselves under leaves, in hollow trees, ditches, and under thick bushes. They feed chiefly on insects, also on slugs, frogs, mice, snakes, and eggs. They have even been accused of killing young levrets; and are said at times to partake of vegetable food. They are nocturnal in their habits. The female produces as many as six, or seven young sometimes, at a birth.

85. Erinaceus collaris.

Gray, figd. Hardwicke, Ill. Ind. Zool.—Blyth, Cat. 236.—Probably *E. Grayi*, Bennett.

The North-Indian Hedgehog.

Descr.—Ears long; spines irregularly interwoven, apiculated with yellow, and ringed white and black; or white on the basal half, and jet black on the upper half, some with the base and tip black, white in the middle; ears, and chin as far as the ears, white; belly and feet pale-brown.

Length, 8 to 9 inches; tail, $\frac{7}{12}$ths.

This hedgehog is found in the North-west Provinces of India, the Punjab, and Sindh. It is stated to occur in the Doab, *i. e.*, between the Jumna and Ganges, but I have only seen it myself west of the Jumna, about Hansi and Hissar. Adams states that, it is found in the Deccan, and also in the lower Himalayan ranges. Hutton, who observed it at Bhawalpore, states that, "their food consist of insects, chiefly of a small beetle of the genus *Blaps*; also of lizards, snails, &c." "They are," says he, "remarkably tenacious of life, bearing long abstinence with apparent ease."

86. Erinaceus micropus.

Blyth, J. A. S. XV. 171.—Cat. 237.—*E. nudiventris*, Horsfield.—*E. collaris*, from Madras, apud Gray.

The South-Indian Hedgehog.

Descr.—Ears moderately large; form somewhat elongated; tail very short, concealed; muzzle rather sharp; feet and limbs very small; head and ears nude, sooty color; belly very thinly clad with yellowish hairs; spines ringed dark-brown and whitish, or whitish with a broad brown sub-terminal ring, tipped white.

Length of one, about 6 inches.

Wagner describes (Schreber, Suppl. II. 22) *E. albiventris*, probably from India: "abdomen and sides clad with white setœ; spines ringed white and yellowish-brown; feet slender." This is perhaps the same as our species.

This hedgehog is stated to be found at Madras, and on the Neelgherries. Many years ago I procured one alive at Trichinopoly, which I gave to Mr. Walter Elliot, and I have reason to believe that this specimen is the supposed *E. collaris* from Madras, now in the British Museum. I never got another specimen from the Carnatic, yet it must be a denizen of the low jungles of the extreme South of India. It has also been obtained on the Neelgherries, and on the Western range of Ghâts; it is said not to be rare near the Missionary Station of Cottayam, inland from Cochin. It is probably one of the two species stated to be found in Ceylon.

Bennett has described *Erinaceus Grayi*, from the Himalayas, the spines yellowish-white, with a blackish ring in the upper half; ears and lower jaw with white hairs; head above brown, with some white hairs intermixed; 6 inches long. The same naturalist has described *E. spatangus*, from the Himalayas; spines parallel to each other, white beneath, blackish above, those on the sides with a small yellow ring near the point; ears and chin white; 3½ inches long. This is probably the young of the former one, and perhaps both are referable to *E. collaris*. Gray has also *E. mentalis* from India, the black-chinned hedgehog, not described. Besides the well-known *E. europœus* of Europe, there are described, *E. concolor*, Martin, from Asia Minor; *E. auritus*, Pallas, from Central Asia; and *E. megalotis*, Blyth, from Afghanistan, perhaps the same as Pallas' species; and there are several from Africa.

The *Tenrecs* from Madagascar, *Centetes*, Illiger, of which there are three or four species, have the body more elongated, the spines feebler, and they cannot roll themselves into a complete ball. *Echinogale*, with one species, from Madagascar, is very closely allied to *Erinaceus*, differing chiefly in its dentition.

Fam. TUPAIADÆ.

Incisors $\frac{4}{6}$; the upper ones remote, the lower ones procumbent, with the four middle ones longest; præmolars $\frac{4-4}{4-4}$; molars $\frac{3-3}{3-3}$; the lower ones divided by a transverse groove and cuspidate; muzzle attenuated, lengthened; ears oval, rather large; feet pentadactylous; tail long, densely clothed with hairs, somewhat distichous; the hair of the body soft and glistening.

The skull differs from that of other Insectivora, in having the bony orbit complete, and moreover they possess a small cœcum. The tree-shrews, as they may be called, are diurnal in their habits, live on trees, which they climb well, and feed both on fruit and insects, which they hold in their paws like squirrels. The female has four mammæ, but according to Cantor only produces one young at a birth.

Gen. TUPAIA, Raffles.

Syn. *Cladobates*, F. CUVIER.—*Hylogale*, TEMMINCK.

Char.—Those of the family of which it is the only genus. Peculiar to South-Eastern Asia.

87. Tupaia Elliotti.

WATERHOUSE, P. Z. S. 1849.—BLYTH, Cat. 241.

THE MADRAS TREE-SHREW.

Descr.—Above pale rufescent or reddish-brown, the hairs being grizzled red and brown; chin throat, breast, and lower parts yellowish-white; which is continued in a narrow line along the underside of the tail. Head shorter than in *T. tana*, or *T. ferruginea;* nails nearly equal.

Length of one, 14 inches; of which the tail is $7\frac{1}{4}$. Another measured, head and body 8 inches; tail 9; head from muzzle to ear $1\frac{8}{10}$ths.

This interesting addition to the Fauna of Southern India, was made by Walter Elliot, Esq., who procured it on the hills west of Madras, the continuation of the Eastern Ghâts. It does not, however, appear to be very common.

88. Tupaia peguana.

LESSON, BELANGER, Voyage.—*T. Belangeri*, WAGNER.—*T. ferruginea.* var. BLYTH, Cat 240.—*Kalli tang-zhing.*—Lepch.

THE SIKIM TREE-SHREW.

Descr.—General hue a dusky greenish-brown, the hairs being ringed brown and yellow; lower parts the same but lighter, and with a pale buff line; a stripe from the throat to the vent, broadest between the fore arms and then narrowing; ears, livid red with a few short hairs; palms and soles dark livid red; nails fleshy.

Length of one, head and body not quite 7 inches; tail $6\frac{1}{2}$; the hair one inch more; head to occipital ridge $2\frac{1}{8}$; ear $\frac{5}{8}$ths; foot $1\frac{3}{4}$; hand about 1. Another measured, head and body $7\frac{1}{2}$ inches, tail $7\frac{1}{2}$.

The Burmese *Tupaia* was considered by Lesson and others sufficiently distinct from the Malayan *ferruginea*, of which Blyth, in his Catalogue, considers it to be only a variety. My specimens differ somewhat from those from Arracan, in having the lower parts much darker, and with the pale central line narrower; in the Burmese examples the whole chin, throat, and breast being buff. I obtained this tree-shrew at Darjeeling, being one of the very few novelties that had escaped the notice of Mr. Hodgson. It frequents the zone from 3,000 to 6,000 feet, and was said, by the natives, to kill small birds, mice, &c. In its colors as well as in size and general appearance, it wonderfully resembles *Scuirus lokriah;* and I see in a note on these animals in the English edition of Cuvier, edited by Blyth, the statement that, "it is remarkable that the squirrels of the same region have very similar fur, both in color and texture."

As a sequel to the history of these animals, I may transcribe part of Cantor's account of the common Malayan species, *T. ferruginea.* "The natural food is mixed insectivorous and frugivorous. In confinement individuals may be fed exclusively on either, though preference is evinced for insects; and eggs, fish, and earth-worms are equally relished. Their disposition is very restless, and their great agility enables them to perform the most extraordinary bounds in all directions, in which exercise they spend the day, till night sends them to sleep in their rudely constructed lairs in the highest branches of trees. . . . . The lateral raised lines of the palms and soles, the posterior part of the first phalanges, and the third phalanx, which is widened into a small soft disk, in fact all the points which rest on the ground are studded with little transversely-curved ridges, or duplications similar to those observed under the toes of some *Geckotidæ*, which fully account for the precision, the aplomb, with which these animals perform the most astounding leaps from below, barely touching with their soles the *point d'appui* above. In a cage the *Tupaia* will continue for hours vaulting from below, back-downwards, poise itself for an instant, continuing back downwards under the horizontal roof, and regain the point of starting, and thus describe a circle, the diameter of which may be three or four times the length of the animal in far shorter time than is required for the description."

Besides the species referred to above, *T. javanica*, *T. tana*, and *T. murina*, are on record, respectively from Java, Sumatra, and Borneo.

There are two peculiar Eastern forms of Insectivora, which make some approach to *Tupaia*, but cannot be included at present in this family. *Ptilocercus lowii*, from Sumatra, has the tail scaly, but some long hairs at the tip arranged like the barbs of a feather. *Hylomys*, with two species, *suillus* from Java, and *Peguensis*, Blyth, from Tenasserim, is stated to be intermediate between *Tupaia* and *Sorex*. *Macroscelides* is an African form of uncertain position, but from its long hair, large eyes, and diurnal habits, makes some approach to the tree-shrews.

Ord. CARNIVORA.

Feræ normales, Gray.—Secundates, apud Blyth.

Incisors, $\frac{6}{6}$; canines large, acuminate; molars uniformly enamelled, with acute uneven crown, and one or more of the hinder teeth tuberculated. Toes mostly cloven for a short distance, but with more or less membrane between them; usually five in front, and four behind.

This order includes all those animals usually called beasts of prey. Their limbs are mostly adapted for rapid exercise, their muscular energy is great, and their circulation and respiration rapid. They are not all exclusively carnivorous, some living partly on vegetable food, and in these the tuberculated teeth exceed the cutting ones in extent. The incisors are of small or moderate size, and cutting, the outer pair always the largest, and medial the smallest, especially in the upper jaw. The canines are stout and separated. The molars graduate from trenchant to tuberculate. The teeth of the lower jaw pass within those of the upper. One of the molar teeth, which exceeds the rest in size, is furnished with a sharp cutting edge, and is the "scissor-tooth" of some naturalists, the "flesh-tooth," "la carnassière" of F. Cuvier. According to Owen, the typical number of præmolars is, $\frac{4-4}{4-4}$; of molars, $\frac{3-3}{3-3}$; but they vary in the different families.

The cranium is characterised by the shortening of the bones of the face and the smallness of the posterior aspect. A strong occipital crest separates it from the anterior portion of the skull. A large median crest exists in many, to afford a strong and extended surface of attachment to the powerful temporal muscles. The orbit and large temporal fossa are confounded in one great excavation. The zygomatic arch is perfect and of great size. The nasal bones are small. The ascending ramus of the lower jaw is large, and is articulated by a hinge joint, which confines the motion to a perpendicular one. In some there is a long process in the internal surface of the cranium, separating the cerebrum from the cerebellum. The clavicle is absent or rudimentary, except in the Bears, and perfect in none. The sternum is usually well developed longitudinally. The two bones of the forearm are distinct.

The stomach is simple; the intestinal canal short; and there is a small cœcum in some, but totally wanting in others. The liver is usually deeply lobed, especially in the Cat-tribe. The cerebellum is almost wholly uncovered, but the optic thalami are concealed. The organ of hearing is well developed, and the organ of smell extensive; the upper and lower turbinated bones being complicated, and covered by pituitary membrane. The tongue of the Cat and Civet tribe is rough, with horny papillæ. There is a scrotum in some; the penis is sheathed and turned backwards in some; it contains a bone in most (except the Hyænas), and in many the female clitoris also has one. The uterus is two-horned. The teats are abdominal, and vary from four to ten in number.

Many possess peculiar organs, secreting an odorous or fetid substance, in some round the anus; in others, between the anus and the tail; in a few between the anus and the genital organs.

In the most active of the order, the bones of the hands and feet are so connected with those above them, as to form a continuous line with them, and the animal rests upon the points of the toes; these are called Digitigrade. In others, a portion of the sole of the hind feet is applied to the ground in walking, hence called Semi-plantigrade: whilst in others, the hands and feet are so united with the bones above them that the animal bears upon its palms and soles, and are hence called Plantigrade. Certain aquatic species (the Seals) have all the feet short, and expanded into broad webbed paddles. These are called Pinnigrade; and they approach the Bears in various parts of their anatomy.

In conformity with these distinctions the Carnivora are here divided into the tribes *Plantigrada*, *Sub-plantigrada*, *Digitigrada*, and *Pinnigrada*.

Tribe, Plantigrada.

Walk on the whole sole of the foot. Five toes to each foot. No cœcum. Most are nocturnal in their habits and of slow action; and those which inhabit cold countries hybernate. This tribe comprises the family of the Bears. Cuvier remarks, that in the absence of the cœcum, their slow and nocturnal habits, &c., they resemble *Insectivora*, which they likewise do in their plantigrade motion.

Fam. Ursidæ.

Incisors normally $\frac{6}{6}$; canines $\frac{1-1}{1-1}$; præmolars $\frac{4-4}{4-4}$; molars $\frac{2-2}{3-3}$. Two tuberculated teeth on each side in the upper jaw; one or two in the lower jaw. Scissor-tooth nearly resembling the tuberculate. Soles of the feet usually devoid of hair; ears small; snout lengthened; tail usually very short.

Bears are mostly large, heavy animals, strictly plantigrade in their walk, and their body covered with long and shaggy hair. Their claws are adapted for digging, being long and stout, and they are mostly expert climbers. Many live almost entirely on fruits and roots, and other vegetable diet; others much on insects, larvæ, honey, &c., a few are more carnivorous in their habits. They conceal themselves in the day-time in caves, holes of trees, and thickets.

Gen. URSUS, Linnæus.

Teeth as in the characters of the family. The false molars small, often deciduous; the penultimate lower tuberculate tooth very large; scissor-tooth with a flat tuberculated crown; snout produced, the cartilage mobile, truncated in front; ears small, erect, rounded; tail very short; mammæ six, four ventral and two pectoral; feet with very strong claws.

Bears are found in both continents. Their cylindrical bones are nearer those of man than those of most animals; the femur, especially, closely approximates the same bone in the human skeleton; and hence the faculty possessed by bears of standing erect, and of dancing. The sole of the foot, as is well known to sportsmen, leaves a mark not unlike that of the human foot. There are three species in our province, two of which are Himalayan.

Bears have been subdivided of late into several sub-genera.

89. Ursus isabellinus.

HORSFIELD.—BLYTH, Cat. 224.—*U. syriacus*, HEMPRICH ? *Barf ka rich*, or *Bhalu*, H.—*Harput*, in Kashmir.—*Drin-mor*, in Ladak. Snow bear—Brown bear—Red, yellow, gray, and silver Bear, of sportsmen.

THE BROWN BEAR.

Descr.—Of large size, general color isabelline or yellowish-brown. In winter and spring the fur is long and shaggy, in some inclining to silvery-gray, in others to reddish-brown; the hair is thinner and darker in summer as the season advances; and in autumn, the under fur has mostly disappeared, and a white collar on the chest is then very apparent. The cubs show this collar distinctly. The females are said to be somewhat lighter in color than males.

A moderate sized one measured 7 feet 6 inches in length, and was above 3 feet in height.

This fine bear belongs to restricted *Ursus* of some writers, being of the same type as the brown bear of Europe. The claws are less powerful than in the other groups, straight and obtuse. It is supposed by some to be identical with the Syrian bear. It is found only on the Himalayas, and at great elevations in summer, close to the snow. In autumn they descend lower, coming into the forests to feed on various fruit, seeds, acorns, hips of rose bushes, &c., and often coming close to villages to plunder apples, walnuts, apricots, buck-wheat, &c. Their usual food in spring and summer is grass and roots. They also feed on various insects, and are seen turning over stones to look for scorpions (it is said), and insects that harbour in such places. In winter they retreat to caves, remaining in a state of semi-torpidity, issuing forth in March and April. Occasionally they are said to kill sheep or goats, often wantonly apparently, as they do not feed on them. They litter in April and May, the female having generally two cubs. If taken young, they are very easily domesticated. This bear does not climb trees well. They abound particularly in the N. W. Himalayas, and in the mountains round Kashmir. Many are killed every year by sportsmen.

To this division belong the Brown bear of Europe, *U. arctos*, L., of which I see it surmised (Nat. Hist. Review, 1865, pt. I.) that our species is only a well marked variety or race; the Black bear of N. America, *U. americanus*; and the huge Grisly bear of the rocky mountains, *U. ferox*.

The next group has been named *Helarctos*, or Sun bears. They are found on mountains in India and Malayana. The claws are larger and more curved than in restricted *Ursus*.

90. Ursus tibetanus.

F. Cuvier. Mammif. pl. 56.—Blyth, Cat. 225.—*U. torquatus*, Schinz.—*U. ferox* apud Robinson, Acc. of Assam.—*Bhalu*, H.—*Bhalak*, Beng.—*Thom*, Bhot.—*Sona*, Lepch.

The Himalayan Black Bear.

Descr.—Black, the lower lip white, also a large crescentric mark on the breast, sending up a branch on each side in front of the shoulder. Of moderate size. Neck thick; head flattened; forehead and muzzle being almost on a straight line; ears rather large; body compact; limbs thick and clumsy.

This bear is only found, within our province, on the Himalayas, but it is also found in the hill ranges of Assam. Its specific name is unfortunate, since it is rare in Thibet. In summer it is generally found at a considerable elevation, 9 to 12,000 feet or so; and often close to snow; but in winter it descends to 5,000 feet, and even lower sometimes. It lives chiefly on fruits and roots, apricots, walnuts, apples, currants, &c., also on various grains, barley, Indian corn, buck-wheat, &c.; and in winter chiefly feeds on various acorns, climbing the oak trees and breaking down the branches; and it is not uncommon to find one early in the morning in an oak tree, close to some dwelling house or village. Occasionally, when urged by hunger, they will destroy the crops of barley, buck-wheat, &c., in broad day-light, also the cucumbers and pumkins planted close to the villages, and trailing over the huts. They are very fond of honey, and occasionally pull down the honey from the hives kept by the hill people, and built into their huts. Now and then they will kill sheep, goats, &c., and are said occasionally to eat flesh. They often visit the village mill, licking up the remnants of flour. During the day-time they take shelter in the interior of some decayed tree, or among rocks, occasionally in some thick clump of trees. The female brings forth her young, generally two in number, in some den or cave among rocks.

This bear has bad eye-sight, but great power of smell, and if approached from windward is sure to take alarm. A wounded bear will sometimes show fight, but in general it tries to escape. It is said sometimes to coil itself into the form of a ball, and thus roll down steep hills, if frightened or wounded. If met suddenly where there is no means of escape, it will attack man at once; and, curious to say, it always mauls the face, sometimes taking off most of the hairy scalp and frightfully disfiguring the unfortunate sufferer. There are few villages in the interior, where one or more individuals thus mutilated are not to be met with. It has been noticed that if caught in a noose or snare, if they cannot break it by force, they never have the intelligence to bite the rope in two, but remain till they die or are killed. In captivity this bear, if taken young, is very quiet and playful, but is not so docile as the next species. Like others of its kind, it is fond of sucking its own or its neighbour's paws. An imperfect skin of a bear from Thibet, termed the "Blue bear," was pronounced by Blyth to be a variety of *Tibetanus*. The fur was softer and longer than in the ordinary race, black with hoary tips, which impart a very characteristic appearance.

Ursus malayanus is a very closely allied species of bear, inhabiting

Burmah, Arrakan, the Malayan peninsula, and some of the islands; whilst *U. euryspilus* of Borneo, is looked on as only a variety of *Malayanus*.

The next species differs a good deal in its type, and has been named *Melursus* by Meyer, *Prochilus* by Illiger. The claws are very large and powerful, the snout very much elongated and mobile, and there only 4 incisors in the upper jaw.

91. Ursus labiatus.

Blainville.—Blyth, Cat. 227.—Elliot, Cat. 14.—*Bradypus ursinus*, Shaw.—Figd. F. Cuvier, Mamm. III. 57.—*Melursus lybicus*, Meyer.—*Bhalu*, H. *Rich* or *Rinch*, H. in south of India.—*Riksha*, Sanscr.—*Aswail*, Mahr.—*Elugu*, Tel.—*Kaddi* or *Karadi*, Can.—*Yerid*, of Gonds.—*Banna*, of the Coles.—Sloth bear of some.

The Indian Black Bear.

Descr.—Black, hair very long and shaggy; muzzle and tip of feet dirty white or yellowish; a white cresceutic, or V shaped mark on the breast.

Length about $5\frac{1}{2}$ feet; height nearly 3 feet; tail about 7 or 8 inches.

This bear is found throughout India and Ceylon, from Cape Comorin to the Ganges, chiefly in the hilly and jungly districts. There never appear to be more than 4 incisors in the upper jaw. Bears are very abundant in some parts of the peninsula, where forest and jungle occur and the hills are rugged and rocky, and especially, as is the case in the Northern Circars, from Goomsoor southwards, and in various parts of Central India likewise, there are many hills formed of huge decomposed masses of granite simulating boulders, (and indeed popularly called so,) which have numberless natural caverns and recesses that suit these animals so well. They ascend the top of the Neelgherries and other high ranges of mountains in spring to feed, especially on the large larvæ of a huge longicorn beetle, that issues from the ground in great numbers later on; and which larvæ the bear sucks out of the ground, having first found the spot and scraped away some of the top earth. Bears are at times dangerous when met in the woods, and in the Vindhian range of mountains, near Mhow, where they are very abundant, woodcutters are very often attacked by them without any provocation, and sadly mauled or killed. Tickell mentions the same occurrence in other parts of India, but attributes it to the bears having their cubs with them at the time. Mr. W. Elliot, in his catalogue, says, "Their food seems to be black ants, termites, beetles, fruit, particularly the seeds of *Cassia fistula*, of the date tree, honey, &c. When pursued they carry their cubs on their backs. In 1833, a bear was chased and killed, having carried her two cubs in this way for nearly three miles. It appears to be a long-lived animal; instances are known of their living in captivity for 40 years." Had Mr. Elliot lived in parts of Central India, he would have learned that there is no fruit* the bear enjoys more than that of the Mohwa (*Bassia latifolia*), which falls in such profusion during the night, and the early sportsmen is sure to find the bears engaged in their pleasant repast under some of these trees.

I have abridged from Tickell's admirable account of this animal the subsequent observations:—"The power of suction in the bear as well as of propelling wind from its mouth is very great. It is by this means it is enabled to procure its common food of white ants and larvæ with ease. On arriving at an ant-hill, the bear scrapes away with the fore-feet until he reaches the large combs at the bottom of the galleries. He then with violent puffs dissipates the dust and crumbled particles of the nest, and sucks out the inhabitants of the comb by such forcible inhalations as to be heard at two hundred yards distance or more. Large larvæ are in this way sucked out from great depths under the soil. Where bears abound their vicinity may be readily known by numbers of these uprooted ants' nests and excavations, in which the marks of their claws are plainly visible. They occasionally rob birds' nests and devour the eggs. In running the bear moves in a rough canter, shaking up and down, but gets with great speed over very bad ground, regardless of tumbles down the rough places. The sucking of the paw accompanied by a drumming noise when at rest, and especially after meals is common to all bears, and during the heat of the day they may often be heard puffing and humming far down in caverns and fissures of rocks." The cause of this has often been speculated on, but Tickell imagines that is merely a habit peculiar to it, and he states "that they are just as fond of sucking their neighbours paws, or the hands of any person as their own paws."

They go with young about seven months, and generally bring forth two, at various times, but most usually about December and January. When taken young they are capable of being most thoroughly tamed, and will then partake of any kind of food. They are very commonly led about to perform various antics. Their pursuit is a favorite sport among Europeans

* It is properly only the sweet fleshy flower that falls off, not the fruit, as popularly called.

in India, and now and then a daring sportsman gets mauled severely by a wounded bear, whilst many others have had narrow escapes of a close embrace of their grisly foe. In the extreme south of India, among the Polygars of the hills, bears used to be hunted by strong fierce dogs, and when held at bay by them, the native sportsmen each thrust a long bamboo loaded with strong bird-lime into the shaggy coat of their quarry, and thus firmly held their struggling prey. This practice I understand has of late years almost fallen into disuse."

The huge Polar bear, *U. maritimus*, L., is the type of *Thalarctos* of Gray. There are some bears on the Andes in South America.

The only other form belonging to the bears which inhabits our province is the following remarkable animal, and which differs sufficiently to have been classed by Gray in a sub-family *Ailurina*.

Gen. AILURUS, F. Cuvier.

Char.—Incisors $\frac{6}{6}$; molars $\frac{5-5}{6-6}$. The crowns of the posterior molars furnished with salient but truncated tubercles; head sub-globose, broad; cheeks tumid; ears short, acute, distant, hairy; eyes well in front near the nose; tail equal to the body, cylindric, with long spreading hair; soles clad with fine down; claws falcate, compressed, sharp, partly retractile.

This curious genus has been considered to have points of resemblance to Badgers and Racoons, and also to *Cercoleptes*, and by some even has been compared in external appearance with certain *Lemurs*, but there is no doubt that its nearest affinities are with the Bears, whilst it has one or two points of affinity with the *Felinæ* or *Viverrinæ*, viz., its semi-retractile talons, and the structure of its genital organs. There is only one known species.

92. Ailurus fulgens.

F. CUVIER, Mamm. III. pl. 52.—BLYTH, Cat. 219.—HARDWICKE, Lin. Trans. XV. 161.—*A. ochraceus*, HODGSON.—*Wáh*, of Nepal.—*Wáh-donka*, Bhot.—*Sunnam* or *Suk-nam*, Lepch.—*Negalya ponya*, of the Nepalese.

THE RED CAT-BEAR.

Descr.—Above deep ochreous-red; head and tail paler, and somewhat fulvous, displayed on the tail in rings; face, chin, and ears within white; ears externally, all the lower surface and the entire limbs and tip of tail jet black; from the eye to the gape a broad vertical line of ochreous-red blending with the dark lower surface; moustache white; muzzle black.

Length of head and body 22 inches; tail 16; about 9 inches high; weight 8 lb.

This very curious and richly colored animal is a denizen of the south-eastern Himalayas, having only been taken in Nepal and Sikim. It is stated to be found from 7,000 feet up to 12,000 feet or so. General Hardwicke was the first to discover this animal, but his description was not published till after Mr. F. Cuvier had described it from a specimen sent to Paris by M. Duvancel. Hodgson has given a full account of it, from which I extract the following observations:—"The Wáh is a vegetalivorous climber, breeding and feeding chiefly on the ground, and having its retreat in holes and clefts of rock. It eats fruits, roots, sprouts of bamboo, acorns, &c.; also, it is said, eggs and young birds; also milk and ghee, which it is said to purloin occasionally from the villages. They feed morning and evening, and sleep much in the day. They are excellent climbers, but on the ground move rather awkwardly and slowly. Their senses all appear somewhat blunt, and they are easily captured. In captivity they are placid and inoffensive, docile and silent, and shortly after being taken they may be suffered to go abroad. They prefer rice and milk to all other food, refusing animal food, and they are free from all offensive odour. They drink by lapping with the tongue, piss and spit like cats when angered, and now and then utter a short deep grunt like a young bear. The female brings forth two young in spring. They usually sleep laid on the side, and rolled into a ball, the head concealed by the bushy tail."

It is not very common now about Darjeeling. The Lepchas there say that it feeds a good deal on insects and larvæ, which it scratches out of the ground. A friend of mine watched a pair seated high up in a lofty tree. They were making the most unearthly cries, he assured me, he ever heard. It was evidently the pairing season.

Hodgson states that one he examined had 14 ribs and dorsal vertibræ, another 15; the radius and ulnæ are distinct and nearly equal in size, and the tibia and fibula also distinct. There is no clavicle: altogether the skeleton was sufficiently ursine. The tongue is rather rough; the stomach is semi-circular, and the intestinal canal nearly five times the length of the body. There are no anal glands; the penis is as in *Felis* or *Viverra*; and the female has eight mammæ.

Other animals placed in this family, but classed in a separate sub-family, *Procyoninæ* by Gray, are the Racoons of North America, *Procyon;* the Coatimondis (*Nasua*), from the warmer parts of the same continent, and the Kinkajou or Potto, *Cercoleptes*, from South America. This last very curious animal has a long prehensile tail, an extensile tongue, and the flesh-tooth tuberculated. The Racoons have three pointed false molars above, and three tuberculated molars. They have a moderately long tail, and live chiefly on animal food, eggs, &c. The Coatimondis have longer tails and sharper snouts than Racoons, and their feet are semi-palmate, but they have similar dentition, and live on worms, slugs, small animals, and birds' eggs, &c.

The animals next in succession do not quite bring the heel to the ground in walking, though they often rest on it, and they constitute the

Tribe, Semi-plantigrada, of Blyth.

They form part of the Plantigrada of Cuvier, and part also of his Digitigrada, and may be divided into *Melidæ* or Badgers, and their affines; and *Mustelidæ* or Weasels and Martens; with a sub-family for the Otters, *Lutrinæ*. Blyth, in his Catalogue, classes them in three sub-families of one great family, *Mustelidæ*. None of them have more than one true molar above, and another below, which, however, vary much in development, and the flesh tooth is most marked in those in which the tuberculate is least developed, and *vice versâ*. The great and small intestines differ little in calibre, and many of them can diffuse at will a disgusting stench.

Melididæ, Badger-like animals.

Molars 4, or sometimes 5 above, 4, 5 or 6 in each side in the lower jaw, only one true tuberculated tooth on each side in the upper jaw; præmolars compressed and cutting; the flesh-tooth usually with a large blunt tubercle on the inside; ears small, or rudimentary; anterior feet with large claws, fossorial in some.

The badgers and their affines differ from the weasels and martens by their heavy form; stout limbs and more inactive gait, by their decidedly fossorial claws (in some), and their harsh coarse hair; and in this group are comprised most of those animals that have the power of diffusing a fetid stench. They are moreover entirely ground animals. They ordinarily erect their tail, and most of them are more or less striped longitudinally.

There are three representatives of this group in India.

Gen. Arctonyx, F. Cuvier.

Char.—Incisors $\frac{6}{6}$; molars $\frac{4-4}{4-4}$ or $\frac{4-4}{5-5}$. Dentition in general like that of *Gulo* or *Meles*. Incisors of moderate size, bluntish, in a regular curve, vertical in the upper jaw, inclined outwards in the lower one. Canines large and strong, and stout at the base: molars compressed; feet plantigrade, pentadactylous, claws strong, compressed, fossorial; claw of the indexa a finger greatly exceeding the others in size. Tail short, attenuated, with rough hairs. Habit that of the badger, but still more robust. Snout somewhat lengthened.

93. Arctonyx collaris.

Cuvier, Mamm. III. t. 60.—Blyth, Cat. 212.—*Mydaus*, apud Gray —Hardwicke, Ill. Ind. Zool. I pl. VI.—A. *isonyx*, Hodgson, P. Z. S. 1856, pl. 4.—*Bhalu-soor*, H., *i. e.*, Bear-pig.

The Hog-badger.

Descr.—Upper parts with the head, throat and breast yellowish-white, more or less grizzled; nape of neck, a narrow band across the breast, anterior portion of abdomen, and the extremities, deep blackish brown; there is likewise a brown band from the middle of the upper lip, gradually widening posteriorly and including the eyes and ears; and another smaller and narrower band arising from the lower lip, passing through the cheek and uniting with the former on the neck.

Length from snout to root of tail 25 inches; tail 7; 1 foot high at the rump.

This very curious hog-badger has been found within our province in the Nepal and Sikim Terais, and also I believe in parts of Eastern Bengal. Its chief localities, however, would appear to be still further east in Assam, Sylhet, Arrakan, &c. Hodgson considered the one he found in the Terai to differ, but this opinion has not been upheld.

It is stated to pass the greater part of the day in profound sleep, but to become active at the approach of night; its gait is heavy and slow, and it readily supports itself erect on the hind feet, having much general resemblance to bears. One kept in captivity preferred fruit, plantains, &c.,

as food, and refused all kinds of meat. Another would eat meat, fish, and used to burrow and grope under the walls of the bungalow for worms and shells.*

Evans found on dissection, the tongue large broad and soft; the stomach simple, no cœcum, 5 lobes to the liver. There was a caudal pouch directly under the origin of the tail (as in the badger) secreting a brown unctuous matter like the wax of the ear. Blyth described a second species, *A. taxoides*, from Sylhet and Assam, much smaller than the last, and with a longer and finer coat.

One of the earliest figures of this animal is to be found in the well known Bewick's Quadrupeds.

Gen. MELLIVORA, Storr.

Syn. *Ratelus*, BENNETT.—*Ursitaxus*, HODGSON.

Char.—Molars $\frac{4-4}{5-5}$; 2 false molars above and 3 below; the tuberculate tooth in the upper jaw transverse, smaller than the flesh-tooth; the lower flesh-tooth with the edge sharp, tricuspidate; the upper one has the anterior and inner tubercles conical; no external ear, only a cutaneous border round the external auditory meatus; head rather short; feet short; tail very short; hair long, rigid; anterior claws very strong.

This is another form very nearly allied to the badgers in general appearance, but still more ursine in its short tail and habit. It was founded on an African animal, the Cape or Honey Ratel, so very similar that it is only lately that they have been allowed to be distinct. The female has 4 teats. The male genital organ is bony and spirally annulated. On each side of the anus there is a hollow gland with a distinct tubular canal opening by a round pore on the caudal margin. Each gland is large enough to contain a walnut, and the secretion is dark, thick, and fetid.

94. Mellivora indica.

Ursus apud SHAW.—HARDWICKE, Linn. Tran. IX. 115, with figure.—*Ursitaxus inauritus*, HODGSON, As. Res. XIX. 60, with figure.—*Ratelus indicus*, SCHINZ.—*M. ratel*, apud BLYTH, Cat. 207.—*Biju*, H., *Biyu khawar*—Tel, in the Hyderabad country.—*Tava karadi*, Tam.—*Bajru bhál*, at Bhagulpore.

* Journal. As. Soc. IX. 732.

The Indian Badger.

Descr.—Above tawny white or light gray, black on the sides and beneath; tail short.

Length of one, head and body 26 inches; tail 6. Another measured 32 inches; tail 5.

The Indian badger has long been considered as the Cape ratel, or Honey-eater, but was recognized as distinct by Schinz; and Blyth, who, in his Catalogue, joined the two, has written me from England, where he has seen both alive, that he now considers them sufficiently distinct. The Indian animal wants the marked white stripe that exist in the Cape species, between the gray of the upper parts and the black lower surface; and its tail is decidedly shorter. A recent writer too, in the Natural History Review, for 1865, vol. I., states it as his opinion from observations of the living animals that they are distinct.

The Indian badger is found throughout the whole of India, from the extreme south to the foot of the Himalayas, chiefly in hilly districts, where it has greater facilities for constructing the holes and dens in which it lives; but also in the north of India in alluvial plains, where the banks of large rivers afford equally suitable localities wherein to make its lair. I never heard of its occurrence on the Malabar coast, nor in lower Bengal, but it is certainly found in most other districts of India, though rarely seen and often not very well known, even to the natives, in the southern parts; but throughout central India it is well known under the name of *Biju*. It is stated to live usually in pairs, and to eat rats, birds, frogs, white ants, and various insects, and in the north of India it is accused of digging out dead bodies, and is popularly known as the grave-digger. It doubtless also, like its Cape congener, occasionally partakes of honey. It is often very destructive to poultry, and I have known of several having been trapped and killed whilst committing such depredations in central India, and in the northern Circars. In confinement the Indian badger is quiet, and will partake of vegetable food, fruits, rice, &c.

The Cape ratel, *Mellivora ratel*, is said chiefly to live on honey, of which it is stated to be immoderately fond. The European badger, *Meles taxus*, is one of the best known animals of this group; and Blyth has described *Meles albo-gularis*, from Tibet, which country also possesses one species of *Taxidea* or Taxel, described and figured by Mr. Hodgson as *Taxidea leucura*, the *Tum-pha*, of the Tibetans. The badger of North America belongs to this last group, which has a much finer fur than the badger and ratels, and a more carnivorous dentition.

The next animal has a less heavy and more lengthened form.

Gen. Helictis, Gray.

Char.—Molars $\frac{5-5}{6-6}$, the upper flesh-tooth three-lobed, with a wide two-pointed inner process; upper tuberculate tooth moderate, transverse; the lower one small. Head and body somewhat lengthened; feet short; soles naked almost to the heel; nails strong, the anterior ones long, compressed, fossorial; tail moderate, cylindric.

This genus was founded on the *Gulo orientalis* of Horsfield, and appears to be a sort of link between the badgers and martens. It is stated to be rather carnivorous in its habits, and to exhale a musky odour. It is not unlike, in general appearance, the *Mydaus meliceps*, figured by Horsfield, of which it has the coloring, viz., pale-brownish with a while dorsal stripe, but it is more slender in its habit and a different dentition, nearly indeed that of *Gulo*.

95. Helictis nipalensis.

Gulo apud Hodgson, J. A. S., V. 237, and VI. 560.—Blyth, Cat. 208.—*Oker* of the Nepalese.

The Nepal Wolverine.

Descr.—Above earthy brown, below with the edge of the upper lip, and insides of the limbs, and terminal half of the tail yellowish; a white mesial stripe from the nape to the hips; and a white band across the forehead, spreading on the cheeks, and confluent with the paler color of the lower surface; tail cylindric, tapering, about half the length of the animal; half the planta naked; fur of two sorts, long, not harsh.

Length head and body 16 inches; tail 7½, 9 with the hair.

The form of this animal, says Hodgson, is decidedly musteline from snout to the tail, with however fossorial fore-feet, and sub-plantigrade, and therefore unsuited either for raptatory or scansorial habits.

There is no account of its habits or food, but Horsfield states of its Malayan representative, *Helictis orientalis*, to which the Nepal animal appears very closely allied, that it is more carnivorous than *Mydaus*, living exclusively on small animals and birds. It does not diffuse the fetid exhalation so characteristic of *Mydaus*. Near here should be placed the Skunks, *Mephitis*. They have the upper tuberculous molar very large, and two tubercles on the inner side of the lower flesh-tooth. They have also long claws adapted for burrowing, and in fact approximate the badgers, but have a fine large bushy tail which they ordinarily erect. They and the Zorillas might be referred either to the badgers or the weasels.

Fam. MUSTELIDÆ, Weasels and Martens.

Four or five molar teeth on each side in the upper jaw; five, rarely six, in the lower: one tuberculate tooth on each side in both jaws; canines slender and curved; flesh-tooth broad and sharp. Feet pentadactylous, slightly sub-plantigrade; claws sharp, but not retractile; snout short, rounded.

This family is here restricted to the weasels and martens, animals of small size, elongated vermiform make, and with very short limbs. The head is rounded in front like that of the cats, but the distance from the orbit to the occipital foreamen is very great, so that the skull has an elongated form posteriorly. They are very active and agile in their movements, and highly carnivorous and blood-thirsty in their habits, destroying vast numbers of small animals and birds, which they generally seize by the back of the head. The fur of many is soft and fine, and is very highly prized. They are most abundant in cold climates, in the northern portion of the old continent; and there is only one species, in our province, south of the Himalayas; but several appear peculiar to this lofty mountain chain.

Gen. MARTES.

Five molars on each side above, and six below. Muzzle more lengthened than in weasels and less rounded; tail rather long, bushy.

The martens are a more or less arboreal group of rather small animals, chiefly found in the northern portion of the world, and many of them are highly prized for their fine fur. Though of larger size, they are less fierce and sanguivorous than their smaller relatives, the weasels. Besides the additional false molar, they have a small tubercle on the inner side of the flesh-tooth, which is not present in the weasels; and what scent they have is not disagreeable. There is only one species in India, which extends into Malayana.

96. Martes flavigula.

Mustela apud Boddaert.—Blyth, Cat. 196.—*Mustela Hardwickii*, Horsfield, Zool. Jour.—*Martes Gwatkinsii*, and *Galidictis chrysogaster*, Jardine, Nat. Libr.—*Mal sampra*, Nepal.—*Tuturala*, in Kumaon.—*Kusiah*, in Sirmoor.—*Huniah*, or *Aniar*, Bhot.—*Sakku*, Lepch.

The Indian Marten.

Descr.—Head and face, ears, and whole upper parts, with the body from the breast, and limbs, glossy blackish-brown, the chin and lower lip white; throat and breast yellow, more or less deep, and inclining to orange yellow, or yellowish-brown in some. The body is at times dirty brownish, or chesnut-brown, or mixed brown with gray, and the middle of the back is sometimes paler than the rest, or the same tint as the sides of the body. In some, the top of the head is pale brown, but it is edged by a dark peripheral line; and in some, there are one or more irregular dark spots between the forelimbs; soles nude.

Length about 20 inches head and body; tail about 12, with the hair.

This marten is found throughout the whole extent of the Himalayas; also on the Neelgherry hills and Ceylon; and, out of our province, it extends from the Khasia hills through Arrakan down the Malayan peninsula to Java. Horsfield, in his Catalogue, applied the synonym *M. Gwatkinsii* to the dark Neelgherry race, but it was originally given to a Himalayan specimen, many of which are equally dark; and Dr. Adams considers that the dark state is merely the summer fur. The Malayan race is paler than the others, and according to Blyth, all specimens from thence are true to the particular coloring.

The Indian marten is chiefly found in the valleys both of the outer ranges and the interior, but also ascends the wooded ridges in summer up to 7,000 or 8,000 feet of elevation. It is sometimes found in pairs, often in small families of five or six, and is not unfrequently met with in the day time, hunting among brushwood, fallen trees, &c. If pursued by dogs it at once takes refuge on trees, in climbing which it is very active. Its food is said to be chiefly birds' eggs; also rats, lizards and snakes sometimes, and even, it is said, the young of the Kakar deer (*Stylocerus*). It is also very destructive to poultry. Adams states that it is easily domesticated, and is very active and playful; and Mr. Bennett, many years ago, gave an account of its manners in confinement in the "Gardens and Menageries of the Zoological Society." It has a very slight unpleasant odour.

Martes toufæus, Hodgson, is stated to have been killed in Tibet, Ladak, &c., at 11,000 feet of elevation, where it chiefly lives in the villages of the inhabitants. It is also found in Afghanistan, and its skin sold in the bazars at Peshawur. Another species, which Blyth is inclined to identify with *Mustela zibellina*, the sable marten, has also been procured from Tibet. This has the soles clad with fur. The former of these has by some observers been taken for the pine marten of Europe, *Martes abietum*.

Gen. Mustela, Linnæus.

Char.—Four molar teeth above on each side, and five below; lower canine with no internal tubercle, upper tuberculated tooth with the crown broader than long; ears short, rounded; feet short; toes separate; claws sharp; tail short or moderate. Of small size; body elongated, vermiform.

Weasels are a well known group of small animals, of lengthened habit of body and very short legs, to which the name vermin is commonly applied. They are, though so small, most sanguinary in their disposition, often killing far more than will satisfy their hunger. They are ground animals, hunting on the ground, and living in holes in walls and such like places. They are chiefly inhabitants of the northern parts of the old world and Northern America; and in India they are only found in the Himalayas.

97. Mustela sub-hemachalana.

Hodgson, J. A. S. VI. 563—Blyth, Cat. 202.—*M. humeralis*, Blyth.
Zimiong, Bhot.—*Sang-king*, Lepch.

The Himalayan Weasel.

Descr.—Uniform light bay or brown, slightly darker along the median line; nose, upper lip and forehead, and the end of the tail dark-reddish brown; edge of the upper lip and chin hoary-white; feet dusky-brown; fur close, glossy and soft; head and ears more closely clad than the body; tail laxly furred, tapering.

Length head and body 12 inches; tail 5½, with the hair 1 inch more.

Blyth described a specimen that had some white spots and mottling on the shoulders and sides of the neck. He also likens this species to the ermine, which is about the same size, but darker in color, and the tip of the tail black.

This weasel appears spread throughout the whole range of Himalayas, from Cashmere to Darjeeling, chiefly on the middle and outer ranges. Adams states that it is common in Cashmere, and very destructive to poultry, &c. A dark variety is indicated in the list of Hodgson's collections.

The stoat or ermine, *M. erminra*, is confidently stated to occur in the Himalayas, in Nepal by Hodgson, and Adams states it to be common in the lower and middle regions of the Western Himalayas; but there do not appear to be Himalayan examples of this species in any of our museums. It is reddish-brown above, white beneath, the extremity of the tail black in winter, changing to yellowish-white, retaining the black tail tip.

98. Mustela kathiah.

Hodgson, J. A. S. IV. 702—Blyth, Cat. 203.—*M. auriventer*, Hodgson.—*Kathia nyal*, Nepal.

The Yellow-bellied Weasel.

Descr.—Deep rich brown above, golden yellow below; chin whitish; ears, limbs and tail, concolorous with body; tail cylindric, tapered, half the length of the animal.

Length, snout to rump 10 inches; tail (minus the hair) 5. The fur is short, shining and adpressed, and the palms and soles are clad in hair.

A horribly offensive yellowish gray fluid exudes from two openings placed near the root of the tail.

This weasel has only been found in the eastern Himalayas, from Nepal, and probably Bootan, as a specimen said to be from Assam is in the Museum of the Asiatic Society, Calcutta.

" This beautiful creature," writes Mr. Hodgson, "is exceedingly prized by the Nepalese for it service in ridding houses of rats. It is easily tamed, and such is the dread of it common to all murine animals, that not one will approach a house where it is domiciled. Rats and mice seem to have an instinctive sense of its hostility to them, so much so that as soon as it is introduced into a house they are observed to hurry away in all directions, being apprized no doubt of its presence by the peculiar odour it emits. Its ferocity and courage are made subservient to the amusement of the rich, who train it to attack large fowls, geese, and even goats and sheep. The latter, equally with the former, fall certain sacrifices to its agility and daringness. So soon as it is loosed it rushes up the fowl's tail or the goat's leg, and seizes the great artery of the neck, nor ever quits its hold till the victim sinks under exhaustion from loss of blood."

99. Mustela strigidorsa.

Hodgson, apud Horsfield, Ann. Mag. Nat. Hist 1855—P. Z. S. 1856, pl. XLIX.

The Striped Weasel.

Descr.—Intense brown, with lips, head and neck inferiorly, and a dorsal and ventral stripe yellowish white or pale aureous.

Length, snout to vent, 12 inches; tail 5½, with the hair 1 inch more.

Larger than *M. kathiah.* Horsfield states that in one specimen sent to the East India Museum, the brown has a shade of chesnut, and the under parts of the head, neck and breast are nearly white, with a slight isabelline discoloration.

This weasel was procured by Hodgson in Sikim. If the dorsal stripe were not uniformly present, it might be taken merely for a variety of *M. kathiah.*

Gray has described *M. Horsfieldii* from Bootan, uniform dark blackish-brown, very little paler beneath; and middle of the front of the chin, and the lower lips white; tail slender, blackish at the tip; half as long as the head and body. This is very probably a dark race of *Mustela sub-hemachalana,* such as was obtained by Hodgson in Nepal, and of which there is a drawing in the British Museum.

Hodgson has described two other weasels from Tibet, *Mustela temon,* brownish-fawn above, pure yellow beneath; head and limbs canescent. Length, head body 9½ inches; tail 6½; fur, short, soft.

M. canigula, cinnamon-red, head and neck below hoary; whiskers small and rigid. Length, head and body, 15½ inches; tail 9½.

A weasel is described from the Malayan peninsula and Java, *M. nudipes,* F. Cuvier; *M. sarmatica,* Pallas, of Northern and Central Asia, has been procured in Afghanistan; and *M. sibirica,* Pallas (*M. Hodgsoni,* Gray), has been sent from China.

M. putorius, L., the polecat of Europe, of which the ferret is considered to be a domestic variety, has been made the type of the genus *Putorius,* F. Cuvier; and a race nearly allied has been described by Hodgson, as *Putorius tibetanus,* olim *Mustela larvata,* from Tibet.

Sub-fam. Lutrinæ, Otters.

Of large size; feet webbed; tail flattened.

Gen. Lutra, Ray.

Char.—Dental formula according to Owen, præmolars $\frac{4-4}{3-3}$; molars $\frac{1-1}{2-2}$. The upper flesh-tooth very large, with a large accessory tubercle internally, the lower one tuberculated posteriorly; otherwise as in the weasels. Ears small, remote; feet palmate, short; body lengthened; tail longish, stout at the base, round, depressed towards the tip, and flat beneath.

Otters are a well marked group of animals, distinguished by their elongated and somewhat flattened form, short and stout limbs, with the toes well webbed and spreading, and with naked soles. The fur is close, fine and short, consisting of a woolly fur beneath, and a layer of smooth glossy hairs above. The eyes are provided with a nyctitating membrane, or additional half-transparent eyelid like that of birds, as a defence to them under water. The teeth are strong and sharp, and the tubercles of the molars very pointed, to secure their prey, which is almost entirely fish, which they hunt for and capture under water with wonderful activity and skill. The skull is said to have something in common with Seals in the short muzzle, and wide and flat cranium; the suborbital foramen is large. The articulations of the extremities are such as to admit of great freedom of motion. The intestines are about six times longer than the head and body.

Mr. Blyth remarks, "the species of this genus are most difficult of determination, and require to be further studied and more elaborately described with reference to their distinctions one from another."

100. Lutra nair.

F. Cuvier.—*L. chinensis* and *L. indica*, Gray.—*L. tarayensis*, Hodgson.—Elliot, Cat. 15—Blyth, Cat. 214—*Pani kuta*, H.—*Nir-nai*, Can. *Neeru-kuka*, Tel., all signifying water-dog.—*Jal manjer*, Mahr., *i. e.* water-cat.—*Ud* or *Hud*, *Udni*, *Ud billau*, Hindi.

The Common Indian Otter.

Descr.—Above hair brown, or light chesnut-brown, in some grizzled with hoary tips, in others with a tinge of isabella yellow; beneath yellowish white, or reddish-white; upper lip, sides of head and neck, chin and throat, whitish, the line of separation between the two colors more a less distinctly marked; in some the throat tinged with orange brown; paws albescent in some, simply of a lighter shade in others; tail brown beneath. F. Cuvier, in his description, mentions some pale facial spots, but these are indistinct, though there is sometimes a faint pale eyebrow.

Total length up to 46 inches, of which the tail is 17, and 3 inches wide at the base.

I have followed Blyth in joining *L. nair* and *L. indica,* though at one time I was strongly inclined to believe them distinct. My impression was that the common otter of most of the rivers of Southern India at all events, was distinct from the generally larger, and more robust otter found in such numbers along the Malabar coast, and in lower Bengal; and that the latter, besides being larger, had the fur more reddish or yellowish-brown, and with the two colors much more distinctly divided; in fact more resembling *Lutra vulgaris;* but in the absence of authentic specimens, I can only draw the attention of observers for future verification.

Accepting the synonymy as above then, this otter is found throughout all India, from the extreme South and Ceylon, to the foot of the Himalayas, and from the Indus to Burmah and Malayana, frequenting alike rivers, and salt water inlets, and from the level of the sea to a considerable elevation. It has its lair under large rocks, among boulders; and, in alluvial countries, excavates extensive burrows, generally in some elevated spot close to the river, with numerous entrances. It is almost always found in parties of five, six, or more, and, though partly nocturnal in its habits, may often be seen hunting after the sun is high, and sometime before sunset. I have seen a party out in the sea, on the Malabar coast, probably making their way from one backwater to another, but as they are very numerous on this coast, they may now and then hunt in the sea. This otter is trained in some parts of Bengal to assist in fishing, by driving the fish into the nets. Young ones are not unusually caught in the fishermen's nets, and are very easily tamed. I had one brought me when very young, whilst at Tellicherry on the Malabar coast, which I brought up with a terrier dog, with whom it became very friendly. This otter would follow me in my walks like a dog, and amuse itself by a few gambols in the water when it had the opportunity, and now and then caught frogs and small fish. As it grew older it took to going about by itself, and one day found its way to the bazar, and seized a large fish from a Moplah. When resisted, it showed such fight that the rightful owner was fain to drop it. Afterwards it took regularly to this highway style of living, and I had on several occasions to pay for my pet's dinner rather more than was necessary, so I resolved to get rid of it. I put it in a closed box, and having kept it without food for some time, I conveyed it myself in a boat some seven or eight miles off, up some of the numerous backwaters on this coast. I then liberated it, and when it had wandered out of sight among some inundated paddy fields, I returned by boat by a different route. That same evening, about 9 P. M., whilst in the town, about one and a half miles from my own house, witnessing some of the ceremonials connected with the Mohurrum festival, the otter entered the temporary shed, walked across the floor, and came and lay down at my feet !

The specific name given by F. Cuvier is unfortunate, it being only the the termination of the common native name *Nir-nai*, or water-dog, and wrongly spelled moreover. Blyth, in his Catalogue, records a specimen from Algeria, quite undistinguishable from specimens from Bengal.

101. Lutra vulgaris.

ERXLEBEN—BLYTH, Cat. 216—*L. monticola*, HODGSON.

THE HILL OTTER.

Descr.—Above bistre brown; below sordid hoary, vaguely defined except on the lips and chin; limbs dark; fur long and rough, not adpressed. Such is Hogdson's description of his *monticola.* Blyth describes a specimen from Darjeeling, as "fur longish, dark colcothar brown, slightly grizzled with a pale ring near the tip; beneath fulvous white, which extends to the tip of the tail; beneath the pale lower parts abruptly separated from the brown above. The second incisor is slightly out of its place behind the others." This is also noticed by Hodgson.

Length head and body 32 inches; tail 20.

Blyth has compared the skull of this otter with that of the European one, and finds them identical. The skull differs from that of *L. nair* in being more compressed between the orbits.

As far as we at present know, the common otter of Europe is restricted, in India, to the interior of the Himalayas.

Hodgson has described a small otter from the hills, as *Lutra auro brunnea.* Size small; habit of body vermiform; tail less than two-thirds of the length of the body; toes and nails fully developed; fur longish and rough. Color rich chesnut-brown above, golden red below, and on the extremities. Length head and body 20 to 22 inches; tail 12 to 13.

Blyth, in his Catalogue, has No. 215, *L.*——, very like *L. nair*, but specimens with adult dentition smaller by one half or nearly so. Found only at great elevations in Ceylon. This is probably the same as the small otter of the Neelgherries, referred to by some writers in the "Bengal Sporting Review," &c.; by some called the black otter, by others the red one; and is perhaps the same as Hodgson's *L. auro-brunnea.*

Hodgson has indicated other otters from the Himalayas. In the Malayan peninsula, besides *L. nair*, there is another, *Lutra barang*, Raffles.

The next otters have the claws very minute, not projecting, but imbedded in the phalanx, the foremost upper præmolars often naturally wanting, and they have been separated generically as *Aonyx*, Lesson. The third and fourth toes exceed the others in length, and are more closely united. It was founded on a Cape species, *Lutra inunguis.* One is found in India extending into Malayana.

102. Lutra leptonyx.

HORSFIELD, Zool. Res., Java, with figure.—BLYTH, Cat. 217.—*Aonyx Horsfieldii*, GRAY.—*L. indigitata*, and *Aonyx sikimensis*, HODGSON.—*Chusam*, Bhot.—*Suriam*, Lepch.

THE CLAWLESS OTTER.

Descr.—Above earthy-brown or chesnut-brown; lips, sides of head, chin, throat, and upper part of breast white, tinged with yellowish-gray. In young individuals the white of the lower parts is less distinct, sometimes very pale-brownish.

Length head and body 24 inches; tail 13; palm $2\frac{5}{8}$; planta $3\frac{1}{2}$.

This otter has been found throughout the Himalayas, from the North-west to Sikim; also in lower Bengal, in Arrakan, down to the islands, &c. I saw one killed close to Calcutta at the edge of the salt-water lake. It had not previously been recorded from lower Bengal.

Tribe, DIGITIGRADA.

Syn. *Cynodia*, Blyth in part.

In walking the digits alone are placed on the ground. These are the most typical of the *Carnivora*, and most of them are very speedy and quick in their actions.

They differ from the previous tribes in having a small cœcum.

The Digitigrade Carnivora are divided into three families—*Felidæ*, *Viverridæ*, and *Canidæ*, or the Cats, the Civet cats, and the Dogs.

Fam. FELIDÆ. The Cat tribe.

Molars $\frac{4-4}{3-3}$, of which, according to F. Cuvier, two are false molars on each side in both jaws, and there is no tuberculate molar in the lower jaw. According to Owen, the dental formula is, incisors $\frac{3-3}{3-3}$; canines $\frac{1-1}{1-1}$; præmolars $\frac{3-3}{2-2}$; molars $\frac{1-1}{1-1}$; total 30 teeth. Fore-feet with five, hind-feet with four or five, toes.

The animals of this family have the smallest number of molars, and hence their jaws are short and strong; the head is rounded, and the limbs powerful. Their teeth are particularly cutting, the canines very large and sharp, the flesh-tooth above three-lobed, with a tubercle on its inner side; and the tuberculated molar above small. All are essentially carnivorous, and they are the type of the tribe and order. Their footfall is noiseless, from the thick pads with which the under surface of their feet is furnished. To preserve their claws sharp, they are habitually kept withdrawn between the toes, by the action of an elastic ligament which acts on the last joint of each toe, bending it upwards. When the animal is about to strike, the flex or tendons pull down this last phalanx, and the claw is thus exserted. Their fur is usually dense and short. Their limbs are of moderate length and very powerful, and they can take astonishing bounds. Their vision is adapted for night as well as for day, and all are nocturnal in habits, or nearly so. Their sense of hearing is very acute, and their long whiskers are delicate organs of touch. The tongue is furnished with rough papillæ, directed backwards and somewhat recurved. The clavicle is rudimentary, and imbedded among the muscles. They usually take their prey by suddenly springing on it from a concealed spot, and if they fail in seizing it rarely pursue. They are generally solitary, but occasionally hunt in families.

The cat tribe are found over both continents, but do not occur in Australia; and the larger species are most numerous in warm countries.

Mr. Blyth has recently published (Proc. Zool. Soc. 1863, p. 181) a Synopsis of the Asiatic species of *Felis*, containing several alterations in the nomenclature from that of his Catalogue, all of which I have here adopted.

The Cat tribe may be popularly divided into Lions, Tigers, Leopards, Cats and Lynxes ; which have been not unfrequently made by late authors into as many genera, but recently have been retained in one large genus. Blyth divides the Asiatic cats into three groups—the Pardine series, with robust skeleton, and rounded and obtuse-ear-conch; Lynxine series; and the hunting Cheeta.

Gen. Felis, Linn.

Char.—Those of the family. Hind-feet with four toes.

1st. Lions, *Leo*, Gray, and others. Unspotted, of large size; pupil round. Lions are distinguished by their enormous head, maned neck, comparatively weak hind limbs, and a shortish, tufted tail.

103. Felis leo.

Linnæus—*F.* (*leo*) *asiaticus* of some.—*F.* (*leo*) *gujratensis*, Smee, Trans. Zool. Soc., with fig.—Bennett, Tower Menagerie, pl. XXIV.—Blyth, Cat. 171., Synops. 2—*Shér*, *Babbar-shér*, H.—*Untia bág* in Guzrat and Cutch, *i. e.* the camel-colored tiger.—*Singha*, H., in some parts.—*Shingal*, Beng.

The Asiatic Lion.

Descr.—Of a pale tawny color without spots or stripes, tail tufted; mane scanty in some, well marked in others.

Length 8½ to 9½ feet; 3½ feet in height; foot 6¼ inches in diameter. The weight of one, 8 feet 9½ inches long, was 35 stone.

The Asiatic lion was long considered to differ from the African one, in being smaller and less powerful, and in wanting the rufous or vinous tinge so general in the African race; but recent observations tend to confirm the specific identity of lions from Asia and Africa, pale colored races being by no means rare in Africa; but it must be allowed that the African lion has generally a finer mane, as well as a median line of lengthened hairs along the abdomen, which is seldom present in the Asiatic lion; and, moreover, has a somewhat different physiognomy. The race from Guzrat was considered distinct by Major Smee, of the Bombay army, and it was supposed that the Indian race wanted the mane altogether. It has, however, been clearly shown by Blyth and others, that the absence of the mane in certain specimens was probably accidental, being torn off in the prickly jungles of those districts of India which it still frequents, and that if allowed to grow that the mane was well developed. Bennett's figure referred to above, was taken from a lion brought from Hurriana.

The lion is found in various parts of India, chiefly the North-west, from Cutch to Hurriana, Gwalior and Saugor, but is now only at all common in Guzrat and Cutch. I have heard of its having been killed south of the Nerbudda many years ago, and I have seen the skins of two that were obtained near Saugor a few years back, near which place, indeed tolerably authentic intelligence was received of their presence in 1856; whilst quite recently two lions were killed most unexpectedly near Gwalior. In former years, lions were much more common in the eastern portion of their present habitat.

Little is recorded of the habits of the lion as found in India. It is said to prey chiefly on bullocks and donkeys, and the fat is highly prized by the natives as a cure for rheumatism. Later and more authentic accounts of the habits of the lion in Africa than those usually found in the older works on natural history, do not quite confirm those accounts of its noble character.

The Puma, *F. concolor*, of South America, the largest of the American feline animals, is sometimes classed with the lions from its uniform coloration, but it wants both the mane and the tail tuft.

2nd. Tigers. Of large size, striped, pupil vertical. Gen. *Tigris*, Gray.

104. Felis tigris.

LINNÆUS.—*Tigris regalis*, GRAY.—BLYTH, Cat. 172, and Synops. 3.—*Bagh*, and *Patayat bágh*, fem. *Bághni*, H.—*Shér* and (female) *Shérni*, in the North of India generally.—*Sela-vagh*, Hindi.—*Go-vagh*, Beng.—*Wuhág*, Mahr.—*Náhar* in Bundelcund and Central India.—*Tút* of the hill people of Bhagulpore.—*Nongya-chor* in Gorukpore.—*Púli*, Tel. and Tam; also, *Pedda púli*, Tel.—*Parain púli*, Mal.—*Húli*, Can.—*Tágh* in Tibet.—*Suhtong*, Lepch.—*Túkh*, Bhot.

THE TIGER.

Descr.—Bright fawn color, more or less tinged with rufous, and with dark stripes.

"The peculiarly striped skin of the tiger," says Blyth, "at once distinguishes it from every other feline animal, and equally so does the intensity of the bright rufous ground hue, so exquisitely set off with white about the head." Again, "unless the lion, no other cat approaches it in the massive proportions of the fore paw, as compared with the hind. Some of both sexes are made more heavily then others, with a greater development of the fold of skin along the belly, which adds to their apparent bulk. The stripes too vary much in different individuals, and occasionally are almost throughout double."

The tiger is found throughout all India, from Cape Comorin to the Himalayas, ascending the hills occasionally to an elevation of 6,000 or 7,000 feet. It is found in all the forests and jungles throughout the peninsula, occasionally visiting the more open and cultivated parts of the country, and harbouring in thickets, long grass, and especially in brushwood on river banks, and on churs covered with tamarisk. In the hot weather, indeed, these are its favorite resorts in many parts of Central India, and from there it sallies forth towards the villages in search of food. In lower Bengal the heavy grass jungles and swamps are his usual lair. Tigers are perhaps more abundant in lower Bengal than in most other parts of the country, and are said to be both larger and more savage than those from other parts of India. Those of Central India, however, are perhaps as large, and quite, if not more ferocious that their Bengal brethern.

The average size of a full grown male tiger is from 9 to 9½ feet in length, but I fancy there is very little doubt that, *occasionally*, tigers are killed 10 feet in length, and perhaps a few inches over that; but the stories of tigers 11 feet and 12 feet in length, so often heard and repeated, certainly require confirmation, and I have not myself seen an authentic account of a tiger that measured more than 10 feet and 2 or 3 inches. Major Sherwill who was for some years in Dinagepore district, told me that the largest he had seen killed was 9 feet 8 inches. The skin is very often measured either when fresh taken from the carcase, or after it has been stretched out to dry; and Mr. W. Elliot records an instance of a lion measured by himself at 9 feet 4 inches. This was noted by one of the party as 11 feet and by another as 12 feet, the first measurement being taken from the skin when taken off; the other from the skin stretched out by pegs for drying.

Mr. Walter Elliot,* has the following remarks on the distribution and habits of this animal in Southern India. "The tiger is common over the whole district, breeding in the forest and mountain tracts, and coming

* Cat. Mammalia, South Mahr. Country.

into the open country when the grain is on the ground. In some places they do much mischief, and have been known to carry off the inhabitants out of the villages whilst sleeping in their verandahs during the night. The female has from two to four young, and does not breed at any particular season. Their chief prey is cattle, but they also catch the wild hog, the sambar, and more rarely the spotted deer. It is naturally a cowardly animal, and always retreats from opposition, until wounded or provoked. Several instances came to notice of its being compelled to relinquish its prey by the cattle in a body driving it off. In one case an official report was made of a herd of buffaloes rushing on a tiger that had seized the herd-boy, and forcing it to drop him. Its retiring from the wild hog has been already adverted to. Though the wild hog often becomes its prey, it sometimes falls a victim to the successful resistance of the wild boar. I once found a full-grown tiger newly killed, evidently by the rip of a boar's tusk; and two similar instances were related to me by a gentleman who had witnessed them—one of a tiger, the other of a panther. It is generally believed a tiger always kills his own food, and will not eat carrion. I met with one instance of a tigress and two full grown cubs devouring a bullock that had died of disease. I saw the carcass in the evening: next day on the report of tigers having been heard in the night, I followed their track, and found she had dragged the dead animal into the centre of a cornfield, and picked the bones quite clean, after which she found a buffalo, killed it, and eat only a small portion of it. Another instance was related in a letter from a celebrated sportsman in Khandeish, who having killed a tigress, on his return to his tents sent a pad elephant to bring it home. The messenger returned, reporting that on his arrival he found her alive. They went out next morning to the spot, and discovered that she had been dragged into a ravine by another tiger and half the carcass devoured. They found him close by, and killed him also. The Bheels in Khandeish say that in the monsoon, when food is scarce, the tiger feeds on frogs, and an instance occurred some years ago in that province of one being killed in a state of extreme emaciation from a porcupine's quill that had passed through his gullet, and prevented his swallowing, and which had probably been planted there in his attempt to make one of these animals his prey. Many superstitious ideas prevail among the natives regarding the tiger. They imagine that an additional lobe is added to his liver every year; that his claws arranged together so as to form a circle, and hung round a child's neck preserves it from the effect of the evil eye; that the whiskers constitute a deadly poison, which for this reason are carefully burnt off the instant the animal is killed. Several of the lower castes eat his flesh."

The late Major Sherwill, of the Revenue Survey, gave me some interesting information on the habits of the tiger, as observed by him in the Dinagepore district—the substance of which is as follows:—

Tigers are very partial to certain localities, and avoid others to all appearance quite as favorable cover. Year after year they will be found in one locality and killed, and never be seen in another close at hand apparently just as suitable. They are very fond of ruins, and may often be seen lying on the top of old walls, temples, &c.; sometimes three or four together. Generally speaking the Bengal tiger is a harmless, timid animal, but when wounded he becomes ferocious and dangerous. He seldom molests man without provocation, and man-eaters are very scarce in Bengal, except in the vicinity of the Sunderbuns. A tigress has from two to four cubs at a time, which remain with her until they are able to kill for themselves. Young tigers are by far the most mischievous, occasionally killing as many as four or five cows at once, whilst an old one seldom kills more than what it requires for its food. An old tiger will kill a cow about once a week, and for this purpose will quit its place of retreat in dense jungle, proceed to the vicinity of a village and kill a bullock or cow. It will remain near the '*kill*' for two or three days, and sometimes longer, gnawing the bones before retreating to deep cover. A tigress deposits her young in good cover. Two taken by Major Sherwill were laid under a thorn bush in dense jungle. Null grass appears to be a favorite place for breeding in. The mother appears much distressed on losing her young, and for three or four nights afterwards remains at the spot roaring all night in a very excited manner.

The few remaining observations must be considered as supplementary to the previous observations of Messrs. Elliot and Sherwill. When once a tiger takes to killing man, it almost always perseveres in its endeavours to procure the same food; and, in general, it has been found that very old tigers, whose teeth are blunted or gone, and the vigour of whose strength is faded, are those that relish human food, finding it a much more easy prey than cattle. In some parts of Central India, however, it appears to be more the rule than the exception; and in the Mundlah district, east from Jubbulpore, in 1856, and previous years, on an average between two and three hundred villagers were killed annually.

So dire was the destruction that Major Erskine, the Commissioner, applied to the Madras Government to furnish an officer for the special work of thinning these cannibals. In the Bustar country, south-east of Nagpore, when I traversed part of that then unexplored district, I found that in several parts the villages were deserted, entirely, as I was informed, from the ravages of tigers, although in some instances, the villages had been surrounded by a high stockade. In the Bengal Sunderbuns too many wood cutters are (or used to be) annually carried off.

Tiger hunting is generally done from elephants in Northern India; and a well trained shikaree elephant will stand the charge of a tiger well, occasionally even rushing to meet it, which is by no means agreeable to the sportsman in the howdah. In Southern India, where there are but few elephants kept, the tiger is often successfully slain on foot; but it is at all times a dangerous sport, and many serious and fatal accidents are well known to have occurred. Occasionally a tiger is shot by night from a platform on a tree, either close to where the tiger has killed, but not eaten all his prey, or, with a fresh bullock picketed near. In the Wynaad one class of Hindoos assemble in large numbers, and forming a large circle, drive the tiger into a net, where it is speared. Various modes of capture are practised all over India, and strychnine has been had resort to occasionally to destroy this animal; but in spite of the numbers killed annually by sportsmen, and by native shikarees for the sake of the Government reward, in many districts its numbers appear to be only slightly diminished.

The native idea about the tiger getting an additional lobe to its liver every year has been fully taken up by English sportsmen, and in the pages of the Bengal Sporting Magazine, &c., the number of lobes in the livers of tigers whose death is there chronicled, are duly recorded. The clavicle lies loosely imbedded among the muscles near the shoulder joint, and is considered of great virtue by natives. The whiskers are, in some parts of Southern India, considered to endow the fortunate possessor with unlimited power over the opposite sex. The claws are mounted in silver and made into bracelets.

The tiger is peculiar to Asia, extending as far west as Georgia, through Persia to Bokhara, and is also found in Amurland, in the Altai region and China; thence extending south through Burmah to the Malayan peninsula, and some of the neighbouring larger islands. It is not found in Ceylon.

Next come the Leopards. Gen. LEOPARDUS, Gray. These are more or less spotted. Of moderate or large size, tail long.

105. Felis pardus.

LINNÆUS.—BLYTH, Cat. 173, Synops. 4.—*F. leopardus*, SCHREBER.—*Leopardus varius*, GRAY.—The Panther and Leopard of the English in India.

THE PARD.

Descr.—Of a rufous-fawn color, more or less deep, with dark spots grouped in rosettes; tail more or less ringed. Varies greatly in size, from six to eight feet, and upwards.

It is still an undecided point among Zoologists, whether there are two distinct species of leopard, or whether they are simply varieties of the same species. Temminck in his monograph of the genus *Felis*, placed them distinct, with the following characters:—*F. leopardus*. The leopard. Tail as long as the body only; fur light-fulvous, the spots moderately distinct from each other, as much as 18 lines in diameter; caudal vertebræ 22. From Asia only. *F. pardus*. The panther. Smaller; tail as long as the head and body; fur deep yellow-fulvous, the spots closely approximate, not more than 14 lines in diameter; caudal vertebræ 28. From both Asia and Africa. Cuvier considered that *F. pardus* was found in Africa and part of Asia; whilst *F. leopardus* was confined to the regions adjacent to the Straits of Sanda: and Sol. Müller, reversing the names, says that *F. pardus* is only found in Sumatra and Java, thus confirming Cuvier's idea of one species being peculiar to these regions. Of late years the two varieties have been classed under one specific name, and Mr. Blyth has joined them in his Catalogue and Synopsis, which arrangement I have also here followed.

The prevalent idea, however, among sportsmen in India, is that there are two distinct races or varieties, and taking Mr. Elliot's remarks as the ground work, I shall briefly notice each.

1st. The larger variety which (with most sportsmen) I shall here call the *Panther*. *F. pardus* apud Hodgson.—*F. leopardus* apud Temminck:—*Leopard* of Sykes.—*Tendwa*, H., throughout India.—*Ténduwá* of Bauris, or cheeta catchers.—*Chita*, and *Chita-bág*; popularly—*Adnára*, Hindi in

Central India.—*Honiga*, Can.—*Asneá*, Mahr. of Ghâts.—*Chinna puli*, Tel. —*Búrkâl* of Gonds.—*Bay-heera* and *Tahir hay* in the Himalayas.—*Sik*, Tibetan.

The color of this large variety is generally pale fulvous-yellow, the belly white; whilst some are deeper and more tawny in hue, and others without any white at all beneath. "As a general rule," says Walter Elliot, "the fur of the *Honiga* is shorter and closer than that of the small variety. The most strongly marked difference of character that I observed was in the skulls. That of the *Honiga* being longer and more pointed, with a ridge running along the occiput, and much developed for the attachment of the muscles of the neck. If this character is universal and permanent, it will afford a good ground of distinction."

Mountaineer, in the Bengal Sporting Review, Vol. VIII., says, "This is a fine and handsome animal. It may be distinguished by its superior size, and the different formation of the head, which is much longer than that of the other;" thus hitting on the same distinctive mark as Mr. Elliot. Horsfield, l. c., says "that this is a taller, larger, slighter animal than the next one, with fewer and more broken spots." Mr. Elliot gives the dimensions as, head and body $4\frac{1}{2}$ to 5 feet; tail $2\frac{3}{4}$ to 3 feet. A fine male, killed near Mhow in 1854, measured 4 feet 9 inches to root of tail, which was 3 feet 2 inches; total 7 feet 11 inches.

My own experience has led me to conclude that this large variety is seldom found in dense forest country, but in more open country, where low hills and deep ravines occur. Mr. Elliot says, "It is found chiefly among the rocky hills to the eastwards. It is a taller, slighter, more active animal, extremely strong and fierce. It is a very formidable assailant, and several instances occurred of as many as four men having been killed by one before it was, put, 'hors de combat.'" Mountaineer says, "It generally keeps aloof from villages, wandering through the forests, and glens of the remoter hills. It preys on all wild animals, wild pigs, monkeys, &c., occasionally seizes on domestic cattle." Baker says, "that in Ceylon (where it is called tiger) he has seen a full grown bull with his neck broken by a leopard who attacked it, and that at Newera ellia they destroy many cattle." Johnson, in his Field Sports of India, gives an account of "a panther or leopard having leapt over a wall 7 feet high, two or three nights in succession, and had killed and carried off a deer each night:" he adds, "I rather think it was a panther, an animal larger than the leopard." I have myself had ponies twice killed close to my own tent, near Mhow, by panthers. Mr. Barnes, of Colgong, informs me that he has known many cases of human beings killed by them in the Bhagulpore district, old women being the chief victims, some of whom were taken out of their huts. Children are not unfrequently carried off in various parts of India. This is the variety usually found in Bengal. It appears to extend through Western Asia as far as the Caucasus, and it is common in the mountainous parts of Afghanistan, but does not accompany the tiger into Northern Asia. In Africa it is often destructive to human life; as also in some parts of the Malayan peninsula.

2nd. The leopard, or smaller variety. *F. leopardus* apud Hodgson.—*F. pardus* apud Temminck.—*F. longicaudata*, Valenciennes.—*Gorbacha*, or *Borbacha*, H., in the Deccan.—*Beebeea-bagh*, Mahr.—*Bibla* of the Bauris.—*Ghur-hay* and *Dheer-hay*, of some of the hill tribes near Simla; but generally called *Lakkar-bagha* throughout the hills, a word in the plains confined to the Hyæna.

W. Elliot says, " The generality of *Kerkals* are dark, whence probably their name, from *kera*, dark; the fur is longer and looser than in the *Honiga*. It is a smaller and stouter animal, and varies much in size, some not being bigger than a large tiger-cat, though the skull proved them to be adult animals. The skull is rounder, and the bony ridge of the *Honiga* wanting. Dimensions from 3 to 3½ feet to root of tail, which is 2½ feet; height 1½ to 2 feet."

Horsfield says, " smaller, stouter, darker, with the spots more crowded." Mountaineer says, " It is smaller, with a round bull-dog head." This is the one most commonly met with, and appears to be the most numerous. It does not confine itself to the forests, but prowls among villages, carrying off sheep, goats, dogs, and sometimes commits great depredations. It is very fearless, frequently seizing a dog in the middle of a village, whilst the inhabitants are still stirring. " Everywhere," says Mr. Blyth, " it is a fearful foe to the canine races, and in general to all the smaller animals—sheep, goats, deer, monkeys, pea-fowl, &c.—and when such animals are penned up and helplessly in its power, it will kill any number of them, seemingly in indulgence of its blood-sucking propensity." Hutton mentions one entering a house and seizing a bull-dog chained to the bed of its master, and I have known it enter tents and carry off dogs in Goomsoor as well as on the Himalayas. At Manantoddy, in the Wynaad, I have known every dog in the station to have been carried off, many in broad daylight. This small variety appear to be most abundant in forest countries, as in Malabar, the Wynaad, Goomsoor, and the more wooded parts of the Himalayas. In winter it is particularly bold, coming on to the roads in some of our hill stations shortly after sunset, and carrying off many dogs. A spiked iron collar is often, however, a sufficient protection, and in the interior of the hills most of the shepherd dogs are thus clad. It always seizes it prey by the back of the neck or the throat, and it is popularly believed in India that it cannot recover from a wound inflicted on it, which would be the case sometimes if it seized a dog from behind. Instances are known of the fine hill dogs killing leopards occasionally in fair fight.

Speaking generally of the pard, without reference to the distinct races, Blyth says, "The pard is a particularly silent creature, very stealthy, and will contrive to dodge and hide itself in places where it would appear impossible that a creature of its size could find concealment." In the Malay Provinces, they are said to attack man not unfrequently, and are said occasionally to climb up to the *machâns** with facility, and carry off people who are watching the grain by night. They are popularly said to be much in the habit of climbing trees, but this habit does not seem to have been much noticed by late observers. The natives assert that they are fearful of water, and will not readily swim, and are therefore rarely found on small islands. Blyth too says that, "it shows great aversion to wetting its feet, and if water be spilt in its cage, will carefully avoid treading on it if possible." Like the tiger, the leopard will, if hungry, eat any dead carcass he can find.

A well marked race is the black leopard, *F. melas*, Peron.—*F. perniger*, Hodgson, Cat Coll. B. M., No. 25. It is of an uniform dull black color, the spots showing in particular lights. Mr. Elliot considered it a variety of the *Honiga* or panther, but it is generally a smaller animal, and is almost always found in forests or forest country, in this more resembling the leopard. It is found sparingly throughout India, from the Himalayas to Malabar and Ceylon, and in Assam, the Malay peninsula, &c.; but I have not seen it recorded from Africa. Mr. Hodgson is inclined to consider it a distinct species.

The name leopard and also panther were originally both given to the Cheeta or hunting leopard, this being the *pard* of the ancients, but they

* Platforms erected on trees.

have been so universally applied to the present species, that it would be vain to attempt to restore these names to their legitimate owner.

106. Felis uncia.

SCHREBER.—BLYTH, Cat. 174, Synops. 5.—HODGSON, J. A. S. XI. 274.—*F. uncioides*, HODGSON.—*F. pardus* apud PALLAS.—*F. irbis*, EHRENBERG.—*Iker*, Tibetan.—*Sáh*, Bhot.—*Páhlé*, Lepch.—*Burrel hay* of the Simla hills.—*Thurwág* in Kunawur.—Snow leopard of sportsmen.

THE OUNCE.

Descr.—Ground color pale yellowish-gray; head, cheeks and back of neck, covered with small irregular dark spots, gradually changing posteriorly on the back and sides into dark rings, running in lines on the back, but irregularly distributed on the shoulders, sides and haunch; from the middle of the back to near the root of the tail on the median line is an irregular dark band, closely bordered on each side by a chain of oblong rings almost confluent; limbs with small dark spots; lower parts pale dingy yellowish-white, with some large dark spots about the middle of the abdomen, the rest unspotted; ears externally black at the base, the tip yellow with a black edge; tail very long, thick and bushy, with incomplete broad bands, or with a double row of large black patches, unspotted below.

Length head and body 4 feet 4 inches; tail 3 feet; height at shoulder barely 2 feet.

The fur throughout is very dense, and it has a well marked though short mane.

The snow leopard, as it is popularly called by sportsmen in the hills, is found throughout the Himalayas at a great elevation, never very much below the snows, at elevations varying with the season, from 9,000 to 18,000 feet. It is said to be more common on the Tibetan side of the Himalayas; and it is found throughout the highland region of chiefly Central Asia, but extending as far west as Smyrna.

The description above was taken from a fine specimen procured in Sikim. It is stated to frequent rocky ground, and to kill the *barrhel*, wild sheep, hence one of its hill names; also *thár*, domestic sheep, goats and dogs; but has never been known to attack man.

107. Felis diardi.

DESMOULINS.—BLYTH, Synopsis 7.—*F. macrocelis*, TEMMINCK—Figd. HORSFIELD, Zool. Res., Java.—*F. nebulosa*, GRIFFITH, ed. Cuvier with figure.—*F. macroceloides*, HODGSON, Cal. J. Nat. Hist., IV. 286.—BLYTH, Cat. 175.—Figd. P. Z. S. 1853, pl. XXXVIII.—*Felis*, n. sp. TICKELL, J. A. S. XII. with figure.—*Tungmar*, Lepch.—*Zik*, Bhot.—*Lamchittia* of the Khas tribe.

THE CLOUDED LEOPARD.

Descr.—Ground color variable, usually pale greenish-brown, or dull clay brown, changing to pale tawny on the lower parts and limbs internally, almost white however in some; in many specimens the fulvous or tawny hue is the prevalent one; a double line of small chain-like stripes from the ears, diverging on the nape to give room to an inner and smaller series; large irregular, clouded spots or patches on the back and sides, edged very dark and crowded together; loins, sides of belly and belly, marked with irregular small patches and spots; some black lines on the cheeks and sides of neck, and a black band across the throat; tail with dark rings, thickly furred, long; limbs bulky, and body heavy and stout; claws very powerful.

Length of one head and body 3½ feet; tail 3 feet; but it grows to a larger size.

This handsome and powerful leopard is found, in our province, only in the south-eastern portion of the Himalayas, usually at a moderate elevation, 5000 to 10,000 feet. It has been found in Nepal? and Sikim, extending through the mountainous regions of Burmah and the Malayan peninsula to Sumatra, Java and Borneo. Hodgson states that it occurs in Tibet, but as it is quite a forest leopard I doubt that, and fancy that his shikarees must have misled him. I obtained the young from the neighbourhood of Darjeeling, and it lived for some time, becoming very tame and playful. It is stated by the Lepchas to be very destructive to sheep, goats, pigs and dogs.

Mr. Blyth notices that some individuals have a cat-gray, and others a fulvous ground hue, and the markings vary to some extent, occasionally even on the two sides of the same animal.

Other Asiatic leopards are *Leopardus japonensis*, Gray; and *Leopardus brachyurus*, Swinhoe; respectively from Japan and Formosa.

Another large leopard is the Jaguar of S. America, *F. onca*, very savage and dangerous, and of which a black variety is by no means rare.

Next come the Cats. Of smaller size, and with shorter tails.

108. Felis viverrina.

BENNETT, P. Z. S. 1833.—BLYTH, Synops. 10.—*F. viverriceps*, HODGSON.—Figd. HARDWICKE, Ill. Ind. Zool. IV. pl. 4.—*F. celidogaster*, TEMMINCK, apud GRAY and BLYTH, Cat. 179.—*F. himalayana*, JARDINE, Nat. Libr. pl. 26.—*F. bengalensis* apud BUCHANAN HAMILTON.—*Machbagrul*, also *Bagh-dasha*, Beng.

THE LARGE TIGER-CAT.

Descr.—Of a mouse gray-color, more or less deep, and sometimes tinged with tawny, with large dark spots more or less numerous, oblong on the back and neck, and in lines, more or less rounded elsewhere, and broken or coalescing; cheeks white; a black face stripe; beneath dull white; chest with five or six dark bands; belly spotted; tail with six or seven dark bands and a black tip; feet unspotted; whiskers either entirely white, or with a white tip.

Length head and body 30 to 34 inches, and sometimes more; tail 10½ to 12½; height about 15 or 16 inches; weight of one 17℔. The ears are rather small and blunt, the pupil circular; the fur coarse and without any gloss; the limbs short and very strong. The nasal bones are somewhat attenuated, causing a narrowness of visage which has suggested the names *viverrina* and *viverriceps*. In old animals the bony orbital rings are complete.

This large tiger-cat is found throughout Bengal up to the foot of the south-eastern Himalayas, extending into Burmah, China, and Malayana. I have not heard of its occurrence in Central India nor in the Carnatic, but is tolerably common in Travancore and Ceylon, extending up the Malabar coast as far as Mangalore. I have had one killed close to my house at Tellicherry. In Bengal it inhabits low watery situations chiefly, and I have often put it up on the edge of swampy thickets in Purneah. It is said to be common in the Terai and marshy region at the foot of the Himalayas, but apparently not extending further west than Nepal. Buchanan Hamilton remarks, "In the neighbourhood of Calcutta it would seem to be common. It frequents reeds near water; and besides fish, preys upon *Ampullariæ*, *Unios*, and various birds. It is a fierce untameable creature, remarkably beautiful, but which has a very disagreeable smell." On this Mr. Blyth observes, "I have not remarked the latter, though I have had several big toms quite tame, and ever found this to be a particularly tameable species. A newly caught male killed a tame young leopardess of mine about double his size." The Rev. Mr. Baker, writing of its habits in Malabar says, "that it often kills pariah dogs; and that he has known instances of slave children (infants) being taken from their huts by this cat; also young calves."

It was considered the same as Temminck's *F. celidogaster* by Gray, in which he was followed by Blyth in his Catalogue; but in his late Synopsis, he states that *celidogaster*, Temminck, is an African species. *F. himalayanus* apud Gray, remarks Mr. Blyth, l. c., is perhaps true *celidogaster*.

109. Felis marmorata.

Martin.—Blyth, Synops. 8.—*F. charltoni*, Gray.—Blyth, Cat. 176.—*F. ogilbii*, Hodgson; probably also *F. duvancelli*, Hodgson, and *Leopardus dosul*, Hodgson, Cat. Hodgson's Coll. B. M., new. ed.—*F. diardi* apud Jardine, Nat. Lib. Felidæ, figd.

The Marbled Tiger-cat.

Descr.—Ground color dingy-fulvous, occasionally yellowish-gray, the body with numerous elongate, wavy, black spots, somewhat clouded or marbled; the head and nape with some narrow blackish lines coalescing into a dorsal interrupted band; the thighs and part of the sides with black round spots; the tail black-spotted, and with the tip black; belly yellowish-white.

Length, 18½ to 23 inches, head and body; tail 14 to 15½; ears, from crown of head, 2.

This prettily marked wild-cat has been found in the Sikim Himalayas, in the hilly regions of Assam, Burmah and Malayana, extending into the islands of Java at all events. It was formerly considered by Mr. Blyth to be the representative of the Malayan *F. marmorata*, but in his Synopsis he his joined it to that species.

In the original edition of Hodgson's British Museum collections, it is not mentioned, and it first occurs in Horsfield's paper on some new contributions by Hodgson, presented in 1853, as *F. charltoni*, with the MSS. name by that gentleman of *F. duvaucelli*. In the recent edition of Hodgson's British Museum Collections, we find No. 26, *Leopardus dosul*. Syn. *F. duvaucelli* and *F. dosul*, Hodgson; but Hodgson himself described it in 1846, in Cal. J. N. H., as *F. ogilbyi*.

I can find nothing recorded of the habits of this cat. Mr. Blyth remarks that it has much the same distribution as *F. diardi*, or not perhaps quite so extensive: and the ground color would similarly appear to become more fulvous with age.

110. Felis bengalensis.

DESMOULINS.—*F. sumatrana* and *F. javanensis*, HORSFIELD, Zool. Res., Java, with figure.—JARDINE, Nat. Libr., pl.—*F. minuta*, TEMMINCK.—*F. undulata*, SCHINZ.—*F. nipalensis* and *pardichrous*, HODGSON.—*F.* ———, ELLIOT, Cat. 29.—*Leopardus chinensis, reevesii, Elliotti*; and *Chaus servalinus*, GRAY.

THE LEOPARD CAT.

Descr.—Ground hue varying from fulvous-gray to bright tawny yellow, occasionally pale yellowish gray or yellowish, rarely greenish-ashy, or brownish-gray; lower parts pure white; four longitudinal spots on the forehead, and in a line with these four lines run from the vertex to the shoulders, the outer one broader, the centre ones narrower, and these two last are continued almost uninterruptedly to the tail; the others pass into larger bold, irregular, unequal, longitudinal spots on the shoulders, back and sides, generally arranged in five or six distinct rows, decreasing and becoming round on the belly; two narrow lines run from the eye along the upper lip to a dark transverse throat band; and two similar transverse bands run across the breast, with a row of spots between; tail spotted above, indistinctly ringed towards the tip; the inside of the arm has two broad bands, and the soles of all the feet are dark-brown. There is generally a small white superciliary line.

Length, head and body, 24 to 26 inches; tail 11 or 12, and more.

From the numerous synonyms it will be seen that this is a variable species, both as to the ground-color of the animal, and the size and boldness of its markings, though all retain much the same pattern as the example here described. Mr. Blyth states that *F. javanensis* differs most from the type, approximating *F. viverrina* in coloring. Those from Southern India appear to have both a richer ground color, and the spots of a bolder pattern than most from the north of India; but I have seen some from the Himalayas very similar. In some the marks have a marbled appearance; in others they appear to be disposed more irregularly and less in rows, and in some the spots are much smaller than in typical specimens.

The original specimen described by Pennant was that of one said to have swam on board ship at the mouth of the Hoogly, and it is said to have coupled with English female cats, and that one of its offspring had as little fear of water as its sire. I cannot help thinking that this must have been a specimen of *F. viverrina* rather than *bengalensis*, especially as Buchanan Hamilton applied the latter name to *viverrina.*

The leopard-cat is found throughout the hilly regions of India, from the Himalayas to the extreme south and Ceylon, and in richly wooded districts, at a low elevation occasionally, or where heavy grass jungle is abundant, mixed with forest and brushwood. In the South of India it is most abundant in Coorg, Wynaad, and the forest tract all along the Western ghâts; but is rare on the east coast and in Central India. It ascends the Himalayas to a considerable elevation, and is said by Hodgson even to occur in Tibet, and is found at the level of the sea in the Bengal Sunderbuns. It extends through Assam, Burmah, the Malayan peninsula, to the islands of Java and Sumatra at all events.

Mr. Elliot says of his *Wagati,** that "it is very fierce, living in trees in the thick forests, and preying on birds and small quadrupeds. A shikaree declared that it drops on larger animals and even on deer, and eats its way into the neck; that the animal in vain endeavours to roll or shake it off, and at last is destroyed." In Coorg, I was informed that it lives in hollow trees, and commits great depredations on the poultry of the villagers. It also destroys hares, mouse deer, &c. Hutton says, "I have a beautiful specimen alive, so savage that I dare not touch her. They breed in May, have only three or four young, in caves or beneath masses of rock." Mr. Blyth says, "I have had many in captivity, none of which ever showed a disposition to become tame and confiding, even though but half grown when they came into my possession, but I never had a small kitten to begin with. It never paces its cage for

* Mr. Elliot did not *name* this cat *F. wagati*, as is generally quoted, even by Blyth, but simply gave it as No. 29, *Felis* ———. *Wagati*, Mahratta of the ghâts.

exercise during the day time at least, but constantly remains crouched in a corner though awake and vigilant." I have seen several caged and now possess one, all of which were quite untameable, and I noticed the same repose during the day that Mr. Blyth observed.

Gray gives *F. wagati* as synonymous with *viverrina*, in which he is quite wrong. *F. nipalensis*, Vigors, sometimes referred to this, is probably a hybrid.

111. Felis Jerdoni.

Blyth, Proc. Zool. Soc. 1863, p. 185; Synopsis, No. 12.

The Lesser Leopard Cat.

Descr.—"Very similar in its markings to the preceding species; but the size of the full grown animal much smaller, that of *F. rubiginosa*; and the ground hue of the upper parts gray, untinged with fulvous.

"Hab. Peninsula of India. I first detected an adult male and a kitten of this species in the Museum at Madras, and find that there is an adult specimen also in the British Museum."

Nothing more is recorded of this cat, which may turn out to be only a small variety of the last, but see further on, page 109.

112. Felis aurata.

Temminck.—*F. moormensis*, Hodgson.—*F. temminckii*, Vigors (young). Horsfield, Cat. 82.—Blyth, Synops. 15.—*F. nigrescens*, Hodgson, Cat. Coll. B. M., new ed., No. 30, black variety.

The Bay Cat.

Descr.—Above deep bay-red; paler beneath and on the sides; a few indistinct dark spots on the sides; throat white; ears internally, and tip of tail black. The lower surface in some is reddish-white, with large and small marroon brown spots; the cheeks are yellowish with two black streaks, and there is a pale black-edged line over the eyes, the whiskers are black with white tips, and the nails are black.

Length, head and body, 31 inches and more; tail 19.

Mr. Blyth has lately determined the identity of Hodgson's "*moormi* cat" with Temminck's *F. aurata*, the origin of which was not known.

Its dimensions are given as, head and body, 3 feet 4 inches; tail 12½; but if Hodgson is right in his measurements, that of the tail must be a mistake. Hodgson does not allude to the spots at all; but Blyth states that a Nepalese specimen in the India Museum is very distinctly and conspicuously spotted. He further writes me that it comes near *diardi* and *marmorata*. There is a very beautiful variety of a saturated brown or black color, of which Mr. Hodgson sent several specimens from Darjeeling to the India House and British Museums. The tip of the tail has a whitish discoloration.

Nothing is known of the habits of this cat, which is stated to inhabit the central region of Nepal and Sikim.

113. Felis rubiginosa.

Is. Geoffroy.—Belanger, Voyage, pl.—*Namali pilli*, Tam.—Blyth, Synops. 13.

The Rusty-spotted Cat.

Descr.—Greenish-gray, with a faint rufous tinge; beneath and inside of limbs white; a white superciliary streak, extending on the side of the nose; two dark face streaks; top of head and nape with four narrow dark brown stripes, becoming interrupted posteriorly, and passing into a series of rusty-colored spots on the back and sides, somewhat longitudinal on the back, but roundish on the sides; tail short, more rufous than the body, and uniform in color, or very indistinctly spotted, the tip not dark; the lower surface, and inside of the limbs with large dark brown spots; feet rufous-gray above, black on the soles; ears small; whiskers long, white; fur short and very soft.

Length 16 to 18 inches, head and body; tail 9½.

This cat varies somewhat, it appears, both in the ground-color of the fur, and the character of the spots. Is. Geoffroy calls the ground-color reddish-gray, and Kelaart describes it as ferruginous grayish-brown. The latter calls the spots on the body dark ferruginous-brown, almost black on the limbs. It appears to be very rare in museums, and I have not had many specimens, but in all, the spots were rusty, and the fur much of the same hue, more or less tinged with rufous.

I have only procured this cat in the Carnatic, in the vicinity of Nellore and Madras. Belanger's specimen was procured in the same district, at

Pondicherry, and I never saw or heard of it in Central India, or on the Malabar coast. It occurs in Ceylon also, but there, according to Kelaart, is found, not in the northern provinces, which resemble the Carnatic, but in the south, and on the hills, even at Newera-ellia. This distribution, and the somewhat different character of the markings, incline me to think that this may be a different species, and I think it possible that it may be *Felis Jerdoni* of Blyth, which that gentleman recently writes me is perhaps the representation of *F. rubiginosa* on the Malabar coast. In the British Museum there is a specimen stated to be from Malacca, but Mr. Blyth is inclined to think that a mistake.

This very pretty little cat frequents grass in the dry beds of tanks, brushwood, and occasionally drains in the open country and near villages, and is said not to be a denizen of the jungles. I had a kitten brought me when very young (in 1846) and it became quite tame, and was the delight and admiration of all who saw it. Its activity was quite marvellous, and it was very playful and elegant in its motions. When it was about eight months old, I introduced it into a room where there was a small fawn of the Gazelle, and the little creature flew at it the moment it saw it, seized it by the nape, and was with difficulty taken off. I lost it shortly after this. It would occasionally find its way to the rafters of bungalows and hunt for squirrels. Mr. W. Elliot notices that he has seen several undoubted hybrids between this and the domestic cat, and I have also observed the same.

Felis planiceps, Vigors, from the Malayan peninsula, is the only other Asiatic cat of this division known at present. There are many from Africa and America, besides the wild cat of Europe, *F. sylvestris*. The North African *F. maniculata* and *F. margarita*, are considered to be two species, from which some of our domestic races may have originated, but several species are known to breed freely with the domestic cat in differents parts of the world.

Other well known species are the Ocelot of South America, the *F. pardalis;* the Serval of Africa, *F. serval*, a very beautiful long limbed cat, allied to the Lynxine group, and there are very many others.

2nd. Lynxine group. Distinguished by a more slender form of skeleton; a somewhat large and pointed ear, which is more or less tufted in general; and a short tail. Mr. Blyth approximates the domestic cats and their affines to this group.

The first is by no means a typical form of Lynx.

114. Felis torquata.

F. Cuvier, fid. Blyth, Synops. 16—*F. ornata*, Gray.—Hardwicke, Ill. Ind. Zool. (bad figure, the color much too pronounced).—Blyth, Cat. 184.—*F. servalina*, Jardine, Nat. Libr. pl.—*F huttoni*, Blyth—*Leopardus inconspicuus*, Gray.

The Spotted Wild Cat.

Descr.—Ground color of the fur cat-gray, more or less fulvescent, or pale grayish-fulvous, with numerous small black roundish spots; on the head, nape and shoulders, the spots are smaller, and tend to form longitudinal lines on the occiput and nape; some distinct cross bands on the limbs, with one or two black streaks within the arm; cheek striped as usual; the breast spotted, but the belly almost free from spots, tail short, with a well defined series of dark rings and a black tip, ears externally dull rufous, with a very small dusky pencil-tuft; cheek stripes as usual; paws blackish underneath.

Length, head and body, about 16 to 18 inches, tail 10 to 11.

The fur is more or less dense, and the markings are much brighter and more distinct in some than in others, but never so much so, that I have seen, as in the figure in Hardwicke's illustrations. Specimens from the Salt range of the Punjab and Hazara, whence sent by Captain Hutton, vary somewhat, and were at one time considered distinct by Blyth. The markings in this variety often form somewhat large transverse ill-defined stripes on the sides and limbs. Length 2 feet; tail 1.

Mr. Blyth first obtained it from the district of Hurriana, near Hansi; and Dr. Scott, who sent the specimens, stated that, "it is very common at Hansi, frequenting open sandy plains, where the field-rat must be its principal food. I hardly ever remember seeing it in what could be called jungle, or even in grass. One of these spotted cats lived long for a time under my hay-stack, and I believe it to have been the produce of a tame cat by a wild one. The wild one I have seen of half a dozen shades of color, and you also frequently see in these cats a tendency to run into stripes, especially on the limbs."

I have procured it at Hissar, where it is common; at Mhow, far from rare; also at Saugor, and near Nagpore, rarely; but it does not appear to extend into the Gangetic valley, and is rare south of the Nerbudda. Those I obtained at Mhow and Saugor were generally killed by my greyhounds in corn and stubble fields, but I have seen it in date groves, though never in jungle. At Hissar it is almost always found among the low sand hills, occasionally in bare fields, usually in the same ground as the desert fox (*Vulpes leucopus*). Here it appears to feed chiefly on the jerboa-rat (*Gerbillus indicus*), so abundant in the sandy tract there.

I have followed Blyth, in his recent Synopsis, in giving this species as the *F. torquata* of F. Cuvier. In his Catalogue, he assigns Colonel Sykes' *F. torquata* also to this species, but in a recent letter to me he writes, that he is inclined to consider Sykes' cat as either a domestic cat run wild, or a hybrid. Colonel Sykes states of his species, that it "frequents the grass roofs of houses, thick hedges, and obscure places in cantonments, shunning the face of man and the light; but it is constantly on the alert at night. It is a pest from the damage it does in poultry yards in the Dekhan." These habits are so perfectly opposed to those of our wild cat, which is constantly abroad all the day in open ground, and whose habitat is so different, that I can only conclude with Blyth, that it is merely a domestic cat run wild, many of which are found in all cantonments. It may indeed be a hybrid between the spotted and the domestic cat. The description by Gray of *F. inconspicuus* differs a good deal, and it is said to have a long tail. The figure in *Jardine's* Naturalist's Library (*F. servalina*), is not a bad representation of the wild cat. Blyth formerly gave Gray's *Chaus servalinus* as a synonym of this cat, but now refers it to *F. bengalensis*.

The next cat is not a typical Lynx, and it has been separated generically as *Chaus*, Gray.

115. Felis chaus.

GULDENSTADT—F. CUVIER, Mamm, 3, pl. 32.—BLYTH, Cat. 186, and Synops. 19.—*F. affinis*, GRAY. HARDWICKE, Ill. Ind. Zool. fig.—*F. kutas*, PEARSON.—*F.* (*lynchus*) *erythrotis*, HODGSON.—*F. Jacquemontii*, IS. GEOFFROY, figd. JACQUEMONT. Voy. pl.—*Chaus lybicus*, GRAY.—*Katás*, Beng. and H.—*Jangli-billi*, H.—*Banberál*, B.—*Birka* of Bhagulpore hill tribes. —*Mant bek*, Can.—*Kada bek* or *Bella bek* of Waddars.—*Mota lahn manjur*, Mahr.—*Bhaoga*, Mahr. of the ghâts.—*Jinka pilli*, Tel.—*Cherru puli*, Mal.

THE COMMON JUNGLE CAT.

Descr.—Yellowish-gray, more or less dark and unspotted, approaching to rufous on the sides of the neck and abdomen, where it unites with the white lower parts; a dark stripe from the eyes to the muzzle; ears slightly tufted, rufous black externally, white internally; limbs with two or three dark stripes internally, occasionally faintly marked externally also; tail short, more or less annulated with black, most conspicuously in the young.

Length, head and body, 26 inches; tail 9 to 10; height at shoulder 14 to 15.

A drawing of this species, in Buchanan Hamilton's collection, has the marks on the limbs very conspicuous externally, and also those on the belly, and the face very rufous; whilst some from Sindh and the Punjab Salt range *(F. jacquemontii)*, have no black markings on the limbs, and there are two or three faint blackish rings at the end of the tail.

This is the common wild cat over all India, from the Himalayas to Cape Comorin, and from the level of the sea to 7,000 or 8,000 feet of elevation. It frequents alike jungles and the open country, and is very partial to long grass and reeds, sugar-cane fields, corn-fields, &c. It does much damage to game of all kinds—hares, partridges, &c.,—and quite recently I shot a peafowl at the edge of a sugar-cane field, when one of these cats sprang out, seized the peafowl, and after a short struggle (for the bird was not dead) carried it off before my astonished eyes, and in spite of my running up, made good his escape with his booty. It must have been stalking these very birds, so immediately did its spring follow my shot. It is occasionally very destructive to poultry.

It is said to breed twice a year, and to have three or four young at a birth. I have very often had the young brought me, but always failed in rearing them, and they always evinced a most savage and untameable disposition. I have seen numbers of cats about villages in various parts of the country, that must have been hybrids between this cat and tame ones; and Mr. Elliot, as quoted by Blyth, says the same.

A melanoid variety is not very rare in some parts. Dr. Scott has procured it both near Hansi and in the neighbourhood of Umballa.

This jungle-cat appears to be found throughout Africa, most abundant perhaps in the north.

The next species is a true Lynx, with the ear pointed and the tuft well developed. The small foremost upper false molar tooth is generally deficient in the adult Lynxes, if not in the young also. Their talons though slender are very sharp. Most have a facial ruff, and pointed tuft and beard, which are both wanting in the Indian species.

116. Felis caracal.

SCHREBER.—BLYTH, Cat. 187; Synopsis 20.—*Caracal melanotis*, GRAY.—WOLF, Zool. Drawings.—*Siagosh*, H., *i. e.*, black-ear.

THE RED LYNX.

Descr.—General color unspotted vinous brown or bright fulvous brown, paler beneath, almost white in many; tail concolorous with the body, tapering, with the tip black; lower parts with some obscure spots, at times distinct, on the belly, flanks and inside of limbs; ears black externally, white within, a long dark ear-tuft; a black spot where the moustaches grow, and another above the eye, also a line down each side of the nose.

Length 26 to 30 inches; tail 9 or 10; ear 3; height 16 to 18 inches.

This handsome animal is found, though rarely, in many parts of India. I have had it from the Northern Circars on the east coast; from the Neermul jungles between Hydrabad and Nagpore; and from the Vindhian range of hills near Mhow. It was sent to Mr. Blyth from Jeypore. It appears to be more abundant perhaps in the west of India, in Kandeish, Gujrat and Cutch; and the Guicowar is said to keep a pack of trained lynxes with which he hunts peafowl, hares, &c. It appears to be quite unknown in the Himalayas and in Bengal, and the countries to the eastward. The Bheels about Mhow assert that it kills many peafowl, hares, &c., in its wild state; and it is occasionally trained to stalk peafowl, hares, kites, crows, cranes, &c., &c. It is found in Persia, Arabia, Tibet, where sometimes trained, and throughout all Africa.

The common lynx of Tibet is *F. isabellina*, Blyth, and there is a small cat-like species in the same country, *F. manul*, Pallas, (*F. nigripectus*, Hodgson). There is also recorded a *F. megalotis*, Temminck, from Timor. Other lynxes are the European red lynx, *F. lynx*, Temminck; the great lynx, *F. cervaria*, L; the pardine lynx, of Spain, *F. pardina*; and the Arctic lynx, *F. borealis*, Temminck; all four found in Europe, and the last in North America also; and the bay lynx, *F. rufa*, peculiar to North America.

The last of the Indian *Felidæ* differs a good deal from the others in having the claws only partially retractile, in being of a much more slender make, and with longer limbs; and it has been separated generally as *Cynailurus*, Wagler.

117. Felis jubata.

SCHREBER.—*F. guttata*, HERMANN.—*F. venatica*, A. SMITH.—*Chita*, H. —*Yuz*, of the trainers.—*Kendua bagh*, Beng.—*Laggar*, in some parts.— *Chita puli*, Tel.—*Chircha* and *Sivungi*, Can.—The *Cheeta*, or Hunting Leopard.

THE HUNTING LEOPARD.

Descr.—Bright rufous fawn with numerous black spots, not in rosettes; a black streak from the corner of each eye down the face; tail with black spots and the tip black; ears short and round; tail long, much compressed towards the end; hair of belly long and shaggy, and with a considerable mane; pupils circular; points of the claws always visible; the figure slender, small in the loins like a greyhound; limbs long.

Length, head and body, about $4\frac{1}{2}$ feet; tail $2\frac{1}{2}$; height $2\frac{1}{2}$ to $2\frac{3}{4}$ feet.

This animal was the original *Panther* and *Leopardus* of the ancients, who considered (with the Arabs of the present day in Northern Africa) that it was a breed between the lion and the pard.

The hunting leopard is found throughout Central and part of Southern India, and in the North-west from Kandeish, through Sindh and Rajpootana to the Punjab.

It is also found in South-western Asia, as far as Syria and Mesopotamia, and throughout Africa. It is stated to exist in Ceylon (fid. Baker ex Blyth), but I doubt extremely its occurring in that island. I have met with it myself in the Deccan, near Jaulna, and near Saugor in Central India, in both cases in tolerably open ground where the common antelope was abundant. In the one instance I turned it out of a small low *bér* bush, along with a jackal that was keeping it company; and near Saugor I saw a pair of them stalking some nil-ghai in mid-day. I had one young one brought to me also at Saugor, only a very few days old. It was clad with long hair of a greenish fawn color without spots, and it was not for several days that I recognised it to be the Cheeta; the cheek stripe was the first mark that appeared. Antelope, gazelle, and nil-ghai are said to be its chief food in the wild state, but it is said occasionally to carry sheep off. Native shikarees assert that it usually has it lair among rocks, and feeds only every third day, sleeping the two others.

I brought up the young one, above alluded to, along with some greyhound pups, and they soon became excellent friends. Even when nearly full grown it would play with the dogs (who did not over relish his bounding at them), and was always sportive and frolicsome. It got much attached to me, at once recognising his name (Billy), and he would follow me on horseback like a dog, every now and then sitting down for a few seconds, and then racing on after me. It was very fond of being noticed, and used to purr just like a cat. It used to climb on any high object, the stump of a tree, a stack of hay, and from this elevated perch watch all round for some moving object. As it grew up, it took first to attacking some sheep which I had in the compound, but I cured it of this by a few sound horsewhippings; then it would attack donkeys, and get well kicked by them; and when not half-grown it flew one day at a full grown tame nil-ghai, and mauled its legs very severely before it could be called off. I had some chikaras (*Gazella bennettii*) caught, and let loose before it to train it. The young cheeta almost always caught them easily, but it wanted address to pull them down, and did not hold them. Occasionally if the antelope got too far away it would give up the chase, but if I then slipped a greyhound, it would at once follow the dog and join the chase. It was gradually getting to understand its work better, and had pulled down a well grown antelope fawn when I parted with it, as I was going on field service.

Its mode of hunting the antelope has often been described; and I transfer an account of it from the pages of the Indian Sporting Review.

"On a hunting party," says Buchanan Hamilton, "the cheeta is carried on a cart, hooded, and when the game is raised the hood is taken off. The cheeta then leaps down, sometimes on the opposite side to its prey, and pursues the antelope. If the latter are near the cart, the cheeta springs forward with a surpassing velocity, perhaps exceeding that which any other quadruped possesses. This great velocity is not unlike the sudden spring by which the tiger seizes its prey, but it is often continued for three or four hundreds yards. If within this distance, the cheeta does not seize its prey he stops, but apparently more from anger or disappointment than from fatigue, for his attitude is fierce, and he has been known immediately afterwards to pursue with equal rapidity another antelope that happened to be passing. If the game is at too great a distance when the cheeta's eyes are uncovered, he in general gallops after it until it approaches so near that he can seize it by a rapid spring. This gallop is as quick as the course of well-mounted horsemen. Sometimes, but rarely, the cheeta endeavours to approach the game by stealth, and goes round a hill or rock until he can come upon it by surprise. This account of the manner of hunting I collected from the conversation of Sir Arthur Wellesley, who, while Commanding Officer at Seringapatam, kept five cheetas that formerly belonged to Tippoo Sultan." Mr. Vigne writes thus: "The hunting with cheetas has often been described, but it requires strong epithets to give an idea of the creature's speed. When slipped from the cart, he first walks towards the antelope with his tail straightened, and slightly raised, the hackle on his shoulder erect, his head depressed, and his eyes intently fixed upon the poor animal who does yet perceive him. As the antelope moves he does the same, first trotting, then cantering after him, and when the prey starts off, the cheeta makes a rush, to which (at least I thought so) the speed of a race-horse was for the moment much inferior. The cheetas that bound or spring upon their prey are not much esteemed, as they are too cunning, the good ones fairly run it down. When we consider that no English greyhound ever yet I believe fairly run into a doe antelope, which is faster than the buck, some idea may be formed of the strides and velocity of an animal, who usually closes with her immediately, but fortunately cannot draw a second breath, and consequently unless he strike the antelope down at once is obliged instantly to stop and give up the chase. He then walks about for three or four minutes in a towering passion, after which he again submits to be helped on the cart. He always singles out the biggest buck from the herd, and holds him by the throat until he is disabled, keeping one paw over the horns to prevent injury to himself. The doe he seizes in the same manner, but is careless of the position in which he may hold her." The natives assert that (in the wild state) if the ground is not very favorable for his approaching them without being seen, he makes a circuit to the place where he thinks they will pass over, and if there is not grass enough to cover him, he scrapes up the earth all round, and lies flat until they approach so near that by a few bounds he can seize on his prey. Mr. W. Elliot says, "they are taught always to single out the buck, which is generally the last in the herd; the meer-shikars are unwilling to slip till they get the herd to run across them, when they drive on the cart, and unhood the cheeta."

I have only to add to this on my own testimony, that I have often seen it, when unhooded at some distance from the antelope, crouch along the ground, and choose any inequality of surface to enable it to get within proper distance of the antelope. As to Vigne's idea of its rush being made during one breath, I consider it a native one and unfounded; and I may say the same of its holding one paw over the horns of the buck. The cheeta after felling the antelope, seizes it by the throat, and when the keeper comes up, he cuts its throat and collects some of the blood in the wooden ladle from which it is always fed: this is offered to the cheeta, who drops his hold, and laps it up eagerly, during which the hood is cleverly slipped on again. My tame cheeta when hungry or left alone (for it appeared unhappy when away from the dogs and with no one near it) had a plaintive cry, which Blyth appropriately calls a "bleat-like mew." Shikarees always assert that if taken as cubs they are useless for training, till they have been taught by their parents how to pull down their prey. This opinion is corroborated, in part at least, by my experiences with the tame one mentioned above.

Out of the fifteen species of *Felinæ* included here, five are common to India and Africa, viz., the Lion, the Pard, the Cheeta, the Chaus, Wild Cat, and the Caracal or Lynx. Seven are common to India and Malayana, including Burmah, Assam, &c., viz., the Tiger, the Pard, the Clouded Leopard, the Marbled Tiger-cat, the Large Tiger-cat, the Leopard Cat, and the Bay Cat, of which three only occur (in our province) in the south-east Himalayas, viz., the Clouded, the Marbled Cat, and the Bay Cat; one, the Ounce, is an outlier of Central Asia; and only three appear peculiar to the peninsula of India, viz., the small Tiger Cat (*Jerdoni*), the Rusty-Spotted Cat and the Spotted wild cat.

Fam. VIVERRIDÆ.

Molars vary in number from $\frac{5-5}{4-4}$ to $\frac{6-6}{6-6}$; feet tetradactylous or pentadactylous.

The civets, as usually recognised, comprise a varied assemblage of animals exclusively confined to the eastern continent, and chiefly to the warmer regions thereof. They most of them possess a pouch under the anus. They are divided into the hyænas and the true civets.

Sub. fam. HYÆNINÆ.

Molar teeth $\frac{5-5}{4-4}$ or $\frac{5-5}{5-5}$; feet tetradactylous; trunk declining backwards from the shoulders; tail short.

In general form hyænas resemble dogs more than cats, and Linnæus classed them with the former, to which they appear united by the *Lycaon pictus* of South Africa. In their dentition they more resemble *Felidæ*. They have three false molars above and four below, all conical, blunt and very large, their upper flesh tooth has a small tubercle within and in front; but the lower one has none, presenting two stout cutting points; behind it is one tubercular molar in the upper jaw, none in the lower jaw. The hind legs are much bent, so that the hind quarters are always lower than the shoulders. The feet have usually four strong claws, which are not retractile. The tongue is rough with recurved spines. They mostly occur in Africa, one only extending to Asia. Blyth considers that they are physiologically most nearly related to the civets, as shown by their rough tongue, the form of their cœcum, the structure of their reproductive organs, their anal pouch and style of coloring.

Gen. Hyæna.

Char.—Incisors $\frac{6-6}{6-6}$; canines $\frac{1-1}{1-1}$; præmolars $\frac{4-4}{3-3}$; molars $\frac{1-1}{1-1}$; feet all with four toes. Other characters those of the sub-family.

Hyænas have a short solid skull, short muzzle, the cervical vertebræ often anchylosed; 15 to 16 pairs of ribs, tibia and fibula very short; claws stout and blunt. Beneath the tail is a deep pouch analogous to that in the civets, but not secreting an odorous substance. Their temporal muscles are very large and powerful, as are those of the neck, and their jaws and teeth are strong enough to enable them to crush large bones. They are quite nocturnal in their habits, living in holes and caverns, and feeding chiefly on the remains of carcases, but they not unfrequently carry off dogs. They are easily tamed, are even susceptible of attachment; and it is stated that tame individuals are occasionally used as watch-dogs.

There is only one species in India which is spread over great part of Asia and Africa.

118. Hyæna striata.

Zimmerman.—*H. vulgaris*, Desmarest.—Elliot, Cat. 24.—Blyth, Cat. 138.—*Taras*, H. (in the South) and Mahr.—*Hundar*, in some parts.—*Jhirak* H., in Hurriana.—*Lakkar-baghar*, H., in the North of India; also *Lokra bág*, or *Lakar bágh;* also *Lakra bágh.*—*Naukra bágh*, Ben.—*Harvágh*, in some parts.—*Rérá* in Central India.—*Kirba* and *Katkirba*, Can.—*Korna gandu*, Tel.

The Striped Hyæna.

Descr.—Of a pale yellowish gray color, with transverse tawny stripes; neck and back maned.

Length of one 8 feet 6 inches to root of tail; tail 17 inches.

The hyæna is common over the greater part of India, most rare in the forest districts, and abundant in open country, especially where low hills and ravines offer convenient spots for the holes and caverns it frequents. It is not enumerated by Kelaart from Ceylon. It is quite nocturnal, sallying forth after dark and hunting for carcases, the bones of which it gnaws, occasionally catching some prowling dog, or stray sheep as a "bonne bouche." Adams says that it is "very destructive to poultry." This I have not heard noticed elsewhere. Now and then one will be found in the early morning making its way back to its den, but in general it is safe in its lair long before sunrise. I have more than once turned one out of a sugar-cane field when looking for jackals, and it very commonly lurks among ruins; but in general its den is in a hole dug by itself on the side of a hill or ravine, or a cave in a rock. The call of the hyæna is a very disagreeable unearthly cry, and dogs are often tempted out by it when near, and fall a victim to the stealthy marauder. On one occasion a small dog belonging to an officer of the Madras 33rd N. I., was taken off by a hyæna very early in the morning. The den of this beast was known to be not far off in some sandstone cliffs (at Dumoh near Saugor), and some sepoys of the detachment went after it, entered the cave, killed the hyæna, and recovered the dog alive, and with but little damage done to it!

A hyæna, though it does not appear to move very fast, gets over rough ground in a wonderful manner, and it takes a good long run to overtake it on horseback unless in most favorable ground. A stray hyæna is now and then met with by a party of sportsmen, followed and speared; but sometimes not till after a run of three or four miles if the ground is broken by ravines. It is a cowardly animal, and shows but little fight when brought to bay. The young are very tameable, and show great signs of attachment to their owner, in spite of all that has been written about the untameable ferocity of the hyæna.

Other species of hyæna are *H. crocuta*, the spotted hyæna, and *H. brunnea*, the woolly hyæna, both from Southern Africa. The *Proteles lalandii*, Is. Geoffroy, also an African animal, most resembles a hyæna in outward appearance, but has an anomalous form of dentition. The canines are moderately large, there are three false molars, and one small tuberculous back molar; and all are small and separated by intervals. It has five toes before and four behind.

Sub.-fam. Viverrinæ, Civets.

Molar teeth mostly $\frac{6-6}{6-6}$, viz., three false molars above, and four below the anterior of which sometimes fall out; two tolerably large tuberculous teeth above, only one below; the lower flesh-tooth with two tubercles on its inner side. Dental formula, incisors $\frac{3-3}{3-3}$; canines $\frac{1-1}{1-1}$; præmolars $\frac{3-3}{4-4}$; molars $\frac{3-3}{2-2}$. The canines are moderately large and sharp, the false molars conical and pointed. Feet mostly digitigrade, the posterior in some, partially plantigrade, with four or five toes, the claws in a few semi-retractile.

The civets are animals of more or less elongated form, with the muzzle produced, and a long and generally tapering tail. The tongue is rough from rigid papillæ directed backwards; and most of them have a large glandular pouch between the anus and the genital organs, secreting an odorous substance. The pupils contract circularly. They are nocturnal in their habits; and, according to their genus, are more or less carnivorous in their habits. Their hair is usually coarse and harsh.

Gen. Viverra, Linn.

Teeth as in the sub-family; feet pentadactylous, the claws small, incurved, blunt, partially retractile; the pollex small and raised. Fur usually spotted.

The anal pouch is large, and divided into two sacs. It secretes a strongly odorous sebaceous substance called *civet*. The pupil is vertical and oblong. They have a more or less erectile mane along the back, and are moderate sized animals, most of them larger than a cat. The female has six teats. Their diet is partly carnivorous, but they will also feed on vegetable substances. There are three species in our province. They are divisible into two sections, which have been made the types of genera.

1st. Size large, does not climb, thumb not remote, s. g. *Viverra*.

119. Viverra zibetha.

Linnæus.—Blyth, Cat. 141.—*V. bengalensis*, Gray.—Hardwicke, Ill. Ind. Zool. 2, pl. 5.—*V. undulata*, Gray.—*V. melanurus* and *V. orientalis*, Hodgson; also *V. civettoides*, ejusdem.—Horsfield, Cat. 87.—*Katás*, H. (used for several other animals as well).—*Mach-bhondar*, Bengal; also

Bágdos and *Pudo-gaula*, in some parts.—*Bhrán* in the Nepal Terai, and *Nit biralu* in Nepal.—*Kúng*, Bhot.—*Saphiong*, Lepch. The Zibet of Shaw.

THE LARGE CIVET-CAT.

Descr.—More or less yellow-gray, or hoary gray, with black spots and stripes; throat white, with a broad transverse band; another on the side of the neck on each side, showing four alternating black and white bands; beneath hoary white; tail with six black rings; limbs nearly black or sooty brown. In some the body is nearly immaculate; in others, marked with numerous dark wavy bands; mane distinct.

Length, head and body, 33 to 36 inches; tail 13 to 20 (with the hair).

This large civet-cat inhabits Bengal, extending northwards into Nepal and Sikim, and into Cuttack, Orissa, and Central India on the south; but replaced on the Malabar coast by the next species. It also extends into Assam, Burmah, Southern China, and parts of Malayana. It is perhaps the large variety of *V. rasse*, indicated by Sykes as found in the country east of the Ghâts; 28 inches long, with more ferruginous in its tint, and the black lines on the neck more marked. It is said to frequent brushwood and grass; also the dense thorny scrub that usually covers the bunds of tanks. It is very carnivorous, and destructive to poultry, game, &c., but will also, it is said, eat fish, crabs and insects. It breeds in May and June, and has usually four or five young. Hounds, and indeed all dogs, are greatly excited by the scent of this civet, and will leave any other scent for it. It will take readily to water if hard pressed.

The drug called civet is produced from the subcaudal gland of this animal, which is $2\frac{1}{2}$ inches in diameter. In some parts the drug is collected periodically from animals kept for this purpose.

120. Viverra civettina.

BLYTH, Cat. 140.—*V. zibetha*, apud WATERHOUSE, Cat. Mus. Zool. Soc.

THE MALABAR CIVET-CAT.

Descr.—"Like the African *V. civetta*, but the mane commences between the shoulders instead of from between the ears." Dusky gray with large transverse dark marks on back and sides; two obliquely transverse dark lines on the neck, which, with the throat, is white; a dark mark on the cheek; tail ringed with dark bands; feet dark. Size of the last, or nearly so.

This species differs chiefly from *V. zibetha* in the more pronounced character of the dark marks, and in the purer gray of the ground color; and it would perhaps be considered by some as a climatal variety; indeed, Mr. Blyth himself, in a note to this species (Cat. p. 44), says "the difference however is scarcely greater from *V. zibetha* than in the most dissimilar examples of *Felis bengalensis.*" All that I have seen, however, were quite true to the particular type of marking, and in no case showed any tendency to the uniformity of coloration sometimes met with in *zibetha.*

The Malabar civet-cat is found throughout the Malabar coast, from the latitude of Honore at all events to Cape Comorin, and very possibly it extends further north. It inhabits the forests and the richly wooded low land chiefly, but is occasionally found on the elevated forest tracts of Wynaad, Coorg, &c. It is very abundant in Travancore, whence I have had many specimens. It is not recorded from Ceylon, but most probably will be found there. I have procured it close to my own house at Tellicherry, and seen specimens from the vicinity of Honore. I never obtained it from the Eastern Ghâts nor in Central India. It is stated by the natives to be very destructive to poultry.

Viverra tangalunga, Gray, is very closely allied to *V. zibetha.* It inhabits the Malayan peninsula and islands as far as the Philippines. *V. civetta*, vera, is from Africa.

2nd group. Size small, vermiform; nails more raptorial; thumb remote; of scansorial habits.

s. g. *Viverricula*, Hodgson.

121. Viverra malaccensis.

Gmelin.—Blyth, Cat. 143.—*V. indica*, Geoffroy.—Elliot, Cat. 20—*V. rasse*, Horsfield, apud Sykes, Cat.—*V. pallida*, Gray (variety), figd. Hardwicke, Ill. Ind. Zool. 2, pl. 6—*Mushak billi*, H.—*Kasturi*, Mahr.; also *Jowádi manjur*—*Gando gaula* or *Gandha gokul*, Beng.—*Púnagin bek*, Can.—*Púnagú pilli*, Tel., these names all signifying musk-cat; popularly *Katás*, Beng.—*Sayer* and *Bug-nyúl*, in the Nepal Terai.

The Lesser Civet-Cat.

Descr.—Tawny gray or grayish-brown, with several longitudinal lines or streaks on the back and croup; the side spotted more or less in rows; some transverse bands on the sides of the neck, and also a few indistinct lines; abdomen without spots; head darker, with a black stripe from the ear to the shoulder; tail long, with eight or nine complete dark rings.

Length, head and body, 22 or 23 inches; tail 16 or 17.

This civet-cat is found over the whole continent of India, from the foot of the Himalayas to Cape Comorin and Ceylon, and extends through Assam and Burmah to the Malayan peninsula and islands. It lives in holes in the ground or in banks, occasionally under rocks, or in dense thickets, now and then taking shelter in drains and out-houses.

Mr. Hodgson says, "these animals dwell in forests or detached woods and copses, whence they wander freely into the open country by day (occasionally at least) as well as by night. They are solitary and single wanderers, even the pair being seldom seen together, and they feed promiscuously upon small animals, birds' eggs, snakes, frogs, insects; besides some fruits or roots. In the Terai a low caste of woodmen, called Musahirs, eat the flesh." The female has six ventral teats, and has usually four or five young at a birth. It is frequently kept in confinement in India, and becomes quite tame, contrary to what Horsfield says of it in Java. I have had several myself perfectly tame, that caught rats and squirrels at times, as also sparrows and other birds. The civet is extracted by the natives from these kept in confinement.

The Genets, *Genetta*, Cuvier, have the pouch very small, and the secretion scarcely discernible, the claws quite retractile, and the pupil vertical. They are smaller and more slender animals than the Civets, with the markings generally more pronounced. There are several species all African, and one extending to the South of Europe.

Near the Genets should be placed the next animal, which at one time was classed along with the *Felinæ*.

Gen. PRIONODON, Horsfield.

Syn. *Linsang*, Müller.

Char.—Molars $\frac{5-5}{6-6}$; false molars three-lobed or serrated; body slender; limbs short; tail very long, cylindrical; feet with the claws quite retractile; a fifth toe on the hind feet; thumbs of both feet approximate to the other digits; soles all well furred.

No anal pouch is present, and the tongue is rough with retroverted prickles. The female has four teats, two pectoral, and two inguinal. This genus was founded by Horsfield on a Malayan animal from Java. It forms quite a link between the cats and civets. The fur is short and close, resembling that of the cats.

122. Prionodon pardicolor.

HODGSON.—Calc. J. N. A. 2, 57, with figure.*—*Zik-chúm*, Bhot.—*Súliyú*, Lepch.

THE TIGER-CIVET.

Descr.—Rich orange buff or fulvous, spotted with black; the neck above with four irregular lines; the body above and on the sides with large entire elliptic or squarish marks, eight in transverse, and seven in longitudinal series, diminishing in size from the dorsal ridge, which has an interrupted dark line, and extending outside the limbs to the digits; below entirely unspotted; tail with eight or nine nearly perfect and equal rings.

Length, head and body, about 16 inches; tail 14; height 6 or so.

This very beautiful animal is said to have the manners of the cats, to spring and climb with great power, to prey on small mammals and birds, and to frequent trees much in search of the former, as well as for shelter. Hodgson says, "equally at home on trees or on the ground, it dwells and breeds in the hollows of decayed trees." It has only been obtained in the south-east Himalayas, in Nepal and Sikim, and does not appear to be at all common, though Hodgson asserts it to be so. I only procured one specimen whilst at Darjeeling. Cantor thus refers to an individual of the Malayan species, to which ours is very closely allied, kept in captivity for some time. "At first the animal was fierce and impatient of confinement, but by degrees it became very gentle and playful, and when subsequently suffered to leave the cage, it went in search of sparrows and other small birds, displaying great dexterity and unerring aim in stealthily leaping upon them."

Hodgson had our species in confinement, and states that it was very gentle and fond of being petted. It was fed with raw meat. It never

* By an oversight in the recent edition of Hodgson's British Museum Collections, this is twice enumerated as 38, *Linsang pardicolor*, and 39, *Prionodon pardochrous*.

uttered any sort of sound. He further states that, "the sharpness of the coronal process of the molar teeth seems to indicate that the animal is somewhat insectivorous, which I hear is actually the fact."

Gen. PARADOXURUS, F. Cuvier.

Char.—Molar teeth $\frac{6-6}{6-6}$ as in *Viverra*; flesh-tooth, especially the lower one, thick, with conical tubercles; all feet with five toes connected by a web, the thumb not raised; sole of the feet bald, tuberculous; claws semi-retractile; tail very long, cylindrical.

The tree-cats are stouter in form than the Genets, with which they have been confounded, and more uniform in their coloration; their gait is plantigrade. Their pupil is elliptic, and they are quite nocturnal in their habits. Their dentition is very similar to that of dogs, but the cerebral cavity is proportionally smaller. The bony orbit is not closed. There is a glandular fold in some between the anus and genitals, secreting a peculiar matter, without the odour of civet or musk;* but not a distinct pouch. They are chiefly inhabitants of the Indian region, and a considerable number of species have been lately made known. They climb trees remarkably well, and roost during the day either on trees or on the roofs of houses, among the rafters. There diet is of a mixed character.

The character of the tail from which the generic name was derived is shown by Blyth to have been the result of some deformity, and not to be a normal state. It can be rolled up, but is not prehensile.

This genus is linked to *Prionodon* by a Malayan species, *P ? derbyanus*, Gray, of which Cantor remarks, "the serrated false molars, the soles hairy under the toes, the somewhat remote thumb, are characters by which this animal differs from *Paradoxurus*, and forms a link between that genus and *Prionodon*." It has indeed been made the type of a distinct genus, *Hemigalea*, by Jourdain.

123. Paradoxurus musanga.

Viverra apud MARSDEN.—BLYTH, Cat. 148.—Figd. F. CUVIER, Mamm. 2, pl. 55.—*P. typus*, F. CUVIER.—ELLIOT, Cat. 23.—*P. Pallasii*, *P. musangoides*, *P. crossii*, and *P. dubius*, GRAY.—*P. prehensilis*, and *Viverra*

* Cantor. Cat. Mamm., Malay.

hermaphrodita, PALLAS.—*Ménúri*, H., in the south.—*Lakáti*, H., in some parts; occasionally *Khatás*.—Vulgo, in Southern India, *Jhár ka kátá*, or tree-dog.—*Ud*, Mahr.—*Bhondar*, Bengal.—*Kéra bék*, Can.—*Mánú-pilli*, Tel.; and *Marra-pilli*, Malyal., both signifying tree-cat.—Toddy cat of Europeans in Madras.

THE COMMON TREE-CAT.

Descr.—General color brownish-black, with some dingy yellowish stripes on each side, more or less distinct, and sometimes not noticeable; a white spot above and below each eye, and the forehead with a whitish band in some; a black line from the top of the head down the centre of the nose is generally observable. In many individuals the ground color appears to be fulvous with black pencilling, or mixed fulvous and black; the longitudinal stripes then show dark; limbs always dark-brown. Some appear almost black throughout, and the young are said to be nearly all black. Some appear fulvous-gray washed with black, the face black, and the tail very dark; and others appear to have the sides spotted. Many of these variations are owing to the state of abrasion of the fur, which is yellowish at the base and blackish at the tip. One is described as "pale grayish-brown with longer black hairs intermixed, and most prevalent on the back of head, neck, and along the back; three black bands on the loins; head brownish with a gray mark above and below the eyes; tail with the terminal fifth yellowish white." I have had several skins with the terminal portion of the tail yellowish white, and one or two with the whole posterior parts of the same hue. Some have the abdomen marked with elongated white spots, and individuals occur with the tail spirally twisted, so that the extremity has the lower surface uppermost; and, according to Blyth, it was an individual similar to this on which the genus was founded, and the name *Paradoxurus* bestowed, which has been translated into *Screw-tail*.

Length, head and body, 22 to 25 inches; tail $19\frac{1}{2}$ to 21; hind foot $3\frac{1}{10}$; weight $8\frac{1}{2}$ lbs.

This tree-cat is a common and abundant animal throughout the greater part of India and Ceylon, extending through Burmah and the Malayan peninsula to the islands. It is most abundant in the better wooded regions, and is rarely met with in the bare portions of the Deccan, Central India, and the North-west Provinces. It is very abundant in the Carnatic, and Malabar coast, where it is popularly called the *Toddy-cat*, in consequence of its supposed fondness for the juice of the palm (*Tari*, H., *toddy*, anglice), a fact which appears of general acceptation both in India and and Ceylon (where it is called the palm cat), and which appears to have some foundation. Kelaart says it, "is a well established fact that it is a consumer of palm-toddy." It lives much on trees, especially on the Palmyra and cocoa-nut palms, and is often found to have taken up its residence in the thick thatched roofs of native houses. I found a large colony of them established among the rafters of my own house at Tellicherry. It also occasionally is found in dry drains, outhouses, and other places of shelter. It is quite nocturnal, issuing forth at dark, and living by preference on animal food, rats, lizards, small birds, poultry and eggs; but it also freely partakes of vegetable food, fruit and insects. In confinement it will eat plantains, boiled rice, bread and milk, ghee, &c. Colonel Sykes mentions that it is very fond of cockroaches. Now and then it will commit depredations in some poultry yard, and I have often known them taken in traps baited with a pigeon or a chicken. In the South of India it is very often tamed, and becomes quite domestic, and even affectionate in its manners. One I saw, many years ago, at Trichinopoly went about quite at large, and late every night used to work itself under the pillow of its owner, roll itself up into a ball, with its tail coiled round its body, and sleep till a late hour of the day. It hunted for rats, shrews, and house lizards. Their activity in climbing is very great, and they used to ascend and descend my house at one of the corners of the building in a most surprising manner.

One, 20 inches long, examined by Kelaart, had the small intestines 5 feet 4 inches long, the large do., 9 inches; cœcum $\frac{3}{4}$ths; liver with seven lobes, &c., &c.

Hodgson has described several new species lately, of which *P. strictus* and *P. quadriscriptus* appear to be merely varieties of color of *P. musanga*. They are figured at plates 47 and 48, of the Proc. Zool. Soc. for 1856. Blyth described the skull of one from the Andaman islands, which had peculiarly large canines. It may possibly be the species lately described by Colonel Tytler, Journ. As. Soc. for 1865, and named after himself, *Paradoxurus Tytleri*. From the description, it is evidently nearly related to *P. musanga*.

The next species were formerly classed under the genus *Paguma*, Gray, differing somewhat from *Paradoxurus* in the form of some of the teeth, in the more attenuated tail; in the fur being dense and woolly, with the coloration more uniform and less variegated.

124. Paradoxurus grayi.

Bennett, P. Z. S. 1835—Blyth, Cat. 154—*P. nipalensis*, Hodgson, Asiatic Trans. Vol. XIX.—*P. bondar* apud Temminck, Mon. t. 65, f. 4-6, skull.

The Hill Tree-Cat.

Descr.—Color above light unspotted fulvous-brown, showing in certain lights a strong cinereous tinge, owing to the black tips of many of the hairs; beneath lighter and more cinereous; limbs ash-colored, deeper in intensity towards the feet which are black; tail of the same color as the body, the end dark, white tipped; ears rounded, hairy, black; face black, except the forehead, a longitudinal streak down the middle of the nose, and a short oblique band under each eye, gray or whitish.

Length, head and body, 30 inches; tail 20.

This animal inhabits the South-east Himalayas only, extending into Assam and Northern Burmah. It has been sent from Nepal, Darjeeling, and the Arrakan hills. Hodgson states that "it is common in the central region of Nepal, keeping to the forests and mountains. It feeds both on small animals and birds, and vegetable food. One shot had only seeds, leaves, and unhusked rice in its stomach. A caged animal was fed on boiled rice and fruits, which it preferred to animal food. When set at liberty it would lie waiting in the grass for mynas and sparrows, springing upon them from the cover like a cat, and when sparrows, as frequently happened, ventured into its cage to steal the boiled rice, it would feign sleep, retire into a corner, and dart on them with unerring aim. Birds thus taken by itself it preferred to all other food. The animal was very cleanly, nor did its body usually emit any unpleasant odour, though when it was irritated, it exhaled a most fetid stench, caused by the discharge of a thin yellow fluid from four pores, two of which are placed on each side of the intestinal aperture."

125. Paradoxurus bondar.

Gray ex Buchanan Hamilton.—*P. hirsutus*, Hodgson, As. Res. XIX. 72.—*P. Pennantii*, Gray.—Hardwicke, Ill. Ind. Zool. 2, pl. 13.—*Ching-*

hár, H.—*Bondar* and *Baum*, Beng.—*Machabba* and *Malwa*, in the Nepal Terai, and neighbouring districts.

THE TERAI TREE-CAT.

Descr.—Color a clear yellow, largely tipped with black, and entirely devoid of marks or lines upon the body; the bridge of the nose, the upper lip, whiskers, broad cheek-band, ears, chin, lower jaw, forelegs and hind feet, and terminal third of the tail, black or blackish-brown; region of the genitals and a zone encircling the eyes, pure pale-yellow; snout and soles of feet brownish fleshy-gray; nude parts of lips, palate and tongue, pure fleshy white. The hair is straight, long, erect, yellow at the base, black tipped; the under wool soft, curly, yellow. Its nails are very sharp and curved, sheathed and mobile. Total length 45 inches of which the tail is about half; weight 6 ℔. The female is somewhat smaller and paler, and has four ventral teats.

This tree-cat is said to be found throughout the Terai of the hills, extending into the neighbouring districts of Bengal and Behar, but of its distribution elsewhere I can find no record. In its habits it is said to be found in inhabited and cultivated tracts, its favorite resort being old abandoned mango-groves, seeking refuge in holes of decayed trees, where it also breeds. It seeks its food as well among the branches of trees as on the ground, and is highly carnivorous, living upon birds, small mammals, mice, rats, and even young hares; also on snakes, but it will not touch frogs or cockroaches. Occasionally it is very destructive to poultry. It will eat ripe mangoes and other fruit. It sleeps rolled up like a ball, and when angered spits like a cat. It is naturally very ferocious and unruly, but capable of domestication if taken young. It has a keen sense of smell, but less acute hearing and vision by day than the mungooses.

Another species allied to these two last, is *Paguma laniger*, Gray, *Martes laniger*, Hodgson, from Tibet, and adjoining snowy Himalayas. *Paradoxurus quinque-lineatus*, Gray, appears to be described from the same specimens as *P. strictus* formerly alluded to; and there are other species described, some of which also appear to be varieties of *P. musanga*.

Ceylon possesses a peculiar species, *P. zeylanicus*, Pallas; and *P. trivirgatus*, Temminck, and *P. leucomystax*, Gray, are found in the Malayan peninsula and islands, in addition to *P. musanga*, and *P. derbyanus*, already alluded to.

The next animal has only a doubtful claim to a place here.

Gen. ARCTICTIS, Temminck.

Syn. *Ictides*, Valenc.

Char.—Molars $\frac{6-6}{5-5}$; canines stout, those in the upper jaw very long, compressed at the base, with a longitudinal groove exteriorly; muzzle short, attenuated; ears short, rounded; body long; legs short; tail nearly as long as the body, partially prehensile; hair long, rough, copious; feet plantigrade; toes five in each foot, with short half-retractile, compressed, strongly-curved claws.

126. Arctictis binturong.

Viverra apud RAFFLES.—Blyth, Cat. 157.—*Ictides ater*, F. CUVIER, Mamm. 3, pl. 50-51, olim *Paradoxurus albifrons*.

THE BLACK BEAR-CAT.

Descr.—General color throughout deep black, with a white border to the ears, and a few brown hairs scattered over the head above, and on the anterior surface of the fore-legs; hairs long, rigid and diverging; tail monstrously thick at the base, tapering to a point, with bristling straggling hairs, exceeding those of the body in length.

Cantor describes it as black, sprinkled with pale ferruginous; head, face and throat whitish and grizzled; a trace of a white spot over the eye in the young; tail black, whitish at the base.

Length, head and body, 28 to 33 inches; tail 26 to 27.

It has a large gland between the anus and genitals, which secretes an oily fluid of an intense but not fetid odour.

This peculiar animal forms a very distinct genus, whose place in the natural system has not been satisfactorily decided. In general form of skull it resembles *Meles*, but the relative position of the bones is more like that of *Paradoxurus*. It deviates from the type of *Viverrinæ* in the more strictly plantigrade character of the feet, and in the partially prehensile tail, approaching *Ailurus* and *Cercoleptes* among the *Ursidæ*. The head is somewhat bulky, and the muzzle slightly turned up, the ears are large, black and prominent, edged with white, and terminated by tufts of black hair. Its habit of body is slow and crouching. In its habits it is quite nocturnal, solitary and arboreal, creeping along the larger branches, and aiding itself by its prehensile tail. It is omnivorous, eating small animals, birds, insects, fruit and plants. It is more wild and retiring than Viverrine animals in general, and it is easily tamed; its howl is loud.

One examined had 14 pairs of ribs; the intestines were 9 feet 9 inches long, and the cœcum ½ inch.

This bear-cat was classed by Cuvier and Cantor among the *Ursinæ*, and it may be considered a sort of link between the plantigrade and digitigrade Carnivora, with some distant analogies to the *Lemurs*. I have followed Blyth in his Catalogue in placing it after *Paradoxurus*. It has been stated to inhabit Nepal, Bhotan, and Assam, but it does not occur in the Catalogue of Hodgson's Collections. It is said to have been obtained from Bhotan by M. Duvaucel, and will probably be found to occur rarely in the north-eastern limit of our province. It is known from the hills of Assam, Arrakan and Malayana.

Other animals belonging to this group of *Carnivora* are *Cryptoprocta ferox*, Bennett, from Madagascar; *Cynogale bennettii*, Gray (*Potamophilus barbatus*, Kuhl), an aquatic species from the Malayan peninsula, Sumatra, &c.

The next group have been separated by Blyth as a distinct sub-family, *Herpestidinæ*. They differ from the *Viverrinæ* by the quality of their fur, which is long and harsh, and generally ringed with pale and dark tints; the tail is thick and bushy at the base, more tapering than in the tree-cats, and they have a large and simple pouch with the anus situated within its cavity. The bony orbits of the skull are perfect in several species. Compared with the *Paradoxuri*, they are much more terrestrial, seeking their prey entirely on the ground, and very rarely climbing trees.

Gen. Herpestes, Illiger.

Syn. *Mangusta*, Fischer.

Char.—Teeth as in *Viverra*, but the molars vary in number, some having $\frac{5-5}{5-5}$, others $\frac{6-6}{6-6}$, and some $\frac{6-6}{7-7}$; ears small, short and rounded; feet all with five toes, with large compressed, incurved, somewhat retractile claws; tail long, thick at the base; hairs long, rigid, often ringed with distinct colors.

The Ichneumons or Mungooses, as they are named in India, have a sharp muzzle, small eyes, short limbs, the hinder ones semi-plantigrade, and the toes connected by a membrane. The female has only four mammæ. The tongue is rough with horny papillæ. Some of the species are stated to have a voluminous simple anal pouch, which does not contain odoriferous matter, and at the bottom of which the vent is pierced. Hodgson states, "that both Nepal species of *Herpestes* have a congeries of small glands surrounding the caudal margin of the anus like a ring, and secreting a thick musky substance, which is slowly protuded in strings like vermicelli, through numerous scattered minute pores; and one species *(nyula)* has also on either side the rectum two large and hollow glands of similar structure, but with a thinner secretion, each of which has a larger and very palpable pore."

The mungooses are very active in their habits, bold and sanguinary in disposition. They are partly fossorial, and in the hot tropical countries of the old continent appear to take the place of the weasels of colder regions.

The bony orbit is often closed by a ring posteriorly, which however is not perpetual, and in some appears to depend on advanced age.

This genus is numerously represented in the Indian peninsula, and extends to Africa.

127. Herpestes griseus.

Geoffroy.—Blyth, Cat. 164.—*H. pallidus*, Schinz.—*Mangusta mungos* apud Elliot, Cat. 21.—*Mangús*, H. and Mahr. in Southern India.—*Néwal*, *Néwara*, in Northern and Central India; sometimes called *Nyúl*.—*Múngli*, Can.—*Yentawá*, Tel.—*Korál* of Gonds.

The Madras Mungoos.

Descr.—Tawny yellowish-gray, the hairs ringed with rufous and yellowish, the general result being an iron gray tinge, with less of the yellow tint than in the next species from Northern India, which it otherwise much resembles in size and form, whilst in the character of its fur it is more like *H. nipalensis*. The muzzle is concolorous with the body, as is the tail, which is not tipped with black, and is nearly equal in length to the body.

Average length, head and body, about 16 to 17 inches; tail 14. It is said occasionally to reach 20 inches and upwards, with the tail 16½.

This mungoos is spread through most of Southern India, replaced in Bengal and the lower Gangetic plains by a nearly allied one, *H. malaccensis.* I am not able to state the limits of each species exactly, but the present animal occurs in the North-west Provinces and the Punjab, and throughout the Deccan up to the Nerbudda river. It frequents alike the open country and low jungles, being found in dense hedge rows, thickets, holes in banks, &c.; and it is very destructive to such birds as frequent the ground. Not unfrequently it gets access to tame pigeons, rabbits, or poultry, and commits great havoc, sucking the blood only of several. I have often seen it make a dash into a verandah where some cages of mynas, parrakeets, &c., were daily placed, and endeavour to tear them from their cages.

It also hunts for, and devours, the eggs of partridges, quails and other ground-laying birds; and it will also kill rats, lizards and small snakes. I do not think it would go out of its way to attack a large snake in its wild state. Colonel Sykes states, that "it is believed by the Mahratta people to have a natural antipathy to serpents, and in its contests with them to be able to neutralize the poison from the bite of serpents by eating the root of a plant called *moonguswail,* but no one has ever seen the plant." This is the prevalent belief throughout all India, and also in Java, and many experiments have been made with a view to test the native idea above referred to, that the mungoos either by virtue of some plant to which it has recourse, or from some other cause, is proof against the bite of a cobra. Many have asserted that after being apparently bitten, it would retire to some hedge side, returning shortly with evident marks of its having eaten some green herb; whilst others have declared that it never attempted anything of the kind even when set free, and that where it was forcibly kept indoors it suffered as little as if allowed its liberty. I of course entirely disbelieve in the efficacy of any herb as an antidote to the serpent's poison; and I do not think that the mungoos habitually has resort to any herb if bitten. The plants are supposed to be *Ophiorhizon serpentinum,* and *O. mungos.* I have witnessed many contests between a mungoos and cobra, and though the mungoos has in general succeeded in killing the serpent, it often declines the combat, or undertakes it somewhat unwillingly. In none of the combats that I have seen has the mungoos suffered, but my belief is that it generally escapes being bitten by its extreme watchfulness and activity; or, if bitten at all, has been so very superficially; and that perhaps its very thick skin may have a certain degree of insusceptibility to poison. Since this paragraph was first penned, a writer in the Indian Lancet confirms this idea, which he says he has practically proved, both by seeing the cobra bite the mungoos, and by forcing the fang of a cobra into the skin of which did not suffer from the experiment. A very recent writer, however, in one of the Indian newspapers, declares that if the fangs are forced *through* the skin into the flesh the mungoos will die.

This little animal is frequently domesticated, and becomes excessively tame, following its owner about like a dog, and effectually clearing a house of rats. Mr. Bennett * mentions that an individual of this species in the Tower, "actually on one occasion killed no fewer than a dozen full grown rats which were loosed to it in a room sixteen feet square in less than a minute and a half." The Egyptian Ichneumon, *Herpestes ichneumon*, is said to have a peculiar penchant for crocodile's eggs. This habit is not noticed with regard to our species, though I dare say it would devour them if it came across any.

128. Herpestes malaccensis.

F. Cuvier, Mammif. 1, pl. 65.—Blyth, Cat. 163.—*H. nyula*, Hodgson.—*Newol* or *Nyul*, H.—*Néwára*, in Central India.—*Baji*, or *Biji*, H., in Behar.

The Bengal Mungoos.

Descr.—General color mixed rich reddish-brown and hoary-yellow, the ears, face and limbs redder, and less maculate; neck and body pure pale yellow; tail concolorous with the body, pointed, and nearly equal in length to the body; the hair harsh, bristly, not closely applied but diffuse.

Length, head and body, 15 inches; tail about 10 or 11.

This mungoos replaces *H. griseus* in Bengal, and other parts of the North of India; and has precisely the same habits as that species. It extends into Assam, Burmah and Malayana. Hodgson states that it affects cultivated fields and grass, and lives in burrows made by themselves. The females produce 3 to 4 young at a birth.

* Tower Menagerie, p. 106.

129. Herpestes monticolus.

W. ELLIOT, MSS.—*Konda yentawa*, Tel.

THE LONG-TAILED MUNGOOS.

Descr.—Colors much as in *griseus*, but somewhat more yellow in its general tone; tail longer, tipped with maronne and black, and more hairy; feet dark reddish-brown; muzzle not dark, slightly tinged with reddish. Larger than *griseus*. Tail nearly equal in length to the head and body.

Length of one 20 inches; tail with hair 19.

This fine species differs conspicuously from *griseus* in its longer and dark tipped tail, which also distinguishes it from *malaccensis*. It differs from *H. Smithii* in its muzzle being concolorous with the body, or nearly so, and prevalent lighter color.

I have only procured this mungoos from the Eastern Ghâts inland from Nellore, where it inhabits forests among the hills.

It most resembles *H. fulvescens*, Kelaart, of Ceylon, but this has a shorter tail with the tip reddish, and has a more prevalent fulvous hue. The muzzle too is blackish and the face ferruginous brown.

130. Herpestes Smithii.

GRAY.—BLYTH, Cat. 162.—*H. Elliotti*, BLYTH.—*H. rubiginosus*, KELAART.

THE RUDDY MUNGOOS.

Descr.—General color ferruginous-brown, in some inclining to grizzled maronne red, brighter where it joins the blackish limbs and black tip of the tail; muzzle dark; face rusty red; head and legs redder than the other parts; feet black, the hairs are ringed black and white, and have a dark reddish tip. It approximates *malaccensis* in the character of the fur and also in size.

Length of one, head and body, 13 to 15 inches; tail 12 to 13.

This mungoos has been taken in forest jungle among the Eastern Ghâts near Madras, and in other parts of the same region. I procured it in forest at the foot of the Neelgherries, but did not obtain it in the Malabar forests, though it most probably will be found there also. It is said to be not rare in Ceylon. The first specimen obtained by Mr. Elliot had an accidental dark collar, and that gentleman named it *torquatus* in MSS. which name is alluded to by Kelaart.

131. Herpestes nipalensis.

GRAY.—BLYTH, Cat. 165.—*H. auro-punctatus*, HODGSON.—*H. pallipes*, BLYTH, olim.

THE GOLD-SPOTTED MUNGOOS.

Descr.—Of an uniform olive-brown color, more or less saturate in different individuals, freckled with golden yellow, paler and somewhat yellowish-gray beneath; cheeks more or less rusty; tail shorter than the body; hairs with five distinct rings of black and golden, the fur short, soft, adpressed.

Length, head and body, 12 to 13 inches; tail 9 to 10.

This species resembles *H. javanicus*, but the ground color is lighter. It is found over the whole extent of the lower Himalayas, from Sikim to Kashmir (and even to Afghanistan); and it also occurs in the plains near the hills, from Bengal to the Punjab, not extending far south. It also inhabits Assam, Burmah, and the Malayan peninsula. Nothing peculiar has been noticed of the habits of this mungoos.

I find a species recorded in Schinz, *H. thysanurus*, Wagner, from Kashmir; hair dark-brown ringed with pale yellow; feet brown; tail ending in a long deep black tuft. This, if correctly described, must be distinct from *nipalensis*. The only mungoos I got in Kashmir was the latter species.

132. Herpestes fuscus.

WATERHOUSE—BLYTH, Cat. 167.

THE NEELGHERRY BROWN MUNGOOS.

Descr.—General color brown, the hair being ringed black and yellow, and tawny at the base; throat dusky yellowish; tail nearly equal in length to head and body.

Length of one, head and body, 18 inches; tail with the hair 17.

I procured this mungoos, many years ago, on the Neelgherries in the dense woods near Ootacamund, and have not seen it from any other locality. My original specimen is in the Museum Asiatic of the Society at

Calcutta. It appears nearly allied to *H. javanicus.* Its distribution is more local than that of any other of the Indian species, no record of its occurring elsewhere existing; and Waterhouse's type specimen also came from the same locality. It probably will eventually be found in other elevated hill regions of Southern India.

The next species has been, with some others, separated as a sub-genus, *Mungos,* having the molars $\frac{6-6}{7-7}$; and the bony orbital ring always complete. It approximates to *Urva.*

133. Herpestes vitticollis.

BENNETT.—BLYTH, Cat. 159.—ELLIOT, Cat. 22, with figure.

THE STRIPE-NECKED MUNGOOS.

Descr.—Of a grizzled gray color more or less tinged with rusty reddish, especially on the hinder part of the body and tail; a dark stripe from the ear to the shoulder; tail rufous black at the tip.

Length of one killed on the Neelgherries, the head and body 21 inches; tail with the hair 15; weight 6 lb. 10 oz.

This fine species of mungoos is found throughout all the forests of the Western Ghâts, from near Dharwar to Cape Comorin. It is rare in the northern parts, and most abundant in Travancore. I have killed it on the Neelgherries, in Wynaad, and seen specimens from various parts of Malabar. From its large size this must be a very destructive animal to game and the smaller quadrupeds. The Malayan region, besides those common to India, viz., *H. malaccensis* and *H. nipalensis,* has *H. javanicus* and *H. brachyurus,* peculiar to that district; and *H. exilis* is recorded, Zool. de la Bonite, from some of the islands. There are many species from Africa, and one extends into Spain.

Gen. URVA, Hodgson.

Syn. *Mesobema,* Hodgson.

Char.—Teeth as in *Herpestes,* but blunter; structure intermediate to that genus and *Gulo*; snout elongate, acute, mobile; hands and feet large; soles nude; nails subequal; digits connected by large crescentic membranes; tail long, cylindric; habit sub-vermiform.

This genus contains only one species.

134. Urva cancrivora.

Hodgson.—Blyth, Cat. 158.—*Gulo urva*, Hodgson (olim).—*Viverra fusca*, Gray, apud Hardwicke, Ill. Ind. Zool. 1, pl. 5.—*Osmetictis fusca*, Gray, Mag. Nat. Hist.

The Crab Mungoos.

Descr.—General color jackal or fulvous iron-gray; inner fur woolly; outer of long straggling lax hairs, generally ringed with black, white and fulvous; in some the coat has a variegated aspect; in others an uniform tawny tint prevails, and in a few dark rusty brown mixed with gray is the prevalent hue; abdomen brown; limbs blackish brown; a white stripe on either side of the neck, from the ear to the shoulder; tail rufous or brown, with the terminal half rufous.

Length, head and body, 18 inches; tail 11; weight 4 lbs.

This curious animal has been found in the South-east Himalayas, extending into Assam and Arrakan. In its habit it is somewhat aquatic, preferring, it is said by Hodgson, frogs and crabs. It lives in burrows in the valleys of the lower and central regions of Nepal. The drawing of the one figured by Hardwicke was taken from a caged individual at Agra. Colonel Phayre informed Mr. Blyth that it was the only mungoos found in Arrakan.

Some details of its anatomy were furnished to Mr. Hodgson by Dr. Campbell. It has two glands about the size of a cherry on each side of the anus, which secrete an aqueous fetid humour, which the animal has the power of squirting out with great force. The female has six ventral teats, remote. The bony orbits are incomplete.

Other genera allied to the mungooses are *Galidia* and *Ichneumonia* of Is. Geoffroy, the former from Madagascar. *Cynictis*, Ogilby, with four toes to each foot, and *Ryzæna*, Illiger, with the same number, both from South Africa; and *Crossarchus*, F. Cuvier, from Sierra Leone.

Bassaris astuta, Lichtenstein, from Mexico, a peculiar digitigrade carnivorous animal, is placed here by some systematists, and it has some likeness to *Paradoxurus*, but it belongs to the sub-plantigrade division, none of the *Viverridæ* occurring in the new continent.

The next group is well marked by anatomical characters as distinct from the other digitigrade carnivora.

Fam. Canidæ. The Dog tribe.

Molar teeth mostly $\frac{6-6}{7-7}$; more rarely $\frac{7-7}{7-7}$ or $\frac{8-8}{8-8}$; two of these in general on each side in both jaws being tuberculous, rarely three; the first of the upper tuberculous teeth very large; upper flesh-tooth with one inner tubercle, lower do. with its posterior portion tuberculous. Fore-feet with five toes, the thumb raised; hind-feet usually with four. Head more or less conical, and pointed in front, the jaws being produced; legs of nearly equal length.

The tongue is smooth; the intestines rather long, and the cœcum of a peculiar spiral form. Some have a dermal gland above the base of the tail; others a sac or hollow gland on each side of the anus, opening by a pore, which secretes a pungent whey-like substance with the peculiar smell of the animal, the contents of which can be made to trickle out on pressure.

In domestic dogs these pores exist, but are evanescent, and without a distinct sac or secretion. In these too there is often a fifth claw on the hind feet, but only connected by skin, and called the dew-claw.

Gen. Canis, Linn. (restricted).

Char.—Dental formula, incisors $\frac{6}{6}$; canines $\frac{1-1}{1-1}$; præmolars $\frac{4-4}{4-4}$; molars $\frac{2-2}{3-3}$. The false molars are $\frac{3-3}{4-4}$; and the tubercular molars $\frac{2-2}{2-2}$; the former small; tail moderately brushed; pupil rounded.

In this group, as here restricted, are classed the Wolf and the Jackal. Linnæus included Foxes and Hyænas as well.

1st. Wolves, *Lupus*, Hamilton Smith.

Of large size. Muzzle obtuse, not much lengthened; tail short; no caudal gland.

135. Canis pallipes.

Sykes, Cat.—Blyth, Cat. 121.—C. *lupus*, var., Elliot, Cat. 17.—*Lándgah*, H., in the South.—*Bherá*, or *Bhériá*, or *Byria*, or *Bharya*, H., in Northern and Central India.—*Nékrá*, in some parts.—*Bighána* in part of Bundelcund.—*Húndár*, or *Húrár*, in other parts.—*Tola*, Can.—*Toralú*, Tel.

THE INDIAN WOLF.

Descr.—Hoary fulvous or dirty reddish-white, some of the hairs tipped black, which gives it a grizzled appearance; somewhat reddish on the face and limbs, the latter paler than the body; lower parts dingy white; tail thinly bushy, slightly black tipped. Ears rather small.

Length of one, head and body, 37 inches; tail 17; height at the shoulder 26 inches.

Elliot and Horsfield have stated that they did not consider the Indian wolf specifically distinct from the European wolf, but Blyth gives it as his opinion that it is so. "The Society's Museum now contains good and characteristic examples of the skulls of the European, Indian and Tibetan wolves, *C. lupus*, *pallipes* and *laniger*, and the specific distinctness appears to be well marked. The European is the largest of the three, with proportionally much larger and more powerful teeth, and the orbital process of the frontal bone is much less developed than in the others. The Indian and Tibetan wolves are more affined to each other than either is to the European one."

This wolf is found throughout the whole of India, rare in wooded districts, and most abundant in open country. "The wolves of the Southern Mahratta country," says Mr. Elliot, "generally hunt in packs, and I have seen them in full chase after the goat antelope (*Gazella bennettii*). They likewise steal round a herd of antelope, and conceal themselves on different sides till an opportunity offers of seizing one of them unawares, as they approach, whilst grazing, to one or other of their hidden assailants. On one occasion three wolves were seen to chase a herd of gazelles across a ravine in which two others were lying in wait. They succeeded in seizing a female gazelle which was taken from them. They have frequently been seen to course and run down hares and foxes, and it is a common belief of the Ryots that in the open plains where there is no cover or concealment, they scrape a hole in the earth in which one of the pack lies down, and remains hid, while the others drive the herd of antelope over him. Their chief prey, however, is sheep, and the shepherds say that part of the pack attack and keep the dogs in play, while others carry off their prey, and that if pursued they follow the same plan, part turning and checking the dogs, whilst the rest drag away the carcase till they evade pursuit. Instances are not uncommon of their attacking man. In 1824, upwards of 30 children were devoured by wolves in one pergunnah alone. Sometimes a large wolf is seen to seek his prey singly. These are called *Won-tola* by the Canarese, and reckoned particularly fierce."

I have found wolves most abundant in the Deccan and in Central India. I have often chased them for several miles, they keeping 50 to 100 yards ahead of the horse, and the only kind of ground on which a horse appeared to gain on them was heavy ploughed land. I have known wolves turn on dogs that were running at their heels and pursue them smartly till close up to my horse. A wolf once joined with my greyhounds in pursuit of a fox, which was luckily killed almost immediately afterwards, or the wolf might have seized one of the dogs instead of the fox. He sat down on his haunches about 60 yards off whilst the dogs were worrying the fox, looking on with great apparent interest, and was with difficulty driven away. In many parts of the North-west of India, they are very destructive to children, as about Agra, in Oude, Rohilcund and Rajpootana, and rewards are given by Government for their destruction. Wolves breed in holes in the ground, or caves, having only three or four young, it is said. The female has ten teats. They are usually rather silent, but sometimes bark just like a pariah dog. The howling after their prey, recorded of the European wolf, is seldom heard in India.

Hodgson has described a wolf from Tibet, *Canis laniger*, sometimes called the "white wolf" by sportsmen who cross the Himalayas. It is the *Cháṅgú* of Tibet, *Chankodi* near the Niti pass from Kumaon; and it is a larger animal than the Indian wolf, with white face and limbs, and no dark tip to the tail, which is fully brushed. The fur is extremely woolly, and the hairy piles few; but this is also to a certain extent apparent in domestic dogs of the same region.

Another species of wolf has recently been described by Gray,* as *Canis chanco*, or the red wolf of Tibet, or golden wolf: "fulvous, head grayish-brown, lower parts pure white. Somewhat larger than the European wolf, to which its skull bears a close resemblance." It is probably the same as the animal in Blyth's Cat. Mamm. No. 119, "large red wolf," referred by that naturalist with doubt to Pallas' *C. alpinus*; but Gray says that that is a fox. The specific name given by Gray is the name also applied to the common wolf of that region, spelt differently.

There are many other species of wolves in various parts of the northern regions of both continents.

* Proceedings Zoological Society, 1863, p. 94.

2nd. Jackals. *Saccalius*, Hamilton Smith.

Of moderate size, gregarious; brush rather scanty.

136. Canis aureus.

LINNÆUS.—BLYTH, Cat. 124.—ELLIOT, Cat. 18.—*Kholá* or *Kolá*, H., in the South of India and Mahr.—*Kolya*, in some parts.—*Gidar* or *Ghidar*, H., in the North.—*Shial* or *Sial*, or *Siár* and *Shialu*, in Bengal and adjacent provinces.—*Nari*, Can.—*Nakka*, Tel.—*Nerka* of Gonds.—*Shigal* or *Sjekal*, in Persia, whence our English word.—*Amú*, Bhot.

THE JACKAL.

Descr.—Fur of a dusky yellowish or rufous gray, the hairs being mottled black, gray, and brown, with the under fur brownish-yellow; lower parts yellowish-gray; tail reddish brown, ending in a darkish tuft; more or less rufous on the muzzle and limbs; tail moderately hairy.

Length, head and body, 28 to 30 inches; tail 10 or 11; height about 16-17 inches.

The jackal varies considerably in the color of its fur according to season and locality. A black variety is by no means rare in Bengal; but I never saw or heard of it in the south of India.

This well known animal abounds throughout all India, and its habits are too well known to require much notice. It occurs also in Ceylon, but is rare in lower Burmah, and said to be only of recent introduction there. It is a very useful scavenger, clearing away all garbage and carrion from the neighbourhood of large towns, but occasionally committing depredations among poultry and other domestic animals. Sickly sheep and goats usually fall a prey to him; and a wounded antelope is pretty certain to be tracked and hunted to death by jackals. They will however partake freely of vegetable food. Sykes says he devastates the vineyards in the west of India; in Bhagulpore he is said to be fond of sugar-cane; and he every where consumes large quantities of the bér fruit, *Zizyphus jujuba*. In Wynaad as well as in Ceylon, he devours considerable quantities of ripe coffee berries: the seeds pass through him, well pulped, and are found and picked up by the coolies; and it is asserted, that the seeds so found make the best coffee!

The female jackal brings forth about four young in holes in the ground, occasionally in dry drains in cantonments. The jackal is easily pulled down by greyhounds, but gives at excellent run with fox hounds. They are very tenacious of life, and sham dead in a way to deceive even an experienced sportsman. I have seen one after being worried by a pack of hounds, and getting a good rap or two on its head with a heavy whip, limp off some time afterwards when unobserved, with apparently a good chance of affording another run on a future day. I have known a jackal come to the aid of his comrade (or mate perhaps) when seized by greyhounds, and attack them furiously, whilst I was close by on horseback. The call of the jackal is familiar to all residents in India, and is certainly the most unearthly and startling music. The natives assert that they cry after every watch of the night. Jackals not unfrequently get hydrophobia, especially in Bengal, and I have known several fatal cases from their bite.

Connected with the old name of the "lion's provider" are the generally credited tales about one always attending the tiger. Mr. Elliot says, "native sportsmen universally believe that an old jackal, which (in the South of India) they call '*Bhâlú*,' is in constant attendance on the tiger, and whenever his cry is heard, which is peculiar and different from that of the jackal generally, the vicinity of a tiger is confidently pronounced. I have heard the cry attributed to the *Bhâlú*, frequently." The "*Kole bhaloo*" is frequently referred to by Lieutenant Rice, in his very interesting work on "Tiger Shooting in Rajpootana," as having been frequently heard and seen by him in company with the tiger. In Bengal the same jackal is called "*Phéall*," or *Phao*, or *Pheeow*, or *Phnew*, from its call, and in some parts *Ghog*, though that name is said by some to refer to some other (fabulous) animal. "It is," says Johnson, in his Field Sports of India, as quoted in the India Sporting Review, N. S. Vol. I, "a jackal following the scent of the tiger and making a noise very different from their usual cry, which I imagine they do for the purpose of warning their species of danger." Again, "soon after the tiger passed within a few yards of us. In a minute or two after he had passed, we plainly saw the jackal, and heard him cry when very near us. I have often heard it said that the Phéall (or provider, as it is sometimes called), always goes before the tiger, but in this instance he followed him, which I have also seen him do at other times. Whether he is induced to follow the tiger for the sake of coming in for part of the booty, or whether merely follows as small birds often follow a bird of prey, I cannot say. Evidently his cry is different from what it is at other times, which indicates danger being near, particularly as whenever that cry is heard the voice of no other jackal is, nor is that particular call ever heard in any part of the country where there are not large beasts of prey. *Phéall*, I believe, was the original, and is now the usual name from its resembling the cry they make, but they are better known in Ramghur by the name *Phinkar*, which means crier—proclaimer—or warner." Mr. Blyth records that, "some time ago I heard a pariah dog upon sniffing the collection of live tigers, before referred to, set up the most extraordinary cry I have ever heard uttered by a dog, and which I cannot pretend to record more intelligibly, but it was doubtless an analogous note to the *Phéall* cry of the jackal." I have often heard this peculiar cry, and seen a jackal following a tiger in various parts of the country; and I have already noted my turning a jackal out of the same bush as a cheeta.

A horn is supposed by the natives in the some parts of India to grow on the head of some jackals, which is of great reputed virtue, ensuring prosperity to its possessor. The same idea is prevalent in Ceylon.

The jackal is found over a great part of Asia, in Southern Europe, and in Northern Africa.

There are several allied species of small or moderate size in Africa and part of Asia.

The domestic dog belongs to this division, but his origin is lost in obscurity, and it is probable that several species of wolf and other animals may have contributed to form this valuable animal. Now and then very jackal-like dogs may be seen about villages, but whether these are hybrids, or simply a reversion to one of the original types, it is impossible to say. In India it is a well known fact that the various breeds of English dogs, if bred in the plains, have a tendency to change towards the pariah dog, the muzzle of the bull-dog as well as his limbs lengthening sensibly in even two generations.

The next animal, though called a dog, differs in its dentition so remarkably that it has been made the type of a distinct genus.

Gen. Cuon, Hodgson.

Char.—General structure and dentition of *Canis*, but the molars only $\frac{6-6}{6-6}$; the second tubercular behind the flesh tooth in the lower jaw being deficient; skull more uniformly arched than in dogs; jaws shorter and stronger. Has the odour and aspect of *Saccalius*, but ears and tail larger, the latter more brushed, the brow and eye bolder, and the muzzle blunter. The shoulder and croup are about level. The female has 12 or 14 teats.

I have followed Blyth in his Cat. Mamm., in keeping this distinct from *Canis*.

137. Cuon rutilans.

Canis apud TEMMINCK.—BLYTH, Cat. 117.—*C. dukhunensis*, SYKES.—Figd. Trans. Roy. As. Soc.—*C. familiaris*, wild variety, ELLIOT, Cat. 16. —*Cuon primævus*, HODGSON.—Figd. also by DELESSERT, Souvenirs d'un Voyage dans l' Inde.—*Jangli kútá*, H., popularly.—*Sona kútá*, i. e., golden dog in Central India.—*Ram kútá*, in some parts.—*Ban kútá*, in the North of India.—*Rahnasay kútá*, of some.—*Kolsun*, *Kolusná*, *Kolsa*, and *Kolasrá*, as variously pronounced by the Mahrattas in different localities.—*Rézá kútá*, Tel., i. e., fierce dog; vulgo *Adavi kútá*.—*Shen nai*, Mal.—*Eram naiko*, of Gonds—*Sakki sarai*, at Hydrabad, (Buchanan Hamilton).—*Ram hún* in Kashmir.—*Sidda-ki*, Tibetan in Ladak.—*Súhú-túm*, Lepch.—*Paóhó*, Bhot.—*Bhaosa*, *Bhoonsa*, *Buansú*, in the Himalayas, generally from Simla to Nepal.—Wild dog of Europeans.

THE WILD DOG.

Descr.—General color bright rusty-red or rufous fawn color, paler beneath; ears erect, rather large, somewhat rounded at the tip; tail moderately brushed, reaching to the heels, usually tipped blackish; limbs strong; body lengthened.

Length, head and body, 32 to 36 inches; tail about 16 inches; height 17 to 20 inches.

I quite agree with Mr. Blyth in considering that the wild dog of Malayana does not differ specifically from the Indian one; and, therefore adopt Temminck's specific name, Sykes' local name, and Hodgson's theoretic one, being alike inapplicable, as well as posterior in date. "A Malayan specimen," says Blyth, "differs only in the considerably deeper tint of the rufous coloring." There is, however, a prevalent belief among sportsmen of the existence of two races of wild dogs in India. In an early notice of the wild dog, in the 1st Vol. of the "Gleanings of Science," two kinds are indicated; one called *Shikari bhowsa*, which hunts its own prey; the other *Lágh*, from eating the offal of its prey. Hamilton Smith says, "besides the *Jangli kútá* of the plains, there are two hill kinds, one larger, the other smaller, but with shorter tails, said to ascend as high as the snow line, and to be very shy."

Blyth gives a description of a wild dog from Darjeeling, which he was informed Mr. Hodgson had considered distinct from the common one; "this one (a female) had a considerably more vulpine aspect with longer and softer fur, with much wool at the base, a considerable ruff round the neck, and much lengthened fur about the jowl; the ears also were densely clad both externally and within; and in a living animal from the same locality, were closely approximated and directed forwards; a remarkably full brush, with much less black than usual on the terminal half, but most of the tail having a nigrescent appearance not particularly noticeable at a little distance. All this may merely indicate the winter vesture as assumed in a cold climate; but the actions of the living animal were decidedly peculiar, and the general appearance as vulpine as that of the ordinary wild dog is jackal-like. It was particularly light, agile and graceful in its movements; still I can discover no distinction in the skull, or in the rest of the skeleton, excepting that the metacarpal bones of the Darjeeling specimen are comparatively shorter. Upon present evidence, I can only regard it as a specimen of the common wild dog in winter vesture as developed in a cold climate."

In the late edition of Hodgson's Collection Brit. Museum, a second species of wild dog is described as *Cuon grayiformis*, with the following description:—"Deep uniform red, deeper than rust, paler and flavescent below; lining of ears, chaffron, and end of tail nigrescent. Hair close and short, no feathering of limbs nor brush to tail. Form slighter than in other species, and larger—that is in largest dimensions." Length, head and body, 3 feet 1 inch; tail 16 inches. This was from Darjeeling. It will be observed that this does not tally with Mr. Blyth's description above. Some young wild dogs were brought to Darjeeling whilst I was there, which did not appear to me at the time to differ in any material point from others I had seen in various parts of India. Specimens from the Eastern Ghâts perhaps differ more from those of other parts. They have the color lighter and more fulvous, the tail less brushed and concolorous with the body, or nearly so; and the hair shorter. Those from Coorg and the Malabar forests have the tail blackish, and moderately bushy, and closely resemble others from Central India, and one represented in a drawing of Buchanan Hamilton's. Mr. Blyth wrote from me Madras, stating that some specimens he had seen in the Museum there, had rather staggered him as to the unity of the species.

Mr. Hodgson gives the following excellent account of his *Cuon primævus* as met with in Nepal. "The *Buánsu* is in size midway between the wolf and the jackal, being 2½ feet long to root of tail and 21 inches in average height. It is a slouching, uncompact, long, lank animal, with all the marks of uncultivation about it, best assimilated in its general aspect to the jackal, but with something inexpressibly but genuinely canine in its physiognomy. It has a broad flat head and sharp visage, large erect ears, a chest not broad nor deep; a shallow compressed barrel, somewhat strained at the loin; long heavy limbs; broad spreading feet, and a very bushy tail of moderate length, straight, and carried low. It stands rather lower before than behind, with the neck in the line of the body, the head unelevated, the nose pointed directly forwards, the fore limbs straightened, the hind stooping; the back inclined to arch, especially over the croup, and the tail pendulous. In action the tail is slightly raised, but never so high as the horizontal line. Though the *Buánsu* be not deficient in speed or power of leaping, yet his motions all appear to be heavy, owing to their measured uniformity. He runs in a lobbing long canter, is unapt at the double, and upon the whole is somewhat less agile and speedy than the jackal, very much so than the fox. The wild dog preys by night and by day, but chiefly by day. Six, eight or ten, unite to hunt down their victim, maintaining the chase by their powers of smell rather than by the eye. They usually overcome their quarry by dint of force and perseverance, though they sometimes effect their object by mixing stratagem with direct violence. Their urine is peculiarly acrid, and they are said to sprinkle it over the low bushes amongst which their destined victim will probably move, and then in secret, to watch the result. If the stratagem succeeds, they rush out upon the devoted animal whilst half blinded by the urine, and destroy it before it has recovered that clearness of vision which could best have enabled it to flee or defend itself. This trick the *Buánsu* usually plays off upon animals whose speed or strength might otherwise foil them, such as the buffalo, wild or tame, and certain large deer and antelopes. Other animals they fairly hunt down, or furiously assail and kill by more violence. In hunting they bark like hounds, but their barking is in such a voice as no language can express. It is utterly unlike the fine voice of our cultivated breeds, and almost as unlike the peculiar strains of the jackal and the fox. The *Buánsu* does not burrow like the wolf and fox, but reposes and breeds in the recesses and natural cavities of rocks." After speaking of some kept alive by him, Hodgson continues; "after ten months confinement they were as wild and shy as at the first hour I got them. Their eyes emitted a strong light in the dark, and their bodies had the peculiar fetid odour of the fox and jackal in all its rankness. They were very silent, never uttering an audible sound save when fed, at which time they would snarl in subdued tone at each other, but never fight; nor did they on any occasion show any signs of quarrelsomeness or pugnacity."

Mr. Elliot has the following remarks on this species:—The "wild dog was not known in the Southern Mahratta country until of late years. It has now become very common. The circumstance of their attacking in a body and killing the tiger is universally believed by the natives. Instances of their killing the wild boar, and of tigers leaving a jungle in which a pack of wild dogs had taken up their quarters, have come to my own knowledge, and on one occasion a party of the officers of the 18th M. N. I., saw a pack run into and kill a large samber stag (*Rusa*) near Dharwar. I once captured a bitch and seven cubs of this species and had them alive for some time."

I have come across the wild dog myself on several occasions, in Malabar, the Wynaad, at the foot of the Ajunteh Ghât in Kandeish, near Saugor, on the Neelgherries, &c., &c. It may be said to inhabit the whole of India where sufficiently wooded to supply it with suitable game. The pack I saw at Ajunteh had just run down a full grown female samber, which our followers at once appropriated. In lower Malabar I came suddenly on a pack that had just killed a tame female buffalo. It was much worried about the throat, and had in the agonies of death given birth to a fœtus a few months old. This is the only instance I have heard of in the south of India of cattle being killed by them; but in the north they are said often to kill calves.

The bitch has twelve to fourteen teats, and has at least six whelps at a birth. They breed from January to March. Colonel Markham mentions that a breeding place was discovered by Mr. Wilson, near Simla, in holes under rocks, several females apparently breeding together. At this time it appears that they endeavour to hunt their game and kill it as near their den as possible. I entirely disbelieve the native story of their capturing their prey through the acridity of their urine.

The wild dog is common in Ceylon, where called the *Dhole* by some, by which name it has been treated of by Hamilton Smith and other writers, and it is found over all the jungles of Assam, Burmah, the Malayan peninsula, and the larger islands. Hodgson asserts that it extends into Tibet.

Gen. VULPES Auctorum, Foxes.

Char.—Muzzle lengthened and very acute; head round; ears large, erect; pupil elliptic, or linear by day; upper incisors less sloping than in dogs and wolves; body long; limbs short; tail thick long and bushy; otherwise as in *Canis.*

Foxes have a gland at the base of the tail above, which secretes a strongly odorous substance. This is called by German huntsmen the *viole.* The female has six teats. Species are found over all the world except in Australia.

There are two types of Foxes in India; the first the foxes of the desert or plains. These are not typical in their characters, having longer ears, longer and more slender limbs, and they have been separated by Hamilton Smith as *Cynalopex.* This is adopted by Blyth in his Catalogue, but I shall only mark it as sectional. The type is *Canis corsac* of Central Asia. They inhabit bare open plains, in which they burrow; are less carnivorous in their habits than true foxes, feeding much on fruit, insects, crabs, &c.

138. Vulpes bengalensis.

SHAW.—BLYTH, Cat. 126.—ELLIOT, Cat. 19.—HARDWICKE, Ill. Ind. Zool. 2, pl. 2.—*C. rufescens,* GRAY.—*C. kokree,* SYKES.—*C. corsac* of India, Auctorum.—*C. chrysurus* and *C. xanthurus,* GRAY.—*Lomri* or *Lúmri,* H.; also *Lokri* in some parts.—*Lokeria* in Central India.—*Kokri,* Mahr.—*Khekar* and *Khikír* in Behar.—*Khek sial,* Bengal.—*Konk,* Can.—*Konka nakka,* or *Gúnta nakka,* Tel.—*Kemp-nari* and *Chandak-nari,* Can.—*Poti-nara,* Tel. at Hydrabad (Buch. Ham.)

THE INDIAN FOX.

Descr.—Reddish-gray, rufous on the legs and muzzle, reddish-white beneath; ears long, dark brown externally; tail long, bushy with a broad black tip; muzzle very acute; chin and throat whitish.

Length, head and body, 21 to 22 inches; tail 12 to 14; weight of a male about 7 lbs.

This pretty little fox varies a good deal in the shades of color in different localities, and according to season. The fur just after it has assumed its winter coat is very beautiful, a purer gray on the body contrasting with the rufous limbs. The legs are remarkably slender. The tail is very bushy. It is usually carried trailing when the fox is going slowly or hunting for food; horizontal when running; and raised almost erect when making a sudden turn.

This fox is found throughout India, rare in the forest countries, very abundant in open country. At night it often comes into cantonments and gardens, but does not appear to molest poultry in general. Mr. Elliot says: "Its principal food is rats, landcrabs, grasshoppers, beetles, &c., &c. On one occasion a half-devoured mango was found in the stomach. It always burrows in the open plains, runs with great speed, doubling like a hare; but instead of stretching out at first like that animal, and trusting to its turns as a last resource, the fox turns more at first, and if it can fatigue the dogs, it then goes straight away."

The burrow which this fox makes has always several openings converging towards the centre, some of them blind, others leading towards a larger central one where the animal breeds. This is often two or three feet below the surface. The burrow is usually situated quite in the open plain, now and then in some thorny scrub. In alluvial plains, the fox takes advantage of any small rise in the ground, to prevent its den being flooded in the rains: and its burrow is frequently found on bunds of tanks and other artificial mounds. I have on two occasions run foxes to holes in old trees, which, from the marks round one of them, had evidently been occupied by the animal for long.

Lizards are a favorite food with the fox, as well as rats, crabs, and various insects, white ants, &c., and it habitually eats melons, bér fruit, and others; now and then pods and shoots of *Cicer arietinum*, and other herbs. I have seen it hunting quail, and it doubtless occasionally kills young birds, and eats eggs.

Foxes couple according to locality from November to January, and the female brings forth almost always four cubs from February to April. At this season the female is rarely to be met with after sunrise, and the cubs are very seldom seen outside their earth till nearly fully grown.

This fox is much coursed with greyhounds in many parts of India, and with Arab or country dogs, or half-bred English dogs, it gives a most excellent course, doubling in a most dexterous manner, and if it is within a short distance of its earth racing the dogs. With good English dogs it stands little chance. Its numerous earths prevent in general much sport being had in hunting it with foxhounds, and its scent is poor.

If taken young, this fox is easily tamed, and it shows a very playful and frolicsome disposition; but it is very generally asserted that tame ones always go mad after a longer or shorter interval, and certainly I have known one or two instances of this.

Vulpes corsac, Pallas, of Central Asia, appears to be nearly allied to this fox, but the ears are represented to be still larger. Some from Africa have yet larger ears, such as the Fennec of North Africa, *V. zerda*, and the *Caama* of the Cape of Good Hope; these have been placed in a distinct genus, *Megalotis*, Illiger.

The next species, though so similar in general appearance to the last, that it is often confounded with it by sportsmen, is placed by Blyth in restricted *Vulpes*.

139. Vulpes leucopus.

Blyth, Cat. 135.

The Desert Fox.

Light fulvous on the face, middle of back and upper part of tail cheeks, sides of neck and body, inner side and most of the fore part of limbs, white shoulder and haunch, and outside of the limbs nearly to the middle-joint, mixed black and white; tail darker at the base above, largely tipped with white; lower parts nigrescent; ears black posteriorly; fur soft and fine as in *V. montanus*, altogether dissimilar from that of *V. bengalensis*. The skull with the muzzle distinctly narrower, and the lower jaw weaker.

One I killed at Hissar had the upper parts fulvous, the hair black tipped; sides paler; whole lower parts from the chin including the inside of the arm and thigh, blackish; feet white on the inner side and anteriorly, with a blackish border on the anterior limbs; legs fulvous externally; all feet white; tail always with a white tip.

Length, head and body, 20 inches; tail to tip 14; weight $5\frac{1}{2}$ lbs.

Mountstuart Elphinstone (quoted by Blyth), writing of the foxes of the Hurriana desert, says, "their backs are of the same color as the common fox; but in one part of the desert their legs and belly up to a certain height are black; and in another white. The line between these colors and the brown is so distinctly marked that the one kind seems as if it had been wading up to the belly in ink, and the other in whitewash." It has been suggested that the female is always white-limbed, and the dog with black limbs; but the variation of color is apparently due to the degree of abrasion of the hairs of the limbs, which are mixed black and white. Some are very light colored above; others are sandy red.

The desert fox inhabits the North-west of India, from Cutch on the

South, to Ferozepore, Umballa, and severals part of the Punjab. It is said to be the only fox in Cutch and some of the Rajpootana States; and where it does encroach on the grounds of the common fox, it is always true to the kind of ground it chiefly haunts. At Umballa, for instance, this desert fox is only found on the sandy downs of the rivers about that station, the common fox occurring in the fields around. Mr. Elliot evidently alludes to this species when he says, " it is remarkable that though the brush is generally tipped with black, a white one is occasionally found, whilst in other parts of India, as in Cutch, the tip is always white."

Dr. Scott, writing from Hansi, says "that this animal is common in the neighbourhood of Hansi in the cold weather only, and rarely seen at other times, whereas *V. bengalensis* is equally abundant at all times. Those that live on sandhills get covered with burrs (from a plant very abundant in such spots), and have much of their fur scratched off." I have now seen this fox at Umballa, near Mozaffurnuggur, and near Hansi and Hissar, almost always on sandhills, or in the broad downy sandy beds of nearly dry rivers. Now and then one may be found in fields near the sandhills, though rarely; but where this fox is the only species, as at Nusseerabad (I am informed) Cutch, Sirsa, and elsewhere, it does not confine itself to the sandy downs, but is also found in open cultivated land.

This fox appears to be more carnivorous than the last, and lives a great deal on the jerboa rat *(gerbillus)*, so exceedingly common among the sandhills and sandy plains. It is I think more speedy than the common Indian fox, and gives a capital run sometimes even with English dogs. When the fur is in good condition it is very handsome.

Vulpes ferrilatus, Hodgson, from Tibet, is a very pretty small fox, which Blyth places, though with doubt, in *Cynalopex*. It is very distinct from *Bengalensis*, with which Gray at one time classed it, but approaches the description and figure of *C. corsac* by Pallas. It has the ears shorter than in *Bengalensis*, the upper fur pale fulvous, and the sides iron-gray or grizzled white.

True foxes. Legs shorter; ears of moderate length.

140. Vulpes montanus.

PEARSON.—BLYTH, Cat. 131.—*V. himalaicus*, OGILBY.—*V. nepalensis*, GRAY, apud HODGSON'S B. M. Collections.*—*Wamoo*, Nepal.—*Loh*, Kashmiri.

* Mr. Blyth appropriates this synonym to *V. flavescens*.

THE HILL FOX.

Descr.—General color pale fulvous, deeper on the sides, and whitish on shoulders; middle of the back dark, inclining to rufous; haunches and tail more gray; ears externally deep velvety black; head mixed with white; a faint eye streak, the cheeks and jowl white; moustaches black; limbs pale fulvous; tail very bushy, white-tipped.

Length, head and body 30 inches; tail 19; height 13½-14.

This is a very handsome animal when in full fur, very like the English fox, but less rufous, paler and more hoary. The fur is exceedingly rich, dense and fine, the longer hairs 2 inches long, the inner fur also long and woolly. It is found throughout the Himalayas, from Nepal at all events to Kashmir, in the central region chiefly. I did not hear of it in Darjeeling, but it may occur in the interior of Sikim, where the climate is drier. In the neighbourhood of Simla it is very common, especially in winter, coming close to houses in search of poultry, and even offal, it is said; and I have seen it at Fagu carry off a fowl in broad daylight. It is also destructive to game, pheasants, partridges, &c. In Kashmir it is very abundant, affecting the cultivated districts in the neighbourhood of hills, and doing much damage to poultry. In 1865, the 7th Hussars had a pack of foxhounds in Kashmir, and killed many of these foxes.

It is stated to breed in April and May, the female having usually three or four cubs.

141. Vulpes pusillus.

BLYTH, Cat. 133.—*V. flavescens*, apud BLYTH, olim.

THE PUNJAB FOX.

Descr.—Similar in color to *V. montanus*, but much smaller, being only a little larger than *Bengalensis*. From the Punjab Salt Range. This may perhaps be only a dwarfed race of the last, caused by a warmer climate, but I have at present followed Blyth in keeping them distinct. The type specimen in the Asiatic Society's Museum, has quite the aspect of *V. montanus*. Dr. Adams suggested that it might be a variety of *V. leucopus*, but it is very distinct from that.

Hodgson in the new edition of his British Museum Collection, has named another species *Vulpes fuliginosus* the "*Thecké*," probably from Tibet or

Sikim, but has given no description. *Vulpes flavescens*, Gray, (*V. montanus* apud Hodgson, olim, and Horsfield,) is a handsome fox from Tibet, of a peculiarly bright light-yellowish fulvous color throughout, with black ears and a superb brush. It is about the size of the English fox, but has the fur finer, longer and denser. It has not I believe occurred on this side of the Himalayas. It is said to be common at Lhassa. Blyth has another species from Afghanistan, formerly referred by him to *V. flavescens*, which he now names *V. Griffithii*, Cat. 134. Beside the well known English fox, *Vulpes fulvus*, there are others in Europe, the *V. melanogaster*, and the Arctic or blue fox, *V. lagopus*, so much esteemed for its fur. There are very many other species generally diffused over both continents.

The Pinnigrada, or *Amphibia*, comprising the Seals and allied animals, are not represented in the Indian seas, being inhabitants of colder regions. Their feet are short and completely enveloped in skin. They have a lengthened body covered with short close fur, a very moveable spine, and are able swimmers. They have no tubercular teeth, all being conic and trenchant, and the true and false molars are alike. Their bones are light and spongy.

They are most abundant in the cold seas of the Arctic and Antarctic regions. The Seals, of which there are several genera, constitute the family *Phocidæ;* and the remarkable Walrus, or sea-horse, *Trichecus rosmarus*, L., is the representative of another family, *Trichecidæ*. Their most natural position would, perhaps, have been following the Otters, between them and the *Felidæ;* but in the present classification they are followed naturally by the Cetaceans.

ORD. CETACEA. The Whale tribe.

Cetæ of some.—*Mutilata*, OWEN.

Anterior feet changed into fins; no posterior extremities. Tail horizontal, flat, continuous with the trunk; no external ears.

Cetaceans are distinguished by the fish-like form of their members, and live in seas and large rivers. They are generally bulky animals, with very large heads, tapering bodies, terminated by a broad tail-fin, which is the principal agent in swimming. It is supported by cartilage only. The head is not separated from the body by a neck. The eye is of very small size, and from the great development of their facial bones, appears in some to be placed nearly in the middle of the body. Their skin is thick and intimately mixed with fat forming the blubber, which serves to preserve the warm temperature of the body in the cold seas they frequent, and at the same time renders them light. Their skin is usually devoid of hair except a few bristles in the fætal state of some, and whiskers in one remarkable genus.

They have spiracles or external nostrils, sometimes on the fore part of the nose, but usually on the top of the head, which can be closed by a conical stopper or valve. The cervical vertebræ are free in some, more or less anchylosed in others. The sternum is short and wide. The ribs are much curved, and very few of them join the sternum. They have no clavicles. The anterior limbs are completely enclosed, forming a fin, but contain the usual bones of the arm of vertebrate animals, sometimes with very numerous phalanges. Two small bones suspended in the flesh near the anus are the only vestiges of posterior extremities. The sacrum is absent, but the first caudal vertebræ are distinguished from the lumbar by the presence of a series of inferior small V-shaped arches.

They have large brains with many and deep convolutions. The arteries are infinitely convoluted, and vast plexures of vessels filled with oxygenated blood occur under the pleura, and between the ribs on each side of the spine. These form a reservoir of oxygenated blood, which supports life whilst their respiration is suspended under water.

The petrous portion of the temporal bone, which contains the internal ear, is separated from the rest of the head. The organ of hearing is of great delicacy. Their sense of smell is little developed. They are either edentulous, or the teeth are of one kind, simple in form, and one set only is developed. (Monophyodont). The stomach has several distinct pouches, usually five. They have several distinct spleens. Many of them have a dorsal fin, which however is only a simple prolongation of skin devoid of any independent movement, and not connected in any way with the vertebræ.

The spiracle, or blowhole, is single or double. This does not serve as an organ of smell, but is used as a respiratory aperture. It has generally been believed that the water taken into the mouth along with their prey is expelled through this aperture in a jet, forming the so called spouting of whales; but of late it is confidently asserted that water is never expelled this way, and that it is simply the moisture of the lungs and air passages expelled along with the expired air which causes the jet or spouting.

The *Cetacea* are divided into the families, *Delphinidæ* or Porpoises, and *Balænidæ*, or Whales, both of which have representatives in the Indian Seas.

Fam. DELPHINIDÆ.

Teeth numerous, conical; nostrils open by a single transverse aperture; head of moderate size; caudal fin notched.

The cranium is broad and high; the nasal passages nearly vertical. The maxillaries are prolonged anteriorly, and also much developed posteriorly, rising anterior to the frontals, over which they are expanded, extending as far as the level of the nasals, which form the summit of the cranium. They have in general no cœcum.

The dolphins, or porpoises, as they are popularly called (the word dolphin being usually restricted to the fish, *Coryphæna*, celebrated for its changeable tints when dying), are found all over the world, inhabiting seas, and many ascending large rivers. They generally associate in flocks or shoals, are very active, swimming and playing near the surface of the sea, and feeding on fishes, crustacea, cuttle-fish, &c. They often accompany ships for miles. There are several genera recognised, one of which is peculiar to the rivers of India.*

Gen. DELPHINUS, Linn.

Char.—Rostrum narrow, of moderate length, continued abruptly from

* Materials for the elucidation of this family as represented in India are very deficient, and I am only able to indicate the names of some. Professor Owen has recently read a paper on those collected by Walter Elliot, on the east coast, describing several new species, but the paper is not yet published. I will introduce, in an Appendix to this volume, the species there described, if published before the work is completed.

the forehead; teeth numerous, slightly recurved, vary from 24 to 60 on each side, both above and below; a median dorsal fin.

142. Delphinus perniger.

ELLIOT apud BLYTH, Cat. 280.

THE BLACK DOLPHIN.

Descr.—26 teeth on each side, above and below, obtuse, slightly curved inwards. Of an uniform shining black above; beneath blackish.

Total length of one 5 feet 4 inches; back to frontal elevation 4 inches; dorsal fin (somewhat posterior) 10¼ inches long, 6 inches high; spread of tail flukes about 14½ inches. This species was taken in the Bay of Bengal and sent to the Museum of the Asiatic Society by Mr. W. Elliot.

143. Delphinus plumbeus.

DUSSUMIER.

THE PLUMBEOUS DOLPHIN.

Descr.—36 teeth on each side in the upper jaw, and 32 in the lower jaw. Of an uniform leaden color, with the lower jaw white. Length of one, 8 feet.

Has been taken on the Malabar coast. Blyth, in his Catalogue, has indicated from the skulls *Delphinus eurynome*, Gray; *Steno frontatus*, Cuvier; *Steno attenuatus*, Gray; and *Neomeris phocænoides* Dussumier, all, from the Bay of Bengal. I shall refer to these in the Appendix.

Gen. PLATANISTA.

Char.—Rostrum very long, compressed, slightly enlarged at the extremity; teeth very numerous, conic and recurved in both jaws, compressed; paddles triangular, fan-shaped; dorsal fin rudimentary; eye minute.

Skull with the maxillary bones bent up in front of the spiracles, forming a vault; the neck long, the cervical vertebræ moveable. Possesses a small cœcum.

This genus is peculiar, as far as known, to India.

144. Platanista gangetica.

Delphinus apud LEBECK.—ROXBURGH, Asiat. Researches, VII., pl. 5.—BLYTH, Cat. 286.—*D. rostratus*, SHAW.—Figd. Ann. Mag. Nat. Hist. 1852, pl. V., &c.—HARDWICKE, Ill. Ind. Zool. fig.—*Susá, Sons, Susá*, H. —*Súsúk* or *Sishúk*, Bengal.—*Sisumar*, Sanscr.

THE GANGETIC PORPOISE.

Descr.—Teeth 28 on each side, 29 below, total 114; one account gives 120. Spiracle linear; aperture of ears small, semi-lunar; eye excessively minute, rudimentary; of a dark plumbous color; when old, with some lighter spots here and there; shining pearl gray when dry.

Length of one 6½ feet; paddle 9 inches by 7; tail 14; eye 1 to 1½ line in diameter. One, 6 feet long had the rostrum 17½ inches long from the gape; whilst another 7 feet long, had the rostrum only 13½ inches. Both these are believed to be females; and Mr. Blyth, Cat. Mammalia, p. 92, note, states that "certain discrepancies of proportion which I had suspected to indicate sexual diversity may yet prove to be of specifical importtance."

This remarkable porpoise is found in the Ganges and its larger tributaries, Jumna, Gogra, &c., up nearly to the hills, most abundant perhaps in the middle portion or lower third; also in the Berampooter. I am not aware of it being found in the Nerbudda, or in any of the large rivers of the South of India. A nearly allied species from the Indus and its tributaries has been discriminated by Blyth. The Gangetic porpoise is very abundant in some localities, large shoals of them may be seen sporting near most of the large towns on the Ganges, rising to the surface to take an inspiration, and dipping down again in a way that is popularly called rolling, and gives an impression of their back being much rounded. I have always found this dolphin most abundant at the junction of rivers with the main body of the Ganges, as it is here that fishes also abound most. I do not think that it ever goes out to sea as conjectured in Erichson's paper, on Dr. Cantor's authority. It feeds on fishes chiefly, also on crustacea, molluscs (cuttle-fish), &c. In one case recorded, some grains of paddy and some small shells alone were found in the stomach; but I should imagine that these came from some bird or animal which the porpoise had picked up. They are rarely taken by fishermen. Two, a male and a female, are recorded by McLelland, to have been killed by the explosion of gunpowder in a wreck in the Hoogly. At Monghyr, a certain caste occasionally catch them; and many are stated to be killed in Dacca by a peculiar tribe called *Garwarus*, who spear them and otters. They eat the flesh and burn the oil, which is also used in rheumatism.

A long account of this animal, with copious anatomical details by Erichson, and translated by Dr. Wallich, is to be found in the number of the "Annals and Magazine of Natural History," quoted above. He considers it most nearly allied to *Hyperoodon*, with relations to the South American genus *Inia*, also found in rivers. The very minute eye, with the very small or almost rudimentary state of the optic nerves, show that this dolphin must be considered to occupy among whales the same place as the mole does among insectivora, and that it seeks its food in places devoid of solar light, owing to the muddy state of the river. It is, however, occasionally found in moderately clear water in the higher parts of the Ganges.

The following species is pronounced by Blyth to be conspicuously distinct.

145. Platanista Indi.

Blyth, Cat. 285.—J. A. S. XXVIII. 493.

THE PORPOISE OF THE INDUS.

Descr.—Larger and more robust than *P. gangetica*, and of a paler color; number of teeth the same, but twice as stout; the depth of the two jaws with the teeth, about their middle, $3\frac{1}{4}$ inches, whilst in *P. gangetica* it is barely $1\frac{3}{4}$ inch.

Length of one 7 feet; skull $20\frac{1}{4}$ inches; greatest width at the zygomata $9\frac{1}{4}$; symphysis of lower jaw 11.

There is a drawing of this porpoise among those of Sir A. Burnes, and there is a skull in the Museum Asiatic Society, Calcutta, presented by the same gentleman, from the river Indus.

Gen. Globicephalus, Lesson.

Char.—Head rounded in front; paddles long, narrow and pointed; teeth few in number, deciduous when old; dorsal fin distinct: intermaxillaries broad.

146. Globicephalus indicus.

BLYTH, Cat. 274.—J. A. S. XIX. 426.—XXI. 358.

THE INDIAN CA'ING WHALE.

Descr.—Of an uniform leaden black color, slightly paler beneath; similar in form and size to *G. deductor* of European seas, but the teeth fewer and larger than in that species, being 6 or 7 above, 7 or 8 beneath.

Length of an adult male 14 feet 2 inches; flippers 2 feet; dorsal fin 2¼ feet long, 11 inches high; breadth of tail flukes 3 feet.

A shoal (*schule* or *school* of mariners) of this species was carried by a current into the Salt-water lake, near Calcutta in July 1852, where Blyth saw them, and procured two specimens. They were floundering about in all directions in the shallow water, and groaning painfully. He was near enough to decide that when spouting, no jet of water was thrown up, only aqueous particles as from a wet syringe; this was whilst the spiracle was above water.

Another of this species was killed in the Hoogly near Serampore, about the same time of year.

There are very many species of this family now described, distributed in numerous genera. One of the most remarkable is the *Narwhal*, or Sea-unicorn, *Monodon monoceros*, L., the long ivory tusk of which is grooved spirally and directed forwards. The germs of two tusks exist, but only one is developed, usually the left.

The Cachalots, or Sperm whales, constitute the sub-family *Catodontinæ*. They have an enormous head with numerous teeth in the lower jaw, the upper teeth being concealed in the gums. The upper part of their huge heads is cellular, and the cavities are filled with a fatty substance, becoming hard when cool, known as spermaceti, for which these whales are chiefly hunted. The substance called ambergris is a concretion found in their intestines.

Blyth, under *Catodon macrocephalus*, remarks, "occasionally hunted at the entrance of the Bay of Bengal, within sight of Ceylon;" species, doubtful however as identical with that inhabiting the Northern Seas. I see that Professor Owen in the paper referred to (page 156), alludes to a new species of this family from Mr. Elliot's collection, which is probably the one referred to. He names it *Physeter (Euphysetes) simus*.

Fam. Balænidæ.

Head enormous; spiracle double; no teeth, but transverse horny laminæ adhering to the upper jaw, forming the *baleen* or whalebone. Conical teeth are found in the fætal state. They possess a cœcum.

Whales are the largest of all known animals, some being nearly 100 feet in length. They produce one young at a birth, which they suckle for a considerable time. Their mammæ are pudendal. They are often found in large shoals sporting on the surface of the ocean. They are most abundant in high latitudes, both arctic and antarctic. . They feed on small fish, cuttle-fish, other mollusca, and small crustacea. The whalebone or baleen, sometimes, in large whales, consisting of six hundred to eight hundred plates 12 to 15 feet long, forms a regular sieve through which the animal strains his food from the vast gulps of water he takes in whilst feeding. The lower jaw has neither teeth nor baleen, but is furnished with fleshy lips.

The skull is characterized by the great predominance of the facial over the cranial portions, and the curvature of the right of the lower jaw, which extend outwards in a convex sweep far beyond the sides of the upper maxilla, and converge to the symphysis, but do not unite. The only Indian species of the family, belongs to a group possessing a dorsal fin, and hence called Finner, Finback, Fin-whale, &c.; also Pike-whale, Rorqual.

Gen. Balænoptera, Lacépede.

Char.—Those of the family, but with an adipose fin on the back; belly marked by longitudinal grooves. Head about one-fourth of total length.

They feed on small fishes, and are found in all seas, tropical as well as cold. The largest animals of the family belong to this genus.

147. Balænoptera indica.

Blyth, J. A. S. XXVIII. 488.—Cat. 288.

The Indian Fin-whale.

Descr.—A whale supposed to be of this species was thrown ashore on the Chittagong coast, said to be 90 feet long and 42 in circumference. Another was cast up dead at Amherst islet, 84 feet in length. Of this last the rami of the lower jaw and a few other bones are now in the

Museum Asiatic Society, Calcutta, and on these remains Blyth founded this species. The length of each ramus is close on 21 feet. It tapers very gradually and evenly, and is remarkably slender for a *Balænoptera*. The radius is $38\frac{3}{4}$ inches long.

Very large whales, most probably of this species, have been stranded near Kurachee; on the Malabar coast (one of which was said to be 100 feet long; and another 90 feet, which got among the reefs off Quilon in Travancore); also on Ceylon, and they are often captured off that island. The Maldives and Seychelles are the head-quarters of the whalers who seek these whales, but they are not so much sought after as the right-whales *(Balæna)*, which yield much more blubber. *Balænoptera boops*, L., is the great Rorqual, and *B. musculus*, L., the Lesser Rorqual, are both found in European seas.

The true *Balænæ* have a still larger head, about one-third the length of the whole body, and have no dorsal fin. They are all from arctic or antarctic seas. *Balæna mysticetus*, the Greenland whale, is the best known. It seldom attains 70 feet in length, and *B. japonica* is the only other one from Northern Seas, but there are at least two from the South, *B. australis* and *B. antarctica*.

Ord. RODENTIA.

Syn. *Glires* of some.

Two incisors only in each jaw, large, incurved, and without roots. No canines. Molars separated from the incisors by an interval, usually few in number, varying from two to six on each side, rarely more than four. Feet unguiculate, generally with five toes.

The so called incisors are, however, by most anatomists considered the representative of canine teeth, the incisors being obliterated except in hares, which have a pair of incisors behind the upper gnawing teeth.*

The Rodents or Gnawers are chiefly characterized by the remarkable conformation of their teeth. Their quasi-incisors have a plate of enamel only in front, often colored yellow or brownish; behind this the anterior plate of true *dentine* is also harder than the posterior layer, though not so hard as the enamel. From this structure a sharp edge is effected by the constant attrition, the teeth acquiring a chisel-shape with the slope backwards. The pulp being persistent, these teeth are always growing, and if from any cause the upper tooth is displaced or lost, its antagonist in the lower jaw has been known to grow on, enter the skull, and cause death. The molars have flat crowns, and the enamelled eminences, which are always transverse, vary from thin lines to blunt tubercles, according as their diet varies from frugivorous to omnivorous. The condyle of the lower jaw is longitudinal, and slides backwards and forwards, and this motion acting on the peculiar chisel-shaped incisors, serves to reduce the hardest substances by a constant filing or gnawing. The orbits are not separated from the temporal fossæ. The intermaxillaries are enormously developed to hold their large incisors, and the maxillaries are therefore pushed far backwards. The nasal bones are greatly elongated. Some possess clavicles, other have none. The os magnum of the carpus is often divided into two, as in some monkeys. The pelvis resembles that of *Carnivora.* The fibula is situated behind the tibia, and consolidated with it in the lower portion in many. The os calcis is much developed.

The stomach is usually simple or in two distinct pouches ; the intestinal canal is very long, and pretty even in diameter; and the cœcum is generally much developed ; and is only absent in one group. The liver is large,

* I shall continue to call these teeth the incisors, or quasi-incisors. Blyth has lately named them the rodential tusks.

and a gall-bladder generally present, but deficient in some rats; and the pancreas is also large. The brain is small, either tapering in front as in birds, or somewhat circular and smooth, and without convolutions. The cerebellum is scarcely overlapped by the cerebrum.

There is no scrotum in most of the rodentia, but the testes increase much in size in the breeding season, and at that time pass into a sort of temporary scrotum. Most possess a bone in the corpus cavernosum of the penis. The uterus has two horns, and in some indeed is actually double.

The rodents are mostly animals of small size, the Capybara, the Porcupines, and the Beavers, being the giants of the order. Their eyes are directed sideways. The opening of the mouth is small, and many have cheek-pouches. The ears are moderate or large. Their limbs are usually short, the hind extremity in many much larger than the anterior. They are usually clad with hair, in a few with bristles or spines. The tail varies much in size, is sometimes hairy, at others naked or scaly. They live chiefly on vegetable substances, often on hard nuts, roots, the bark of trees, &c.; and many are nocturnal in their habits. Many of them build artificial nests, and a few manifest a constructive instinct in association; whilst others are remarkable for their migrations. They are very prolific, often producing several litters in the year, and the young quickly attaining maturity. Many hybernate like reptiles. In many of their anatomical features, as well as in their habits, we are reminded of birds, and they manifest a decided inferiority of type. *Cheiromys*, a Lemurian form already alluded to, is the only animal that possesses teeth similar to the rodents, with which it was classed by some. Blyth considers that "perhaps the nearest affinity of the *Rodentia*, is with the Elephant among the *Pachydermata*."*

The division of the rodents into groups is attended with some difficulties, and various classifications have been proposed. I shall here group the Indian rodents in four families—*Sciuridæ*, squirrells; *Muridæ*, rats; *Hystricidæ*, porcupines; and *Leporidæ*, hares; which, indeed, are considered by some to embrace the whole of the order; to which has recently been added the *Saccomyidæ*, or pouched rats, † whilst many systematists make separate families of the dormice, *Myoxidæ;* jerboas, *Dipodidæ;* voles, *Arvicolidæ;* mole-rats, *Aspalacidæ* and *Bathyergidæ;*

* Cuvier's Animal Kingdom. Transl. p. 109. † *Vide* Sclater, Quarterly Jour. Science, October 1865, p. 617.

all included in the MURIDÆ; and the *Caviadæ*, *Octodontidæ*, and *Hydrochæridæ*, belonging to the HYSTRICIDÆ.

The two first families possess clavicles, and have the projecting angle of the lower jaw subquadrate.

Fam. SCIURIDÆ, Squirrels.

Quasi-incisors smooth, compressed; molars usually $\frac{5-5}{4-4}$ or $\frac{4-4}{4-4}$; enamelled continuously, or complex, and furnished with roots. Feet either all pentadactylous, or the fore-feet with four toes and a thumb-wart or tubercle. Tail typically long, bushy; clavicles perfect.

The squirrels form a well marked group of elegant animals, mostly with arboreal habits, and widely distributed both in the old and new world. One group only is quite terrestrial, the marmots. The additional molar of the upper jaw is early deciduous. The most striking feature of the skull of the squirrels is the distinct post-orbital process; and the palate is larger than in other rodents. The molars are variously tubercled, some with blunt, others with sharp points. Of five well marked generic groups, three occur within our province; one however only as an outlier from the central Asian plateau.

Gen. SCIURUS, Linn.

Char.—Præmolars $\frac{2-2}{1-1}$; molars $\frac{3-3}{3-3}$; quasi-incisors smooth in front, brown or orange colored, the lower ones compressed, acute; fore-feet with only four toes, and a tubercle on the site of the thumb; claws compressed, incurved; tail very long, bushy, the hairs directed more or less laterally.

Squirrels have a large head, and prominent eyes, a large body, and moderately long limbs. They are mostly quite arboreal in their habits, exceedingly active and lively, feeding on buds, fruit, nuts, and other vegetable substances; and building a large rude nest of leaves, grass, &c. They hold up their food to their mouth between the two thumb-tubercles. They are found over both continents, most rare in the Neotropical region.

There are three well marked groups in India, distinguished by size, coloration, and habits.

1st group. Large squirrels.

These are squirrels of very large size, rich coloration, and more or less pencilled ears. They are peculiar to South-eastern Asia, including the Archipelago as far as Borneo, attaining their maximum in India. Of these Blyth, though retaining them as species, remarks in a foot note, Cat. Mammal, p. 98, "It is difficult to conceive of the whole series as other than permanent varieties of one species."* There are to two or three nearly allied species or races inhabiting the peninsula of India, wherever there are large and lofty forests, but the specific distinctions and the exact geographic limits of each yet require much investigation.

148. Sciurus malabaricus.

SCHINZ.—*S. maximus*, apud BLYTH, Cat. 307.—HORSFIELD, Cat. 209.—*Jungli gilheri*, H.

THE MALABAR SQUIRREL.

Descr.—Ears, nape, back of neck, the back and sides of the body, bright maroon chesnut; the posterior part of the back, rump, and upper portion of all the limbs, and the tail, black; forehead and interocular regions brownish; muzzle and cheeks rufous; neck, breast, and lower parts dingy-yellow; feet rufous in front, yellow internally; ears small, rounded, very hairy.

Length, head and body 16 to 18 inches; tail with the hair 20–21.

This race inhabits the southern portions of Malabar, the Wynaad, slopes of the Neelgherries, Travancore, &c., &c.

149. Sciurus maximus.

SCHREBER.—ELLIOT, Cat. 43.—*Sc.* No. 308, BLYTH, Cat. (sine nomine). —*Kát berrál*, Bengal.—*Kondeng* of Coles.—*Karrát*. Hindí.—*Rasú* and *Ratuphar*, at Monghyr.—*Bet-údatá*, Tel.—*Per-warsti* of Gonds.

THE CENTRAL INDIAN RED SQUIRREL.

Descr.—Similar to the last, but there is never any black on the croup or thighs, and less on the fore limbs; the tail more or less black or deep maroon above, usually with a pale yellowish tip; the under parts are more or less deeply colored.

* Theoretically I quite agree with Blyth, but practically we must distinguish them as species, as indeed he himself does; and the same remark might be applied with more or less reason to many other groups of animals.

About the same size as the last. This race inhabits Central India, whence often brought alive to Calcutta. I have seen it in the forests at the foot of the Puchmurri hills, near Seonee, and in the vast jungles of Bustar, where it is very abundant; also in Goomsoor.

Blyth remarks that it is very constant to its particular type of coloration, "apparently never varying."

150. Sciurus Elphinstonei.

SYKES, Cat.—*S. bombayanus*, apud SCHINZ.—ELLIOT, Cat. 43, var.—*Shekra*, Mahr. of the Ghâts.—*Kés annalú*, Can. of the Halapyks.

THE BOMBAY RED SQUIRREL.

Descr.—Ears and the whole upper surface of the body, and halfway down the tail, outside the hind legs, and halfway down the fore legs outside, of an uniform rich reddish chesnut; the whole under surface of the body from the chin to the vent, inside of the limbs and lower part of the forelegs, crown of head, cheeks and posterior half of the tail, of a fine reddish-white, the two colors being separated by a defined line, and not merging into each other; feet light red; forehead and nose reddish-brown, with some white hairs intermixed. Ears tufted.

Length of one, head and body 20 inches; tail 18.

The Bombay red squirrel is found in the northern portion of the Western Ghâts, extending into north Malabar. It is probably the species found on the Mahableshwar hills. Mr. Elliot records *S. maximus* as being the species of the forest of the Southern Mahratta country, but alludes to this as a variety found in the Ghâts.

These three well marked races or species have similar habits, dwelling in lofty forests, and making a large nest near the top of the tallest trees. Their voice is a loud quickly-repeated cry, which Sykes syllabizes as *chook-chook-chook.* Many are taken young and brought to Calcutta and other large towns for sale, and they become very tame. They are awkward in their gait on the ground, but most active on trees, jumping from bough to bough with amazing agility. I am unable to define the geographic limits of each race more than what I have noted under the species. Many years ago I saw a large colony of one of these races in a wood near Kotagherry, on the Neelgherries, which was perhaps *S. malabaricus;* but I have an impression that it might have been *S. macrourus*, or *S. tennantii.*

151. Sciurus macruroides.

HODGSON.—*S. bicolor*, var. *indica*, HORSFIELD, Cat. 204.—BLYTH, Cat. 309.—*S. giganteus*, MCLELLAND.—*Shingsham*, Bhot.—*Lé-hyúk*, Lepch.

THE BLACK HILL SQUIRREL.

Descr.—Uniform dark blackish-brown or black above, beneath and round the lower part of the limbs fulvous white; posterior limbs wholly black externally, and the anterior ones black behind, and more or less so externally; a black cheek-band; cheeks fulvous-gray with a large triangular patch; a rusty-red spot between the ears, which are sometimes pretty densely tufted.

Length, head and body 15 inches; tail with the hair 16.

The fur is more glossy and less wavy than in *S. macrourus.* The pelage is sometimes blanched and rusty on the back towards the rump; and, in the young, it is said to be always thin and pale on the croup.

I have here, with Hodgson, considered the south-east Himalayan squirrel, with its well-clad ears, as distinct from the Malayan race which has the ear-conch almost nude. It is found in the south-east Himalayas, Nepal and Sikim, also in the hill regions of Assam and Burmah. Near Darjeeling I found it at about 5,000 feet of elevation, but by no means common. It has been stated to occur in Southern India; and a well marked race or species *S. tennantii*, is found at high elevations in Ceylon. This may have been the one observed by me near Kotagherry. The nearly allied *S. bicolor* is found in the Malayan peninsula, Sumatra, &c. It is *S. affinis* of Raffles, *S. aureiventris*, Is. Geoffroy.

152. Sciurus macrourus.

FORSTER.—BLYTH, Cat. 313.—HORSFIELD, Cat. 211.—HARDWICKE, Ill. Ind. Zool. 2, 19.—*S. ceylonensis*, BODDAERT.—Figd. PENNANT'S Indian Zoology.

THE GRIZZLED HILL SQUIRREL.

Descr.—Head and neck, basal half of tail, and limbs externally, dull maroon black, much grizzled with white, especially on the haunches, sides, croup and tail, the apical end of which is brown with a whitish grizzle; lips, cheeks, neck in front and on the sides, belly, and limbs internally, yellow or yellowish white. Ears ovate, acuminate, with short hair, not tufted, or whitish externally with a very small black tuft.

Length, head and body 12 to 13 inches; tail 12, or with the hair 13½.

The fur is coarse, slightly waved, and varies from maroon-black to rufous brown, and the hairs are often grizzled and tipped white and yellow. In many specimens the anterior half is black or nearly so, and the posterior parts light brown. One that was sent to me from Travancore was of a grizzled yellow-brown color above, slightly darker on the top of the head, beneath dirty straw color, the toes blackish-brown.

Length 11 inches; tail 10.

Blyth mentions a ruddy-white or whitish isabelline variety from Ceylon.

This squirrel is stated to have been sent from the jungles of Mysore and the Neelgherries. I have only had it myself from Travancore, and cannot speak with certainty of its geographic limits.

S. ephippium, S. Müller, from Borneo, is another species of this division.

The next group consists of squirrels of medium size, with grizzled fur. They are peculiar to South-eastern Asia and its islands, and, as Blyth remarks, are extraordinarily developed in the Indo-Chinese countries and Malayan peninsula, where the species, or permanent races, would seem to be almost endless, differing more or less in size and coloring. In India they are confined to the south-east Himalayas, and the provinces north-east of Bengal.

153. Sciurus lokriah.

HODGSON.—BLYTH, Cat. 327.—*S. subflaviventris*, MCLELLAND.—*Lokria*, Nepal—*Zhámo*, Bhot.—*Killi* or *Kalli tingdong*, Lepch.

THE ORANGE-BELLIED GRAY SQUIRREL.

Descr.—Above dark grizzled olive-brown, the hairs tipped with orange color; beneath and thighs deep orange yellow; tail concolorous with the body above, ferruginous beneath, distichous, flattened, rather broad, with a double margin of black and hoary.

Length, head and body about 8 inches; tail 6½ to 8 (with the hair).

154. Sciurus lokrioides.

HODGSON.—BLYTH, Cat. 328.—*S. lokriah*, apud GRAY.

THE HOARY-BELLIED GRAY SQUIRREL.

Descr.—Very similar to the last, lower parts rufous-hoary, instead of orange; thighs usually concolorous with body above; tail narrower and devoid of the marginal bands; upper parts not so dark, with less of the rufescent tinge observable in *S. lokriah;* thighs occasionally tinged with rufo-ferruginous. Of the same size as the last.

This species is nearly allied to *S. assamensis*, McLelland, but differs in wanting the black tip to the tail, and in some other points of coloration.

These two squirrels, *lokriah* and *lokrioides*, are not distinguished from each other by the natives of Sikim, and there is a great resemblance between them. *S. lokriah*, I think, ascends to a higher elevation than the other species. They are both found in the south-eastern Himalayas, Nepal, Sikim, and Bhotan, the former extending into the hill regions of Assam and Arrakan. *S. lokrioides* has been considered by some identical with *assamensis*, which occurs in the neighbourhood of Dacca, Sylhet, &c. About Darjeeling neither are very abundant in individuals. Most are seen in the autumn when the chesnuts ripen, of which they are very fond.

Of this group, *Sciurus ferrugineus*, F. Cuvier, *S. erythræus*, Pallas; *S. erythrogaster*, Blyth; *S. hyperythrus*, Blyth; *S. chrysonotus*, Blyth; *S. hyperythrus*, Is. Geoffroy; *S. Phayrei*, Blyth; *S. Blanfordi*, Blyth, and *S. atrodorsalis*, Gray, inhabit various localities, from the Khasya hills to Tenasserim; and there are several others from the Malayan peninsula and islands.

The next group is that of the striped squirrels, which, from the best known species, *S. palmarum*, has been named by some the *Palmists.* They are of small size, and affect the ground more than any other of the Indian squirrels, and in this, as in general appearance, nearly approach the group of ground squirrels called *Tamias.*

155. Sciurus palmarum.

GMELIN.—BLYTH, Cat. 339.—ELLIOT, Cat. 42.—*S. penicillatus*, LEACH, Zool. Misc. fig.—*Gilheri*, H.—*Berál*, also *Lakki*, Bengal.—*Kharri*, Mahr.—*Alalu*, Can.—*Vodata*, Tel.—*Urta* of Waddurs.

THE COMMON STRIPED SQUIRREL.

Descr.—Above dusky greenish-gray with three yellowish-white stripes along the whole length of the back, and two fainter lines on each side; beneath whitish; tail with the hairs variegated with red and black; ears rounded.

Length about 13 to 14 inches, of which the tail is nearly half.

This well known little squirrel is common throughout the whole peninsula of India, except in some parts of Malabar, and the north-eastern part of Bengal; and from its familiarity and shrill voice is quite a pest at times, especially to invalids. It does not occur out of India, nor in Ceylon. It enters houses freely, picking up crumbs, grains of rice, &c., and, indeed, often has its permanent abode in bungalows and out-houses, building its nest on the eaves, rafters, and in the thatch. It resorts much to the ground for its food, and it is often carried off by the dwarf-eagle, *Aguila pennata*, which stoops on it when thus employed. It usually constructs a bulky nest of grass, wool, cotton, &c., which it takes no pains to conceal among the branches of trees, or in the eaves of houses, on cornices, &c. Why it was named the "palm squirrel" has often puzzled the Indian naturalist, for though occasionally seen on palm trees it is so exceedingly rarely. The female has from two to four young at a birth. Mr. Blyth has noticed that the call of this squirrel, but more particularly that of the next closely-allied one, reminded him of the chirping of birds, which, says he, is also noticed of the allied form *Tamias*.

This squirrel is easily caught in a common rat trap. If taken when young it becomes very tame. Great numbers used to be taken at Trichinopoly, and the skins very nicely tanned for sale to Europeans. An Indian legend runs that when Hunamán was crossing the Ganges, it was bridged over by all the animals. A small gap remained which was filled by this squirrel, and when Hunaman passed over, he placed his hand on the squirrel's back, and the marks of his five fingers remained ever since on its back. When alarmed the hairs of its tail are erected at right angles, like a bottle brush.

Gray has applied the synonym of *S. penicillatus* to the next species but it certainly appertains to this one, the type having been taken in a house in Madras.

156. Sciurus tristriatus.

WATERHOUSE, P. Z. S. 1839.—*S. palmarum*, var. b., dark variety, ELLIOT, Cat. 42.—BLYTH, Cat. 340.—*S. brodiei*, and *S. kelaarti* LAYARD.

THE JUNGLE STRIPED SQUIRREL.

Descr.—Very similar to the last, but generally darker, the face, forehead, back and haunches, more or less tinged with rusty-red, or reddish brown; the stripes small, narrower than in the common one, and not extending the whole length of the back; tail beneath distinctly rusty; sides darker than in *palmarum*.

Length, head and body 7½ inches; tail 7½.

Mr. Blyth says he observed no difference in size. I have always found this species slightly larger and conspicuously heavier than *palmarum*.

This species is so exceedingly similar to the last that many would only look on it as a slight variety, but it differs very remarkably in its voice, which is much less shrill, and indeed quite different in character. This was first noticed by Mr. Blyth, and I can fully confirm his statement. It is found in most of the forest districts of India, from Midnapore to the extreme south and Ceylon, where it quite replaces *S. palmarum*, as indeed it does in some parts of Malabar. I have not seen specimens from the Eastern Ghâts, nor did I notice it in the Bustar jungles. Mr. Blyth remarks that specimens from Midnapore quite resemble others from Ceylon. Although generally, as Mr. Blyth remarks, the tendency of this species is to avoid human habitations as much as that of the other is to affect them, yet at Tellicherry, where I resided for some time, and at other stations on the Malabar coast, where the whole country is densely wooded, it does occasionally enter and even take up its abode in houses. A pair frequented my own house at Tellicherry, but they were much more shy than their ally, and always endeavored to shun observation.

With reference to the very great similarity of these two squirrels, Mr. Blyth well remarks, "the slight differences of form and color between these two species so distinct in their voice and habits, should indicate the the extreme caution necessary ere we conclude other allied races to be merely varieties of the same from their general similarity of size and coloring."

157. Sciurus Layardi.

BLYTH, Cat. 341.—J. A. S. XVIII. 600.

THE TRAVANCORE STRIPED SQUIRREL.

Descr.—Much darker than the last, being of a dark dingy olive color with a tinge of ashy; middle of back, black with a short yellowish streak in the middle and a faint and shorter streak on each side; tail tipped black, rusty in the middle; lower parts somewhat ferruginous.

Size of the last or a trifle larger.

This well marked race is found in the mountains of Travancore, and in Ceylon. I have had skins from the former locality, but know nothing peculiar in its habits, nor is its call recorded.

158. Sciurus sublineatus.

WATERHOUSE, P. Z. S. 1838.—BLYTH, Cat. 342.—*Sc. delesserti*, GERVAIS, Mag. de Zool. 1842, and Zool. Voyage de DELESSERT, with figure.

THE NEELGHERRY STRIPED SQUIRREL.

Descr.—Of a dark grizzled olive color, tinged with tawny above, and with three pale lines alternating with four dark ones on the back and croup, the outer dark lines narrower and somewhat less dark than the others; beneath lighter, more mixed with tawny; tail grizzled dusky olive and ferruginous. Fur remarkably dense, close and soft.

Length, head and body 5½ to 6 inches; tail 6.

I first procured this small squirrel on the Neelgherries in the dense woods there; where, however it is by no means common. I have since killed it in Wynaad and Coorg, but only at considerable elevations. It has been sent to Mr. Blyth from the mountains of Travancore, and is also found in Ceylon, at Newera-ellia, and other localities. Blyth remarks that this squirrel is somewhat allied to *S. insignis*, Horsfield, from Java.

159. Sciurus McClellandi.

HORSFIELD, P. Z. S. 1839.—BLYTH, Cat. 344.—Perhaps *Sc.* No. 135, HODGSON, New edit. British Mus. Collection, called in the preface *S. chikhura ?* olim *S. Pembertoni*, BLYTH.—*Kalli Gangdin*, Lepch.

THE SMALL HIMALAYAN SQUIRREL.

Descr.—General hue dull brownish-fulvous grizzled with black; under parts whitish-brown; a black stripe on the nose anterior to the whiskers; a black mesial stripe from near the shoulders to the croup, and a narrow lateral black stripe, with a broader fulvous one external to it from the sides of the neck; tail grizzled dark above, fulvous beneath; ears small, black-edged, fulvous-white within, and with a small white tuft externally.

Length, head and body 5 inches; tail 4.

This little squirrel is found in Sikim, Bhotan and the hill ranges of Assam, the Khasya hills, &c. I procured several in the neighbourhood of Darjeeling, at an elevation of from 4,000 to 6,000 feet chiefly, but it is not abundant. It does not appear to extend to Nepal.

S. Barbei, Blyth, from Tenasserim, is nearly allied to this, but more brightly colored; and *S. plantani*, Horsfield, from Java, is another similar species. *S. berdmorei*, Blyth, from Mergui, is the representative of *S. palmarum*.

Sc. europæus, L., the European squirrel, is found in Northern and Central Asia, and a skin from Tibet, received by Mr. Hodgson, was named by him *Mustela calotes*. Adams states that he thinks he observed it in Kashmir, but did not obtain a specimen. *Rhinosciurus tupaioides*, Gray. (*S. laticaudatus* of S. Müller), is a peculiar long-snouted squirrel of Malayana; and a group of African squirrels have been named *Xerus* by Ehrenberg, *Geosciurus*, by Dr. A. Smith.

The next group is that of the Flying-squirrels.

These are divided into two smaller groups, one of large size, and with the tail round and hairy throughout, *Pteromys;* the other of smaller size with the tail flat, and the hairs distichous, *Sciuropterus*.

Gen. PTEROMYS, Cuvier.

Char.—Dental formula as in *Sciurus;* molars complex, the first upper ones very small, placed inside the second. Feet as in *Sciurus*. The skin of the flanks extended between the fore and hind feet, forming when expanded a wide parachute; tail rounded, hairy all round, as long as the body or longer.

They have long osseous or cartilaginous appendages to the feet, which serve to support the lateral membrane. This genus is restricted to south-east Asia and the islands of Malayana. There are three species in our province, one in the peninsula, the other two, respectively, from the north-west and south-east Himalayas.

160. Pteromys petaurista.

PALLAS.—BLYTH, Cat. 291.—*P. philippensis*, apud ELLIOT, Cat. 44.—

P. oral, Tickell, Calc. J. N. H. 2, pl. XI.—*Orál* of the Coles.—*Pakya*, Mahr. of Ghâts.—*Parachaten*, Mal. (Buch. Hamilton).

The Brown Flying-squirrel.

Descr.—Upper parts dusky-maroon black grizzled with white, the membrane and limbs above somewhat brighter and more rufous; the feet, the muzzle, and round the eyes, and terminal half of the tail, dark brown or black, the last sometimes with a little white towards the tip; under parts dingy brownish-gray or nearly white. Mr. Elliot calls its upper color a beautiful gray, caused by the intermixture of black with white and dusky hairs. The male is distinguished by an irregular patch of rufous on the sides of the neck, which in the female is a sort of pale fawn.

Length, head and body 20 inches; tail 21; breadth 24.

The female has six mammæ, two pectoral, and four ventral.

This flying squirrel is found throughout the peninsula of India wherever there are extensive lofty forests. I have observed it in Malabar, in Travancore, where very abundant; in the forest of Bustar in Central India, and in the Vindhian mountains, near Mhow; and I have seen specimens from the Northern Circars. It also extends from the Midnapore jungles through great part of Central India. It is found in Ceylon. It frequents the loftiest trees in the thickest parts of the forests, and is quite nocturnal in its habits, usually making its appearance when quite dusk. The natives discover its whereabouts by noting the droppings beneath the trees it frequents. It is said to keep in holes of trees during the day, and breeds in the same places. In the Wynaad many are killed, and a few captured alive by the Coorumbars, a jungle race of aborigines who are usually employed to fell the forest trees in clearing for coffee; and I have had several sent to me alive, caught in this way, but could not keep them for any time. It lives chiefly on fruits of various kinds, also on bark, shoots, &c.; and Tickell says, "occasionally on beetles and the larvæ of insects." Mr. Elliot says, "it is very gentle, timid, and may be tamed, but from its delicacy is difficult to preserve."

Tickell also states, that "when taken young it becomes a most engaging pet. It can be reared on goat's or cow's milk, and in about three weeks will begin to nibble fruit of any kind. During the day it sleeps much, either sitting with its back bent into a circle, and its head thrust down to its belly, or lying on its back with the legs and parachute extended, a position it is fond of in sultry weather. During the night time it is incessantly on the move. In spite of its flying paraphernalia the oral is by no means so agile as other squirrels; its pace on the ground is a hobbling or hopping kind of gallop, nor is it particularly nimble even in trees, the parachute flapping about and impeding its movements in moving from branch to branch. In its wild state it scrambles in this manner all over a tree, and when wishing to pass on to another at some distance, does not descend to the ground, but leaping from the top-most branches sails through the air by means of the parachute, and reaches the lower part or trunk of the adjacent tree. These leaps or flights can be extended, I am told, to ten yards or upwards, always of course in a diagonal and lowering direction. I myself have never witnessed them."

I have on several occasions seen both this species and the next take flights, and on one occasion an individual of the present species went over a distance, from tree to tree, of above sixty yards. Of course it was very close to the ground when it neared the tree, and the last few feet of its flight were slightly upwards, which I have also noticed at other times.

"The voice of the oral," says Tickell, "is seldom heard. It is a weak, low, soft monotone, quickly repeated, so low that in the same room you require to listen attentively to distinguish it. It is to the Koles a sound ominous of domestic affliction. When angry the oral seldom bites, but scratches with it fore-claws, grunting at the same time like a guinea-pig." The fur of this species is, when in good order, very beautiful and soft, and is highly prized.

161. Pteromys inornatus.

IS. GEOFFROY, Zool. Voyage de JACQUEMONT, pl. IV.—BLYTH, Cat. 293.—*P. albiventer*, GRAY?—*Rusi gugar*, Kashmiri, *i. e.*, the Flying-rat.

THE WHITE-BELLIED FLYING-SQUIRREL.

Descr.—Above grizzled reddish-brown, or dark gray with a rufous tinge and white speckled, the sides, parachute, and outer edge of limbs darker, nearly maroon red; the head, neck and breast light grayish-rufous, cheeks gray; chin and throat white; lower parts from the breast white, faintly tinged with rufous on the belly, and more strongly on the lower surface of the parachute, the posterior outer edge of which has a border of grayish-white; a band across the nose, orbits, whiskers and feet black, tail round, bushy, brownish-rufous, tip nearly black.

Length of one, head and body 14 inches; tail 16.

This flying squirrel is found throughout the north-west Himalayas, from Kashmir to Kumaon, usually at a considerable elevation, from 6,000 to 10,000 feet, lower in winter; and in Kashmir it is stated to hybernate during the season. It is often killed near Simla and Landour.

162. Pteromys magnificus.

HODGSON.—BLYTH, Cat., page 95.—*P. chrysothryx*, HODGSON.—*Sciuroptirus nobilis*, GRAY (variety).—*Biyom*, Lepch.

THE RED-BELLIED FLYING-SQUIRREL.

Descr.—Above dark chesnut, or ochreous-chesnut mixed with black, in some with a golden-yellow mesial line, and an external border of the same; shoulders and thighs golden-yellow or red; all the lower parts orange or golden red, ochreous on the limbs and on the margin of the parachute; tail somewhat depressed, slightly paler than the back, tipped black for about two inches; a black zone round the eyes, and mystaceal region also black, between which the nose is pale golden color; chin pale with a black triangular spot; ears red. The pelage thick, soft and glossy.

Length of one, head and body 16 inches; tail 22; of another, head and body, 15; tail 18.

This splendid flying-squirrel is found in the south-east Himalayas, from Nepal to Bhotan, and also in the Khasya hills, and hill ranges of Assam. It is not very uncommon near Darjeeling, and used to be more so before the station was so denuded of its fine trees. It frequents the zone from 6,000 to 9,000 feet or so, and feeds chiefly on acorns, chesnuts, and other hard fruit; also on young leaves and shoots.

In one examined, the intestinal canal was 14 feet long, and the cœcum 20 inches, very capacious and sacculated.

Various other species are found in the Indian region, viz., *Pteromys cineraceus*, Blyth, from Burmah; *P. nitidus*, Geoffroy; from the Malayan peninsula; *P. elegans*, S. Müller, from Java; *P. philippensis*, Gray, from the Philippines, &c., &c.

Gen. SCIUROPTERUS, F. Cuvier.

Char.—Tail shorter than the body, flat, and the hairs more or less distichous; molar teeth tuberculated. Usually of smaller size, otherwise as in *Pteromys*.

163. Sciuropterus caniceps.

GRAY, Ann. Mag. Nat. Hist. X. 262.—BLYTH, Cat. 296.—*Pteromys senex*, HODGSON.—*Biyom chimbo*, Lepch.

THE GREY-HEADED FLYING-SQUIRREL.

Descr.—Entire head iron-gray; orbits and base of ears deep orange fulvous; whole body above, with parachute and tail, a mixture of blackish and golden yellow; limbs deep orange-ochreous; margin of parachute albescent; beneath, the neck whitish, rest of the lower parts pale orange-red; tip of tail black; ears nearly nude; tail sub-distichous.

Length of one, head and body 14 inches; tail with the hair 16½.

This species by its long and only slightly distichous tail, its large size, and coloration, is quite a link between *Sciuropterus* and *Pteromys*, and I would have preferred classing it with the latter, but for the sake of uniformity with Blyth's Catalogue have placed it as the first of the former group. The pelage is not so fine as in true *Pteromys*.

It has been found in Nepal and Sikim. I got one or two specimens only near Darjeeling and it was said to frequent a somewhat lower zone than *P. magnificus*, viz., from about 4,000 to 6,000 feet.

Horsfield, in his Catalogue of Mammalia, has *Pteromys Pearsoni*, Gray, like *caniceps*, about one third smaller, paler above and below, head colored like the back, no orange spot over the eye or at base of ears; tail flatter and broader. From Darjeeling. I fancy that this must be the young of *S. caniceps*, or it may be *S. villosus*, q. v. Blyth does not notice it in his Catalogue.

Sc. Layardi, Blyth, from Ceylon, is stated to be somewhat allied to *S. caniceps*.

164. Sciuropterus fimbriatus.

GRAY, Mag. Nat. Hist. N. S. 1, 584.—BLYTH, Cat. 298.—*Pteromys Leachii*, GRAY?

THE GRAY FLYING-SQUIRREL.

Descr.—Fur above pale rufous-brown, or soft gray, varied with black, like the color of the wild rabbit, the hairs being lead-colored at their base, the rest brown with a black tip; face whitish; orbits black; whiskers very long, black; chin and lower parts yellowish-white; tail broad, rather tapering, fulvous, the hairs near the base black-tipped, and the tail black at the end; feet broad, the outer edge of the hind-feet with a broad tuft of hair.

Length of one, head and body 10 to 11 inches; tail 8 to 9, but it is said to attain larger dimensions.

This flying-squirrel is found throughout the north-west Himalayas from Simla to Kashmir, and is said to extend still further west into Afghanistan. Blyth has named a flying squirrel *Sc. baberi*, from the drawings of Sir A. Burnes, which is probably the same species, or a very nearly allied one.

165. Sciuropterus alboniger.

Hodgson.—Blyth, Cat. 302.—*Sc. Turnbulli*, Gray.—*Khim*, Lepch.—*Piam-piyu*, Bhot.

The Black and White Flying-squirrel.

Descr.—Above black faintly shaded with hoary or rufous, tail concolorous, distinctly distichous; beneath white with a slight tinge of yellowish; nude lips, ears, and feet fleshy-white.

Length, head and body 11 inches; tail 8¼ to 9. The young is pure black and white.

This flying-squirrel is found from Nepal to Bhotan, generally at an elevation of from 3,000 to 5,000 feet. I procured it near Darjeeling, but it is not common now.

166. Sciuropterus villosus.

Blyth, J. A. S. XVI. 866.—Cat. 299.—*S. sagitta* from Assam, Walker.

The Hairy-footed Flying-squirrel.

Descr—Upper surface bright ferruginous, grizzled with some pale tips intermingled; tail strongly rufescent, pale towards the base; under surface of parachute deep ferruginous, which more or less imbues the whole under surface; ears small, clad with a tuft of long fine hair surrounding them; feet, especially the hind-feet, with brushes of hair impending the claws, and densely hairy.

Length of one, head and body 8 inches; tail 8.

The long haired flying-squirrel has been found in Sikim, Bhotan, and the hill regions of Assam. It is more rare than *alboniger* at Darjeeling, and is found from 3,000 to nearly 6,000 feet.

167. Sciuropterus fusco-capillus.

JERDON apud BLYTH, J. A. S. XVI. 867.—BLYTH, Cat. 300.

THE SMALL TRAVANCORE FLYING-SQUIRREL.

Descr.—Upper parts a rufescent-fulvous or dark-brownish isabelline hue, the hairs being fuscous with a fulvous tip; head darker and fuscous; lower parts rufous-white, as are the cheeks and under lip; margin of the membrane rufo-fulvous; tail concolorous or nearly so with back above, with a whitish tip, and the lower surface blackish-brown. Ears small, almost nude. Tail bushy, the hair above one inch long at base, hardly distichous; moustaches long and black; fur long, porrect, very fine.

Length of one, head and body $7\frac{1}{2}$ inches; tail $6\frac{3}{4}$ with the hair.

I had a skin of this flying-squirrel sent to me from Travancore, which I forwarded to Mr. Blyth. He subsequently had other specimens sent him by the Rev. Mr. Baker, also from the same country. Nothing is recorded of its particular habitat. At one time Mr. Blyth was inclined to think it identical with a Ceylon *Sciuropterus*, which has since been named as distinct, *S. Layardi*, Kelaart, apud Blyth.

Sciuropterus spadiceus, Blyth, is a small species from Arrakan, and *S. Phayrei*, Blyth, inhabits Pegu and Tenasserim; whilst *S. sagitta*, L.; *S. Horsfieldii*, Waterhouse, and *S. genibarbis*, Horsfield, inhabit Malayana.

One *Sciuropterus* is found in the North of Europe and Asia, the skin of which is occasionally brought to Peshawur; and there are others in North America.

The genus *Tamias*, or ground squirrel, already alluded to, possesses cheek-pouches and burrows in the ground. It thus appears to form a sort of link to the Marmots. The species are found in the northern regions of both continents.

Sub-fam. ARCTOMYDINÆ, Marmots.

Dental formula, incisors $\frac{1-1}{1-1}$; præmolars $\frac{1-1}{1-1}$; molars $\frac{4-4}{3-3}$; incisors smooth in front, rounded; molars enamelled continuously, marked by transverse tubercles on the crown; the first upper tooth smaller than the rest. Ears short, rounded, scarcely apparent. Fore-feet with 4 toes, and an unguiculate hallucar wart; hind-feet with 5 toes; claws strong, incurved. Tail short or moderate.

Marmots are heavy-bodied animals with short tails, of social habits, and strictly terrestrial, burrowing extensively in the ground, and inhabiting elevated districts in the north of both continents, more particularly North America. There are only two genera in the sub-family, one distinguished by the presence of cheek-pouches, and not represented in our limits. The other is

Gen. ARCTOMYS, Gmelin.

Char.—Those of the family; tail short; head and eyes large; no cheek pouch; body stout; ten to twelve mammæ in the female.

168. Arctomys bobac.

SCHREBER.—BLYTH, Cat. 348.—PALLAS, *Glires* t. 8.—*A. tibetanus*, HODGSON, olim *A. himalayanus*—*A. caudatus*, JAQUEMONT, Voyage.—*Brin* of Kashmir.—*Kadia-piu*, in Tibet.—*Chibi*, Bhot.—*Lho* or *Pot-sammiong*, Lepch.—White Marmot of Adams.

THE TIBET MARMOT.

Descr.—Color a clear fulvescent cat-gray, like that of *Felis chaus*, fading into pure rufescent-yellow beneath; limbs and ears the same, but darker; chaffron and end of tail, dark-brown; fur close and thick, both hairy and woolly; tail cylindric, bluff pointed.

Length, head and body 23 to 24 inches; tail 5 to 6.

This marmot, which inhabits Eastern Europe and Central Asia, is only a scanty outlier in our province, crossing over the snowy Himalayas only for a short distance, but found on the Indian side along the whole length of the range, from Kashmir to Sikim, though less abundantly than on the Tibet side, never at a lower elevation than 12,000 feet; often up to 16,000 feet. It burrows in the ground, living in small societies, and feeding on roots and vegetables. It lifts its food to its mouth with its fore-feet. It is easily tamed. One was brought alive to Calcutta some years ago, and did not appear, says Mr. Blyth, to be distressed by the heat of that place. It was quite tamed and fearless, and used to make a loud chattering cachinnation. It was fond of collecting grass, &c., and carrying it to its den. Travellers and sportsmen often meet with this marmot, and speak of its sitting up in groups and suddenly disappearing into their burrows. The cured skins form an important article of commerce, and are brought to Nepal, and in great numbers to China.

169. Arctomys hemachalanus.

HODGSON, olim *A. tibetanus*.—*Sammiong*, Lepch.—*Chipi*, Bhot.—*Drun* of Kashmir.

THE RED MARMOT.

Descr.—General color dark-gray with a full rufous tinge, which is rusty and almost ochreous red on the sides of the head, ears and limbs, especially in summer; bridge of the nose and last inch of the tail dusky brown; head and body above strongly mixed with black, which hue equals or exceeds the pale one on these parts; claws long; pelage softer and fuller than in the last.

Length, head and body about 13 inches; tail 5½.

This species is not fully recognised, and Blyth states that the specimens of the Asiatic Society did not enable him to determine the point. Hodgson, however, insists on their distinction, and some skins which I saw at Darjeeling incline me to consider this a distinct species. The Lepchas distinguish the Tibet marmot from this one by a prefix, signifying mountain, from its occurring at higher elevations. Adams moreover distinguishes the two, stating of this one that it is found at elevations varying from 8,000 to 10,000 feet in Kashmir and the North-west Himalayas, inhabiting fertile and secluded spots, forming burrows on gentle slopes among stones, and emitting a loud wailing cry.

Hodgson kept some of this species in his garden for sometime. They were somnolent by day, active at night, and did not hybernate in Nepal. They were fed on grain and fruit, and would chatter a good deal over their meals, but in general were silent. They slept rolled up into a ball, were tame and gentle usually, but sometimes bit and scratched like rabbits, uttering a similar cry.

The marmot of the Alps and Pyrennees, *Arctomys marmota*, is the best known of the group; and there are others in Northern Asia, and many in North America, of which the so-called Prairie dog, *A. ludovicianus*, is one of the most remarkable. The genus *Spermophilus* differ from *Arctomys* in having a longer tail, and possessing cheek-pouches. One species is found in Europe, and others in Central Asia and North America.

The next family comprises all the remaining rodents with tolerably perfect clavicles, and sub-quadrate lower jaw. They are usually divided into several distinct families, but were all included, of late, by Waterhouse* and others in one group, *Muridæ*. Blyth classes them in the families *Myoxidæ*, *Dipodidæ*, *Muridæ*, *Arvicolidæ* and *Bathyergidæ;* only two of which have representatives in India, viz., the *Muridæ*, and *Arvicolidæ*, which will be here considered as sub-families.

Fam. MURIDÆ.

Incisors compressed or rounded; molars 3 or 4 on each side; fore-feet usually with 4 toes; hind-feet with 5. Tail very various.

Two of the groups comprising this family are somewhat related to the squirrels, and may be said to form the transition between them and the rats. One of these is the Dormice, *Myoxidæ*, Auct. These have 4 molars on each side, the crown divided by closely folded lines of enamel, and the lower incisors pointed. They are pretty little animals with soft fur, hairy and tufted tail, and live on trees. They are remarkable as being the only rodents that do not possess a cœcum. Blyth classed a peculiar rodent from south India in this family, but this location has not been upheld by late writers.

The Jerboas, *Dipodidæ* or *Jerboidæ*, Auct., have teeth similar to the true *Murinæ*, but with an occasional small tooth in front of the upper molar. Their hind limbs are much lengthened, and the metatarsus of the three middle toes is formed of a single bone. The fore-feet have each 5 toes. The tail is long and tufted. Some, in which the hind-feet have 5

* *Vide* Sclater, South American Mammals. Quarterly Journal of Science.

toes as usual, have been separated as *Alactaga*, Gray, one species of which, *Alactaga indica*, Gray, inhabits Afghanistan, and its habits have been described by Hutton. Most of the jerboas are from Africa, a few from Central Asia. They make most surprising jumps.

Sub-Fam. MURINÆ, Rats and Mice.

Incisors compressed laterally, the lower ones acuminate, awl-shaped; molars, $\frac{3-3}{3-3}$; rooted, uniformly covered by enamel, the anterior one of each series the largest, the posterior the smallest; the upper molars shelve somewhat backwards, the lower ones forwards. Fore-feet with 4 wide-set toes, and a hallucar unguiculate wart; hind-feet with 5 toes. Tail usually long and thinly clad or nude, short, and hairy in a few. Cosmopolite.

This comprises the true rats and mice. Mr. Blyth, just before his departure from India, wrote a valuable memoir on the rats and mice of India, which has been my chief guide in treating of these little animals. Much yet remains to be done in elucidating this group, and determining the value of many of Mr. Hodgson's species.

Gen. GERBILLUS, F. Cuvier.

Char.—Upper incisors grooved; molars equably enamelled with transverse ridges, forming when worn oval figures. Ears oval. Head lengthened and somewhat pointed; hinder tarsus and toes elongated. Tail long, hairy, with a tuft of hair at the tip.

These field rats have small fore limbs and well developed hinder limbs. Their form is somewhat slender and their eyes are large. They are extraordinarily agile, and form extensive burrows in plains, especially in sandy districts, and also in sand hills, but not generally in cultivated fields. They are found in Africa and Asia.

170. Gerbillus indicus.

Dipus apud HARDWICKE, Lin. Tr., VIII. pl. 7.—Ill. Ind. Zool.—BLYTH, Cat. p. 110.*—ELLIOT, Cat. 32.—*G. Hardwickii*, GRAY, and *G. Cuvieri*, WATERHOUSE.—*Hurna mús*, H., *i. e.*, Antelope rat.—*Jhenku indúr*, Sansc. and Bengal.—*Yeri yelka*, of Waddurs.—*Tel yelka* of the Yanadees.—*Billa ilei*, Can.

* The printer has played such pranks with the subsequent numbers n Blyth's Catalogue, that henceforth I will only cite the page.

THE INDIAN JERBOA-RAT.

Descr.—Above light fulvous-brown, or bright fawn color, somewhat paler on the sides, beneath white; eyebrow whitish; whiskers long, black; tail blackish towards the tip, which is clad with a tuft of long blackish hairs; ears large, almost nude. The hairs of the back are light pumbeous at the base with fulvous tips, with some thin black hairs intermixed, most conspicuous on the sides and cheeks.

Length, head and body 7 inches; tail $8\frac{1}{2}$; ear $\frac{3}{4}$ths. Another measured, head and body 7 inches; tail $8\frac{1}{10}$; ear $\frac{9}{10}$ths; fore-foot $\frac{5}{10}$ths; hind-foot 2; weight $6\frac{3}{4}$ oz.

The jerboa-rat is very abundant in most parts of India, frequenting the bare uncultivated plains, and sandy downs, where it forms extensive burrows; occasionally near the roots of shrubs or bushes, but very generally in the bare plain. "The entrances," says Mr. W. Elliot, "which are numerous, are small, from which the passage descends with a rapid slope for 2 or 3 feet, then runs along horizontally, and sends off branches in different directions. These galleries generally terminate in chambers from half a foot to a foot in width, containing a bed of dried grass. Sometimes one chamber communicates with another, furnished in like manner, whilst others appear to be deserted, and the entrances closed with clay. The centre chamber in one burrow was very large, which the Wuddurs attributed to its being the common apartment, and said that the females occupied the smaller ones with their young. They do not hoard their food, but issue from their burrows every evening, and run and hop about, sitting on their hind legs to look round, making astonishing leaps; and on the slightest alarm flying into their holes."

This rat eats grain, various seeds, but chiefly roots and grass. It is the common prey of foxes, owls and snakes. The female brings forth numerous young ones, usually 8 to 12, occasionally it is said as many as 16 to 20. It is certainly the most elegant and graceful of its family, and well deserves the name of the antelope-rat, equally from its color, activity, and fine, full, gazelle-like eyes.

It is found over all India and Ceylon, but is not in general found at high elevations. Blyth states that it also occurs in Afghanistan.

171. Gerbillus erythrourus.

GRAY, Ann. Mag. Nat. Hist. 1842? New species?

The Desert Jerboa-rat.

Descr.—Much smaller than the last, with the tail also comparatively shorter and the ear smaller. Above pale rufous or sandy with fine dusky lines, the hairs being blackish at the base, the rest fawn colored with a minute dusky tip; a few longer piles on the rump and thighs; sides slightly paler with fewer dusky lines; all the lower parts whitish, tinged more or less with fawn-color on the belly, the line of demarcation of the two colors not strongly marked; limbs pale fawn; tail yellowish-rufous or fawn color throughout, with a line of dusky-brown hairs on the upper surface of the terminal half, gradually increasing in length to the tip; orbits pale; whiskers mostly white, a few of the upper ones dark.

Length, head and body 5 inches; tail $4\frac{1}{2}$; ears $\frac{3}{8}$; palm $\frac{1}{2}$; hind-foot 1.

I have not at present access to Gray's description of *G. erythrourus*, of which there is no specimen in the Museum of the Asiatic Society, so merely conjecture it to be the same from the specific name applying to the Indian one, and its habitat being not far removed. At any rate it differs conspicuously from the common jerboa-rat of India, and if not the same as Gray's species, may be designated as *Gerbillus Hurrianæ.* When I first observed this rat, I thought that it must be a casual variety of the common kind, especially after Blyth's emphatic statement that he had seen *Gerbillus indicus* from every part of India without any decided variation; but I have seen it since in vast numbers over a large extent of country, all pretty constant to the description and measurements above given. Its habitat is the sandy tract of country west of the Jumna, Hurriana and adjacent districts. Whether it extends much further south, or through the Punjab, I cannot now say, but should imagine that it will be found throughout Rajpootana, part of Sindh, and the Punjab, thence extending into Afghanistan. It is exceedingly numerous in the sandy downs and sand-hills of Hurriana, both in jungles and in bare plains, especially in the former, and a colony may be seen at the foot of every large shrub almost. I found that it had been feeding on the kernel of the nut of the common *Salvadora oleifolia*, gnawing through the hard nut, and extracting the whole of the kernel. Unlike the last species, this rat, during the cold weather at all events, is very generally seen outside its holes at all hours, scuttling in on the near approach of any one, but soon cautiously popping its head out of its hole and again issuing forth. In the localities it frequents it is far more abundant than I have even seen *G. indicus* in the most favorable spots.

There are many other species of Gerbill on record, both from Asia and Africa.

Near the Gerbills should be placed the genus *Meriones*, F. Cuvier, from North America. It differ from the former in having still longer hind-feet, the tail being nearly naked, and in having a very small tooth in front of the upper molars, as in the true Jerboas.

Gen. Nesokia, Gray.

Char.—Incisors very large, flat in front, and smooth: the anterior upper molars large, with three transverse ridges; the middle ones oblong; and the posterior the smallest, narrowed behind and with two ridges; the three middle toes subequal, long; claws small, compressed; ears moderate, nude; tail short, naked.

" This genus," says its founder, " is easily known from *Mus* by the large size of the cutting teeth, and the comparative shortening of the tail; it appears to be intermediate to the Rats and *Rhizomys*." On this Mr. Blyth remarks that he can perceive no particular approximation, but I fancy Mr. Gray only meant the general resemblance of a large bluff head, large teeth, and a short naked tail. This bluff aspect led him formerly to class the best known species as an *Arvicola*.

172. Nesokia indica.

Mus apud Geoffroy.—Blyth, Cat. p. 112.—*Arvicola indica*, Gray, figd. Hardwicke, Ill. Ind. Zool.—*M. kok*, Gray.—*M. providens*, Elliot, Cat. 31.—*M. pyctoris*, Hodgson.—*Kok*, Can.—*Golatta koku*, Tel. of Yanadees.

The Indian Mole-rat.

Descr.—Fur long and somewhat harsh, brown mixed with fawn, the short fur softer and dusky; paler beneath and tinged gray; the color generally being like that of the common rat, but with more fawn or red intermixed, and lighter beneath; head short and truncated; ears small, nearly round, covered with a fine down or small hairs; tail naked, nearly as long as the body without the head; whiskers long and full; incisors orange yellow.

Length, head and body 7 inches; tail 6; head $1\frac{8}{10}$; ear $\frac{9}{10}$ths; fore-palm $\frac{4}{10}$ths; hind-palm $1\frac{4}{10}$. Another measured, head and body $8\frac{1}{2}$; tail 6; hind-foot $1\frac{3}{4}$.

Hodgson describes his *M. pyctoris* as follows:—"Characterized by its bluff face with short thick muzzle, and by its short tail. Pelage of two sorts, with the long piles sufficiently abundant; color dusky brown with a very vague rufous tinge; below fulvescent; long hairs black, rest with hoary bases and black points; inner piles mostly dusky. Length, snout to vent, 7 inches; tail $4\frac{1}{2}$; head $1\frac{7}{8}$; ears $\frac{13}{16}$ths; palm $\frac{5}{8}$ths; planta $1\frac{1}{4}$. I think there can be very little doubt that this is the same as the *kok* of Southern India, but I do not think that the specimen in the British Museum, with that name attached, described by Gray, is the same, but rather that of one of the allied species.*

This large field-rat is found throughout India, ranging up to a considerable altitude, above 7,000 feet, and also in Ceylon, but is not hitherto recorded from the east of the Bay of Bengal.

Mr Elliot has given the following interesting account of the habits of this rat:—

"In its habits it is solitary, fierce, living secluded in spacious burrows, in which it stores up large quantities of grain during the harvest, and when that is consumed, lives upon the *huryalee* grass and other roots. The female produces from eight to ten at a birth, which she sends out of her burrow as soon as they are able to provide for themselves. When irritated, it utters a low grunting cry like the bandicoot.

The race of people known by the name of Wuddurs or tank-diggers, capture this animal in great numbers as an article of food, and during the harvest they plunder their earths of the grain stored up for their winter consumption, which in favorable localities they find in such quantities as as to subsist almost entirely upon it, during that season of the year. A single burrow will sometimes yield as much as half a seer (1 ℔.) of grain containing even whole ears of jowaree (*Holchus sorghum*).

The *kok* abounds in the richly cultivated black plains or cotton ground, but the heavy rains often inundate their earths, destroy their stores, and force them to seek a new habitation. I dug up a winter burrow in August 1833, situated near the old one, which was deserted from this cause. The animal had left the level ground, and constructed its new habitation in the sloping bank of an old well. The entrance was covered with a mound of

* *Vide*, p. 192.

earth like a mole-hill, on removing which the main shaft of the burrow was followed along the side of the grassy bank at a depth of about 1 or 1½ foot. From this a descending branch went still deeper to a small round chamber, lined with roots, and just large enough to contain the animal. From the chamber a small gallery ran quite round it, terminating on either side in the main shaft at the entrance of the chamber, and the passage then continued down to the bottom of the bank and opened into the plain. Near the upper entrance and above the passage to the chamber was another small branch which terminated suddenly, and contained excrement. But these burrows are by no means on an uniform plan. Another occupied by an adult femále was likewise examined in the same neighbourhood. It was much more extensive, and covered a space of about 15 feet in length by about 8 in breadth, also in a grassy mound, of which it occupied both sides. Six entrances were observed (and there may have been many more), each covered with bare earth. The deepest part of the burrow near the chamber was about 3 feet from the surface; the chamber raised a little above the shaft, which terminated abruptly, and was continued from the upper part of the chamber. The chamber itself was lined with roots of grass and bark of the date tree. The branching galleries, of which there were six, from the principal shaft, appeared to have been excavated in search of food.

"A variety found in the red soil is much redder in color than the common *kok* of the black land. Another variety is said to frequent the banks of nullahs and to take the water when pursued, but the specimens I have seen differed in no respect from the common kind (of which they appeared to be young individuals) except in size."

I have seen many burrows of this rat in all localities, but especially in pasture and meadow land on the Neelgherries and elsewhere, much more extensive than those recorded by Mr. Elliot, not unfrequently covering a space nearly 15 to 20 yards in diameter, and covered with huge mounds of the earth thrown out, forming unsightly heaps in a grassy compound, or on a hill side. This rat is occasionally destructive to tea trees, biting the roots just below the surface; more, I believe, because they come in the way of their burrows, then to feed on them. In the Government Tea Garden near Dehra, many trees are destroyed by these rats, and the Superintendent is obliged to keep some men employed to dig them out whenever they betray their presence by the rat-hills of loose earth. Several that I procured from Dr. Jameson were of a very large size, and corresponded somewhat to the description of Hodgson's *M. macropus*, but that species is said to have a fine pelage, and the Dehra rat has the usual harsh hair of the *kok*.

173. Nesokia Hardwickei.

Mus apud GRAY.—Mag. Nat. Hist. 1837, 585.—*Nes. Huttoni*, BLYTH, J. A. S. XV., 139?—Memoir on Rats, &c.

THE SHORT-TAILED MOLE-RAT.

Descr.—"Reddish or yellow brown with longer dark-brown hairs intermixed on the rump; sides grayer and paler; hairs lead-colored at the base." Such is Gray's original brief description. Elsewhere it is described, as "yellowish-brown, paler beneath, with numerous bristles tipped black; incisors broad." Gray says, "very like *kok*, skull wider, stronger and larger; cutting teeth nearly twice as wide, grinders very little larger." Blyth writes me that the "cutting teeth of a specimen in the British Museum are large, smooth, yellow, flat in front; the thumb of the fore-feet small, clawed, grinders about the same size as in *kok*; tail shorter."

Blyth described *N. Huttoni* as follows:—"Bears a near resemblance to *M. indica* (v. *kok*), but the tail is shorter, and the general color lighter, resembling that of the gerbilles. On comparison of the skulls, the zygomatic arch is seen to be conspicuously broader anteriorly, and the palate is much narrower and contracted to the front; but the most obvious distinction consists in all the teeth, both incisive tusks and grinders being considerably broader and stronger. In other respects the skulls of these species bear a very close resemblance. Length, head and body about 6 inches; tail (vertebra) 4; tarsus with toes and claws $1\frac{3}{8}$; ears posteriorly $\frac{1}{2}$. Fur soft and fine, blackish for the larger basal half of the piles, the surface pale rufescent-brown, deepest along the crown and back, pale below and whitish on the throat; whiskers small and fine, chiefly black; tail naked, feet light-brown; incisive tusks buff-colored." It will be observed that *Hardwickei* and *Huttoni* are both described as differing from *kok or indica* by the broader skull, and especially the broader incisors, and also by a shorter tail; which, however, is stated by Blyth (in epistola) to be only $2\frac{1}{4}$ inches in a specimen of *Hardwickei* in the British Museum; but the total length of that individual is not given, and the description does not imply such a very short tail as typical of the species. Blyth in addition writes me, that the fur of this specimen is dense, shortish, and of uniform length. On the whole I see no reason against these two being considered identical. *Hardwickei* is stated to inhabit India, *gardens;* and *Huttoni* occurs "south of Bahawulpore; and is abundant in Afghanistan, throwing up the mould after the manner of the mole. In the *gardens* and along the sides of water-courses in the fields at Kandahar, their earth heaps are abundant. It feeds on herbs and seeds, and burrows in the ground beneath hedge-rows and bushes, as well as along the banks and ditches. Its nest is deep-seated, and it constructs so many false galleries immediately below the surface, that it is difficult to find the true passage to its retreat, which dips down suddenly from about the middle of the labyrinth above."*

Nesokia Griffithii, Horsfield, also from Afghanistan, ought to be closely allied to this, but it is said to have the cutting teeth *nearly white;* but they are represented to be as in *Huttoni*, large, flat anteriorly, and broad; tail nearly naked, short; ears moderately large; thumb of fore-feet very minute; fur soft and silky; above dusky chesnut-brown with streaks of a plumbeous tint, chin, chest and under parts of a lighter tint, passing into grayish-leaden color on the abdomen. Length of specimen 6 inches; tail 3; but the "body probably stretched and tail shrunk." Blyth in a copy of his Memoir forwarded to me, puts this as "probably young of *N. indica*," but it appears to me just as likely *N. Hardwickei* vel *Huttoni*. Closely allied to this species must be Hodgson's *Mus? hydrophilus*, olim *Arvicola*, now *Nesokia hydrophila*, Gray. Hodgson described his species (which, however, was evidently a young one) as characterized by its small ears, hardly above one-third the length of the head, also by its short tail, and by a pelage that is short and fine; above dusky-brown, below and limbs nearly white; long piles inconspicuous. Length, head and body $3\frac{1}{2}$ inches; tail $2\frac{3}{4}$; palm $\frac{1}{2}$; planta $\frac{7}{8}$ths. Gray, describing a specimen in the British Museum says, "gray-brown, beneath whitish; fur very soft, with rather elongated, very slender, soft longer hairs, ears moderate, rounded; whiskers black at base, slender; front cutting teeth broad, yellow; grinders very large; hind-feet large ($1\frac{3}{12}$ inch), but length of animal not recorded. This measurement corresponds to the dimensions of the foot of *M. macropus*.

Hodgson calls this the small water-rat of Nepal, dwelling in holes on the margins of ponds and rivers. His *M? macropus*, he calls the large water-rat, "like the last, but twice as large, distinguished by the largeness

* Hutton, Journal Asiatic Society.

of its feet, and also by the fine pelage and proportions of *hydrophilus;* above smoky-black, below smoky gray; legs dark. Length, head and body $7\frac{1}{4}$ inches; tail 6; ears $1\frac{1}{16}$th; palm 1 (?); planta $1\frac{13}{16}$ths."

Blyth examined the specimen of *Hydrophilus* in the British Museum, and writes me that the "fur is soft, much finer than in *Indicus;*" so that we must conclude that this rat of Hodgson, is certainly distinct from *Nesokia indica;* and if the dimensions of the ear and feet are correct, also from *Hardwickei.*

I recently examined a single specimen of a field rat, *Nesokia*, procured by Colonel Tytler in Umballa. It has the incisors white, fur fine and soft, the hairs fawn-brown above, plumbeous at base, mixed with some long, slender, white, bristly hairs; the tail almost quite nude; whiskers mostly black, slender, some of them white.

Length, head and body 5 inches, tail $3\frac{1}{2}$; ears $\frac{5}{8}$ths nearly; palm $\frac{3}{4}$ths; hind-feet $1\frac{1}{4}$.

This differs from *Huttoni* vel *Hardwickei* in the incisors being white, and in the long hairs being white in place of brown, black-tipped. It also differs from the description of *M. hydrophilus* in the white incisors, but agrees with it in other characters; but as I only have seen one specimen, it would be premature to increase the list of names of this perplexing group. It certainly differs conspicuously from *Nesokia indica;* though it approaches most nearly to Gray's description of *M? pyctoris*, from the British Museum specimen, already alluded to. "Fur soft, dark brown, minutely gray-varied, with scattered narrow white bristles; lower cutting teeth very narrow, rounded in front, middle of belly whitish; tail very slightly hairy. Length, head and body 7 inches; hind-feet $1\frac{3}{12}$; tail $4\frac{1}{2}$." The most obvious difference is the slightly larger foot of the Umballa specimen.

From the above notices and descriptions, it appears to me obvious that besides *Nesokia Hardwickei* and *N. indica*, there is at least one other species of this group in northern India, but, with the few specimens hitherto examined, it is at present impossible to decide whether the differences noted depend on imperfect descriptions, nonage, or are of specific value.

The next group is that of the true rats.

Gen. Mus, L. (restricted).

Char.—Incisors usually smooth in front. Ears more or less rounded, somewhat naked, exsert. Tail long, scaly, usually thinly haired. Otherwise as in the characters of the sub-family.

The genus, as here restricted, comprises the house rats and mice, and some field rats of more or less allied form, and the various species may be grouped together according to their size and habit.

1st Group. Rats more or less allied to the common brown rat, *Mus decumanus*, L.—*Chúhá*, H.—*Yelka*, Tel.—*Illi*, Can.—*Kallok*, Lepch.—*Pitsi*, Bhot.

174. Mus bandicota.

BECHSTEIN.—BLYTH, Cat. p. 112.—*M. giganteus*, HARDWICKE, Lin. Trans. VIII. t. 18.—*M. malabaricus*, SHAW.—*M. nemorivagus*, HODGSON.—*M. perchal*, SHAW?—*M. setifer*, HORSFIELD, fid. BLYTH.—ELLIOT, Cat. 30.—*Indúr*, Sansc.—*Ghous* or *Ghus*, H. and Mahr.—*Ikria* or *Ikara*, Beng.—*Heggin*, Can.—*Pandi koku*, Tel. *i. e.*, the pig-rat, whence the word *Bandicoot* is derived.

THE BANDICOOT-RAT.

Descr.—Dark dusky olive-brown color above, with some black bristly hairs intermixed; beneath lighter mixed with gray.

Length of a large individual, head and body, 15 inches; tail 13; weight 3 lbs. Hardwicke's specimen figured was, head and body $13\frac{1}{2}$; tail 13. Average size in Bengal, head and body $10\frac{3}{4}$ inches; tail $8\frac{3}{4}$. Hodgson gives dimensions of *nemorivagus* as, snout to rump 12; tail $9\frac{1}{2}$; weight 20 oz.

The incisors are dark olive-green at the base, becoming yellow at the extremities. The molars have strong alveolar processes; the anterior (præmolar) is divided into three portions by transverse ridges of enamel, the middle ones into two, and the posterior ones only partially so. They become quite tubercular when old. The tail is scaly, with a few scattered, short, adpressed, bristly hairs. The female has twelve teats.

This well known rat is found throughout India, also in Ceylon, and many parts of Malayana, the *M. setifer* of Horsfield being identical with this species, according to information lately received from Mr. Blyth. It appears to be more abundant in the south of India and Ceylon than in the north; and Mr. Blyth states it to be rare in Calcutta. In the fort at Madras it is exceedingly numerous, living during the day in drains, and entering houses at night. During my residence in Fort St. George, I killed a great many in my own house, some of which were of large size and showed great fight. It is found in all towns and large villages in the south, frequenting granaries and stack-yards, and is very destructive to the stores of grain, on which it chiefly feeds. It burrows under walls and often injures the foundations of houses. Besides grain it will feed on fruit and various other vegetable matter, and even at times it is said animal food. At Newera-ellia in Ceylon, it is said to be very destructive to potatoes, peas, &c. It does not occur to my knowledge in the Neelgherries, a similar climate. Kelaart says that it occasionally attacks poultry also. When assailed it grunts like a pig, hence its Telugu name. It is eaten by some classes of natives. Hodgson in his first account of *M. nemorivagus* stated that it avoids houses, and dwells in burrows in fields and small woods. He subsequently stated that it was a house-rat, and most likely identical with the bandicoot.

Mus andamensis, Blyth, is, according to that gentlemen, in an annotated copy of his Memoir sent to me, the *M. setifer* apud Cantor, and inhabits the Andaman islands, probably the Nicobars, (in which case *M. nicobaricus*, Scherzer,) and the Malayan peninsula.

In Blyth's MSS. notes, above alluded to, he gives "a small pale specimen (of *M. andamanensis*) in the British Museum, marked *M. kok* from India? Perhaps an allied species." Is it possible that this is Hodgson's *M. rattoides*, instead of that being referred to *M. rattus*, which we know to be rare except near the coast.

175. Mus rattus.

LINNÆUS.—BLYTH, Cat. p. 113.—ELLIOT, Cat. 34.—*M. rattoides*, HODGSON.

THE BLACK-RAT.

Descr.—Grayish black above, dark ashy beneath, tail longer than the body, long piles numerous, somewhat flattened.

Length of one, head and body $7\frac{1}{4}$; tail 8 inches.

The muzzle is sharper than that of the brown rat, the ears more oval, and it is lighter in its make, and with much longer hair.

Hodgson describes his *M. rattoides*, as "above dusky or blackish brown, below dusky hoary. Limbs dark, fingers pale; tail longer than head and body; long piles sufficiently numerous. Length, snout to vent $7\frac{1}{2}$ inches; tail $8\frac{3}{4}$; ears $\frac{7}{8}$ths; palm $\frac{13}{16}$ths; sole $1\frac{1}{2}$. Gray at one time referred Hodgson's species to *M. indicus*, Geoffroy, which he apparently considered distinct from *Nesokia indica* vel *kok*. Blyth describes *M. andamensis* as, "ears much as in *Decumanus;* fur a shade darker on the back, paler on the sides, and dull white below; the long piles distinguished by their flattened spinous character. Length 8 inches; tail the same." This would appear to differ from Hodgson's species chiefly in the shorter tail.

The black-rat of Europe has been occasionally found in various parts of India, chiefly in large towns near the coast, where it has probably been introduced by shipping. Blyth notices a brown variety obtained at Calcutta, which, however, he subsequently referred to another species. Elliot notices it as occurring rarely, and Kelaart obtained it in Trincomalee only.

If my suggestion hold good as to *M. andamensis* being the same as Hodgson's *M. rattoides*, it will probably be found extending from the Malayan peninsula through Burmah to the south-east Himalayas.

176. Mus decumanus.

Pallas, Glires, 91.—Blyth, Cat. p. 113.—Elliot, Cat. 33.—*M. norveyicus*, Buffon.—*M. decumanoides*, Hodgson?—*Ghur-ka-chúhá*, H.—*Demsa indur*, Beng.—*Manei ilei*, Can.

The Brown-rat.

Descr.—Above dusky cinereous brown with a tinge of yellow, the shorter hairs being slaty at the base with a yellow tip, and the longer ones dusky-blackish; beneath dirty pale ashy; ears as broad as long, rounded tail naked and scaly.

Length of one, head and body 8 inches; tail 6; ears $\frac{3}{4}$ths: of another head and body, $10\frac{1}{2}$ inches; tail $8\frac{1}{4}$.

Blyth remarks that "Calcutta specimens are undistinguishable from British," and the same may be said of specimens from other parts of the country. It is yet a doubtful point from what country this pest has spread itself over the greater part of the world. Mr. F. Buckland remarks "that it is now agreed by most naturalists, that it is a native of India and Persia; that it spread onwards into European Russia, and was thence transferred by merchant ships to England and elsewhere." On this Blyth observes: "If an indigenous inhabitant of India, it would undoubtedly be more generally diffused over this, if not also the neighbouring countries. I suspect that the Trans-Baikalian region of east Asia has at least as good a claim to the *discredit* of originating the abominable brown rat as any other." Again, "whatever the extremes of temperature and climate *M. decumanus* contrives to find itself a home, and to increase and multiply about human abodes and granaries, to the serious detriment of not quite all-subduing man."

I have found the brown rat throughout great part of India, more abundant near large towns, as it appears to be particularly a parasite on man and his belongings. It is most omnivorous in its propensities, and particularly carnivorous, destroying pigeons, chickens, &c., &c., and showing great ingenuity sometimes in reaching the cages of tame birds, &c. It also destroys a vast number of bird's eggs. Sykes states that it migrates sometimes in thousands, destroying the crops in its progress.* I never heard of similar migrations in other parts of India. Blyth states that though it is common at Akyab, it is not found at Rangoon or Moulmein, or at Mergui.

One or two other rats, with tails shorter than the head and body, are recorded by Hodgson.

177. Mus plurimammis.

Hodgson, Ann. Mag. Nat. Hist. 1855., p. 112.

The Nepal-rat.

Descr.—Color above brown with a rufescent shade; fur soft, consisting of brown and rufous hairs intermixed in equal proportions, forming an uniform upper surface; a rather obscure band extending from the gape over the cheek, terminating under the ears; and the abdomen and adjoining parts rufous-gray. Head proportionally short, muzzle abrupt, ears moderate. Tail equal in length to the body, tapering to a sharp point, minutely annulated. Length of head 2½ inches; body 5½; tail the same." "The distinguishing character," says Horsfield, "according to Mr. Hodgson rests on the number of teats exceeding that of other species; but the number is not stated. From the Nepàl Terai and adjacent plains.

Blyth in his MSS. notes before referred to, writes, "good species, specimen in British Museum. Fur uniform, with a few longer piles."

* Perhaps this refers to the ravages of *Golunda meltada*, q. v.

Hodgson has a *Mus tarayensis*, which appears to be not far removed from *M. decumanus*. It is thus described by Dr. Horsfield, A. M. N. H., 1855. "Nearly allied to *M. brunneusculus*. Color of the body and head above dark-brown, delicately variegated with blackish and rufous hairs; a very slight gloss on the surface. Outer sides of the extremities rather darker. Under parts from the chin to the vent, and inner parts of the extremities, grayish-brown with a rusty shade. Tail shorter than the body, tapering to an abrupt tip. Head lengthened and compressed, muzzle gradually tapering to an abrupt tip. Mr. Hodgson's collection contains a single specimen, and further observations are required to confirm the distinctness of this species."

Another rat that might be placed here is the following—

178. Mus infralineatus.

Elliot, MSS.—Blyth, Memoir.—*M. Elliotti*, Gray, Br. Mus. Cat. Mamm. (not *Golunda Elliotti*).—*M. fulvescens*, Gray, Cat. Hodgson's Coll. ?

The Striped-bellied Field-rat.

Descr.—Above the fur fulvous with the shorter hairs lead colored; throat, breast and belly, pure white, with a central pale fulvous-brown streak; tail slightly hairy.

Length of one, head and body $5\frac{1}{2}$ inches; tail not quite 5. Another, about 5 inches; tail $4\frac{1}{4}$; hind-foot $1\frac{1}{16}$.

I think it exceedingly probable that Gray's *M. fulvescens*, from Nepal, is the same. It is described as, "fur pale fulvous, hairs very soft, lead-colored, with bright yellow tips, and interspersed slender black bristles; throat, belly and beneath, pure white; in one specimen with a central yellow streak." This is not included in the British Museum Cat. Mamm.; but there is a *Mus Elliotti* (distinct from *Golunda Elliotti*) not described, which may be the same.

Kelaart's rat referred by him to *M. asiaticus*, may be the same. "Fur soft, above pale brown mixed with black, the sides ashy-gray; beneath pure white; tail thinnish, shorter than head and body; ears large, slightly hairy; limbs slender. Length, head and body 6; tail $5\frac{1}{4}$."

I saw specimens of this field-rat in Mr. Elliot's possession in 1848, procured in the neighbourhood of Madras; and I have twice obtained it myself, on both occasions lying dead on a path in the forest country of Bustar in 1857.*

Mr. Blyth places this field-rat among the field-mice, but, if it does not belong to the true rats, it appears to me related to the *Mus meltada* group, and *M. plurimammis* may be somewhat allied. Another similar rat is described in the same place as *Mus morungensis*, Hodgson. "Hairy covering of the body above minutely striated with black and rufous hairs nearly equally mixed, giving the animal a blackish rufous aspect; abdomen and extremities paler, rufescent gray. Body proportionally robust and stout; head large and thick, and muzzle short and abrupt; ears large and rounded; tail cylindrical, gradually tapering to the point and delicately annulated, equal in length to body and head; fur above soft, hairs longer than in *M. plurimammis*. Length, head and body 4½ inches; tail 4½. From the Nepal Terai and adjacent plains."

Next come a group of rats with the tail usually fully as long, or longer than the head and body. Some of these have quite arboreal habits, building nests among the branches of trees, among the rafters of houses, &c., and not burrowing in the ground.

179. Mus brunneus.

HODGSON, Ann. Mag. Nat. Hist. 1845.—*M. nemoralis*, BLYTH, J. A. S. XX.—Cat. 114.—*M. æquicaudalis*, HODGSON?

THE TREE-RAT.

Descr.—Above reddish-brown, or rusty-brown, with a few long bristles intermixed; beneath dull whitish, or pale rusty with a hoary tinge, or pale grayish-brown; tail as long, or a little longer than the head and body; feet pale fleshy; ears rather long, and head somewhat lengthened.

Length of one, head and body 9½; tail 9: another measured 8½ inches; tail the same: and another 8½ inches, tail 9½.

Some have the upper parts dark brown, with only a slight rufescent tinge.

This rat appears to be found throughout India and Ceylon, not habitually living in holes, but coming into houses at night; and, as Blyth

* These were unfortunately lost during the Mutiny with many other valuable specimens from the same district.

remarks, often found resting during the day on the *jhil-mil*, or venetian blinds. It makes a nest in mango trees, or in thick bushes and hedges. Hodgson calls it the common house-rat of Nepal, and Kelaart also calls it the small house-rat of Trincomalee. Blyth writes me that it comes very near *Mus alexandrinus* of Africa.

I have given Hodgson's *brunneus* as the name of this species on Blyth's authority. Whether *M. æquicaudalis* be the same or not is yet doubtful. He describes it as "pure dark brown above, with a very slight caste of rufescent in some aspects; underneath, from chin to vent, with interior of thighs, yellowish white; head and ears long."

180. Mus rufescens.

GRAY, Mag. Nat. Hist. 1837.—*M. flavescens*, ELLIOT, Cat.—BLYTH, Cat. p. 115.—*M. arboreus*, BUCHANAN HAMILTON apud HORSFIELD, Cat. Mamm.—*M. brunnensculus*, HODGSON.—*Gachua indur*, Beng.

THE RUFESCENT TREE-RAT.

Descr.—Pale yellowish-brown or rufescent brown above, white beneath, with numerous bristles on the back tipped with black. Head long, muzzle pointed; face narrow; eyes large; incisors yellow; ears very large, subovate, nude.

Length of one, head and body 5½ inches; tail 6½: another measured, head and body 7½; tail 8½, and some are recorded as even larger than that.

It varies a good deal in the character of the upper fur, some being described as above dark-iron gray, with the lower parts white, the hairs black and tawny, the former the most numerous. This variety, however, may be a distinct species, *M. niveiventer*, q. v. Some are much browner than others, and the lower surface is sometimes very white, often pale yellow, at other times not much paler than the upper surface. The white is generally abruptly separated from the hue above, rarely gradually blending. It comes very near the last, but differs in its smaller size, in the more general rufescent tone of coloring, and the lower parts being whiter. In the south of India, specimens are generally pale rufescent above, yellowish-white below, and it is rare to meet with dark brown specimens, as is said to be often the case at Calcutta. Perhaps some of these varieties may be hybrids, as it has been lateiy shown* that, in London, *M. decumanus*, *M. rattus*, and *M. alexandrinus* interbreed and commingle, yielding fertile hybrids of all degrees of intermediateness.

This rat is found over great part of India. Mr. W. Elliot observed it at Dharwar, frequenting stables and out-houses only, but abundant there. It is common at Calcutta, but there vary more than in Southern India. I have met with it in various localities, at Madras, at Nellore, on trees generally, and on the Malabar coast; but most abundantly at Secunderabad in the Deccan, frequenting the beams and rafters of houses, verandahs, &c.

It is perhaps Hodgson's *M. brunneusculus*, which he says, "closely resembles *brunneus* (vel *nemoralis*), but considerably smaller; rusty brown above, rusty below, extremities pale."

Buchanan Hamilton states that at Calcutta it frequents cocoa-nut trees and bamboos, making a nest with the branches, and bringing forth five or six young in August and September. They eat grain, which they collect in their nest, also young cocoa-nuts. They enter houses at night, but do not live there.

181. Mus niviventer.

HODGSON, Ann. Mag. Nat. Hist. 1845.—BLYTH, Memoir.

THE WHITE-BELLIED HOUSE-RAT.

Descr.—Above blackish-brown, shaded with rufous; below entirely white, tail and all.

Length of one, head and body $5\frac{1}{4}$ inches; tail 6: another 6 inches head and body; tail 7; hind-foot nearly $1\frac{1}{2}$. A female 7 inches long; tail $7\frac{1}{2}$.

This rat is stated by Hodgson to be a house-rat in Nepal, but not very common. It is the rat very generally found in most hill stations, and I found it very common at Darjeeling. Blyth also received it from Mussoorie, from Colonel Tytler, and noticed it as "a well marked species, rather larger than as originally described." In his Catalogue he gives it doubtfully as a variety of *M. rufescens*. I have occasionally obtained it in various other localities.

Hodgson states it to have the proportions and character of his *rattoides*, but to be less, with a shorter tail, and the long piles of the pelage rarer.

* Proc. Linn. Soc. 1862.

Two specimens from Landour were considered by Mr. Blyth as doubtfully belonging to this race, being very like *rufescens*, but with coarser and sub-spinous fur of duller coloring.

Blyth has a *Mus robustulus* (*M. rufescens*, variety olim) and *M. rattus*, brown variety olim, from Pegu and Tenasserim, the common house-rat there, very like M. *rufescens*, but darker, less rufescent, and the tail about equal to the head and body. A variety he described as *M. berdmorei* with peculiarly hispid fur; and one specimen differed from the other in having very dark upper parts, and very white lower parts, also smaller front teeth. This specimen would appear to accord with Gray's description of a specimen of *M. niviventer*, "dark-brown, cutting teeth narrow and slender," of which Blyth remarks, probably not the same as the above (*niviventer*).

182. Mus nitidus.

HODGSON.—BLYTH, Cat. p. 116.

THE SHINING BROWN-RAT.

Descr.—Dusky brown above, dusky hoary below; distinguished by its smooth coat, wherein the long hairy piles are almost wanting; short piles cinereous below with pale rufous tips; long piles basally horny, apically black.

Length, head and body $6\frac{1}{2}$ inches; tail $7\frac{1}{4}$; ears $\frac{3}{4}$ths; palm $\frac{11}{16}$ths.

Blyth states that one, of eight specimens, from Darjeeling, has the lower parts pure white, abruptly defined. They are especially distinguished by the fineness and softness of the fur. Hodgson says that it is a house-rat, and I procured several specimens of this rat at Darjeeling, mostly in houses.

Hodgson has another small rat, apparently of this group, *Mus horeites*. "A small species with fine pelage, tail longer than head and body; color above sordid brown, below sordid white. Length, head and body, 4 inches; tail $4\frac{1}{4}$; ears $\frac{7}{10}$ths; palm $\frac{1}{2}$; sole $1\frac{1}{8}$."

This has not been recognized by Mr. Blyth.

183. Mus caudatior.

HODGSON apud HORSFIELD—*M. cinnamomeus*, BLYTH, Cat. p. 115.

THE CHESNUT-RAT.

Descr.—Above bright cinnamon or chesnut-brown, with a rufous shade, the hairs with inconspicuous black tips, under parts white, abruptly divided from the upper color, sometimes yellowish-white. Muzzle rather sharp; ears long; tail long: Like M. *rufescens*, but smaller, with proportionally longer tail and softer fur.

Length of one, head and body 6 inches; tail $7\frac{3}{4}$; hind-feet $1\frac{1}{4}$.

Blyth has recently identified Hodgson's species with the one described by himself from Burmah. Hodgson's specimens were from Nepal. I procured one or two individuals at Darjeeling. Those from Nepal are said by Blyth to be "much darker than those from Burmah, but otherwise similar." This is considered by Blyth as one of the best marked species of this group. The only other rat of this section noticed by Blyth is *Mus concolor*, Blyth, the "common small thatch-rat of Pegu and Tenasserim." He states, however, that *Mus palmarum*, Scherzer, from the Nicobar islands, probably belongs to this group.

Another group consists of some small arboreal, long-tailed mice, diminutives of the last, which constitute the genus *Vandeleuria* of Gray. This he characterizes as having the upper incisors triangular, grooved in front, ears hairy, hind-feet very long, slender, claws small; tail long, with scattered hairs, more crowded at the tip; the fur soft with long bristles interspersed.

184. Mus oleraceus.

SYKES.—BLYTH, Cat. p. 120.—ELLIOT, Cat. 37.—*M. dumeticola*, and *M. povensis*, HODGSON.—*Marad ilei*, Can.—*Meina yelka*, Tel. of Yanadees.

THE LONG-TAILED TREE-MOUSE.

Descr.—Above light rufous or pale chesnut; lips, feet, and lower parts, pure white; tail almost nude, very long; muzzle slightly rounded; head of moderate length; ears ovate.

Length of one, head and body, $2\frac{1}{2}$ inches; tail 4; of another 3; tail $4\frac{1}{2}$; another measured 3; tail $4\frac{2}{10}$; head 1; ears $\frac{1}{2}$.

This very pretty little mouse has been found in all parts of India from the Himalayas to the extreme south, but is not recorded from Ceylon. I have found it most abundant in the south of India, where it frequents trees, and very commonly palm trees, on which it is said to make its nest generally. It, however, occasionally places its nest in the thatch of houses, on beams, &c. It is very active and from its habits difficult to procure.

Colonel Sykes merely observes that, "it constructs its nest of leaves of oleraceous herbs in the fields." This I have not observed myself, but had once a nest sent to me at Trichinopoly, said to have been found in a garden on some low shrub.

Hodgson's descriptions agree well enough with the characters of this mouse. He merely observes that it frequents woods and coppices.

185. Mus nilagiricus.

JERDON.—New species?

THE NEELGHERRY TREE-MOUSE.

Descr.—Above deep but bright chesnut-brown, beneath bright fawn-yellow, with a distinct line of demarcation between the two colors; head rather elongated; ears long, oval: tail somewhat hairy.

Length of one head and body, $3\frac{1}{2}$ inches; tail 5; head $1\frac{1}{10}$; ear $\frac{7}{10}$ths.

I have on several occasions found this tree-mouse in woods on the summit of the Neelgherries, near Ootacamund. The first I observed was brought into the house by a cat. I afterwards on two or three occasions found the nest, a mass of leaves and grass, on shrubs and low trees, from 4 to 6 feet from the ground, and on one occasion it was occupied by at least eight or ten apparently full-grown mice.

Blyth has *Mus badius* and *Mus peguensis*, of this group from Burmah, and *M. gliroides* from the Khasia hills. Gray has also described *Mus castaneus*, from the Philippine islands, similar in color to the Neelgherry mouse.

The following group chiefly comprises house-mice, and perhaps a few field ones. It has been named *Musculus* by Hodgson and others.

186. Mus urbanus.

HODGSON.—BLYTH, Cat. p. 118.—*M. musculus* apud ELLIOT, Cat. 39, and KELAART.—*M. dubius*, HODGSON.—*M. manei*, GRAY (undescribed).

THE COMMON INDIAN-MOUSE.

Descr.—Above dusky reddish-brown, below paler and more or less rufescent; feet paler.

Length of one, head and body, $2\frac{3}{4}$; tail $3\frac{3}{4}$; head $1\frac{1}{16}$ths; ear $\frac{6}{16}$ths; palm $\frac{3}{8}$ths; sole $\frac{1}{2}$: of another, 3; tail 4.

Blyth says that this differs conspicuously from the common English mouse in its smaller ears, and much longer tail. It has also larger eyes, and smaller feet. The fur too is of very different texture.

This mouse is found throughout India in houses in the plains, and also in Ceylon; and its habits do not differ from those of its English congener. *M. dubius*, Hodgson, is considered the young of this one.

187. Mus homourus.

HODGSON.—BLYTH, Cat. p. 118.—Olim, *M. nipalensis*, HODGSON.

THE HILL-MOUSE.

Descr.—Dark rufescent brown above, rufescent white below; hands and feet fleshy white; tail equal in length to head and body; "fur more gerbille-like in character than in *M. musculus*, the piles less dense and sinuous."

Length of one, head and body $3\frac{1}{2}$ inches; tail $3\frac{1}{2}$, head $1\frac{1}{16}$; ears $\frac{9}{16}$ths. Hodgson states that the female has only eight teats, whilst other mice have ten.

This is the common house-mouse of the Himalayan hill stations, from the Punjab to Darjeeling.

I obtained a specimen of what I considered the English house-mouse at Tellicherry on the Malabar coast, where it may have been introduced from the shipping, but I shall not give it a place here.

188. Mus crassipes.

BLYTH, J. A. S. XXVIII. 295.

THE LARGE-FOOTED MOUSE.

Descr.—Like *M. homourus*, but with the tail rather longer than the head and body, the feet particularly large, and like the tail well furnished with coarse short setæ.

Length $2\frac{3}{4}$ inches; tail $3\frac{1}{4}$; hind-feet $\frac{3}{4}$ths. From Mussoorie.

Some years ago I obtained one or two specimens of a mouse in a house on the Neelgherries which certainly differed both from *M. urbanus*, and *M. homourus*. It was larger, with large head and ears, and very large feet, and had more the appearance of a small rat than a mouse, but my specimens were lost before I had taken a more detailed description.

189. Mus darjeelingensis.

HODGSON, apud HORSFIELD, Cat. 168.

THE DARJEELING-MOUSE.

Descr.—Above dusky brown with a slight chesnut reflection, underneath pale yellowish white. Proportions of body, tail and extremities, comparatively slender; ears long.

Length of one, head and body, 3 inches; tail $2\frac{1}{2}$. From Darjeeling.

A white-bellied house-mouse is found frequently in the plains at various stations. I have also seen it on the Neelgherries. Its colors are dark mouse brown above, white beneath. It differs structurally from *M. urbanus* in its shorter tail, longer ears, and more slender feet. It is also usually smaller. I have found it common at Jaulna in the Deccan, at Nagpore, and other places. Length of one, head and body $2\frac{1}{2}$ inches; tail $2\frac{2}{10}$; ear $\frac{9}{20}$ths; fore-foot $\frac{5}{20}$ths; hind-foot $\frac{6}{10}$ths. It bears some resemblance to the descriptions of *M. darjeelingensis*, having the same propertional length of tail, slender feet, and longer ears.

The next mice have the color of field-mice.

190. Mus Tytleri.

BLYTH, J. A. S. XXVIII. 296.

THE LONG-HAIRED MOUSE.

Descr.—Fur unusually long and full, of a pale sandy mouse-color above, isabelline below, and pale on the well-clad limbs, and also on the tail laterally, and underneath. Whiskers exceedingly fine in texture and of a whitish color.

Length $2\frac{3}{4}$ inches; tail the same. From Dehra Doon. Apparently very nearly allied to the next, but kept distinct by Blyth in his Memoir. It should be compared with *M. homourus*.

191. Mus bactrianus.

BLYTH, J. A. S. XV. 140.—*M. gerbillinus* and *M. Theobaldi*, BLYTH, Cat. p. 119.

THE SANDY-MOUSE.

Descr.—Upper parts light isabelline, or sandy-brown, the extreme tips of the hairs dusky, and the basal two-thirds deep ashy; entire under parts and feet white; tail thinly clad with minute setæ. Fur dense and long.

Length of one, head and body, $2\frac{3}{8}$; tail $2\frac{5}{8}$; hind-foot $\frac{3}{4}$ths; ear conch barely $\frac{1}{2}$; of another, head and body $2\frac{7}{8}$; tail $2\frac{5}{8}$; ears $\frac{1}{2}$; tarsi $\frac{11}{16}$ths.

This mouse has been sent from Pind Dadun Khan in the Punjab, and from Kashmir, and it is stated to be the common house-mouse of Kandahar.

Blyth has in this group *Mus nitidulus* from Burmah; and *M. cunicularis* and *M. erythrotis*, from the Khasia hills.

Next field-mice. Tail shorter than head and body; fur not spinous.

192. Mus cervicolor.

HODGSON.—BLYTH, Cat. p. 119.—*M. albidiventris*, BLYTH.

THE FAWN FIELD-MOUSE.

Descr.—Above dull fawn or yellowish-gray; below sordid white; lining of ears and extremities pale; tail short; ears large, hairy.

Length of one, head and body $3\frac{1}{2}$ inches; tail $2\frac{7}{8}$; head 1; ears $\frac{9}{16}$ths: another $3\frac{1}{4}$; tail $2\frac{3}{4}$.

Blyth described his *M. albidiventris* as light-mouse color above, paling to grayish-white on the lower parts.

This field-mouse has been found in lower Bengal, in Nepal, and in south Malabar, although this last locality is given with doubt by Blyth.

It appears to me that Hodgson's *M. strophiatus* is nearly allied, if not the same. He describes it as, "bright fawn above, pure white below, a cross or gerget on the breast. Length $3\frac{1}{8}$; tail $2\frac{7}{16}$. A field-mouse closely allied to *M. cervicolor*, but seemingly distinct."

There is a nearly allied species in Ceylon, *Mus fulvidiventris*, Blyth, (*M. cervicolor* apud Kelaart).

193. Mus terricolor.

BLYTH, J. A. S. XX. 172.—Cat. p. 119.

THE EARTHY FIELD-MOUSE.

Descr.—Above variable according to the soil, light fawn brown, more or less rufescent; under parts white, abruptly separately from the hue of the upper parts.

Length of one, head and body $2\frac{1}{2}$ inches; tail $2\frac{1}{8}$; ears $\frac{1}{4}$th; hind-foot $\frac{9}{16}$ths. Much resembles *M. lepidus* of Elliot, but the fur is short, soft and not spinous in the least degree. Those from the alluvium of the Ganges are darker than specimens from the ferruginous soil to the westward.

"This," says Blyth, "is the most common field and garden-mouse in lower Bengal." It has been also found in Midnapore, and in southern India, a specimen having been sent to Mr. Blyth by Walter Elliot, along with a lot of *Mus lepidus*, from which he did not distinguish it.

The following species are a group of field-mice, the fur of which is mixed with spines. They have been placed in a distinct genus by Gray, which is practically adopted by Blyth in his Memoir.

Gen. LEGGADA, Gray.

Char.—Molars high with somewhat convex crowns, the cross ridges of the crown of the upper grinders deeply three-lobed; the front one with an additional lunate lobe at the base of its front edge; fur fine mixed with numerous spines, somewhat flattened.

This group was founded on a mouse first described by Colonel Sykes.

194. Leggada platythrix.

Mus apud SYKES.—BLYTH, Cat. p. 121.—ELLIOT, Cat. 40.—*Legyade* and *Kál yelka* of Waddurs.—*Gijeli-gadu*, Tel. of Yanadees.—*Kal ilei*, Can.

THE BROWN SPINY-MOUSE.

Descr.—Above light sandy brown or light brown mixed with fawn; beneath pure white, the white separated from the brown by a well defined pale fawn line: The flattened spines are transparent on the back, beneath smaller, and form with the fur a thick close covering. The head is long, the muzzle pointed, the ears rather large, oblong, rounded.

Length, head and body $3\frac{1}{2}$ inches; tail $2\frac{1}{2}$; hind-foot $\frac{3}{4}$ths; ear $\frac{1}{2}$.

This mouse is found only in southern India, and Mr. W. Elliot has given a full account of it habits. "The Leggyade lives entirely in the red gravelly soil in a burrow of moderate depth, generally on the side of a bank. When the animal is inside the entrance is closed with small pebbles, a quantity of which are collected outside by which its retreat may always be known. The burrow leads to a chamber in which is collected a bed of small pebbles on which it sits, the thick close hair of the belly protecting it from the cold and asperity of such a seat. Its food appears to be vegetable. In its habits it is monogamous and nocturnal.

In one earth which I opened, and which did not seem to have been originally constructed by the animal, I found two pairs; one of which were adults, the other young ones about three parts grown. The mouth of the earth was very large and completely blocked up with small stones; the passage gradually widened into a large cavity from the roof of which some other passages appeared to proceed, but there was only one communication with the surface, viz., the entrance. The old pair were seated on a bed of pebbles, near which, on a higher level, was another collection of stones, probably intended for a drier retreat. The young ones were in one of the passages, likewise furnished with a heap of small stones."

I have often opened the burrows of this rat, and can confirm Mr. Elliot's account. The Yanadees of Nellore state that one variety uses small sticks to sit on instead of stones, and give it a distinct appellation, but I did not notice any difference in the few specimens they brought me, though it is possible that they might have been of the next species.

195. Leggada spinulosa.

BLYTH, J. A. S. XXIII. 734.—Cat. p. 121.

THE DUSKY SPINY-MOUSE.

Descr.—Nearly affined to the last, but of a dark dusky color above, with fulvous tips to the softer fur; below, and all the feet dull whitish, Upper rodential tusks orange, the lower white.

Whiskers long and fine, the posterior and longer of these black for the basal half or more, the rest white.

Length of adult, head and body 3¾ inches; tail 3; foot ⅞ths.

This species was originally described by Blyth from specimens sent from the Punjab, and specimens were afterwards received from south Malabar, "quite similar, unless rather larger, and there is little difference in the color of the upper and lower tusks.''

196. Leggada Jerdoni.

BLYTH, Cat. p. 121.—Memoir on Rats, &c.

THE HIMALAYAN SPINY FIELD-MOUSE.

Descr.—Above bright dark ferruginous, pure white below ; some fine long black tips intermingled among the spines of the back; limbs marked with blackish externally; the feet white.

Length 4 inches ; tail $3\frac{1}{2}$; hind-feet $\frac{7}{8}$ths.

I procured specimens of this large field-mouse at Darjeeling; and lately in the valley of the Sutlej in Kunawur, at an elevation of nearly 12,000 feet, living under large stones.

197. Leggada lepida.

Mus apud ELLIOT, Cat. 41.—*Leggada booduga*, GRAY.—*Chitta burkani*, *Chit yelka*, *Chitta ganda*, Tel., of Wuddurs.—*Chitta yelka*, Tel., of Yanadees.

THE SMALL SPINY-MOUSE.

Descr.—Above pale sandy brown, pure white below, separated from the upper color by an exact line. The spines are small, fine, transparent, and of a dusky tinge tipt with fawn. The head very long, and muzzle pointed. Ear large ovate, naked. Tail naked. Limbs rather long, fine.

Length of a large individual, head and body $2\frac{9}{10}$ inches ; tail $2\frac{7}{10}$.

This pretty little mouse lives in pairs in the red soil, but sometimes a pair of young ones is found in the same burrow with the old ones.

I have found this species in gravelly soil, in gardens and in woods, in most parts of Southern India, making a small burrow, which generally has a little heap of stones placed at a short distance from the hole. It is preyed on now and then by the common Indian roller or jay, and it is very generally used as a bait to catch that bird with bird-lime.

Near these spined mice perhaps should come the "curious spiny-rat of south Malabar," which Mr. Blyth considered as belonging to the dormouse family, *Myoxidæ*, but which location Professor Peters has recently* called in question, stating it to be a true Murine type.

* Proc. Zool. Soc. 1865.

Gen. PLATACANTHOMYS, Blyth.

Char.—Molars $\frac{3-3}{3-3}$; equal in size except the last upper one, which is smaller than the rest, surrounded with enamel, with three or four transverse folds; incisors smooth, compressed; muzzle acute; ears moderate, nude; tail hairy, the hairs arranged distichously; whiskers very long; upper parts densely covered with sharp flat spines, mixed with an exceedingly delicate, thin undercoat; a few spines also on the lower part but smaller and finer; hallux nail-less. Blyth states that the rodential tusks are quite those of *Myoxus*, and that its whole habit is myoxine. Professor Peters too says the resemblance of this genus to the dormouse at first sight is very striking, principally on account of the long haired tail; but in other respects, in its smaller eyes, very thin ears, and the well developed, although very short, thumb of the fore-foot, it more approaches several murine genera of tropical India. The peculiarities of the skull, in which it deviates from the murine type are, according to Peters, the small and narrow foramina incisiva, formed only by the intermaxillary bones, the imperfect perforate palate, and the very short coronoid process of the lower jaw.

198. Platacanthomys lasiurus.

BLYTH, Proc. As. Soc. Calc. 1859. Cat. p. 109.

THE LONG-TAILED SPINY-MOUSE.

Descr.—General color a somewhat light rufescent-brown; under fur paler. On the forehead and crown, where the hair is very full, the color is more rufescent; whiskers chiefly black; lower parts dull or subdued white. The hairs on the tail darker than the body color, infuscated, except at the tip of the tail, where they are dull white, forming a conspicuous pale tail-tip.

Length of one, head and body 6 inches; tail $3\frac{1}{2}$, $1\frac{1}{2}$ more to the end of the hair; ear posteriorly $\frac{1}{2}$, ovoid and all but naked; hind-foot 1.

This very interesting addition to the Fauna of Southern India was found by Rev. Mr. Baker, in the hill ranges of the Western Ghâts of south Malabar, and also in Cochin and Travancore. "I was ignorant of the existence of this animal," says Mr. Baker, "till about a year ago when I found it in a range of hills about 3,000 feet high. It lives in the clefts of the rocks and hollow trees, is said to hoard ears of grain and roots, seldom comes into the native huts, and in that particular neighbourhood the hill-men tell me they are very numerous. I know they are to be found in the rocky mountains of Travancore; but I never met with them on the plains." In a further communication he remarks: "I have been spending the last three weeks in the Ghâts, and among other things had great hunt for the new spiny-dormice. They are most abundant I find in the elevated vales and ravines, living only in the magnificent old trees there found, in which they hollow out little cavities filling them with leaves and moss. The hill-people call them the 'pepper-rat', from their destroying large quantities of ripe pepper (*Piper nigrum*). Angely and jack-fruit (*Artocarpus ovalifolia* and *integrifolia*) are much subject to their ravages. Large numbers of the *Shunda palm* (*Caryota*) are found in the hills, and toddy is collected from them; these dormice eat through the covering of the pot as suspended, and enjoy themselves. Two were brought me in the pots half drowned. I procured in one morning sixteen specimens. The method employed in obtaining them was to tie long bamboos (with their little branches left on them to climb by) to the trees, and when the hole was reached, the man cut the entrance large enough to admit his hand, and took out the nest with the animals rolled up in it, put the whole in a bag made of bark, and brought it down. They actually reached the bottom sometimes without being disturbed; it was very wet cold weather, and they may have been somewhat torpid; but I started a large brown rat at the foot of one of the trees which ran up the stem into a hole, and four dormice were out in a minute from it, apparently in terror of their large friend. There were no traces of hoarding in any of the holes, but the soft bark of the trees was a good deal gnawed in places. I noticed that when their tails were elevated the hairs were perfectly erect like a bottle-brush.

Another rat has been made the type of

Gen. Golunda, Gray.

Char.—Molars when perfect low, with a broad flat crown; the cross ridges of the crown of the upper grinders divided into three distinct, slightly raised tubercles; upper incisors grooved.

Two species are classed under this by Blyth, which are apparently sufficiently distinct in general feature as well as in habits.

199. Golunda Elliotti.

GRAY, Mag. Nat. Hist. 1837.—BLYTH, Cat. p. 121.—*Mus hirsutus* ELLIOT, Cat. 36.—*M. coffæus*, KELAART.—*Gulandi*, Can.—*Gulat yelka*, of Waddurs.—*Sora-panji-gadur*, Tel. of Yanadees.

THE BUSH-RAT.

Descr.—Above olive-brown mixed with fulvous, giving a dusky fulvous tint; beneath yellowish-tawny or light yellowish gray; the tail somewhat villose; the head long, muzzle blunt, rounded, and covered with rough hair, as are the face and cheeks; ears round, hairy; whiskers long and very fine.

Length of one, head and body $6\frac{2}{10}$; tail $4\frac{3}{10}$; head $1\frac{1}{10}$; ear $\frac{6}{10}$ths.

This rat is found only in southern India and Ceylon. I have only met with it myself in the Carnatic, Malabar, and the Deccan.

"The *gulandi*," observes Mr. Elliot, "lives entirely above ground, in a habitation constructed of grass and leaves, generally in the root of a bush, at no great height from the ground; often indeed touching the surface." Again: "The *gulandi* lives entirely in the jungle, choosing its habitation in a thick bush, among the thorny branches of which, or on the ground, it constructs a nest of elastic stalks and fibres of dry grass, thickly interwoven. The nest is of a round or oblong shape, from 6 to 9 inches in diameter, within which is a chamber about 3 or 4 inches in diameter, in which it rolls itself up. Round and through the bush are sometimes observed small beaten pathways along which the little animal seems habitually to pass. Its motion is somewhat slow, and it does not appear to have the same power of leaping or springing, by which the rats in general avoid danger. Its food seems to be vegetable, the only contents of the stomach observed being the roots of the haryalee grass. Its habits are solitary except (when the female is bringing up her young) and diurnal, feeding in the mornings and evenings."

The Yanadees of Nellore catch this rat, surrounding the bush and seizing it as it issues forth, which its comparatively slow actions enable them to do easily. I have always found the nest on the ground or very close to it, in the midst generally of a thorny mass of *Zizyphus nummularia.*

This is the coffee rat of Ceylon, so destructive to coffee trees, whole plantations being sometimes deprived of buds and blossoms by these rats.

"They are found," says Kelaart, "in all the higher parts of the Kandian provinces. They appear to be migratory; and are not always seen in coffee estates; when they do visit the cultivated parts, their numbers are so great that in one day more than a thousand have been known to be killed on one estate. In clearing forests, the nests of these rats are met with under the roots of trees."

200. Golunda meltada.

GRAY, Mag. Nat. Hist. 1837.—*Mus lanuginosus*, ELLIOT, Cat. 35.—*Mettade* of Wuddurs.—*Metta yelka*, Tel., of Yanadees.—*Kera ilei*, Can.

THE SOFT-FURRED FIELD-RAT.

Descr.—Above reddish brown with a mixture of fawn, lighter beneath. The fur fine, close and soft, with a few longer hairs projecting. Head short; muzzle sharp; ears large; tail shorter than body.

Length of one, head and body $5\frac{6}{10}$; tail $4\frac{3}{10}$; ear $\frac{8}{10}$ths.

This rat has only been found in southern India. "The *mettade*," says Mr. Elliot, "lives entirely in cultivated fields in pairs or small societies of five or six, making a very slight and rude hole in the root of a bush, or merely harbouring among the heaps of stones thrown together in the fields, in the deserted burrow of the *kok*, or contenting itself with the deep cracks and fissures formed in the black soil during the hot months. Great numbers perish annually when these collapse and fill up at the commencement of the rains. The monsoon of 1826 having been deficient in the usual fall of rain at the commencement of the season, the *mettades* bred in such numbers as to become a perfect plague. They ate up the seed as soon as sown, and continued their ravages when the grain approached to maturity, climbing up the stalks of jowaree and cutting off the ear to devour the grain with greater facility. I saw many whole fields completely devastated, so much so as to prevent the farmers from paying their rents. The ryots employed the Wuddurs to destroy them, who killed them by thousands, receiving a measure of grain for so many dozens, without perceptibly diminishing their numbers. Their flesh is eaten by the tank-diggers. The female produces from 6 to 8 at a birth."

The physiognomy of this rat in so distinct from that of the last, as is also the character of the fur and the habits, that I much doubt if they ought to be included in the same group.

Kelaart has a *Golunda newera*, which he considers allied to this last species, and found in the black soil of Newera-ellia, where it is a great destroyer of peas and potatoes.

It appears to me that Hodgson's *Mus myothrix* has some affinities for *Golunda Elliotti.* It is described as, "fur yellow brown, minutely black varied, hair rather short and rigid, lead colored with yellow tips and with scattered narrow black bristles; beneath yellowish white, tail slightly hairy, yellow. Length of one 6 inches, tail $3\frac{3}{4}$; head $1\frac{1}{2}$. Tenants the woods only, dwelling in burrows under the roots of trees, but not gregariously."

Blyth has described a *Hapalomys longicaudatus* from Burmah.

The next animal has been referred by Gray to another group, the *Aspalacidæ*, but this is not agreed to by Blyth and Waterhouse, who consider it as a murine type.

Gen. RHIZOMYS, Gray.

Syn. *Nyctocleptes*, Temminck.

Char.—Incisors very large, long, somewhat triangular, sharp, molars $\frac{3-3}{3-3}$, rooted, subcylindric, the crown with somewhat parallel cross ridges; upper molars with a lobe internally; head large; body massive; eyes small; ears naked, conspicuous; feet short, strong; tail short, thick, naked. Chiefly from the Indo-chinese region and Malayana. One species extends into our north-eastern limits.

201. Rhizomys badius.

HODGSON.—BLYTH, Cat. p. 122.—*R. minor*, GRAY.

THE BAY BAMBOO-RAT.

Descr.—Above of a bay or chesnut color, the fur being slaty gray with rufous-brown tips; below dark ashy-gray; feet dark.

Length 9 inches.

This small bamboo-rat has been taken only in the Terai of Sikim, and the adjoining parts of the Nepal Terai. It eats the roots of bamboos and other trees, constructing burrows under the roots. It is said to be very bold and easily taken.

Rhizomys pruinosus, Blyth, is from the Khasia hills; *R. castaneus*, Blyth, from Burmah; and *R. sumatrensis*, from the Malayan peninsula and islands. *R. sinicus*, Gray, from China, is figured in Hardwicke's Illustrations.

There are many genera of true rats found in the new world, and a few in Africa. From the old continent there are several peculiar forms, some of which deserve particular mention. Among these are the hamsters, genus *Cricetus*. They have the teeth of *Murinæ*, but their tail is short and hairy, and they have cheek-pouches. They belong to the Palæarctic region.

The Beaver, *Castor fiber*, L., is one of the most remarkable *Muridæ*, and is, by some, placed in a distinct sub-family. It has four molars on each side, and five toes on all the feet. Its flattened tail, webbed hind-feet, together with its aquatic habits and peculiar habitations, are described in all popular works on natural history. Their fur is highly prized, and much sought for, and it is now all but extinct in Europe. The substance called *Castor* is a peculiar pungent secretion of a glandular pouch, terminating in the prepuce; and the organs of generation of both sexes terminate within the rectum.

The genus *Helamys*, F. Cuvier (*Pedetes*, Illiger), from South Africa, is a peculiar animal, isolated in its position. It is called the jumping hare, has a large head and eyes, a long tail, short fore-feet, with 5 toes, having long pointed nails; and lengthened hind-feet, with only four toes, having large claws like hoofs. The mole-rats, *Aspalacidæ*, chiefly from Africa, have the incisors broad, large and exserted; three molars as in rats, heavy bodies with short limbs and tail, very small eyes, concealed in some, and the ears small. They live underground, and feed entirely on roots. *Bathyergus*, of South Africa, is made the type of a distinct family by Blyth, *Bathyergidæ*. They have four molars on each side, small eyes, and a short tail.

The pouched-rats are considered by some to form a distinct family, equal in rank to the other four large families. They are the *Saccomydidæ* of authors. They have four molars on each side; the upper incisors are grooved; the anterior median nails very long and trenchant. They have deep cheek-pouches, opening externally, and are all from North America.

Sub-fam. Arvicolinæ, Voles, &c.

Snout blunt, rounded; ears small, more or less concealed in the hair; molars $\frac{3-3}{3-3}$, composed of alternating triangular prisms, without roots; incisors rounded; tail generally short.

This family comprises several forms mostly Palæarctic, one or two species only occurring in the Himalayas, of the same genus as the water-rat and meadow vole of Britain.

Gen. ARVICOLA, Lacepede.

Syn. *Hypudæus*, Illiger.

Char.—Incisors smooth in front; snout short, bluntish; eyes small or moderate; anterior feet with four toes and a hallucar wart, posterior feet five toed; nails curved; tail short or moderate, hairy; otherwise as in the character of the sub-family.

202. Arvicola Roylei.

GRAY, Ann. Mag. Nat. Hist. 1842.—Figd. ROYLE, Ill. Bot. Himal.—BLYTH, Cat. p. 125.

THE HIMALAYAN VOLE.

Descr.—Above ashy-brown with a tinge of rufous more or less apparent; beneath pale brownish-ashy; ears moderately large, rounded, hairy; tail clad with rigid pale hairs; incisors yellow in front.

Length of one, head and body $3\frac{1}{2}$ inches; tail $1\frac{2}{12}$; hind-foot $\frac{9}{12}$ths. One procured by myself measured, head and body $3\frac{3}{4}$; tail $1\frac{3}{8}$.

The Himalayan Vole is noted by Blyth only from Kashmir and Pind Dadun Khan, in the Punjab. I obtained it in Kunawar, near Chini, at an elevation of nearly 12,000 feet, and again on the south side of the Barendo pass, at about the same height, in great numbers in a fine meadow, where it was burrowing lightly close to the surface, and several were caught in digging a light trench round my tent. I also observed it in the Pir Punjal pass. Its occurring at such a low level as Pind Dadun Khan is remarkable, as it is only found on the Himalayas at great elevations.

In the recent edition of Hodgson's British Museum Collections, there is No. 116, *Arvicola thricotis*, new species, Darjeeling, in woods near houses; but it is added, compare with *Neodon sikimensis*.

Gen. NEODON, Hodgson.

Char.—Nearly allied to *Arvicola*; incisors similar; grinders both above and below disposed in a regular compact series with slightly elevated ridges or folds; anterior grinders of the upper jaw larger than the others, and having an additional ridge more than *Arvicola.* Molars of lower jaw more uniform, with a very slight decrease posteriorly, otherwise as in *Arvicola.*

This genus is very close to *Arvicola.* I have not had an opportunity of examining the teeth.

203. Neodon sikimensis.

HODGSON, Ann. Mag. Nat. Hist. 1849.—BLYTH, Cat. p. 125.

THE SIKIM VOLE.

Descr.—Fur very soft and silky; above deep brownish-black, with a slight rusty shade, minutely and copiously grizzled with hairs of a deep ferruginous tint, giving a general shade of dark rufescent-brown; beneath dark bluish-gray or ashy with a slight ferruginous or fulvous shade. All four feet very slender. Ears moderate, hairy.

Length of one, head and body 4¾; tail 1½; head 1¼; hind-foot ¾ths. Another was 5 inches long. The female has six teats.

This Vole differs from the last in its much darker tints. It has only been procured in Sikim, near Darjeeling, at heights varying from 7,000 to 15,000 feet. It is said by Hodgson to breed in hollow decayed trees, or among the roots of trees, making a saucer-shaped nest of moss or soft grass. The female brings forth three or four young only.

Compared with the *Arvicola,* it is more a denizen of forests. Mr. Atkinson found it under fallen trees and stones, on the top of Tonglo, near Darjeeling, 10,000 feet; whence, also, I had a specimen brought me.

Some of this family are nearly related to the beavers, and the fur of one, *Fiber zibethicus,* the *Musquash* or *Oudara* of North America, is highly prized. It has semi-palmated hind-feet and a long scaly tail. The Lemmings, *Myodes,* are another well known genus of *Arvicolinæ.* They occur in the northern parts of both continents in immense numbers, and their migratory habits are familiar to all. They quite resemble voles, but are more heavily formed, with very short ears and tail. They have five distinct nails on the fore-feet.

The peculiar genus *Geomys,* perhaps belongs to this sub-family. Blyth described a *Phaiomys leucurus,* from Tibet.

The remaining rodents have the clavicle imperfect in many, almost wanting in some. They form two groups, *Hystricidæ* and *Leporidæ.*

Fam. HYSTRICIDÆ.

Clavicles typically imperfect; the lower angle of the lower jaw acute; usually 4 equal molars on each side with roots.

This family comprises a large number of rodents of varied form and habits, by far the greater number being from America, and only one sub-family occurring in the old world.

Sub-fam. HYSTRICINÆ Porcupines.

Incisors large, usually colored, not grooved anteriorly; molars $\frac{4-4}{4-4}$ in adults, complex, with undulated striæ of enamel in the crown; body more or less clad with acuminate spines; fore-feet tetradactylous with a very small wart-like thumb; hind-feet with 4 or 5 toes.

Porcupines possess clavicles, which, however, are only attached to the sternum and not to the scapula. The skull is remarkable for the great size of the infra-orbital foramen. They have usually 14 pairs of ribs. The length of the tail is very various.

Porcupines are burrowing animals of strictly nocturnal habits, feeding on roots, fruit, bark, and young shoots. The most typical forms of the sub-family belong to the old world.

Gen. HYSTRIX, Linnæus.

Char.—Hind-feet with five unguiculate toes; all the claws stout; body armed with rigid spines, mixed with some longer flexible ones; tail very short, with a bundle of open tubes at the end; muzzle truncated.

Porcupines are a well known group, which take their popular name, signifying spiny-pig, from their large size and grunting voice. They are found in the warmer regions of the old continent. The peculiar open tubes of the tail are supported on slender stalks, and they make a rattling noise when shaken.

204. Hystrix leucura.

SYKES.—BLYTH, Cat. p. 128.—ELLIOT, Cat, 45.—*H. hirsutirostris*, BRANDT.—*H. cristata indica*, GRAY, HARDWICKE, Ill. Ind. Zool. 1. pl.

14.—*H. zeylanensis*, BLYTH.—*Sahi*, *Sayal*, *Sarsel*, H., in various parts of the country.—*Sajru*, Bengal.—*Saori* in Gujrat.—*Salendra*, Mahr. of the Ghâts, *Yed*, Can.—*Yeddu pandi*, Tel.—*Dumsi*, in Nepal.—*Ho-igu*, of Gonds.

THE INDIAN PORCUPINE.

Descr.—Muzzle clad with short stiff bristly hairs, and a few white spines on the face; spines on the throat short, grooved, some with white points forming a demi-collar; crest full, long, chiefly of black bristles, a few of them only with long white points; the larger quills on the back black; many annulated with white at base and middle, and some with white points; the long thin quills mostly white at tip; the quills on the loins mostly all white, the pedunculated quills of the tail yellowish-white; some of the quills of the sides and lumbar regions flat and striated; whiskers long black, a few tipped white.

Length of one, head and body 32 inches; tail 7.

The Indian porcupine closely resembles the porcupine of Africa and the South of Europe, but differs, according to Waterhouse, in "the quills of the lumbar regions being white in *leucura*, and chiefly dusky in the *cristata;* and the bristles of the crest of the latter have all long white points, whereas in *leucura* only some have white points, the rest are entirely brown. The long quills of the back have the white more extended in *leucura*."

This porcupine is found over a great part of India, from the lower ranges of the Himalayas to the extreme south, but does not occur in lower Bengal, where it is replaced by the next one. It forms extensive burrows, often in societies, in the sides of hills, banks of rivers and nullahs, and very often in the bunds of tanks, and in old mud walls, &c., &c. In some parts of the country they are very destructive to various crops, potatoes, carrots, and other vegetables. They never issue forth till after dark, but now and then one will be found returning to his lair in daylight. Dogs take up the scent of the porcupine very keenly, and on the Neelgherries I have killed many by the aid of dogs, tracking them to their dens. They charge backwards at their foes, erecting their spines at the same time, and dogs generally get seriously injured by their strong spines which are sometimes driven deeply into the assailant. The porcupine is not bad eating, the meat, which is white, tasting something between pork and veal.

This species is common in Ceylon, whence Mr. Blyth formerly named a young specimen as distinct. It occurs also in Afghanistan, and probably in other parts of Asia.

205. Hystrix bengalensis.

Blyth, J. A. S. XX. 179.—Cat. p. 128.—*H. malabarica*, Sclater. P. Z. S. 1865 (fid. Blyth).

THE BENGAL PORCUPINE.

Descr.—Smaller than *leucura;* crest small and thin, the bristles blackish; body spines much flattened, and strongly grooved, terminating in a slight seta; slender flexible quills much fewer than in *leucura*, white with a narrow black band about the centre; the thick quills basally white, the rest black, mostly with a white tip; a distinct white demi-collar: spines of lumbar region white; as are those of the tail and rattle; muzzle less hirsute than in *leucura*.

Length of one, head and body 28 inches; tail 8.

Blyth compared this species with the hill porcupine, which it resembles in its smaller crest, and also in its general characters, but it more resembles *leucura* in the proportion of the large quills and other points. He has quite recently written me from England that he considers the porcupine recently described by Sclater as *H. malabarica*, to be the same as his *bengalensis*. Sclater describes it as having a great general resemblance to *leucura*, but differing in the less bristly snout, and the longer tail, as also in many of the quills being orange colored in the place of white, especially some of the spines of the back and tail, whilst others were black and white as in the common kind. If Mr. Blyth is right in his identification of the two species, the orange color of the quills would appear to be only a local variation, and even this does not appear to be constant; for Mr. Day, who first noticed the orange porcupine, states that in captivity they lose much of their orange color, and its vividness greatly decreases when they are ill. Besides the general points of distinction between *leucura* and *malabarica*, Mr. Sclater points out a few slight peculiarities in the form of the skull of the latter.

The Bengal porcupine is found in lower Bengal, extending into Assam and Arrakan; and also in south Malabar, if Blyth's identification be correct. Nothing peculiar is recorded of its habits. Mr. Day states that he procured specimens of the orange porcupine from various parts of the Ghâts of Cochin and Travancore, and that the flesh of this kind is more highly esteemed for food than the common variety. The native sportsmen declare that the aroma from these burrows is quite sufficient to distinguish the two species.

206. Hystrix longicauda.

MARSDEN.—BLYTH, Cat. p. 129.—*H. alophus*, HODGSON.—*H. Hodgsonii*, GRAY.—*Acanthion javanicum*, F. CUVIER.—*Anchotia dumsi*, in Nepal; *i. e.*, the crestless porcupine.—*Sathung*, Lepch.—*O'—e'* of the Limbus.

THE CRESTLESS PORCUPINE.

Descr.—No crest; head, neck, fore-half of the body, entire belly and limbs covered with black spinous bristles, 2 to 3 inches long, shortest on the head and limbs; the large quills of the back and croup vary from 7 to 12 inches long, mostly white with one central black ring; the tail conico-depressed, with some quills about 5 inches long, and the rattle consisting of 35 to 40 hollow cylinders, some closed, others open. A narrow and vaguely marked white color.

Length of one, head and body 24 inches; tail 4, or with the quills $5\frac{1}{2}$.

This porcupine is found in the central region of Nepal and Sikim, and extends through Burmah into the Malayan peninsula and islands. Sclater in a Synopsis of the species of *Hystrix*, separates *H. Hodgsoni* from *H. javanicum*. I have followed Blyth in uniting these two.

Hodgson states that they are "very numerous and very mischievous, depredating greatly among the potatoes and other tuberous or edible rooted crops. They are most numerous in the central region, but are common to all three regions. They breed in spring, and usually produce two young, about the time the crops being to ripen. They are monogamous, the pair dwelling together in burrows of their own formation. Their flesh is delicious, like pork, but much more delicate-flavored, and they are easily tamed so as to breed in confinement. All tribes and classes, even high-caste Hindoos eat them, and it is deemed lucky to keep one or two alive in stables, where they are encouraged to breed."

I saw several skins of this species at Darjeeling that had been killed in some tea plantations between 4,000 and 5,000 feet of elevation. The name given to this animal by the Limbus of Sikim (according to Hodgson), viz., *O'—e'*, is singularly like that which the Gonds of Central India apply to the common one *Ho-yú.*

Hodgson gives a few interesting anatomical details of this species. There are two glands which almost surround the anus, secreting a pus-like fluid devoid of any odour, which is carried off by several pores. The penis is sheathed and pointed backwards, and has a bone 1½ inch long; the testes are internal. The intestines of one were 30 feet long, and the cœcum 12.

The only other recorded species of *Hystrix*, besides *H. cristata* of Europe, is *H. Africæ australis* of Peters.

Atherura fasciculata, is another species of porcupine found on the Tippera hills, and thence southwards to the Malayan peninsula. It has a much longer tail than the true porcupines, and the spines of the back are less elongated. The tail ends in a tuft of long bristles.

The American porcupines belong to a different group, called *Cercolabinæ*, by some; *Philodendreæ* by others. They are more or less arboreal, have long tails, prehensile in some, and the spines are short and mixed with hair.

The remaining animals of this family are, with one or two exceptions, exclusively American, and the great majority from the Neotropical region.

The sub-family CAVINÆ, comprises the Cavies and the Capybara. The former, Gen. *Cavia*, have short ears, and little or no tail, and the nails of the toes are large. They are terrestrial and burrow. The guinea-pig is a domesticated variety of one of the species. The capybara, *Hydrochærus capybara*, is one of the giants of the order, and has much the appearance of a small pig. It has 4 toes in front, the three toes to the hind-feet united by a short membrane, and is quite aquatic in its habits.

The *Dasyproctinæ* comprise the Agoutis and the Paca. The former, *Dasyprocta*, have 4 toes before, and three or two behind; whilst the latter, *Cœlogenys*, have small additional ones, making five on both feet. They somewhat resemble hares and rabbits.

The ECHIMYINÆ comprise a somewhat more varied group of animals. Some have spines mixed with their fur, and one, *Myopotamus coypus*, has much the form of the beaver, and has often been classed with it. It has the hind-feet webbed, and 5 toes to all the feet. The fur is used by hatters, and many are imported into Europe for that purpose.

Two African genera, *Aulacodon* and *Petromys*, are usually classed in this division.

The OCTODONTINÆ have rootless molars, and usually 5 toes to each foot, with large claws. They have mostly large ears, and a long or moderate hairy tail. They are of small size, and burrow. Their general aspect is intermediate to that of chinchillas and voles. The chinchillas (CHINCHILLINÆ) have rootless molars and stout claws, as the last; but the number of toes is usually less. The tail is moderate and hairy, and held recurved, and the ears are generally conspicuous. The clavicles are developed in this and the last group. The chinchilla, *Chinchilla laniger*, whose fur is so highly prized; and the viscacha *Lagostomus trichodactylus*, are the best known species. They burrow in the ground, and live in numerous societies. The hind-feet are usually considerably larger than the anterior, and the animals hold their food, like the squirrels, between the short fore-paws. All the species of the two last sub-families are exclusively confined to South America.

Fam. LEPORIDÆ, Hares.

Syn. *Duplici-dentata*, Van der Hoeven.

Upper incisors 4 in number, there being two thin teeth placed behind the anterior and larger teeth. Molars 5 or 6 on each side above, and 6 beneath on each side, rootless, and formed of two laminæ joined together by a transverse ridge of enamel. Fore-feet with five toes, hind-feet with 4, all with hairy soles; nails long, compressed; tail short or none.

This family is distinguished from all other rodents by the possession of a small additional incisor placed behind each of the large incisive tusks of the upper jaw. These small teeth are considered to be the true incisors, the front teeth, being as before stated, the representatives of the canines. Their orbits communicate with each other through an aperture in the septum as in birds. They have an enormous cœcum lined internally with a spiral layer throughout its entire length. There are only two well marked generic forms, *Lepus* and *Lagomys*.

Gen. LEPUS, Linnæus.

Char.—Incisors, $\frac{2-2}{1-1}$; præmolars, $\frac{3-3}{2-2}$; molars $\frac{3-3}{3-3}$. The last molar above small and simple; ears typically very long; tail short, recurved. Hind-legs much longer than the fore-legs. Their clavicles are imperfect.

Hares are found thinly scattered over all the world, except in Australia but are most abundant in the northern temperate zone.

The habits of hares are well known; their timidity, watchfulness, increased by the situation of their eyes, which are so placed that they can see all round, and their great speed. In some, as in hares, the young are born with their eyes open; in the rabbits with their eyes closed. There are two well marked species of hare in India, and a third of a peculiar type.

207. Lepus ruficaudatus.

GEOFFROY—BLYTH, Cat. p. 131.—*L. indicus* and *macrotus*, HODGSON.—*Khargosh*, H.—*Kharra* in Central India and part of Bengal.—*Sasrú*, also in Bengal.—*Lamma*, Hindi of some—*Molol*, of Gonds.

THE COMMON INDIAN HARE.

Descr.—General hue rufescent mixed with blackish on the back and head; ears brownish anteriorly, white at the base and the tip brown; neck, breast, flanks and limbs, more or less dark sandy rufescent unmottled; nape pale sandy rufescent; tail rufous above, white beneath; upper lip, small eye mark, chin, throat, and lower parts, pure white.

Length of one, head and body 20 inches; tail with hair 4; ear externally nearly 5; breadth of ear when expanded 2¾. Weight rarely exceeds 5 lbs.

This hare is found from the foot of the Himalayas southwards to the Godavery river on the east, and on the west as far south as the Taptee river at all events, perhaps further. It extends from the Punjab to Assam. It is stated by the Rev. H. Baker also to occur in South Malabar along with the next species, but no specimens appear to have been sent, and I rather doubt its occurrence there. It is also supposed to extend into Afghanistan, the skull of a hare from Kandahar being very similar to that of our hare; perhaps, however, Mr. Blyth suggests, that of a nearly allied species.

Hairs are very abundant in parts of the North-west Provinces, and excellent coursing is had near Delhi and especially in Hurriana. They are less common in the Punjab.

Both this and the next species take to earth readily when pursued, and appear to be well acquainted with all the fox holes in their neighbourhood.

208. Lepus nigricollis.

F. CUVIER,—BLYTH, Cat. p. 132.—ELLIOT, Cat. 46.—*L. melanauchen*, TEMMINCK.—*Khargosh*, H.—*Malla*, Can.—*Sassa*, Mahr.—*Músal*, Tam. *Kúndéli*, Tel.

THE BLACK-NAPED HARE.

Descr.—Upper part grayish-rufescent, slightly mottled with black; large nuchal spot extending to near the shoulders velvety black; ears grayish-brown internally, dusky posteriorly, black at the base, and white-fringed at the apex; lower neck yellowish, chin and abdomen white; tail grizzled black and yellowish-gray above, white beneath.

Length of one, head and body 19 inches; tail $2\frac{1}{2}$; ear $4\frac{3}{4}$.

The black-naped hare is found throughout the South of India, extending north to the Godavery river on the east, and on the west coast as high as the Taptee river, and perhaps further, for Adams states it to be found in Sindh and parts of the Punjab, but this much requires confirmation. It is the hare of Ceylon also, and has been introduced into Java and the Mauritius. It is very abundant in many parts of the Madras Presidency, more especially on the east coast and in parts of the Deccan.

Lepus peguensis, Blyth, is found in Upper Burmah, and *L. sinensis* in China.

Lepus pallipes, Hodgson, J. A. S. XI. 288, with plate (*L. tolai*, Pallas apud Gray) is found in Tibet, along with *L. tibetanus*, Waterhouse (*L. oistolus*, Hodgson), if indeed they be distinct. The latter is described as pale fawn above, whitish below and on the limbs; the croup grayish-blue, and the tail white. They are both represented as frequenting rocky places, and running from rock to rock. It is possible that a few individuals may occasionally cross to the Indian side of the passes, but I have not observed them myself on this side. The Bhotia name is *Ribong*, or hill-ass.

The next species differs somewhat in general appearance and structure, and was formerly separated generically by Blyth, and I think with justice; but he has in his Catalogue merely marked it as a section. The characters of the sub-genus, *Caprolagus* are,—large head, small eyes, short ears, small and subequal limbs, strong, straight and sharp claws, harsh hair and inconspicuous whiskers. The skull is very strong, and the incisors larger comparatively than in the common hare.

209. Lepus hispidus.

PEARSON.—BLYTH, Cat. p. 133.

THE HISPID HARE.

Descr.—General color dark or iron gray with an embrowned ruddy tinge; limbs and body shaded externally with black; the tail rufescent both above and below; the inner fur short, soft, downy, of an ashy hue; the outer longer, hispid, harsh and bristly, some of the hairs annulated black and yellow-brown, others pure black and longer, the wholly black hair more abundant than the lighter ones. The ears are very short, and broad.

Length of one, head and body $19\frac{1}{2}$ inches; tail with the hair $2\frac{1}{8}$; ear $2\frac{3}{4}$.

This curious hare is of a very dark hue, of a heavy make, with small eyes, make more rabbit-like, with small eyes, short and stout limbs, and short whiskers. It is popularly called the black rabbit at Dacca and elsewhere, and it is said to burrow in the ground like rabbits. It inhabits the Terai at the foot of the Himalayas, from Goruckpore to Assam, extending south to Dacca, and probably still further, and even it is said to the Rajmahal hills. It frequents jungly places, long grass, bamboos, &c., shunning observation; and, from its retired habits, is very difficult to observe and obtain; and it perhaps has a more extended distribution through lower Bengal than that noted above. I have only seen it near Dacca. The flesh is stated to be white like that of the rabbit.

The next group is a Northern or Arctopolitan form.

Gen. LAGOMYS, Cuvier.

Char.—Incisors double as in hares; molars $\frac{5-5}{5-5}$; ears short, rounded; claws curved; no tail; limbs short and slender; clavicles perfect. Of small size. This genus, called by some the calling hare, by others, the barking mouse, is composed of a few species from the northern regions of both continents, one of which crosses the ridge of the Himalayas. They are called by some travellers tailless-rats. They construct curious and intricate burrows, and have a peculiar piping call, heard to a great distance.

210. Lagomys Roylei.

OGILBY, figured in ROYLE's Ill. Bot. Himalayas, pl. 4.—*L. nipalensis*, HODGSON.—*L. Hodgsoni*, BLYTH.—*Rang-rúnt*, or *Rang-dúni*, in Kunawar.

THE HIMALAYAN MOUSE-HARE.

Descr.—General color deep rabbit-gray or brown with a yellowish gray tinge, more or less rufous on the head, neck, shoulders, and sides of body; ears elliptic, roundish at tip, nearly nude, with some long white hairs externally; muzzle hairy, brown; lower lip pale; under parts dingy whitish; whiskers long and fine, white anteriorly, the posterior ones blackish, $2\frac{1}{2}$ inches long. The hairs of the body are dark-bluish at the base, with a broad gray ring and a dark brown point, some of them slaty-black, then rufous-brown, finally tipped dark; the fur delicately soft and fine.

Length varies from 6 to nearly 8 inches; of one 7 inches long the head 2; ears $\frac{7}{8}$ths; hind-feet $1\frac{1}{4}$.

Some specimens have much more rufous than others. Hodgson described his *L. nipalensis* (which Blyth identifies with *Roylei*) as deep bay from snout to mid-body, black freckled with paler rufous thence to the vent; below chin and belly, pale bay, limbs the same. This indicates a somewhat darker coloration than is usually met with.

This species of *Lagomys* was first made known from skins sent home by Royle from the Chor mountain, not far from Simla. This hill, I may observe, is some distance south from the snowy range, and on one of the outer ranges of the Himalayas. I have observed it in Kumaon also at some distance on this side of the Snowy range, near the Borendo pass, and elsewhere, at heights varying from 11,000 to 14,000 feet. It has been found all along the Himalayas at suitable elevations, from Kashmir to Sikim. It is also found on the other side of the snowy range, but in some parts is replaced by another species. It lives always in rocky ground or among loose stones, several pairs together. They come out to to feed, but dart into their holes on the smallest alarm. It is said that they hibernate during winter.

Lagomys Curzoniæ has been lately described by Hodgson from Tibet and the interior of Sikim. This species replaces the common species in Ladak, and other countries beyond the snowy range.

Lagomys rufescens, Gray, is another species from Afghanistan, and there are others in Northern and Central Asia, and one or two in North America.

Ord. UNGULATA, L.

Feet with hoofs instead of claws.

The feet being used only as supports they have no clavicles, and their fore-arms are constantly in a state of pronation, whence they are reduced to live on vegetables. Their forms and mode of life show much less variety than unguiculated animals. They were divided into two large groups or orders by Cuvier, the non-ruminating, or *Pachydermata*, and the *Ruminautia*. More recently they have been divided into several tribes or sub-orders, viz., *Proboscidea*, *Perissodactyla*, and *Artiodactyla*, the two former, together with one family of the latter, constituting the Pachydermatous division; and the remander of the *Artiodactyla* comprising the ruminating animals. Linnæus divided them into *Bruta*, *Bellua*, and *Pecora*; the former comprising the elephant and rhinoceros; the *Bellua*, the horse, the hog and the *Hippopotamus;* and the last the ruminants.

Tribe, Proboscidea, Cuvier.

This comprises only one family.

Fam. Elephantidæ.

Two large incisive tusks in the upper jaw; none in the lower jaw: molars large, with the crown elongated; feet with 5 toes, with nails surrounded by a thick callous skin; snout elongated into a long prehensile proboscis or trunk; mammæ two, pectoral.

The cranium of the elephants is much elevated vertically, the intermaxillary bones being much developed to support the tusks which are sometimes enormous, and curved upwards, and to give origin to some of the numerous muscles which support the proboscis. This organ, which is flexible in every direction, and endowed with great sensibility, enables the elephant to procure his food from the ground or high trees, sucks up the water he drinks, and conveys it to his throat. The brain occupies but a small space in the huge cranium, which has numerous sinuses or air-cavities extending through the frontal, parietal, and temporal bones, even to the occipitals. The nasal bones are so shortened, being pushed up by intermaxillaries, that the nostrils (in the skeleton) are situated in the upper portion of the face, but in the living animal terminate in the end of the proboscis. In a fossil genus when immature, the lower jaw possesses incisors. The carpus has the same number of bones as in man, and there are five complete bony phalanges. The stomach is simple; the intestines voluminous, and the colon and cœcum are enormous. The testes of the male are deeply situated in the abdomen near the kidneys. The brain has numerous small but deep convolutions, and the cerebellum is very large. There are two genera of elephants distinguished by the form of the molars, but one of them is now extinct.

Gen. Elephas, Linnæus.

Char.—Molars usually 2 on each side above and below, the crown flattened. They are formed of a number of vertical lamellæ consisting of bone, enamel, and another substance, called cortical or crusta petrosa.

The huge tusks are cylindrical with a conical tip, like the so-called incisors of rodents; which, as before stated, they closely resemble, and they grow from a persistent pulp which is constantly forming new ivory. They are formed of ivory and enamel only. The laminæ of the molar teeth are arranged transversely to the direction of the jaw; also as in rodents. The grinders succeed each other from behind forwards, so that each tooth as it becomes worn is pushed forwards by the one behind it, and thus at times the elephant has only one, at other times two molars on each side, according to its age. It is said that these molars are renewed eight times in some elephants. The tusks are only renewed once, between the first and second years of age. The skin is very thick and nearly devoid of hairs.

Elephants are huge unwieldy animals with large ears, long and thick limbs, and a long tail. They only occur now in the tropical regions of the old world, but in former ages were also denizens of even the northern portions of the old continent. There are two well marked species, one from Africa, the other Indian, and a third species is indicated.

211. Elephas indicus.

Cuvier.—Blyth, Cat. p. 134.—Elliot, Cat. 48.—*E. asiaticus*, Blumenbach.—*Hathi*, H.—*Ani*, Tam., Tel., Can., and Mal.—*Yenu*, of the Gonds.

The Indian Elephant.

Descr.—Head oblong with a concave forehead; crowns of the molars presenting narrow transverse ridges; 4 toes to the hind-feet; ears moderate; tusks large in the male, small in the female. Compared with the African elephant this species has much smaller ears. In the former the head is more rounded; the grinders present broad lozenge-shaped eminences on their crowns; and they have usually only 3 toes on their hind feet. The number of pairs of ribs is, 19 in the Indian elephant, and 21 in the African, and there are 33 caudal vertebæ in the Indian, and never more than 26 in the African. In some males only one tusk is developed; and in Ceylon many male elephants have the tusks very small.

The elephant is still tolerably common in most of the large forests of India, from the foot of the Himalayas to the extreme south. It is found in the Terai from Bhotan to Dehra Doon, and the Kyarda Doon. It used not many years ago, to occur in the Rajmahal hills, and it abounds in many parts of Central India, from Midnapore to Mundla, and south nearly to the Godavery. On the west coast it is abundant in many localities from the extreme south, Travancore to north latitude 17 or 18 degrees, all along the line of Western Ghâts, more especially on the Animally hills, named from that circumstance; in the Coimbetore hills, Wynaad, the slopes of the Neelgherries, Coorg and parts of Mysore and Canara. The Shervaroys and Colamallies, and other detached ranges to the east, have occasionally small herds on them. It is numerous in Ceylon and in Assam, southwards to the Malayan peninsula.

Now and then considerable damage is done by wild elephants to various crops, and a single male individual at times becomes savage, and kills any one that comes in his way. Such individuals often occupy a line of road, and rush out at all passers by, and not unfrequently prevent the dâk runners from passing. As a general rule, however wild elephants are most timorous, and shun the presence of man as carefully as deer do. Some years ago large rewards were given by the Madras Government for elephants being killed in the Malabar forests, and several sportsmen earned considerable sums by shooting them, only however taking the Government rewards for females, or young males, as the value of the tusks of old males generally exceeded that of the Government reward. Two or three of our best sportsmen almost always succeeded in killing elephants with a single shot, never firing till within a few yards.

Elephants used to be captured by Government establishments, both in the south of India near Coimbetore, and in the north at Dacca; some were taken in huge pit-falls dug for the purpose, and carefully concealed;

others were driven, after days of preparation, into large enclosures; and occasionally one or two were captured by female decoys taken out for the purpose. The elephant rarely breeds in confinement. The female has generally one young at a birth.

Of the value of the tame elephant, its docility, intelligence, &c., numerous popular accounts have been written, and are familiar to all. Sir J. Tennent has given the most recent and authentic history of the elephant in Ceylon.* Tigers are almost always shot from off elephants, and a well-trained one will stand the charge of a tiger without flinching, though naturally one of the most timorous of animals. Elephants are used in India occasionally to drag heavy pieces of ordnance, but their chief use is in carrying tent equipage for troops, and to assist in the transport of logs of timber from forests to river banks.

A peculiar race or species, *E. sumatranus*, Schlegel, is stated to occur in Sumatra, and the Ceylon elephant was by some considered to be of this race, but that opinion was opposed by Dr. Falconer.

The Sumatran elephant has twenty pairs of ribs, and the laminæ of the teeth are wider than in the Indian species. It is said to be of more slender make, and to be more remarkable for its intellectual development than the Indian.

The African elephant, *Elephas africanus*, Cuvier, is not now tamed in Africa, though it appears to have been so in the time of the Carthaginians. The tusks are very large, and are nearly of the same size in the male and female.

The Mammoth, *Elephas primogenius*, appears to have been tolerably well clad with hair of two kinds, and was therefore probably an inhabitant of cold climates. It has been found in both continents. The Mastodons, which are quite extinct now, have the molar teeth with large conical tubercles, and there are small tusks in the lower jaw of the immature animal. They have been found in both continents.

Tribe, Perissodactyla, Owen.

With an uneven number of toes on the hind-feet at least. This tribe comprises part of the *Pachydermata ordinaria* of Cuvier (excluding those with cloven feet, the hippopotamus and pigs) and the *Solidlungula*.

The crown of some of the præmolars is complex like that of the molars;

* Wanderings in Ceylon, and Natural History of Ceylon.

the stomach is simple, and the cœcum is large and complicated. It comprises the families of *Rhinocerotidæ*, *Tapiridæ*, *Hyracidæ*, and *Equidæ*, or the Rhinoceroses, Tapirs, Coneys and Horses. Their molars are six or seven or each side, both above and below.

Fam. Rhinocerotidæ.

Syn. *Nasicornia*, Illiger.

Incisors persistent in both jaws in some, in others disappearing with age; no canines; molars tuberculate, the crown marked by narrow eminences, usually $\frac{7-7}{7-7}$; feet with three hoofed toes; one or two horns, placed one behind the other on the median line of the muzzle; tail short; skin very thick, marked by deep folds.

Gen. Rhinoceros, Linnæus.

Char.—Those of the family, of which it is the only genus.

The animals composing this genus are large ungainly and unwieldy looking, with long heads and a short tail, and the hide very thick with several folds. The incisors vary somewhat both in number and in size, and they are stated to bear an inverse ratio to the horns. Canines in a rudimentary state exist in the mature fœtus, but early disappear. The molars are implanted by distinct roots. The crowns of the upper molars, are subquadrate with two transverse eminences, joined by a crest to the outer margin; the crowns of the lower ones are longer, narrower, with two lunate lines, having the convexity outwards. The nasal bones are very strong and arched to support the horn, which is composed of longitudinal fibres, as if of hairs closely compacted together without any bony structure. The upper horn, when present, is fixed in the frontal bone. The upper lip is somewhat prolonged. The stomach is simple, and the cœcum large and sacculated. The intestines are about eight times longer than the body, and the villi are very large. The females have two inguinal mammæ. Rhinoceroses are found only in the tropical regions of the old world. Three species occur in India and Malayana, two of which are found within our limits; and four or five others inhabit Africa.

212. Rhinoceros indicus.

Cuvier.—Blyth, Cat. p. 136.—*R. unicornis*, Linnæus.—*R. asia-*

ticus, Blumenbach.—*R. inermis*, Lesson.—Figured F. Cuvier, Menag. de Museum d'Hist. Nat.—*Genda*, *Gonda*, *Ganda*, and *Genra*, H.

The Great Indian Rhinoceros.

Descr.—Of large size; only one horn; skin with a deep fold at the setting on of the head, another behind the shoulder, and another in front of the thighs; two large incisors in each jaw, with two other intermediate small ones below, and two still smaller outside the upper incisors, not always present. General color dusky black.

Length, about 9 to 10 feet, occasionally it is said 12 feet; tail 2; height 4½ to 5 feet; horn occasionally 2 feet.

Compared with the next species, this rhinoceros has the condyle of the lower jaw proportionally much more elevated, imparting a conspicuously greater altitude to the vertex when the lower jaw is *in situ*. The skull of one specimen was 2 feet long; the height of the condyle of the lower jaw one foot. The tubercles of the hide are also much larger than in *R. sondaicus*.

This huge rhinoceros is found in the Terai at the foot of the Himalayas; from Bhotan to Nepal. It is more common in the eastern portion of the Terai than the west, and is most abundant in Assam and the Bhotan Dooars. I have heard from sportsman of its occurrence as far west as Rohilcund, but it is certainly rare there now, and indeed along the greater part of the Nepal Terai; and although a few have been killed in the Sikim Terai, they are more abundant east of the Teesta river. As far as is at present known, this species does not extend to the south of the region adjoining the Himalayas, though it is possible that it may cross the Berrampooter river, and occur on the north of the range of hills that bound that valley to the south.

It frequents swampy ground in the forests, and dense jungles. The rhinoceros is almost always hunted for on elephants, and a wounded one will occasionally charge and overthrow an elephant. The very thick hide of this animal requires a hard ball, and a steel-tipped bullet was frequently used before the introduction of the deadly shell, now in general use against large game. Jelpigoree, a small military station near the Teesta river, was a favorite locality whence to hunt the rhinoceros, and it was from that station Captain Fortescue of the late 73rd N. I., got his skulls, which were, strange to say, the first that Mr. Blyth had seen of this species, of which there were no specimens in the Museum of the Asiatic Society, at the time when he wrote his Memoir on this group.

213. Rhinoceros sondaicus.

SOL. MULLER.—BLYTH, Cat. p. 137.—*R. javanicus*, F. CUVIER, Mammif., pl. 85-86.—HORSFIELD, Zool. Res. Java, pl.

THE LESSER INDIAN RHINOCEROS.

Descr.—Much smaller than the preceding; with one horn; two large incisors in each jaw; folds in the skin less prominent and fewer; hide covered with square angular tubercles, much smaller than those of *R. indicus.*

Length 7 to 8 feet; height $3\frac{1}{2}$ to $3\frac{3}{4}$.

As in the last, there is a short and broad type of skull, and a narrow type, the broad type being the kind found in our province. Length of the skull of one $1\frac{3}{4}$ feet; height of condyle of lower jaw 9 inches. The fold at the setting on of the head, so prominent in *Indicus*, is at most but indicated in *Sondaicus*.

The lesser rhinoceros is found at present in the Bengal Sunderbuns, and a very few individuals are stated to occur in the forest tract along the Mahanuddy river, and extending northwards towards Midnapore; and also on the northern edge of the Rajmahal hills near the Ganges. It occurs also more abundantly in Burmah, and thence through the Malayan peninsula to Java and Borneo. Several have been killed quite recently within a few miles of Calcutta.

One of these species formerly existed on the banks of the Indus, where it was hunted by the Emperor Baber. Individuals of this species are not unfrequently taken about the country as a show.

The only other Asiatic rhinoceros is the two-horned one, *Rhinoceros sumatranus*, which has been shot as high as north latitude 23° or so, near Sandoway, and is suspected by Blyth to extend as far north as Assam. Though with two horns, it is quite of the same type as the one-horned species, having strong incisors, and not like the African two-horned species, which have deciduous incisors. It is the most common rhinoceros in the Indo-Chinese territories, extending to Sumatra only among the islands. It appears from information received by Blyth, that the horns of this species are sometimes much longer than such as are usually met with, and he suspects that *R. crossii*, Gray, is this species.

Africa possesses four or five species of rhinoceros, all of them double-horned, and without incisors.

The curious genus, HYRAX, is usually placed near the rhinoceros family. It forms the family *Hyracidæ*, and the tribe *Lamnunguia*, Wagner. They are animals of small size, about that of a rabbit, and have quite similar molars to the rhinoceroses; the upper jaw has two stout incisors curved downwards, and during youth two very small canines; the lower jaw has four incisors and no canines. The fore-feet have 4 toes; the hind-feet 3, all furnished with flat hoof-like nails; they have no tail, have a short muzzle, and they are covered by hair. Several species are known from Africa, and one from Arabia and Palestine, supposed to be the coney of our version of the Scriptures, *Hyrax syriacus*. It was considered by the Jews one of the animals that chew the cud.

The Tapirs, TAPIRIDÆ, have six incisors and two canines in each jaw, separated from the molars by a wide interval. The fore-feet have 4 toes, and the hind-feet 3. The snout is prolonged into a short fleshy trunk, and the skin is covered with short close hair. The tail is very short, and the ears are small and upright. They are animals not unlike pigs in their general form; frequent damp forests, and are fond of the water.

One species is found in the Malayan peninsula and islands, *Tapirus malayanus*, and it has been killed in Southern Tenasserim. The only other two species are inhabitants of South America, *Tapirus americanus*, and *T. villosus*, of the Andes.

The remarkable fossil genus, *Dinotherium*, was at first described as a tapir. It is now considered to have been an aquatic animal, like the dugongs; and this would perhaps be the best place to intercalate the family of *Sirenia*, or herbivorous *Cetacea*, but I will describe them at the end of the next tribe.

Fam. EQUIDÆ, Horses.

Syn. *Solidungula* and *Solipedes*, Auct.

Incisors $\frac{6}{6}$; canines $\frac{1-1}{1-1}$; molars $\frac{6-6}{6-6}$ or $\frac{7-7}{6-6}$. The two anterior toes are soldered together, forming a single perfect toe, covered by a broad undivided hoof.

The molars are complex, with square crowns marked by laminæ of enamel; and, in young individuals, there is often a small anterior molar which is deciduous. The incisors have their crowns furrowed by a groove. The canines are only present in males. The tail is moderately long with long hair, the ears rather large and pointed, and there is a mane. The female has two inguinal mammæ.

The skull is elongated, and the lower jaw is of great size and strength. The humerus and femur are short, the fore-arm and shank are long and partially anchylosed, and there is only one metacarpal and metatarsal bone, the others however being represented by small bones called the splint bones. Three phalanges complete the foot, the last of which bears the hoof. The stomach is simple, the intestinal canal long and capacious, and the cœcum enormous.

The animals of this family are peculiar to the old world. They comprise horses, asses and zebras, which are usually placed in one genus.

Gen. Equus, Linnæus.

Char.—Those of the family, of which it is the only genus.

It subdivides into horses properly so called, *Equus;* asses, *Asinus*, Gray; and zebras, *Hippotigris*, Hamilton Smith. Wild horses of a truly feral type are at present unknown, but they have become almost wild in the Pampas of South America.

Asses. Gen. *Asinus*, Gray.

Asses are distinguished from horses by their longer head and ears, by the tail being covered with short hairs at the base and furnished with a tuft of long hairs towards the tip and on the sides only, not throughout as in horses. They also want the peculiar hard horny excrescences found on the legs of horses, and have almost invariably a dark longitudinal dorsal stripe. Several species of wild ass are now known to exist, one of which is a native of the western parts of India.

214. Equus onager.

Pallas.—Blyth, Cat. p. 135.—Figd. F. Cuvier, Mammif. 2, pl. 92 —*E. hemionus* of India, Auct.—*Asinus indicus*, Sclater.—*Ghor-khur*, H. —*Ghour*, of Persians.—*Koulan*, of the Kirghiz.

The Wild Ass of Cutch.

Descr.—Of a pale isabella or sandy color above, with a slight but distinct rufescent tinge; muzzle, breast, lower parts, and inside of limbs white; a dark chocolate brown dorsal stripe extending from the mane to the tail; tail-tuft and short mane blackish-brown; frequently a dark short cross stripe on the shoulders, sometimes two; and limbs usually faintly barred, now and then strongly so; a narrow dark ring over the hoof; ears sandy externally, white internally, with a black tip and outer border.

Height at shoulder 11 to 12 hands.

The head is heavy but well formed, the ears longish, the neck rather short, and the croup higher than the withers.

It is now generally acknowledged that this wild ass is quite distinct from the *kiang*, or wild ass of Tibet, *Equus hemionus* of Pallas; yet Mr. Blyth in a paper on wild asses,* stated that the two species were so alike that he found it difficult to characterize them apart. "Indeed," he says, "instead of being strongly distinguished apart, as has been asserted, they bear so exceedingly close a resemblance that no decided specific distinction has yet been pointed out satisfactorily, however probable that such distinction may exist." Sportsmen and travellers however who have seen both the *kiang* and the *ghorkhur*, always assert their marked distinction; and Sclater in his brief paper on wild asses, states the *ghorkhur* to be "obviously distinct from the Tibetan animal, though apparently hardly separable from the next species, *Asinus hemippus*." Dr. J. Hooker too, asserts that the *kiang* "differs widely from the wild ass of Persia, Sindh, and Beluchistan." Perhaps some of Mr. Blyth's hesitation about the distinctness of the two species arose from the mistake he made in considering the wild ass, figured by Dr. Walker (from a drawing from life by Dr. Cantor), to have been a *ghorkhur;* whereas, as Colonel Strachey pointed out, it was in reality a *kiang*.

The following distinctive marks have been pointed out. The dorsal stripe is generally broader on the back in the *ghorkhur* than in the *kiang*, but narrower over the tail, and not extending so low down, for in the kiang it is continued down to the tail tuft. In the *ghorkhur* too it is more or less conspicuously bordered with white, which extends broadly towards the tail, and along the hind margin of the buttocks. The stripe on the shoulder is much more strongly marked in the *ghorkhur*, being often only faintly visible, and not dark or blackish in the *kiang*. The markings on the limbs, though not always present in the *ghorkhur*, are denied to be

* Journ. As. Soc. 1859, p. 229, *et seq.*

ever traceable in the *kiang*. The white of the under parts extends higher upwards, in some joining the white border of the dorsal streak, and thus isolating the isabelline hue of the haunch; and the muzzle has more white than in the *kiang*.

The *ghorkhur* is found sparingly in Cutch, Guzrat, Jeysalmeer and Bikaneer, not being found further south, it is said, than Deesa, or east of 75° feet longitude. It also occurs in Sindh, and more abundantly west of the Indus river, in Beluchistan, extending into Persia and Turkistan, as far north as north latitude 48°. It appears that the Bikaneer herd consists at most of about 150 individuals, which frequent an oasis a little elevated above the surrounding desert, and commanding an extensive view around. A writer in the Indian Sporting Review, writing of this species as it occurs in the *Pât*, a desert country between Asnee and the hills west of the Indus, above Mithunkote, says, "they are to be found wandering pretty well throughout the year; but in the early summer when the grass and the water in the pools have dried up from the hot winds (which are here terrific), the greater number, if not all of the *ghorkhurs* migrate to the hills for grass and water. The foaling season is in June, July and August, when the Beluchis ride down and catch numbers of foals, finding a ready sale in the cantonments for them, as they are taken down on speculation to Hindustan. They also shoot great numbers of full grown ones for food, the ground in places in the desert being very favorable for stalking." In Bikaneer too, according to information given by Major Tytler to Mr. Blyth, "once only in the year, when the foals are young, a party of five or six native hunters, mounted on hardy Sindh mares, chase down as many foals as they succeed in tiring, which lie down when utterly fatigued, and suffer themselves to be bound and carried off. In general they refuse sustenance at first, and about one third only of those taken are reared; but these command high prices, and find a ready sale with the native princes. The profits are shared by the party, who do not attempt a second chase in the same year lest they should scare the herd from the district, as these men regard the sale of few *ghorkhurs* annually as a regular source of subsistence."

This wild ass is very shy and difficult to approach, and has great speed. A full grown one has however been run down fairly and speared, more than once. It was generally believed that almost all the males shot or otherwise procured were castrated, and that the old males thus treated all the young ones which they could manage to overcome in fight. This idea is of course erroneous, and simply arose from the fact of the testes being drawn up close to the abdomen.

The voice of the *ghorkhur*, according to Blyth, who heard it in some individuals taken to Calcutta by Colonel Tytler, is "a shrieking bray," and was considered by Colonel Tytler to resemble exceedingly the cry of the mule.

Equus hemippus, Is. Geoffroy, inhabits the countries to the west of *E. onager*, viz., Syria, Mesapotamia, North Arabia, &c., and is the wild ass of our version of the Scriptures. Mr. Sclater remarks that it can barely be distinguished from *E. onager*, but Blyth considers them distinct. He says that the *ghorkhur* differs from *hemippus* in the latter having a smaller head and shorter ears. The voice of this species is said by Blyth to be much more like the bray of the common ass than that of *E. onager;* and St. Hilaire also notices the difference of voice of the two animals. This wild ass of Western Asia is considered by Blyth to have been the *Hemionus* of the ancients, and their *Onager*, the veritable wild *E. asinus*, which is found in north-east Africa and southern Arabia, so that the specific names given by Pallas are unfortunately applied. To this last species, Dr. Sclater applies the name *Asinus tæniopus*, Heuglin.

The *kiang* or *dzightai* of Tibet and Central Asia, *Equus hemionus*, Pallas, is met with across the snowy Himalayas in Ladak and other parts, and has frequently been killed by sportsmen. It is much darker in hue than the *ghorkhur*, the upper parts being of a dull ruddy-brown or chesnut-rufous hue, approaching to bay, especially on the head, and distinctly darker on the flanks, where it abruptly contrasts with the white of the belly. Cunningham calls it the wild horse, and says that it neighs, and does not bray; and others assert the same, or that the voice of the *kyang* is "as much like neighing as braying." On the other hand, Moorcroft, Col. Strachey, and many sportsmen say that his cry is more like braying than neighing. The evidence of Colonel Strachey, an accomplished and scientific traveller, is valuable on this point. He says, "my impression as to the voice of the *kyang* is that it is a shrieking bray, not like that of the common ass, but still a real bray and not a neigh." Again: "the *kyang* so far as external aspect is concerned, is obviously an ass and not a horse." How any one can call it a wild horse after looking at its tail I cannot understand, (though Colonel Chesney even calls the *hemippus* the wild horse); but I can imagine that its darker color, shorter ears, and large size compared with the ordinary domestic ass, may give this animal, at a distance, something of the aspect of a horse.

There are several species of this genus in Africa, known as zebras and quaggas, some of them very beautifully striped, and hence named by H. Smith, *Hippotigris*.

ARTIODACTYLA, Owen.

With an even number of toes. The crowns of the præmolars smaller and less complex than those of the true molars. The stomach is complex and the cœcum small.

This group comprises the pigs and hippopotamus, *i. e.*, the *Pachydermata ordinaria*, of Cuvier, and the great tribe of ruminants. It is generally adopted, I believe, by Zoologists, but is I think rather an artificial group, and I would prefer keeping the non-ruminating *Artiodactyles* in a separate tribe, which has indeed been long ago named by Blyth.

Tribe, CHÆRODIA, Blyth.

Incisors in both jaws; canines directed outwards, and usually rubbing against their fellows in the opposite jaw. They comprise the families *Suidæ* and *Hippopotamidæ*, the latter of which is not represented in India.

Fam. SUIDÆ.

Incisors various; canines in both jaws, large; molars vary from $\frac{3-3}{3-3}$ to $\frac{7-7}{7-7}$; feet with the hoofs insistent, with 4 toes usually on all feet, the hind-feet sometimes with 3; snout truncate, mobile, prominent; tail short.

Pigs have a somewhat moveable snout with a firm cartilaginous tip, which they employ in turning up the ground in search of roots, &c. The incisors, always small, sometimes fall out with increase of age, and the lower ones always slant forwards. The canines, very large in the males, project from the sides of the mouth, except in the American peccaries. The two middle toes are large, armed with strong hoofs, and the animal walks on them alone, the two upper lateral toes with their hoofs not touching the ground. The eyes are small, the ears moderate and upright, and the skin is clad with strong bristles.

The occipital bone terminates abruptly above in a broad crest to form an attachment for the strong muscles of the neck. There are four metacarpal bones, the two middle ones of which are long, and much larger than the others, and only the two middle phalanges touch the ground. The same arrangement exists in the metatarsal bones and phalanges.

Most of the animals of this family (unlike most of the *Pachydermata* and ruminants) are very prolific. They are found in the warm and temperate portions of both continents.

Gen. Sus, Linnæus.

Char.—Incisors $\frac{4}{6}$ or $\frac{6}{6}$; the lower ones procumbent or slanting forwards; canines large in the males, exsert, directed upwards; molars six or seven on each side in both jaws, tuberculate; all the feet with 4 toes, which are enclosed in separate hoofs.

215. Sus indicus.

Schinz.—*S. cristatus*, Wagner.—*S. scropha*, Linnæus.—Blyth, Cat. p. 139.—Elliot, Cat. 49.—*S. vittatus*, Schlegel.—*Súr* or *Súwar*, H; sometimes *Búra janwar*, or *Bad jánwar*, H., *i. e.*, the bad or unclean animal.—*Dúkar*, Mahr.—*Handi*, *Mikka*, and *Jewadi*, Can.—*Pandi*, Tel. —*Paddi*, of Gonds and Mharis.—*Kis* of Bhagalpore hill tribes.

The Indian Wild Boar.

Descr.—Head longer and more pointed than in the European boar; the plane of the forehead straight and not concave; ears small and pointed; tail more tufted; the malar beard well marked.

Length of a tolerably fine boar, 5 feet to root of tail which is 1 foot. Stands a little over 30 inches high at the shoulder.

"The color of the adult," says Mr. Blyth, "is brownish-black, scantily covered with black hairs. Besides the black recumbent mane of the occiput and back, and the whiskers and the bristles above and below the eyes, there is a bundle of long black bristles on the throat, and the hairs of the throat and chest are reversed. The tail is scantily covered with short hairs, and the apex compressed, with long lateral bristles like those of the elephant, arranged like the rings of an arrow. The young is more hairy, of a tawny or fulvous color and striped with dark brown. The hairs of the throat, chest, abdomen and elbows (in the two latter places very long) are black on the basal and white at the apical half."

Mr. Blyth, in his Catalogue, has given the Indian boar only as a variety of the common wild boar of Europe, but he allows it to be a well marked race, and I think is worthy of specific separation as many other recognised species. Mr. Elliot states that the Indian wild hog differs considerably from the German one, the former of which is altogether a more active looking animal, the German having a stronger, heavier appearance. He was the first, I believe, to point out the differences, some of which moreover are perceptible in domesticated individuals of the two countries.

Gray too in describing a *Sus indicus* from Madras, says bristles more abundant on the front part of the body, legs slender, covered with a few bristles; skulls of the Indian one have the hinder part of the forehead less high and dilated.

There appear to be two or three varieties of type in India. Blyth has indicated two different forms of skulls. One skull $14\frac{1}{2}$ inches long, was only $1\frac{3}{8}$ inch wide at the vertex, flat and narrow, with the lower tusks $7\frac{1}{2}$ inches long: the other one was $2\frac{1}{4}$ inches wide at the vertex, and the whole vertical aspect of the cranium wider and more convex. The latter he distinguished as *Sus bengalensis*, and the former as *S. indicus*. The frontal region is flat in the latter, somewhat convex and broad in the former. The skull of one of the Bengal type was nearly 16 inches long. It is found all over Bengal to the foot of the Himalayas, Arrakan, and probably Assam, Sylhet, &c. *Sus indicus*, apud Blyth, is the wild hog of India generally and Ceylon. Gray has indicated* another race, from the Neelgherries, as *Sus neelgherriensis*. The wild boar of Bengal is said to be larger, and to stand higher on its legs than those from other parts of India, some large individuals being said to stand nearly 40 inches high at the shoulder.

The wild hog is found throughout India, from the level of the sea to 12,000 feet of elevation, wherever there is sufficient shelter either of long grass, low jungle, or forest. It is very numerous in some parts, and does much damage to various crops. It associates in more or less numerous herds, called "*sounder*" technically, in sporting language in the Deccan, but isolated individuals are frequently met with especially in long grass.

Where this form their chief shelter, they construct a sort of rude abode by cutting a lot of grass and spreading it out carefully on the ground. They then creep under this and raise it up to the proper height, and they remain in these lairs during the day which afford a good shelter from the heat of the sun. I have seen numerous lairs of this description in various

* Cat. of Osteological Specimens, British Museum.

parts of Bengal, and often turned the hogs out of them. They travel great distances for their food in some parts of the country, and the early traveller in Nagpore and other parts, often sees a herd returning to their abode in the jungle an hour or so before sunrise. The root of a particular kind of sedge *(Carex)* is much sought for by wild hogs, and the edges of tanks and jheels may be seen covered with their excavations. Though in general almost entirely vegetable feeders, at times a somewhat carnivorous habit has been observed. Wild pigs have been detected feeding on the carcase of a dead elephant in Southern India.

Spearing the wild boar is one of the favorite sports of India wherever it can be pursued, and is one of the most exciting pursuits, the dash of danger intermingled with the excitement of the chase, giving it a zest wanting in fox-hunting; and the greater address and personal skill required giving it also the palm over tiger-shooting. The speed of the wild hog for a short distance must be tried on a good horse before it can be realized. In Madras and Bombay a long spear is used lance-wise, but in Bengal a short leaden-topped jobbing spear is preferred. Now and then, as before stated, even the tiger has fallen a victim to the impetuous dash of the wild boar, and the sudden onslaught of a wounded hog when brought to bay, occasionally proves too speedy to be avoided even by a timorous and active horse.

Wild pigs are found over great part of Asia and the North of Africa, as well as in Europe, but recent information is required on the particular races inhabiting such extensive areas.

Mr. Blyth has indicated a particular race from the Tenasserim provinces, like the *Sus indicus* of India generally, "but one-fifth smaller in linear dimensions, the tusks of the boar well developed." Another race is named *Sus zeylanensis* by Blyth, from Ceylon. It has the vertex very narrow, and the last molar very large. A skull measured $16\frac{1}{4}$ inches; vertex 1; last molar $1\frac{3}{4}$ inches + $\frac{15}{16}$ths. The same Zoologist has described a small race from the Andamans, as *Sus andamensis.*

Near this small Andaman race should come the next little-known pig.

Gen. Porculia, Hodgson.

Char.—Incisors $\frac{6}{6}$; canines $\frac{1-1}{1-1}$; molars $\frac{7-7}{7-7}$. Canines small, straight, scarcely cutting, but not ordinarily exserted from the lips; the fourth toe on all the feet small and unequal; tail very short.

This genus, it will be remarked, makes an approach to the American peccaries, in the non-exserted canines, the short tail, and the small fourth toe.

216. Porculia salvania.

HODGSON.—J. A. S., XVI. 423, and XVIII. 476.—HORSFIELD, P. Z. S. 1853, pl. 37.—*Sano banel*, Nepal.—*Chota súwar*, H.

THE PIGMY HOG.

Descr.—Blackish-brown, slightly and irregularly shaded with sordid amber; iris hazel; nude-skin, dirty flesh color; hoofs glossy brown.

Length, snout to vent 26 inches; tail little more than 1; height 10; weight 7 to 10 lbs., rarely 12 lbs.

There is no mane, but the general pelage is ample, and there is a mystaceal tuft. The false molars are compressed, and the face is proportionally less long than in *Sus*. The female has only 6 mammæ, and the tail is not so long as the hair of the rump. It wants the normal nasal bones of *Sus*. The stomach is narrower and the orifices more terminal; it has also a smaller cœcum and shorter intestines.

The pigmy hog is found in the Nepal and Sikim Terai, probably extending into Assam and Bhotan, but it is rare and with difficulty procurable. Mr. Hodgson had long heard of its existence before he got a single specimen. It is exclusively confined to the deep recesses of the primæval forests. The full grown males live constantly with the herd, which consists of from five to twenty individuals, and are its habitual and resolute defenders against harm. They eat roots, bulbs, &c., but also birds' eggs, insects, and reptiles. The female has a litter of three to four young ones.

The above account is taken entirely from Mr. Hodgson's descriptions. I endeavoured in vain to procure a specimen from the Sikim Terai whilst at Darjeeling.

The babyroussa *(Sus babyrussa)*, remarkable for its long slender, curved tusks, is found in Malayana, and *Sus papuensis* is from new Guinea. A peculiar species exists in Africa and Madagascar, *Sus larvatus*, forming the genus *Potamochærus* of F. Cuvier; and the same region produces the curious wart-hogs, *Phascochærus*, F. Cuvier, with huge tusks, an immense head, with a thick fleshy lobe hanging from their cheeks. Their molars are renewed and succeed one another from behind as those of elephants do.

The peccaries, *Dicotyles*, Cuvier, represent this family in America.

They have only three toes to the hind-feet; the canines do not project; they have no tail. Their metacarpal and metatarsal bones are soldered together as in ruminants, and their stomach is also divided into several sacs, presenting a marked analogy to that family.

To this division of the *Ungulata* belong some remarkable fossil genera, viz., *Palæotherium*, *Anoplotherium*, &c. The former somewhat resembled tapirs, and the latter presents, according to Cuvier, most singular relations with the different tribes of *Pachydermata*, approximating in some respects to the order *Ruminantia*. Their teeth form a continuous series without any intervening space, a disposition seen elsewhere in man only.

The family *Hippopotamidæ* contains one genus only, the hippopotamus, with one or two species. They are huge unwieldy animals, with immense heads, four incisors in each jaw, those of the lower one projecting; large canines, especially the lower one, and six or seven molars on each side above and below. They have four toes on all the feet, nearly equal, and ending in small hoofs, a short tail and small eyes and ears. Their stomach is divided into several sacs. Their skin is naked, and they are very aquatic in their habits. The common species is *Hippopotamus amphibius*, L., and a second species has been lately made known, *H. liberiensis*, Morton, distinguished generically by Leidy as *Chæropsis*.

Tribe, Ruminantia.

Feet with two toes with hoofs, and two supplementary hoofs in many. Upper incisors generally wanting; six or eight (apparently) in the lower jaw: canines in the upper jaw sometimes present: four stomachs.

The camels alone of all the ruminating animals have incisors in the upper jaw. In all other they are completely wanting, their place being supplied by a hardened and somewhat callous gum. The incisors have simple trenchant crowns, slanting forwards. The outermost of the lower incisors, when more than 6, are the representative of the canines, and there are besides upper canines in a few. There is generally a wide space between the incisors and molars. The molars are almost always six in number on each side, above and below, and their crowns are marked by double crescentic ridges of enamel. The crowns of the præmolars are smaller and less complicated than those of the true molars, which are of a quadrilateral form with a somewhat convoluted margin.

The two hoofs present a flat surface to each other, and appear like a single hoof cleft in two, hence the names of bisulcate, cloven-footed, applied to these animals. This form of hoof imparts lightness and elasticity to the spring, and aids them in soft ground, expanding when sinking, and closing when being extricated. Many have a sebaceous gland between the toes, whose office is to lubricate the digits and prevent injury from friction; and being hollow, are often called feet-pits. They have received the name of ruminants or chewers of the cud, from the circumstance of their having the faculty of masticating their food a second time, it being returned to their mouth by one of their four stomachs. The first of these, or the paunch, receives the food as it is plucked, and in the second it undergoes a good maceration. It is then returned to the mouth in pellets or boluses to undergo a complete trituration by the molars; then passed into the third stomach, where it undergoes an additional preparation, and is lastly received into the true digestive stomach. The object of this provision of nature is obviously to enable them to crop a large quantity of food quickly, to be masticated at leisure, to obviate the many interruptions they are liable to from beasts of prey and other alarms, as all are excessively timid and wary.

The tribe of ruminating animals comprises most of the animals useful to man, viz., camels, deer, cattle, and sheep, and of all the *Ungulata* they are the most truly and exclusively vegetable feeders. They break or tear rather than cut their food, and this action is accompanied by a swinging motion of the head forwards. To assist them in their watchfulness their eyes are so placed laterally that they have a great range of vision. Their ears are large, placed well back, and very mobile; and their smell is very acute. The speed of most is great. Many of them are docile and can be easily tamed, but they show very little intelligence. Most of them possess horns.

The nasal bones vary much, and the intermaxillaries are usually much lengthened; the lachrymals are directed forwards, and occupy a considerable extent of the cheeks. The lower jaw is very long, and is narrowed in the space between the canine and first præmolar. The dorsal vertebræ are twelve to fifteen in number, and they have long spinous processes. The metacarpal and metatarsals form a single *cannon bone*, with one or two splint bones in most of tribe; and there are phalangeal bones to each toe. The olecranon and os calcis are both large.

The salivary glands are large. The paunch or first stomach is capacious, of a somewhat square form, with two well-marked constrictions. The second stomach, small and globular, is situated between the paunch and the third stomach, and appears to be a sort of terminal dilatation of the œsophagus. It is called the reticulum or honey-comb-bag, being lined with polygonal acute-angled cells. The third stomach, the monyplies of the Scotch, is small and sub-globular, but is much increased in capacity internally by the folding of the lining membrane. The fourth stomach is the true digestive sac, about one-third of the size of the paunch, and of an elongated pyramidal form. The intestinal tube is very long, and the large intestines are very much wider than the small ones. The cœcum is bulky, smooth and obtuse. The liver is simple, and there is a gall-bladder in all except in the *Cervidæ*. The urinary bladder is large; the testes are enclosed in a scrotum; and the mammæ are inguinal, with two to four teats. Many are provided with a hollow gland below the eye, called the eye-pit, tear-pit or lachrymal sinus, or infraorbital sinus. This secretes a waxy sort of substance, and, in some of the tribe, it is very mobile and can be opened at pleasure, or even reversed. Their use is not exactly ascertained, but they are generally considered subservient to sexual purposes. Many also possess hollow inguinal glands, or groin pits.

Ruminants form five groups,—*Camelidæ*, *Camelopardidæ*, *Moschidæ*, *Cervidæ*, and *Bovidæ*.

Camels, CAMELIDÆ, forming the *Ancerata* of Blyth, have a cleft upper lip which is prehensile, two toes encased in skin with nail-like hoofs, and the whole surface of the toes touches the ground. They have two upper incisors, and six in the lower jaw, and two canines in each jaw. They have usually 18 to 20 molars, there being generally one more molar above on each side than in the lower jaw. In the true camels, the foremost molar is placed considerably in advance of the others. This family includes the camels of the old world, and the alpacas of the new world. The former have the two toes united below almost to the point by a common sole, and humps of fat on the back. Two species are known, both of large size, *Camelus dromedarius*, L., the one-humped camel or dromedary; and the two-humped or Bactrian camel, *C. bactrianus*, L. They are now completely domesticated. The former is supposed to have spread from Arabia into North Africa, India, &c.; the latter is considered to have spread from Central Asia. Their humps are reservoirs of fat, which become absorbed during long fasts, and enable them to take long journeys on very little food. Their flat feet are admirably adapted for treading on loose sand.

The Llamas of South America have their toes divided, are of smaller size, and lighter make, than camels. There are two wild species, *Auchenia llama* and *A. vicunna;* and two domestic races, the *llama* and *alpaca*, the latter with long woolly hair.

The other families of ruminants constitute the *Pecora* of Blyth and others. They comprise the *Camelopardidæ*, *Cervidæ*, *Moschidæ* and *Bovidæ*. The Giraffe, *Camelopardus giraffa*, L., is the only species of the *Camelo pardidæ*. It is a native of Africa, with the dentition of deer, but with permanent short horns in both sexes, covered with a hairy skin, and without any accessory hoofs. The neck is immensely long, its fore-legs are disproportionately long, and it has a moderately long tail, ending in a tuft of long black hair.

Fam. CERVIDÆ, the Deer tribe.

Elaphii, Van der Hoeven; *Cervina*, Gray. Horns usually in the males only, deciduous; incisors $\frac{0}{6}$ apparently $\frac{0}{8}$; canines present occasionally in the upper jaw.

Deer are remarkable for their fine horns, or osseous prominences, which are shed and renewed annually, more or less cotemporaneously with the renewal of the hair, and are called antlers. In the rein-deer alone of all the family the females possess horns normally, though very rarely old and barren females of other species have been known to assume them.

The feet touch the ground only at the extremity of the two principal toes, and there are usually two rudimentary toes with small hoofs at the back of the foot. The end of the muzzle is bare in almost all deer, and is sometimes called the muffle. Eye pits, or so called lachrymal sinuses, are constantly present, but inguinal or groin-pits are vague or wanting. There are one or two glands, covered with a small tuft of hair, on the hind leg (metatarsus), the presence of which, in some cases at least, furnishes a good character to distinguish females of this family from hornless female antelope; and there are feet-pits also, either in all four feet, or only in the hind-feet. The female has four teats, and the gall-bladder is absent.

The metacarpus and metatarsus have each two "splint bones," attached to which are two small digits, each consisting of three phalangeal bones.

When the horns first appear they are covered with a hairy skin, commonly called the velvet, which becomes dry and is thrown off; and at each successive renewal of the horns, they become larger and more developed, getting additional branches in some, till excessive age when they diminish at each renewal. During the renewal of the antlers a strong determination of blood to the head takes place, the vessels enlarge much, and a fibro-cartilaginous matrix is secreted on the summit of the cone, taking the form of the antler of each species. In their early condition the horns are soft and yielding, with a highly vascular periosteum, and delicate integument, the cuticular portion of which is represented by fine, closely set hairs, (the velvet). As development goes on, progressive ossification takes place, the periosteal veins become enlarged, grooving the external surface, the arteries are enclosed by hard osseous tubercles at the base of the horns, which coalesce and render them impervious, and the supply of nutriment being thus cut off, the envelopes shrivel up and fall off, and the animals perfect the desquamation by rubbing their horns against trees, technically called "burnishing."

There is a remarkable sympathy between the generative organs and the horns. The rutting season immediately follows the development of the antlers, and it appears to owe its energy to the determination of the blood, now no longer required for the formation of the horns, to the generative system. If castrated, deer shed their horns as usual, which are succeeded by others that never drop off, but grow weakly, irregularly, and with the velvet more or less permanent. If castrated very young, horns do not appear at all. The popular opinion, as expressed by Buffon, was, that if castrated, they do not shed their horns at all, and it is possible that this may be the case if they are castrated immediately after the appearance of the horns.

The deer found in India mostly belong to a peculiar group, occurring chiefly in the tropical and subtropical regions of Asia; but two species of elaphine deer occur within our limits.

Sub.-fam. CERVINÆ. True Stags.

These comprise the red deer of Europe and its affines, the rein deer, and the fallow deer; and are chiefly found in the northern parts of both continents. They possess a median tine or royal antler, found (with very rare exceptions) in no other deer. Body longer, and with a somewhat different carriage.

Gen. CERVUS, Linn. (restricted).

Char.—Horns of adults typically with two basal tines, a median tine, and the summit more or less branched; muzzle somewhat pointed; muffle broad; with a hairy band above the lip; eye-pits moderate; tail very short with a disk round it; hair coarse. Of large size.

The red-deer of Scotland is the type of this group, and the Indian Fauna includes two species, both outliers of Northern and Central Asia, one in the extreme north-west, and the other in the extreme north-east corner of the province. Some species have only one basal tine.

217. Cervus Wallichii.

CUVIER.—BLYTH, Cat. 481.—Figd. F. CUVIER, Mammif. 2, pl. 103.—*C. pygargus*, apud HARDWICKE.—*C. caspianus* and *C. cashmiriensis*, FALCONER.—*C. elaphus* of Asia apud PALLAS.—*C. nareyanus*, HODGSON, (young).—*Hangul* or *Honglu*, in Kashmir.—*Barasingha*, H.

THE KASHMIR STAG.

Descr.—Horns with the extremity usually trifurcate in adults. General color brownish-ash, darker along the dorsal line to the rump; small caudal disk white, contrasting strongly with the blackish border that merges into the body color; sides and limbs paler; lips and chin white; ears whitish; eyes surrounded by a white circle; hair on the ridge of the neck long, thick and bushy, and browner than the rest.

Length, about 7 to 7½ feet; height 12 to 13 hands; tail about 5 inches.

In summer the pelage is bright rufous passing into liver brown, or "bright pale rufous-chesnut." The belly of the male is dark brown contrasting with the pale ashy hue of the lower part of the flanks. The legs have a pale dusky median line. In females the whole lower parts are albescent. In old males the hair of the lower neck is long and shaggy. The horns have frequently twelve points, *i. e.*, a brow antler, bez-antler, median tine and a trifurcated tip; but, sometimes other small points, and occasionally a doubly forked tip. Fifteen and sixteen, and even eighteen, points have been counted, but such horns are very rare, and ten points are the average of by far the greatest number killed. The average length of the horns may be stated at about 40 inches, but they are stated to reach 4 feet in length. In one pair 40 inches long, the extreme divergence of the snags was 41 inches, and the nearest points at the tip were 24 inches apart.

The Kashmir stag nearly approaches the red deer of Europe. It somewhat perhaps exceeds the European animal in size, and it has the horns less rough, and somewhat larger than those of most specimens of the European deer, and the second basal tine is generally present, which it is not in young stags of *C. elaphus* of the same age. The horns too of the Kashmir stag are more divergent and bowed, converging again at the crown, whilst the European animal has them conspicuously straighter in the beam, and the crown generally finer and more ramifying.

The *Barasingha* of Kashmir, as it always called by sportsmen (and generally by the native shikarees also), is only found, within our limits, in Kashmir, where it inhabits the magnificent pine forests, usually at a height in summer of 9,000 to 12,000 feet, but descending much lower in autumn and winter. Most of the individuals of this deer have shed their horns before the time when Europeans are allowed to enter Kashmir, viz., 15th April, and many have the new horns perfect early in October, at which time the rutting season commences, and the stags may be heard bellowing in the woods all day long, and they are then easily stalked. The females give birth to their young in April, and the young are spotted.

This stag is found throughout great part of Western and Central Asia, and has been found as far as the eastern shores of the Euxine sea. It is common in some parts of Persia, where called *Maral*, and it was long ago described by Pallas as the *C. elaphus*. He stated that it appeared to be larger than the European stag, and that it was very abundant in Caucasus, in the woods at the foot of the Altai mountains, round lake Baikal, and on the river Lena.

Specimens of this deer are living in the gardens of the Zoological Society, London, and the female has bred there.

218. Cervus affinis.

HODGSON.—BLYTH, Cat. 480.—*Shou*, of Tibet.

THE SIKIM STAG.

Descr.—Of very large size; horns bifurcate at the tip in all specimens yet seen; horns pale, smooth, rounded. Color a fine clear gray in winter with a moderately large white disk; pale rufous in summer. Length about 8 feet.

Stands 4½ to nearly 5 feet high at the shoulder. Hodgson thus describes the horns: "Pedicles elevate; burrs rather small; two basal antlers nearly straight, so forward in direction as to overshadow the face to the end of the nasals, larger than the royal antler; median or royal antler directed forwards and upwards; beam with a terminal fork, the prongs radiating laterally and equally, the inner one longest and thinnest."

Compared with the Kashmir stag this one has the beam still more bent at the origin of the median tine, and thus more removed from *C. elaphus*; and, like *C. Wallichii*, the second basal tine or bez-antler is generally present, even in the second pair of horns assumed. Moreover, the simple bifurcation of the crown mentioned above, is a still more characteristic point of difference, both from the Kashmir *Barasingha*, and the stag of Europe. The *Shou* nearly approaches the Wapiti, *Cervus canadensis*, in size and general character, but the horns of the latter converge less at the tip, or do not tend to converge at all, and the crown consists mostly of "successively diminishing tines on the same plane, thrown off and upward from the continuation of the beam that inclines backward."

One pair of horns measured 54 inches along the curve, and 47 inches in divergence between the two outer snags; the longest basal tine 12 inches, the median 8; and still larger ones have been seen.

Hodgson first made known this fine stag, but was misled by his shikarees to believe it to be an inhabitant of the sâl forest of the Nepal Terai. Blyth, from imperfect materials, long denied the existence of this species as distinct from *C. Wallichii*, but latterly (1861) fully acknowledged his former error. It inhabits Eastern Tibet; and, as I was informed by Dr. Campbell, the valley of Choombi on the Sikim side of Tibet, formerly the summer retreat of the Sikim Rajas.

It is probably also the great stag of Northern China, the *Irbisch* of Siberia, and the *Alain* of Atkinson. How far west it extends we have no exact information, but it probably extends to the longitude of the western boundary of Nepal, at least, on the other side of the snowy range. Indeed, it has been stated by Blyth, that he saw some "horns of this deer brought from Ladakh, but that does not prove that they were killed there."

It is a question whether the individual from which the figure of *Cervus Wallichii* was taken belonged to this species or the Kashmir stag. The individual stag was living in the Barrackpore Menagerie, and was stated to have been brought from Muktinath, near Dewaligiri, to the east of the Gundhuk river, but north of the snowy range. When Mr. Blyth first obtained a specimen of the "*Shou*" from Dr. Campbell, he stated that, "most decidedly it is that well figured in M. F. Cuvier's work by the name *C. Wallichii.*" He subsequently, however-says, "this animal died at Barrackpore, and we still possess what were evidently his horns. I have now compared them carefully with mature horns of both *Hungal* and *Shou;* and though it is impossible to pronounce with confidence, I incline rather to assign them to the former, considering also the locality and the dimensions of the young buck as given by Hardwicke."

Judging from the figure alone, I am inclined to think that it represents *Cervus affinis*, both from the peculiar light color of the pelage, and the larger white disk. In this case the *Shou* would stand as *C. Wallichii*, and the Kashmir stag as *C. cashmiriensis*, Falconer. It is a point reserved for future travellers and sportsmen to ascertain the limits of *C. Wallichii* east, and *C. affinis*, west; for, as Dr. Sclater remarks, "it would be contrary to all analogy to find two species of the same type inhabiting one district." In the new edition of the Catalogue of Hodgson's Collections, the native names given are *Sia rupchu*, and *Shou* of Tibet. I presume that this is a misprint, and that *Sia* is given as the name of this deer in Rupchu, which would be a more western locality than hitherto recorded.

Other species of true elaphine deer are besides the Wapiti and the red-deer, *Cervus barbarus*, Bennett, from North Africa; *C. sika*, Schlegel, from Japan; *C. mantchuricus* and *C. taiouanus*, Swinhoe, respectively from from Mantchuria and Formosa. Of these *C. barbarus* and *C. sika*, appear never to show the second basal tine. All the spècies, except *C. affinis*, are now living in the Zoological Gardens, London.

The rein-deer, *Tarandus rangifer*, from the glacial regions of both continents, and the fallow-deer, *Dama vulgaris*, spread through Europe, belong to this sub-family; and both of them have the horns more or less flattened. The former has no muffle. The elk or moose deer, *Alces machlis*, Ogilby, from the marshy forests of the north of both continents, has the horns still more flattened, and is the giant of the deer tribe. It has a small muffle. It is said to stand 6 feet high, and some pairs of horns are known to weigh 66 lbs., and to have fourteen points on each horn. It is placed by some in a separate sub-family, *Alcinæ*.

Sub-fam. Rusinæ.

With one basal tine and no median tine. Summit more or less branched, generally with only one subterminal tine. Muffle high.

This group, which includes the Samber, the spotted deer, and the Kakur or muntjac, is peculiar to the tropical and subtropical regions of Asia and its archipelago, or to the Indian kingdom, taken in its widest sense.

The first on the list is one that makes some approach in the number of its branches to the true deer, and in aspect is intermediate between *Cervus* and *Rusa.*

Gen. RUCERVUS, Hodgson.

Char.—Horns moderately slender, smooth, pale, large, with one basal process, no median; the summit in maturity much branched; muzzle pointed; canines in the males only.

219. Rucervus Duvaucellii.

Cervus apud CUVIER.—BLYTH, Cat. 487.—F. CUVIER, Mammif. 2, pl. 104.—*C. elaphoides* and *C. bahraiya*, HODGSON.—*C euryceros*, Knowsley Menagerie.—*Barasingha*, H.—*Baraya*, of the Nepal Terai; also *Máhá* of many parts at the foot of the Himalayas.—*Jhinkár*, in Kyarda Doon. *Potiya haran*, at Monghyr.—*Goen* or *Goenjak* (the male) in Central India; *Gaoni*, the female.—Swamp-deer of many Europeans, generally *Barasingha* of sportsmen in Bengal, Oude, &c.

THE SWAMP DEER.

Descr.—Horns very large and moderately stout, curving well outwards; pale, with basal antler, and a more or less branched summit, the lower branches sometimes simulating a median tine. Form altogether lighter than that of the Samber, especially the neck and fore-quarter; hair finer and more woolly; tail moderately short. Color dull yellowish-brown in winter, bright rufous-brown or chesnut in summer, paler below and inside the limbs; white under the tail. The female is lighter, of a pale dun or whity-brown color. The young are spotted.

Length, nearly 6 feet; tail 8 to 9 inches; height 11 hands to 11½ (44 to 46 inches).

Average length of horns 3 feet, or a little more. Fourteen and fifteen points are not uncommon in old stags, and I have seen them with seventeen.

This fine deer is found in the forest land at the foot of the Himalayas, from the Kyarda Doon to Bhotan, and is very abundant in Assam, inhabiting the islands and churrs of the Berrampooter, extending down the river in suitable spots to the eastern Sunderbuns. It is also stated to occur near Monghyr, and thence extends sparingly through the great forest tract of Central India. It is rare to the south of the Nerbudda, but it has to my knowledge been killed between the Nerbudda and Nagpore, not far from Seonee, and it is tolerably abundant in the open forest land between Mundlah and Omerkuntak at the source of the Nerbudda. To the east of this forest tract it has been killed near Midnapore, and in the highlands of Goomsoor; but does not, as far as is known, extend so far west as the road between Mirzapore and Jubbulpore. It is very gregarious, being often found in large flocks feeding in plains near the forests, and when pursued often keeping in a close pack till they gain the shelter of the forest. A writer in the Indian Sporting Review, thus speaks of these deer as he saw them in Central India. "The plain stretched away in gentle undulations towards the river, distant about a mile, and on it were three large herds of barasinghas feeding at once time: the nearest was not more than five hundred yards away from where I stood; there must have been at least fifty of them, stags, hinds, and fawns, feeding together in a lump, and outside the herd grazed three most enormous stags. . . . Then the herd went off in earnest, showing a perfect forest of antlers, and the clatter of their hoofs on the hard ground was like the sound of a squadron of cavalry going to water."* According to Hodgson, it never enters the mountains of the Himalayas, nor even habitually frequents the depths of the forests. His lair is on the skirts of large forests amidst swampy and grassy glades. It is found sparingly in the forests of the Dehra and Kyarda Doons, and here it is occasionally found on the low hills as well as on the valleys. I have seen it in Dehra Doon in long grass, and in forest in the Kyarda Doon. It is said to be exceedingly numerous in Assam, enormous herds occurring in the grassy churs of rivers. It is stated to feed both on grass and on the bark and young shoots of trees.

The name *Maha* sometimes applied to this deer is also given to the Samber stag, and it is occasionally called *Jhánk*, a name usually applied to the male spotted deer. This deer is now living in the Zoological Society's Gardens, London, and has bred there.

A remarkable deer that approaches the last in size and some of its characters is the *Panolia Eldi*, Guthrie, Blyth's Cat. 486, the *Cervus frontalis*, McClelland, and *C. dimorphe*, Hodgson, the Burmese or brow-antlered deer. Gray, in his Catalogue of Hodgson's Collection, gives both *Panolia Eedii*, and *Rusa dimorpha*, from Nepal, as distinct species. The basal antler is directed forwards, and is very long, and the horns are very divergent, with fewer terminal branches than the last. It is found in Munnipore, where called *Sung-nai* or *Sing-nai*, and thence southwards

* Indian Sporting Review, vol. XVIII., p. 49.

throughout Burmah to Siam, and the Malayan peninsula. It is the *Thamin* or *Té-min* of Burmah. Hodgson asserts that he obtained it from the sál forest of the Nepal Morung, where called *Gour* and *Ghos*, and he also gives another name *Séving*. He was most probably deceived by his shikarees who brought him the animal, and it will be observed that that the name *Séving* is probably a mispronunciation of the Burmese name. The name *Ghos* is also probably the same as the *Ghous*, by which the Samber is called in Dacca and eastern Bengal. The horns of *dimorphe*, as described by Hodgson, are considered by Blyth to be "abnormal as developed in captivity."

Gen. RUSA, Ham. Smith.

Char.—Horns with one basal and one upper tine, thick, dark and rugose. Muffle large; eye-pits large and reversile; no feet pits. Of large size. Canines in the upper jaw in both sexes; the males heavily maned.

This genus is spread over the Indian region from the Himalayas to the Philippine islands.

220. Rusa Aristotelis.

Cervus apud CUVIER.—BLYTH, Cat. 488.—Figured F. CUVIER, Mammif. 1, 104 and 3, 93.—*C. hippelaphus*, *C. equinus*, and *C. Leschenaultii*, CUVIER.—*C. niger*, BLAINVILLE.*—*C. jarai* and *C. heterocercus*, Hodgson. *C. saumur*, OGILBY.—*Sámbar*, H. and Mahr.—*Jarai* and *Jerrao*, in the Himalayas.—*Máhá*, in parts of the Terai.—*Mérú*, Mahr. of the Gháts.—*Ma-ao*, of Gonds.—*Kadavi* or *Kadaba*, Canarese.—*Kannadi*, Tel.—*Ghous* or *Gaoj*, in Eastern Bengal; the female, *Bhalongi*.

THE SAMBER STAG.

Descr.—Horns with a basal antler springing directly from the burr or base of the horn, and pointing forwards, upwards and outwards, the beam bifurcating at the extremity, a snag separating posteriorly and pointing obliquely to the rear. Color dark brown, in summer somewhat slaty; the chin, limbs within, tail beneath, and irregularly marked patch on the buttocks pale yellowish, or orange yellow; neck and throat with long hair, forming a sort of mane; tail moderately long. Female and young dusky olive-brown, lighter than the buck.

* I think it doubtful whether this name was originally given to a *Rusa* or *Axis*. C. H. Smith; Griffith's Cuvier, Vol. IV., p. 114.

Length, 6 to 7 feet; height 13 to 14 hands at the shoulder; tail 12 to 13 inches; ears 7 to 8. Some are stated to be larger than this even.

It has been for long a disputed point whether the Himalayan Jerrow was distinct from the Samber of Central India or not. Horsfield, in his Catalogue of Mammalia, gives three species, *R. equina*, from Southern India; *R. hippelaphus*, and *R. aristotelis*, from the Himalayas. Hodgson makes three races from the hills alone, viz., *C. hippelaphus*, the samber, or *Phursa jarai*, *i. e.*, the hoary jerrow; *C. aristotelis*, the *Rato jarai*, or red jerrow; and *C. heterocercus*, the *Kalo jarai*. The former is said to have a dark hide copiously sprinkled with hoary; the basal antler recurved towards the beam, and the posterior process of the bifurcation much longer than the anterior one. *C. aristotelis* is said to have the frontal branch elongate, the rump very rufous, and the posterior terminal snag very small and approximate to the other. The animal is also said to be smaller. *C. heterocercus*, is stated to have the upper part of the beam simple; the body color very dark, almost black; and to be much smaller than the two last. Gray, in his Catalogue of Mammalia of the British Museum, gives *R. aristotelis*, *hippelaphus* and *equinus*. *R. equina*, by some restricted to Southern India, by others looked on as the *Rusa* of the Malayan countries, is said to differ from *hippelaphus* in having the basal antler directed forwards, and in the upper branch of the summit being small and directed backwards; and *C. leschenaultii*, stated to be from Southern India, is described as being not so dark as the *Rusa* of Bengal, with the horns angulated and more rugose, and the caudal disk more developed. Colonel Sykes too, in his Catalogue, speaking of the race of Western India, says, "not so large nor so dark as *C. niger* of Bengal."

Blyth was at one time inclined to consider that the Himalayan *Jerrow*, *C. aristotelis*, differed from *C. hippelaphus* of Central and Southern India, stating that the *Jerrow* was larger, of a darker color, and with the hair on the head and neck more lengthened. The horns too were considered to be generally larger and more diverging than those of Southern India, and the forehead to be broader. Latterly however, and in his Catalogue, he looked upon them as all belonging to one species; and after seeing these deer in the Himalayas, in Central India, and in Southern India, I quite agree with this decision. The chief distinctions relied on in naming these races are a difference of size of the animals, and of their horns, the comparative size of the basal and terminal snags, different shades of color, with the more or less developed mane, and the more or less marked caudal disk. Many of these differences are, however, observed in individuals from the same part of the country, and others appear due to age or climate. Elliot, in his Catalogue, considered all to be varieties of one species. He says, "the horns of different individuals present great diversities of form. I have met with instances of medial antlers, of trifurcated extremities, and in one case with the extremity showing a fourfold division." I have seen many Sambers in Southern India with a trifurcate extremity to one or both horns, and more rarely a horn without the terminal snag, corresponding to Hodgson's *heterocercus*.

The horns vary much in thickness and length, some being very massive but of no great length, others being comparatively thin but long, and the divergence of the horns varies much, as well as the degree of curvature, and the relative size of the terminal snags. The horns are considered to attain their complete form in the fourth year, and after that go on increasing in size for several years more, without any normal alteration of form. The length of the horns rarely exceeds 40 inches (indeed the generality are under 3 feet), but some are recorded 4 feet along the curvature. The basal antler 10 to 12 inches or more. The thickest pair of horns in the Museum Asiatic Society, Calcutta, came from near Cuttack, and are extraordinarily massive and heavy. An immense pair killed in Mysore, is alluded to by Colonel W. Campbell, in his "Indian Journal," which he states (from recollection however) to have been nearly 18 inches in circumference at the base!

The color too varies a good deal even in the same locality, some being much darker than others. Mr. W. Elliot says, writing of the Samber of the Southern Mahratta country, "the color varies from dark-brown to grayish-black or slate-black, with the chin, the inner sides of the limbs, the under part of the tail, and the space between the buttocks, yellowish-white passing into orange-yellow, but never extending into a large circular disk on the buttocks. In several instances I have met with the hinds of a pale yellow or light chesnut color. The neck and throat are clothed with a long mane."

The *Samber* or *jerrow*, is found in all the large forests of India, from the extreme south to the Himalayas, ascending these mountains to 9,000 or 10,000 feet of elevation. Among other localities may be named the Western Ghâts throughout their whole extent, the Wynaad, Coorg, the Neelgherries, many parts of Mysore, the Eastern Ghâts, the Vindhya and Sautpoora ranges of hills, and all Central India where sufficient cover is afforded by the forests. Also, the whole range of Himalayas, not only at their base but far within the hills. As a rule they prefer hilly ground to flat land, but if the forest is dense, are frequently found on comparatively level country. They rarely leave the coverts of the forests, but in elevated and cool districts, as on the Neelgherries and Himalayas, &c., they may not unfrequently be seen morning and evening outside a patch of jungle, grazing on the new grass that springs up after the old grass is burnt off. They are generally more or less gregarious, being often found in herds, varying from four or five to twenty and upwards; but both males and females are occasionally found alone. In the day time they seek the most sheltered spots, especially in hot districts, and in the hot weather, and are very impatient of the sun's rays. They feed both on grass, on young shoots, and on various fruits. They travel wonderfully over rocky and stony ground.

The stags drop their horns in April, sometimes earlier, and the new horns are not perfected till the end of September, about which time the rutting season commences, and their peculiar call may be heard, especially morning and evening. Mr. Elliot says that, "the stags are then fierce and bold. I have seen one when suddenly disturbed face the intruder for a moment, shaking his head, bristling his mane, distending the suborbital sinus, and then dashing into the cover." The females produce one young at a birth.

The eye-pit or suborbital sinus is very large in these deer, and when the animal is excited or angry or frightened, it is opened very large, and can be distended at pleasure. Hodgson says that it is completely reversile.

The pursuit of this large stag is a favourite sport in India, its great size and fine horns causing it to be greatly prized by sportsmen. It is either stalked in the forests, or when seen feeding outside a patch of jungle; but is generally driven by a line of beaters, the gunners being posted at intervals. The clattering of a herd of samber over the stones may often be heard for some distance before they come in view, usually following one another in single file and giving a succession of shots. The action of this animal is by no means elegant, but it gets over a great deal of rough ground very rapidly, with an apparently heavy, lumbering, lobbing gallop. I have known it killed by fox hounds on the Neelgherries; and large powerful deer hounds will bring it to bay occasionally. When hard pressed it often takes to water. As previously mentioned I have known it killed by the wild dog. In the interior of the Himalayas many are killed in winter in the snow, the hill men mobbing them, and knocking them on the head with clubs. I have seen some very fine horns in Kumaon procured thus. The flesh of the Samber is rather coarse, and rarely fat, but sometimes well tasted. The specific names *hippelaphus* and *Aristotelis* were given under the impression that this stag was the *Hippelaphus*, *i. e.*, the horse-deer of Aristotle, but most naturalists think that the *Nylghai* was intended, and not this animal.

This deer is found in Ceylon, in Assam, Burmah, the Malayan peninsula, and some of the islands. Blyth remarks that, "the race seems rather smaller in Burmah, the Malayan peninsula and Sumatra, being the *R. equina*, Auct.; but it does not appear to me to be fairly separable. I have never seen really fine horns from the eastward of the Bay of Bengal."*

Several individuals of this deer are living in the Zoological Gardens, where it has bred for some years.

Rusa tunguc, Vigors, (*Cervus rusa*, S. Müller,) from Sumatra, is another well marked species of this group; and *C. Moluccensis*, Müller, from the Moluccas, and *C. peronii*, Gray, from Timor, are also considered distinct by Dr. Sclater, though stated by Blyth to be barely separable from the Javanese stag. All three are also living in the London Zoological Gardens.

Gen. Axis, Ham. Smith.

Char.—One basal and one subterminal snag; beam a good deal bent, pale and somewhat smooth. Muffle large, eye-pits large; inguinal glands; feet pits in the hind legs only. Canine teeth in the upper jaw in the males only, or in both sexes. Of small or moderate size. Pelage more or less spotted. Tail moderately long.

221. Axis maculatus.

Gray.—Blyth, Cat 490.—Figd. F. Cuvier, Mammif. 1, 98-99.—*Cervus axis*, Erxleben.—*C. nudipalpebra*, Ogilby (melanoid variety).—*Axis major* et *medius*, Hodgson.—*Chital*, H.—*Chitra* or *Chitri*, in some parts; the male, *Jhánk*.—*Chatidah*, of Bhagulpore.—*Boro khotiyá*, Beng. at Rungpore.—*Buriyá*, in Goruckpore.—*Saraga*, Can.—*Dupi*, Tel.—*Lupí*, of Gonds.

* Lieutenant R. Beavan assures me that the largest pair of Samber's horns which he has seen were from Burmah.

THE SPOTTED DEER.

Descr.—General color yellow or rufous-fawn with numerous white spots, and a dark dorsal streak from the nape to the tail; head brownish and the muzzle dark; chin, throat and neck in front white; lower parts and thighs internally, whitish; ears brown externally, white within; tail longish, white beneath. The basal tine is directed forwards, and in old individuals has often one or two points near the base.

Length, about 4½ to nearly 5 feet; height at shoulder 36 to 38 inches.

Hodgson insists that there are two species of spotted deer, which he named respectively, *Axis major*, and *Axis medius*, the latter as being intermediate in size to the larger kind, and the hog-deer, *Axis minor* apud Hodgson. These are ignored by Blyth and Gray, but I am inclined to agree with Hodgson in this from my personal knowledge of the spotted deer of Malabar and of Central India. When I first saw horns of the spotted deer killed in Central India, and subsequently killed it myself, I was astonished at their size and their greater smoothness as compared with specimens of the Southern Indian *Axis*, and on making the proper references, found that Hodgson had distinguished them. From want of specimens, however, I am at present unable to point out their specific differences except in a general way, and have therefore allowed both to stand under *Axis maculatus*.

It appears to me very probable that Kelaart's *Axis oryzeus* is either the same, or a still smaller race of spotted deer. Blyth, indeed, classes the Ceylon animal as a variety of the hog deer, but states that it is somewhat lighter in form, with the menilling more distinct in summer vesture, and the horns perhaps longer on the average, with the inner prong of the terminal fork branching at a less abrupt angle, all tending to approximate nearer to *Axis maculatus*. Now, if these differential points be extended a little more, they would tally nearly with the spotted deer of Malabar. This animal has the horns much longer than in the hog-deer, slender in make, and rougher externally than those of the deer of Central India, with the bifurcated extremity as described by Blyth of the Ceylon deer, and the basal antler longer and more directed upwards. I never saw, in the South of India, any disposition to throw off points on the basal tine as in the large *Axis*. It always retains its spotted pelage, and is a good deal smaller than the northern deer, standing about 30 to 34 inches in height, and is a light and graceful animal, very unlike the hog-deer in habit. As however, I have no specimens, and have lost my notes of measurements, &c., I can do no more here than point out the supposed difference, and leave it to future observers for verification. It appears that Pennant also long ago distinguished it from the large one, calling it the middle-sized *Axis*. Where Hodgson observed his *Axis medius*, and what are its peculiar characters and haunts, we are unfortunately ignorant. He calls it the *Jhao lugna* or *Laghuna*, which would indicate that it frequented the sandy beds of rivers, in which the jhow *(Tamarix)* grows, but it is impossible to say whether his *Axis medius* is the same as the Malabar spotted deer or not; but, if really distinct, it very probably will be found to be the same, and in that case Hodgson's name, *Axis medius* would stand for the small race, whether identical or otherwise with *A. oryzeus* of Celyon.

The large spotted-deer is found in many of the forests and jungles in Central India, both in hilly ground and level plains, and is very abundant on both sides of the Nerbudda in suitable places; also in many localities along the Western Ghâts and Eastern Ghâts, Northern Circars, &c., &c. It is also abundant along the lower and outer ranges of the Sub-Himalayas, and in the forests and jungles that extend into the plains, and along the course of the large rivers. It is also numerous in the Bengal Sunderbuns, but is not found wild on the other side of the Bay of Bengal, nor does it extend into the Punjab. Where numerous, they are very gregarious. Early in the morning they may be found feeding in the open glades, but soon retire to rest in the more shady and retired spots.

The Malabar spotted deer occurs in forest all along the Malabar coast, coming to open glades or patches of rice land during the night, where it commits great depredations, and where it may sometimes be shot early in the morning before it has retired to the forest. I have seen herds of above a hundred of these deer at the foot of the Neelgherries, and nearly as numerous ones in Malabar, and in the Wynaad.

The next deer has been separated as a sub-genus, *Hyelaphus*.

222. Axis porcinus.

Cervus apud ZIMMERMAN.—BLYTH, Cat. 491.—Figd. F. CUVIER, Mammif. 3, 91-92.—*C. oryzeus*, KELAART apud BLYTH.—*C. dodur*, ROYLE.—*C. niger* apud BUCH. HAM. MSS., dark variety.—*Párá*, H.—*Khar laguna*, of Nepal Terai.—*Sugoria* also, in some parts.—*Nuthrini haran*, in some parts of Bengal, unless this name be properly applied to the small spotted deer.

THE HOG-DEER.

Descr.—General color a light chesnut or olive brown, with an eye-spot, the margin of the lips, the tail beneath, limbs within, and abdomen white. In summer many assume a paler and more yellow tint, and get a few white spots; and the old buck assumes a dark slaty color. The horns resemble those of a young spotted deer, with both the basal and upper tines very small, the former pointing directly upwards at a very acute angle, and the latter directed backwards and inwards, nearly at a right angle, occasionally pointing downwards.

Average length of a full grown buck from 42 to 44 inches, from muzzle to root of tail; tail 8; height at shoulder 27 to 28 inches. Average length of horns 15 to 16 inches.

The hog-deer is found throughout the Gangetic valley in suitable spots, extending to the foot of the hills, and more rarely into Central India. It is also found in the Punjab and Sindh, and is abundant in Assam, Sylhet, and Burmah. It has been stated to inhabit south Malabar and Ceylon, but the race from the latter country differs somewhat and is probably distinct, and neither Mr. Blyth nor myself have actually seen specimens from Malabar, though I was resident in north Malabar for some time. It is very abundant in Bengal, in many parts near the foot of the Himalayas, in Deyra Doon, and near the Ganges, Jumna, Sutlej, and other large rivers, frequenting chiefly long grass and jhow jungle. It rarely seeks the shelter of forests, though frequenting grassy grounds in open forests and open glades in the thicker jungles. It lies sheltered during the day in thick patches of long grass, or in thick bushes in the grassy plains, and lies very close, often getting up within a few feet of the elephant or beaters. It runs with its head low and in a somewhat ungainly manner, hence its popular appellation in India of hog-deer. It is not gregarious, both sexes lying solitary in general, though at times two or more may be put up together. From the nature of the ground it frequents, high grass, &c., it is generally shot from off elephants. It is not very speedy, and if it breaks into a patch of open ground can be run down by dogs.

The buck drops his horns in April generally, and ruts in September and October. The young are beautifully spotted.

Both this and the spotted-deer are living in the Zoological Gardens, and have bred there.

Gen. CERVULUS, Blainville.

Syn. *Styloceros*, SMITH; *Muntjacus*, GRAY.

Char.—Horns raised on high hairy pedicles, with only one small basal snag. Large canines in the upper jaw in both sexes; muffle large; two conspicuous longitudinal facial creases: tail rather short; eye-pits very large and mobile; large feet-pits in the hind-feet; no inguinal pits; no calcic tuft.

The muntjacs are deer of small size, inhabiting dense forests, and are peculiar to the Indian kingdom. By their long canines and small antlers they be said to form a link to the *Moschidæ*, or musk-deer, but they do not, I think, enter that family as Blyth has placed them.

223. Cervulus aureus.

HAM. SMITH.—*C. vaginalis*, BODDAERT apud BLYTH, Cat. 492.—*C. ratwa*, HODGSON, As. Res. XVIII. 130, with figure.—*C. styloceros* apud OGILBY, ROYLE's Ill. Bot. Himal. pl. 5 f. 2.—*C. albipes*, WAGLER.—*C. muntjac*, apud ELLIOT, Cat. 53.—*C. moschatus*, BLAINVILLE apud HORSFIELD, Cat. 276.—*Muntjacus vaginalis*, GRAY, Cat. Mamm., and Cat. Hodgson's Coll.—*Kakur*, H., throughout Northern India.—*Maya*, Beng., in Rungpore.—*Ratwá*, Nepal.—*Karsiar*, Bhot.—*Sikkú* or *Súkú*, Lepch.—*Gutra* and *Gutri* (m. and f.) of Gonds, in Central India.—*Bekra* or *Bekur*, Mahr.—*Kán-kuri*, Can.—*Kúká-gori*, Tel.—*Jangli-bakra*, vulgo of Mussalmans of Southern India, hence the name of *jungle sheep* in the Madras Presidency. Barking-deer of sportsmen in Bengal; rib-faced deer of Pennant; red hog-deer in Ceylon.

THE RIB-FACED OR BARKING DEER.

Descr.—Color a bright rufous-bay; limbs internally, pubic region, and tail beneath, white; chin and lower jaw whitish; some white spots in front of the fetlocks of all four legs; facial creases dark brown.

Average length of male 3½ feet; tail 7"; height 26 to 28 inches; horn 8 to 10 inches.

The doe is a little smaller, and has bristly black tufts of hair on a knob in the spot where the horns of the buck are.

It is yet undecided whether the *Kakur* of India is distinct from the *muntjac* of Java and Malayana. Blyth, in his Catalogue, has considered them the same, as Elliot had previously. Horsfield, in his Catalogue of Mammalia, puts them distinct, but says that the specific distinctions are by no means strongly marked. Schinz, in his Synopsis Mamm., gives three species from continental India, viz., *C. styloceros* of Royle's Illustions, and *C. ratwá*, Hodgson, both from the Himalayas; and *C. albipes* from Poonah; all of which he considers distinct from *C. muntjac* of Malayana. Gray also considered the Malayan race distinct, stating that it was generally darker than the Indian animal. Dr. Sclater, from observation of the living animals in menageries, says that they appear sufficiently distinct; and this is the view I have long taken.

The rib-faced deer is found in all the thick jungles and forests of India, from the extreme south to the Himalayas, and from a low level to 8,000 or 9,000 feet in the Himalayas. It is most abundant in hilly countries, and it is quite a forest animal, only coming to the skirts of the woods morning and evening to graze. It is a solitary animal, very rarely even two being found together. It carries its head and neck low, and as its hind quarters are high, its action in running is peculiar and not very elegant, somewhat resembling the pace of a sheep, hence its popular but very erroneous name in Southern India. "It has," says Hodgson, "no powers of sustained speed and extensive leap, but is unmatched for flexibility and power of creeping through tangled underwood. It has, indeed, a weasel-like flexibility of spine and limbs, enabling them to wend on without kneeling, even when there is little more than 6 inches? of perpendicular passage room, thus escaping their great enemy the wild dog."

In the Himalayas, near Darjeeling, two or three bowmen with three or four common hill dogs, will often chase one to death in an hour or so. I have seen it hunted with fox hounds on the Neelgherries, and run down with tolerable ease, the woods there being very open, and if it be driven out of the woods a greyhound will quickly pull it down. It is easily stalked, and on the Himalayas many are killed during the winter when the snow is on the ground. It gets its name of barking-deer from its call, which is a kind of short bark like that of the fox, but louder, and it may be heard in the jungles it frequents both by day and by night. Colonel Markham says that, "as it runs a curious rattling noise may often be heard like that from two pieces of loose bone knocked together sharply." It is excellent venison, but rarely carries any fat.

Its tongue is very long and extensile, and it often licks its whole face with it. Hodgson states that the vertebræ of the back and neck are very mobile, and the spinous processes of the dorsal vertebræ are unusually short and of uniform height, the humerus and femur are nearly as long respectively as the radius and ulna, and the metacarpus and metatarsus are short.

Dr. Sclater says that the *Cervulus vaginalis* of Java and Sumatra is a larger and finer animal than the India *Cervulus*. Another species is recorded from China, *C. Reevesii*, Ogilby.

The deer found in America constitute a peculiar group, placed by Blyth in a distinct sub-family, but without a name. One group has the horns considerably branched, and to this belong the Virginian and Mexican deer, *Cariacus virginianus* and *C. mexicanus;* and a peculiar group are called Brockets, having the horn simple, *Coassus* of Gray.

The little roe-deer of Scotland, *Capreolus europæus*, is the type of the sub-family *Capreolinæ*. It is stated to be monogamous, wants the eye-pits, and has a very short tail. An allied species is found in Northern and Central Asia, *C. pygargus*, Pallas, somewhat larger and with longer hair.

Fam. MOSCHIDÆ. Musk-deer.

Without horns. Canines in the upper jaw; feet very much cloven and large false hoofs.

This group includes the musk-deer and the mouse-deer. They are mostly of small size with very slender limbs, and are found in the Indian region and Northern Asia. They are stated to differ from other deer in possessing a gall-bladder.

Gen. MOSCHUS, Linnæus.

Char.—Canines in both sexes, very long and slender in the male; false hoofs very large, acute, touching the ground. Muffle large; no eye-pits nor feet-pits, nor inguinal pits; a posteal calcic tuft; hair exceedingly rough, long and bristly.

This genus comprises the true musk-deer, celebrated as producing the musk of commerce and medicine.

224. Moschus moschiferus.

LINNÆUS.—BLYTH, Cat. 498.—*M. saturatus, M. chrysogaster*, and *M.*

leucogaster, HODGSON?—*Kastúrá*, H.—*Rous* or *Roos* and *Kasturé*, Kashmir.—*Lá* and *Láwá*, in Tibet.—*Ríb-jo*, in Ladak.—*Béná*, in Kunawur.

THE MUSK-DEER.

Descr.—Color usually dark fuscous-brown, paler beneath, the hairs being long and harsh, with hoary rings and a black tip; ears internally and chin whitish; ears large and erect; tail very short, hairy in females, almost naked with a tuft of hair at the end in males.

Length of male nearly 3 feet; height 22 to 23 inches.

The color varies a great deal, perhaps according to age and season. Markham describes it as a dark speckled brownish-gray, nearly black on the hind quarters, edged down the inside of the thighs with reddish yellow, the throat, belly and legs lighter gray. Hodgson describes his *chrysogaster* as bright sepia-brown above, sprinkled with golden red; orbitar region, lining and base of ears, whole body below and insides of limbs, rich golden red or orange; a dark brown patch on the buttocks; legs fulvescent. Adams says, "others are yellowish-white all over, the upper parts with the belly and inner side of the thighs white." One I got in Kashmir had the back sepia-brown with grizzled gray spots in lines on the back; head more or less grizzled, edges and insides of ears, rump, tail, lower parts and limbs, grizzled gray, very pale and almost white on the rump and tail; posterior limbs with a dark brown stripe as far as the knee. The young are spotted with white.

The hairs are long, thick, bristly, very thick-set, white at the base and for more than half their length. The canines of the male are about 3 inches long, about as thick as a goose quill. The tail of the male has a peculiar gland, the secretion from which glues the hairs together. The legs are long and slender, and the toes long and pointed, with the false hoofs very long, touching the ground.

The musk-deer is found throughout the Himalayas, always at great elevations, in summer rarely below 8,000 feet, and as high as the limits of forest. It extends through the Himalayas to Central and Northern Asia, as far as Siberia.

Hodgson says that the musk-deer is "solitary, living in retired spots near rocks, or in the depths of the forests. They leap well but cannot climb nor descend slopes well.* They rut in winter, and produce one or

* This is contrary to the experience of most sportsmen.

two young, usually in the cleft of a rock. In six weeks the young can shift for themselves, and are driven off by the mother. They can procreate ere they are a year old. They are easily tamed."

Colonel Markham says that the musk-deer is exclusively a forest animal, keeps much to the same ground, and makes a sort of form, like the hare, to lie on in the sun. It usually runs in bounds on all fours, and often makes most astonishing bounds, occasionally 60 feet on a gentle slope for several successive leaps, jumping over considerable bushes at each bound. Adams too states that, "its mode of progression is performed by series of jerking leaps." It is wonderfully sure-footed, and over rocky and precipitous ground perhaps has no equal. It appears to eat but little, chiefly grasses and lichens. If twins are produced the two are kept apart, it being very solitary in its habits, even in infancy. The musk is milky for the first year or two, afterwards granular: the dung of the males smells of musk, but the body does not, and females do not in the slightest degree. The flesh is dark-red and not musky, and the young is considered to be the best venison in India.

The musk deer is much sought after for its musk, many being shot and snared annually. A good musk-pod is valued at from 10 to 15 rupees. The musk as sold is often much adulterated with blood, liver, &c. One ounce is about the average produce of the pod.

A few anatomical details of great interest by Dr. Campbell are here given.

"The musk bag lies at the end of the penis, and might be termed a præputial bag. It is globular, about 1½ inch in diameter, and hairy, with a hole in the centre about the diameter of a lead pencil, from which the secretion can be squeezed. The orifice of the urethra lies near this, a little posteriorly. Round the margin of the opening of the gland is a circle of small glandular looking bodies. The musk when fresh is soft, not unlike moist gingerbread.

"The anus is surrounded by a ring of soft hairs, the skin under which is perforated by innumerable small pores, secreting an abominably offensive stuff, which pressure brings out like honey. The scrotum is round and naked.

"There is, besides, a peculiar organ or gland on the tail, which indeed is composed almost wholly of it. The tail of the male is triangular, nude above, thick, greasy, partially covered with short hair below and with a tuft of hairs at the end, glued together by a viscid liquor. It has two large elliptical pores beneath basal and lateral, the edges of which are somewhat mobile, and the fluid, which appears to be continually secreted, has a peculiar and rather offensive odour. The liver consists of a single lobe, and the gall bladder is constantly present."

The next group have the canines much shorter, and want the musk-bag. They form the family *Tragulidæ* of some authors. They are peculiar to the Indian region, and are among the smallest ruminants known. The most typical form, *Tragulus*, Bennett, is found in the Malayan peninsula and islands. It has the hinder part of the metatarsus bald and callous. Our province contains one member of this group, slightly differing from *Tragulus*.

Gen. MEMIMNA, Gray.

Char.—Canines only in the males, small, not exserted; false hoofs of ordinary make and size; tail very short: ears moderate; hinder edge of metatarsus covered with hair; no eye-pits nor groin-pits nor feet-pits.

These are animals of very small size and with the hairs smooth. Their limbs are exceedingly slender, and their hind quarters are high, causing their action to be very inelegant. They frequent only the thickest forests. But one species is known.

225. Memimna indica.

GRAY.—BLYTH, Cat. 494.—*Moschus memimna*, ERXLEBEN, ELLIOT, Cat. 50.—*Moschiola mimenoides*, HODGSON.—*Pisuri, Pisora, Pisai*, H. and Mahr.—*Mugi*, in Central India.—*Jitri haran*, Beng.—*Gandwa*, of Oorias.—*Yar*, of Koles.—*Kuru-pandi*, Tel.

THE MOUSE-DEER.

Descr.—Above olivaceous mixed with yellow gray; white below; sides of the body with yellowish white lines formed of interrupted spots, the upper rows of which are joined to those of the opposite side by some transverse spots; ears reddish-brown.

Length of body about 22 to 23 inches; tail $1\frac{1}{2}$; height 10 to 12 inches; weight 5 to 6 ℔s.

The color of this mouse-deer varies somewhat in different localities.*

* The note in Blyth's Catalogue, p. 155, placed after this species, belongs to the barking deer, and should be placed in the previous page, after *C. ratwa*, Hodgson.

The Indian mouse-deer is found in all the large forests of India from the extreme south to the foot of the Himalayas, but it does not occur at any great elevation, and I have rarely seen it from higher altitude than about 2,000 feet. It is much more abundant in the south of India than towards the north, and is certainly rare in the Himalayan Terai. It is not included among the list of Hodgson's Collections, presented to the British Museum, but Blyth says he has seen it from Nepal, and certainly Mr. Hodgson named it as above. I made many enquiries about it in various parts near the foot of the hills, but could get no precise information as to its actually occurring there. It is unknown in the countries to the eastward of the Bay of Bengal. It abounds in the forests of Malabar, and also occurs in some of the denser portions of the woods of the Eastern Ghâts. It is by no means rare in Central India, and Tickell has given some interesting details of its habits, from which I have taken the subsequent account.

The animal walks on the tips of its hoofs, which gives the legs a rigid appearance, and the natives say that it has no knee-joint, and that, in order to rest, it is obliged to lean against a tree. It never ventures into the open country; keeps a good deal among rocks; and it is said not to go out much about the fall of the leaf, as its sharp hoofs penetrate the leaves which clog its movements. They rut in June and July, and the female brings forth two young towards the end of the rains, or beginning of the cold weather.

The mouse-deer is timid but easily domesticated, and has bred in confinement.

Four or five species of *Tragulus* are known from the Malayan province, one of which, *Tragulus kanchil*, occurs as high north as the Tenasserim provinces.

We next come to the numerous and important tribe of the hollow-horned ruminants, *Cavicornia* of some, to which belong, cattle, goat, sheep, and antelope. In all these the horn consists of a conical bony process of the frontal bone, covered by a sheath of horny matter which is permanent, and is mostly present in both sexes. Their dentition is the same as that of deer. They form one family.

Fam. Bovidæ.

Canines rarely present. Horns in both sexes, or in the males only, composed of a bony nucleus or core, and a persistent horny sheath;

muffle generally present. Feet-pits usually in all four feet. Inguinal pits in some; eye-pits usually present. Four mammæ in most.

This family comprises antelope, goats, and cattle, which may form as many sub-families. They are entirely wanting in South America and Australia.

Sub-fam. ANTILOPINÆ, Antelopes.

Horns in both sexes or only in the males. Eye-pits in all, and feet-pits in most. The bony nucleus of the horn is generally solid, and often has a sinus at the base within. The horns are seated below the crest of the frontals, and are usually considerably apart at the base. There are inguinal pits in many, and the muffle is often wanting. The mammæ are in most cases four. The occipital plane of the skull forms an obtuse angle with the frontal plane. They resemble deer in the lightness of their make, but they are of still more slender form, with finer limbs, and possess still greater speed, but physiologically they are far removed from them.* Their hair is generally finer and more smooth than in deer.

The horns of antelopes are variously bent, usually ringed at the base, and round and smooth at the tip, situated well forwards, almost over the edge of the orbits. They are never branched, except in one species, the prong-horned antelope of North America, which, by its harsh hair and tail, evidently forms a sort of link between the antelope and deer, and which, I have noticed, has been removed by a recent writer to the deer family. One small group has four horns. The eye is usually very large, deep brown or almost black, contrasting with the light eye of the *Caprinæ*. It is situated at the upper margin of the forehead, remote from the nostrils. The head is lengthened owing to the elongation of the nasal bones; the ears are seated well back and are long. Antelope mostly live in more or less numerous herds, and are found chiefly in the old continent, by far the greatest number being from Africa, with many types.

Antelopes have been variously grouped. Blyth, in his Catalogue, distributes them in the sub-families, *Tragelaphinæ*, *Cephalophinæ*, *Adenotinæ*, and *Antelopinæ*, of which the first and the last alone have representatives of the Indian Fauna. Taking their habits as well as structure, the Indian members of this sub-family may be classed into bush antelope and desert antelope.

Bush-antelope, *Tragelaphinæ* apud Blyth.

Horns smooth, unknotted, spiral in some; females usually without

* Throughout the Bengal Presidency all antelope are popularly called deer.

horns; muzzle bovine; four teats; usually white ringed markings above the hoofs, and many with white spots on the face and body.

There are two types of this group in India, and many in Africa, the white markings being most highly developed in an African antelope, *Tragelaphus scriptus*. The Indian species both frequent jungly ground.

Gen. PORTAX, C. H. Smith.

Syn. *Damalis*.

Char.—Horns only in males, short, recurved, distant, smooth; eye-pit rather small; upper lip broad, ample; nostrils approximate; tail long, tufted; a short erect mane, and a tuft of hairs on the throat of the male. Of large size.

There is a slight pit in front of the orbit, and anterior to this a small longitudinal fold in the middle of which there is a pore, through which exudes a yellow secretion from the gland beneath. In the only species of this genus the back is rather short, and slopes downwards from the high withers, and the neck is deep and compressed like that of a horse.

226. Portax pictus.

Antilope apud PALLAS.—Figured F. CUVIER, Mamm. 3, 100-101.—*A. tragocamelus*, PALLAS.—BLYTH, Cat. 512.—*Damalis risia*, H. SMITH.—ELLIOT, Cat. 57.—*Tragelaphus hippelaphus*, OGILBY.—*Roz* or *Rojh*, H., in Northern India.—*Rú-i*, Mahr. and H., in the south.—*Nil-gai*, generally; the male often called simply *Nil* or *Lil.*—*Gúrayi* and *Gúriya*, of Gonds. —*Maravi*, Can.—*Mánú-potú*, Tel.

THE NIL-GAI.

Descr.—Male of an iron-gray color; lips, chin, lower surface of the tail, stripes inside the ears, rings on the fetlocks, and abdomen, white; head and limbs tinged with sepia-brown; mane, throat tuft, and tip of tail, black.

The female is a good deal smaller than the male, and tawny or light brown.

Length of a male about 6½ to 7 feet; height at the shoulder 4 feet 4 inches to 4½ feet; horns 8 to 9 inches, rarely 10; ear 7, very broad; tail 18 to 21 inches.

The Nil-gai is found throughout India, from near the foot of the Himalayas to the extreme south of Mysore, but is rare to the north of the

Ganges, and also in the extreme south of India. It is most abundant in in Central India, and in the country between the Jumna and Sutlej, but is rare in the Punjab, according to Adams. It does not occur in Ceylon, nor in Assam or the countries to the east of the Bay of Bengal.

It frequents thin forests, and low jungles, and is often found in tolerably open plains with only a few scattered bushes. It does not affect a hilly country, but does not avoid low hills clad with thin forest. It is indifferent to the sun, except during the hottest weather. It associates in small herds, varying from 7 or 8, to 20 and upwards. It appears to go at a lumbering ungainly pace, yet it requires a good horse and a hard run to overtake one, and the only way to succeed certainly, is to press the animal with the utmost speed at first and blow him.

The Nil-gai is not much sought after by the Indian sportsman, nor is its flesh highly esteemed, yet at times it is excellent and juicy, and gives a good beef steak.

It is often caught young and becomes very tame, many being allowed to wander about at large. They are apt however to get vicious at times. It browzes a good deal, and is very fond of many kinds of fruit. Mr. Elliot says that those he kept used to drop on their knees to feed, and attacked and defended themselves by butting with the head. A very dark, almost black one, was lately seen by more than one sportsman near Umballa. Blyth, Ogilby, and other naturalists, consider that the Nil-gai was probably the *hippelaphus* of Aristotle, and not the Samber-deer, which opinion I quite endorse.

Gen. TETRACEROS, Leach.

Char.—Horns in the males only, erect, slightly bent forwards at the tip, round, subulate, slightly ringed at the base, situated far back on the frontal bone; an additional pair of small horns situated between the orbits, short, conical, sometimes replaced by a mere bony knob; eye-pit moderate, linear; muffle large; feet-pits in the hind-feet only; no inguinal pits; canines in the males; four mammæ in the females.

The form of these animals is not so elegant as that of the true antelope, and their hair is harsher. They frequent jungles and thin forest, and do not associate in herds, but are monogamous, and often found in pairs.

This genus is strictly Indian, and there is only one well marked species known.

227. Tetraceros quadricornis.

Antilope apud BLAINVILLE.—BLYTH, Cat. 513.—Figured F. CUVIER, Mamm. 3, 99.—*A. chickara*, HARDWICKE, Linn. Trans. XIV. pl. 15.—*T. striaticornis*, LEACH.—*T. iodes*, HODGSON, Calc. J. N. H. VIII. 88, with fig.—*T. paccerois*, HODGSON.—*A. sub-quadricornutus*, ELLIOT, Cat. 56, variety ?—*Chouka* and *Chousingha*, H.—*Bekra*, Mahr.—*Bhirki*, at Saugor.—*Bhirkúra* (the male) and *Bhir* (the female), of Northern Gonds.—*Bhirul*, of Bheels.—*Kotri*, in Bustar.—*Kúrús*, of Bustar Gonds.—*Kondgúri*, Can.—*Konda-gorí*, Tel.—Vulgo, *Jangli bakra*, H., in the Deccan.

THE FOUR-HORNED ANTELOPE.

Descr.—Color an uniform brownish bay above, beneath lighter, and whitish inside the limbs and in the middle of the belly; forelegs dark, also the muzzle and edge of the ears, which are white within, with long hairs; fetlocks dark within, with more or less distinct whitish rings.

Length from 40 to 42 inches; tail 5; ear $4\frac{1}{4}$; height at shoulder 2 feet to 26 inches; at the croup a little higher. Anterior horns up to $1\frac{1}{2}$ inches; posterior horns 4 to 5.

The color varies a good deal acccording to locality. Some are much browner than others; many are light fawn with a darker shade on the back and hind quarters, and some are very pale yellowish fawn. The anterior horns vary much in development. Those in the South of India generally have rarely more than a knob or corneous tip, which often falls off, leaving a black callous skin. Many from the North of India have the anterior horns well developed, thick, conic and straight, not exceeding $1\frac{1}{2}$ inches in length. The posterior horns are nearly straight, or curve very slightly forwards at the tip, and have three or four wrinkles at their base.

Hodgson separated *A. chickara* from *quadricornis*, and named two additional species, but these now are all looked on as identical.

I was at one time strongly inclined to consider Mr. Elliot's species distinct from the northern animal, as all those which I procured from the Eastern Ghâts had only a vestige of an anterior horn, and were very pale colored, but in deference to Mr. Blyth's matured opinion I have followed him in uniting them. The four-horned antelope is found throughout all India, to which it is exclusively limited, not being known in Ceylon nor the countries to the east of the Bay of Bengal. It frequents jungly hills and open forests in the plains, not occurring in the dense woods of Malabar, nor in lower Bengal. It abounds in the hills of the Eastern Ghâts from near Madras northwards, whence it extends over all the wooded parts of Central India; and on the west is found in parts of Mysore, and in the jungles that border the Western Ghâts. It is unknown in the valley of the Ganges, but occurs at the foot of the Himalayas, in the more open forests. It is said by Adams to occur, though rare, in the Western Punjab and Sindh.

The *Chousingha* never frequents open plains, but may be seen in open glades in the forests, and in bushy ground at the skirts of denser woods, and is always found single or in pairs, being strictly monogamous. Rarely I have seen five or six scattered not far from each other. It is not a mountain animal, but is quite at home on rocky and jungly hills. When first disturbed it sometimes bounds off in a succession of short leaps, but generally runs with its neck low. It is stated to rut (in Central India) during the rains, and the female to bring forth her young in the cold weather.

The specific name, *Chickara*, applied to this antelope by Hardwicke, is quite erroneous, as that name is throughout all India applied to the *Indian gazelle.* The venison of this antelope is rather dry, and is not held in much esteem.

Other antelope belonging to the *Tragelaphine* section are the *Elands*, *Oreas canna*, and *O. derbianus;* the Gnoos, *Catoblepas gnu*, and *C. gorgon*; the *Koodoo*, *Strepsiceros kudu;* the harnessed antelope, the *Grysbok*, *Klipspringer*, and many others, all from Africa. No other Asiatic form is known.

The next group is that of the true antelope, or antelope of the desert, restricted *Antilopinæ* of Blyth. They have more or less ovine muzzle, and ringed horns, generally present in the female also. They occur both in Asia and Africa. The teats of the female are generally only two in number. The two best known Indian antelope belong to this group.

Gen. ANTILOPE, Linnæus (restricted).

Char.—Horns in the males only, long, annulated with strong rings, the tip smooth, spirally twisted, approximate at the base; no muffle; eye-pits moderate, somewhat linear; no canines; large inguinal pits; feet-pits present; small knee-brushes; female with two mammæ.

228. Antilope bezoartica.

ALDROVAND.—BLYTH, Cat. 528.—*A. cervicapra*, PALLAS, and ELLIOT,

Cat. 54.—Figured HARDWICKE, Ill. Ind. Zool., and F. CUVIER, Mamm. 3, 102-103.—*Mirga*, Sansc.—*Mirga*, the male, and *Harna*, the female, of some Hindus.—*Haran*, male, and *Harnin*, female, H. and generally; also Mahr.—*Harin*, in Bengal.—The black buck called *Kalwit*, H., and *Phandayat*, Mahr.—*Guria* or *Goria*, in Tirhoot, the male being called *Kálá*.—*Kálsar* and *Baoti*, male and female, in Behar.—*Burěta*, in Bhagulpore.—*Barout* and *Sásin*, in Nepal.—*Chigri*, Can.—*Irri*, the male, and *Ledi*, the female (but also applied to both), Tel.; also *Jinka*, Tel (generic name).—*Alali*, male, and *Gandoli*, female, of Baoris.

THE INDIAN ANTELOPE.

Descr.—Horns long, diverging, with five flexures in old individuals; rings strong at the base, tip smooth; color of adult male rich dark glossy brown color above and on the sides, beneath and inside of the limbs white; hind head, nape, and back of neck hoary-yellowish; nose and lips, and a large mark round the eyes white.

Length about 4 feet to root of tail which is 7 inches; height at shoulder 32 inches; ear $5\frac{1}{2}$. Horns from 20 to 27 inches long, 9 to 81 inches divergent at tip.

The female is somewhat less and is pale yellowish fawn-color above, white beneath and inside the limbs, and with a pale streak from the shoulder to the haunch.

"The horns of the males in the Southern Mahratta country," says Mr. Elliot, "seldom exceed 19 or 20 inches in length. The largest I have seen was 22 inches with four flexures in the spiral twist; but I saw a pair from Hydrabad 24 inches long with five flexures and fifty rings, and another pair from Kattywar, which were 25 inches." In many parts of Central and Northern India, the average length of the horns of black buck exceeds those of Southern India, and in Hurriana, and especially in the country between the Sutlej and Hissar, horns of 23 and 24 inches are by no means uncommon, and I have seen them only 22 inches long with more than five flexures. I have seen several pairs 26 inches long, and heard of others 27, and I heard of one pair killed in the Deccan that were said* to be close upon 30 inches. The horns vary much in the size of the rings, in the degree of spiral twist, and in divergence. Three instances of females with horns are now on record. They were however

* This much requires confirmation.

thin and much curved, "gyring round like those of *Ovis ammon*." One buck is also mentioned in which one of the horns curved round, and Blyth suggested that the testis of that side had probably been injured.

This beautiful antelope is found throughout India in suitable localities, and does not occur out of our province. It is rare in Bengal, a few only extending into Purneah and Dinagepore, north of the Ganges; and it does not occur in the richly wooded Malabar coast. It is abundant in the Deccan, in parts of the Doab between the Jumna and Ganges, also in Hurriana, Rajpootana, and neighbouring districts. It is found in the Punjab, but does not cross the Indus. I have seen larger herds in the neighbourhood of Jalna, in the Deccan, than anywhere else, occasionally some thousands together, with black bucks in proportion. Now and then, Dr. Scott informs me, they have observed in the Government cattle farm at Hissar in herds calculated at 8,000 to 10,000. Generally throughout the country, smaller herds are more common, where one black buck is accompanied by his harem of ten to twenty does or even more. With these herds younger bucks that have not turned black are occasionally seen, the lord of the herd driving off the other bucks as soon as they begin to turn black.

Mr. Elliot says, "the rutting season commences about February or March, but fawns are seen of all ages at every season. During the spring months the buck often separates a particular doe from the herd, and will not suffer her to join it again, cutting her off and intercepting every attempt to mingle with the rest. The two are often found alone also, but on being followed always rejoin the herd.

"When a herd is met with and alarmed the does bound away for a short distance and then turn round to take a look, the buck follows more leisurely, and generally brings up the rear. Before they are much frightened they always bound or spring, and a large herd going off in this way is one of the finest sights imaginable. But when at speed the gallop is like that of any other animal. Some of the herds are so large that one buck has from 50 to 60 does, and the young bucks driven from these large flocks are found wandering in separate herds, sometimes containing as many as 30 individuals of different ages.

"They show some ingenuity in avoiding danger. In pursuing a buck once into a field of *toor*, I suddenly lost sight of him, and found after a long search that he had dropt down among the grain, and lay concealed with his head close to the ground. Coming on another occasion upon a buck and doe with a young fawn, the whole party took to flight, but the fawn being very young, the old ones endeavoured to make it lie down. Finding however that it persisted in running after them, the buck turned round and repeatedly knocked it over in a cotton field until it lay still, when they ran off endeavoring to attract my attention. Young fawns are frequently found concealed and left quite by themselves."

When a herd goes away on the approach of danger, if any of the does are lingering behind, the buck comes up and drives them off after the others, acting as whipper-in, and never allowing one to drop behind. Bucks may often be seen fighting, and are then so intently engaged, their heads often locked together by the horns, that they may be approached very close before the common danger causes them to separate. Bucks with broken horns are often met with caused by fights; and I have heard of bucks being sometimes caught in this way, some nooses being attached to the horns of a tame one. I have twice seen a wounded antelope pursued by greyhounds drop suddenly into a small ravine, and lie close to the ground, allowing the dogs to pass over it without noticing, and hurry forward. This antelope, and indeed all the Indian species, have the habit of always dropping their dung in the same spot.

Buck-shooting is one of the favorite sports of India, and gives fine opportunities for testing the skill of the sportsman. Where they are very abundant and the ground is favorable, shots can generally be had with a little trouble in stalking, at from 100 to 150 yards, and sometimes closer; but, in very open ground, shooting must be practised at from 200 to 300 yards. During the heat of the day antelope usually lie down to rest and and chew the cud, and a single one may then often be stalked successfully, but if there is a herd, one of the females is always on the alert.

A wounded antelope gives occasionally an excellent course with greyhounds, and I have known one with a broken fore-leg get away from half-bred dogs in the middle of the day when the sun was rather powerful. Spearing a wounded buck off horseback is rather exciting work, and I have known one, also with a broken leg, give a run of three miles before be was overhauled, and that on tolerably good ground. Greyhounds are very keen after a wounded antelope, and occasionally get savage and fight over it when pulled down, seeming to take pleasure in sniffing and biting at the groin-pits.

Very rarely good greyhounds have pulled down this antelope unwounded, on ordinary ground; but there are at least three localities where this coursing used to be practised successfully. One at Pooree, on the east coast, south of Cuttack, where the antelope are found in the morning on an extensive plain of heavy sand, and if the dogs are slipped favorably, they are sometimes pulled down before they can get on to hard ground. Another is in the desert near Sirsa, where the ground is entirely sandy. The third locality is at Point Calymere, also on the east coast, very far south, not far from Trichinopoly, where there is a tract of fine pasture land always green and elastic, and on which first-rate English dogs have repeatedly pulled down black buck. I rather think that the antelope here are in somewhat soft condition, the grass being always green, and that from this cause they are more easily caught than elsewhere. During the rains, indeed, if antelope are found in the fields where the soil is very soft and heavy, they fall an easy prey to good dogs.

The venison of this antelope is at times excellent, the meat very fine-grained, but not fat. Colonel W. Campbell says, that of old bucks is infinitely superior to that of young ones. If taken young this antelope becomes very tame, and will follow its owner about, or wander forth by itself all day and return at evening. I have often seen one accompanying a regiment on the line of march.

This antelope is living in the Zoological Gardens, in London. A large herd of them is kept in the park round Government house, at Madras. It is one of the constellations of the Indian zodiac, and is sacred to Chandra. There is no other species of this genus.

Gen. GAZELLA, H. Smith.

Syn. *Tragops*, Hodgson (partly).

Char.—Horns rather short, lyrate, ringed, approximate at the base, diverging at the tip, present in the female but very small; ears long, acuminate; tail moderate; eye-pits small, obliquely transverse; groin-pits distinct; large feet-pits in all feet; knees tufted, and calcic tuft posteal.

This genus comprises the gazelles, so called from the Arabic word, *Al-ghazal*, the name of the *Antilope dorcas*. They are animals of rather small size, with large eyes and very active and graceful, inhabiting bare and desert countries, chiefly in Africa, Arabia and Persia, one species at least extending to India. Several species are known.

Hodgson separated the Indian gazelle under the generic name ot *Tragops*, but on erroneous grounds, as the eye-pits (on the absence of which he grounded his genus) are present, though small.

229. Gazella Bennettii.

Antilope apud SYKES, Cat.—BLYTH, Cat. 533.—*A. arabica* apud ELLIOT, Cat. 55.—*A. dorcas*, var. SUNDEVALL.—*A. Christii* GRAY?—*A. hazenna*, IS. GEOFFROY, Voy. JACQUEMONT, Zool. pl. VI.—*Chikára*, H., throughout India.—*Kal-púnch*, H., and *Kal-sipi*, Mahr., *i. e.*, black-tail.—*Tiska*, Can.; also *Budári* and *Mudari*, Can.—*Búrúdú-jinka*, Tel.—*Porsya*, male, and *Chári*, female, of Baoris.—*Hazenne*, near Chittor in Malwa (JACQUEMONT).—Ravine-deer of sportsmen in Bengal.—Goat-antelope in Bombay and Madras.

THE INDIAN GAZELLE.

Descr.—Color above deep fawn brown, darker where it joins the white on the sides and buttocks; chin, breast, lower parts and buttocks behind white; tail, knee tufts and fetlocks behind black; a dark brown spot on the nose, and a dark line from the eyes to the mouth, bordered by a light one above.

Length of a buck 3½ feet; tail 8½ inches; height 26 at shoulder 28 at the croup; ear 6 inches; head 9; horns 12 to 13.

The horns vary much in thickness and lyration. I have seen several 14 inches long with 23 rings; but Adams states that he has seen them in the Punjab 18 inches;* as a rule very few exceed 14 inches, and most are below this. The tip sometimes curves much forward. The horns of the female are small, rarely longer than 6 inches, usually 4 to 5, slender, slightly wrinkled at the base, inclining backwards with the tip bent forwards.

The Indian Gazelle is found throughout India in suitable localities, unknown in lower Bengal and the Malabar coast, and most abundant in the desert parts of Rajpootana, Hurriana, and Sindh. It is never found in forest country, nor in districts having a damp climate, but is often met with in low thorny jungle. As a rule, however, it prefers the open bare plains, or low rocky hills or sand-hills; and a barren country to a richly cultivated one. It occurs generally in small herds, rarely more than 7 or 8, except in the extreme north-west, where I have seen 20 or more

* I think there must be some mistake in this, either that the measurement is wrong, or that a different species is meant.

together. Usually I think there are several bucks if the herd is large, but the young expelled bucks are also often found in separate herds. Single individuals are also of common occurrence.

Mr. Elliot says, "when two bucks fight they butt like rams, retiring a little and striking the foreheads together with great violence. When alarmed it utters a sort of hiss by blowing through the nose and stamps with the fore-feet, whence its Canarese name, '*Tiska.*'"

Dr. Scott informs me that in Hurriana, during the rainy season, a sort of maggot or bot is constantly found under the skin of the gazelle, only near the root of the tail. It was never observed on the antelope.

The Gazelle is occasionally hunted by dogs with the aid of the *Saker* falcon *(Falco cherrug)*, which strikes the antelope on the head, and confuses it, so that the dogs come up and catch it. Without this aid dogs have very little chance, though now and then I have known one pulled down. It is considered better eating than the black buck.

Gazella Christii, Gray, from Sindh and Cutch, is said to be paler in color, and with the horns more slender and smaller than in the Indian gazelle, and with the tips abruptly bent inwards. This is joined by Blyth to *Bennettii.* I have seen one or two heads of gazelles considered distinct from the *chikára*, called "the desert antelope," smaller, and with the horns more bent forwards. I only looked on them at the time as a dwarf or stunted *chikâra*, but it is possible that there may be another species extending from Beloochistan across Sindh into the plains of Rajpootana, either *G. sub-gutturosa*, or *G. Christii*, if distinct from *Bennettii.* Indeed, Mr. Blyth, in a note, p. 172 of his Catalogue (transposed with another on the opposite page) says, "an animal marked *Gazella Christii*, Gray, in the London United Service Museum, appeared to me to be *G. sub-gutturosa.* It was labelled from Sindh, but might have been brought thither from beyond the passes."

Gazella dorcas of Arabia, to which Blyth unites *A. arabica*, *G. cora*, *kevella*, and *corinna* of H. Smith, is sometimes brought alive to this country, and has been considered by some to be really found in Western India. Mr. Blyth, in a note, p. 173,* Cat. Mammalia Asiatic Society's Museum, says, "after elaborate study of these specimens I have been obliged to bring all of them together, and suspect that the whole of the animals (*i. e.*, specimens in the museum that had died in captivity) had been brought to India from Aden and Muskat."

* This note, attached to *G. Bennettii*, has been transposed with another on the opposite page, under *G. dorcas*.

Gazella sub-gutturosa of Persia and Afghanistan, (*A. dorcas*, var. *Persica* of Rüppell,) may, as above stated, occur in Sindh and Beloochistan. The horns of this are said by Hutton and Blyth, to be abruptly hooked in at the tip. Other species of gazelle occur in Africa.

The *Chiru* of Tibet, *Kemas Hodgsonii*, is a fine antelope, of a somewhat pale yellowish-white color, with very long and nearly straight horns. It is considered to be the *Kemas* of Ælian. It is probable that this animal may have given rise to the belief in the unicorn; for, at a little distance when viewed laterally, there only appears to be one horn, there is so little divergence throughout their length.

Another antelope allied to the gazelles is the pretty *Procapra picticaudata* of Hodgson, the *Goá* and *Rá-goá*, of Tibet. *Antilope gutturosa*, Pallas, of China and Central Asia, is by some classed as a *Procapra*. It has the larynx dilated and swollen, and covered externally with long hair. It has also a præputial bag. The female is without horns.

The *Saiga* antelope, *Saiga tartarica*, has a most peculiar, vaulted, cartilaginous muzzle, and very open nostrils. It is found in the deserts of Tartary and other parts of Central Asia, and extends into Eastern Europe.

There are many other antelope belonging to this division in Africa, some of them very fine, and with magnificent horns; among others the *Oryx* group, *Oryx leucoryx*, and *O. gazella*; the *Harte-beest*, *Boselaphus caama*; *Aigoceros niger*, and *A. equinus*; the *Addax* group, and many other types.

The group of *Cephalophinæ* apud Blyth, are mostly small species peculiar to Africa, somewhat resembling the *Muntjacs* and mouse-deer. They have a pig-like form, slender limbs, short horns slightly ringed at the base, with a tuft of lengthened hair between the horns; and some have a long extensile tongue. The females are mostly hornless, and have four teats.

The *Adenotinæ* apud Blyth, are another group peculiar to Africa, with bovine muzzle, and with semi-ringed horns curving forwards. Some are large with coarse hair, others small with a soft coat. The females are hornless and have four teats.*

The two first animals of the next group are by some classed among the antelope; but I think, taking all their characters, habits and haunts into consideration, they more properly pertain to the next sub-family.

Sub-fam. CAPRINÆ, Goats and Sheep.

Horns usually in both sexes, or in the males only, more or less com-

* Blyth, Cat. p. 167 and 168.

pressed, usually angulated, rugose, and curving backwards, or spiral; the bony cores of the horns thick, porous and cellular. No canines. Muffle generally absent. Feet-pits in all feet, or in the fore-feet only, or none. Eye-pits rare. Groin-pits not usual. Teats generally two, rarely four.

The horns are seated on the crest of the forehead, and are closely approximate, covering the top of the head. The occipital plane of the skull forms a more or less acute angle with the frontal plane. Eyes usually pale.

This sub-family may be divided into the capricorns, the goats, and the sheep.

1st. Capricorns, or Antelope Goat, or Mountain Antelope.

Horns somewhat rounded, conical, curving backwards, of small size, found in both sexes. Compared with antelope these animals have a heavy body, stronger limbs, large hoofs and false hoofs. Dr. Sclater, who places them among the antelope, says, "the mountain antelopes which form the transition between the *Antilopinæ* and the goats and sheep, are a group distributed over the northern regions of the two hemispheres, of which the well known *Chamois* is a somewhat aberrant European representative." Blyth and Hodgson class them among the goats, as I have done.

Gen. NEMORHŒDUS, H. Smith.

Syn. *Capricornis* and *Kemas*, Ogilby.

Char.—Horns in both sexes, round, black and ringed; a small muffle; eye-pits wanting or small; large feet-pits in all feet; no inguinal pits nor calcic tufts; tail short, hairy; four mammæ.

This genus was founded by H. Smith upon *A. sumatrensis*, and therefore must be retained for this group, even if we separate the *Goral* as is done by Blyth and others, who apply Ogilby's generic name, *Capricornis*, to the *Serow*, retaining *Nemorhœdus* for the *Goral*.

230. Nemorhœdus bubalina.

Antilope apud HODGSON.—BLYTH, Cat. 536.—*A. thar*, HODGSON, olim; also *Nemorhœdus proclivus*, HODGSON.—*Thar*, in Nepal.—*Sarao*, *Serou* or *Sarraowa*, in the hills generally.—*Eimú*, on the Sutlej.—*Rámú*, in Kashmir.

The Serow or Forest Goat.

Descr.—Above black more or less grizzled and mixed on the flanks with deep clay color; a black dorsal stripe; forearms and thighs anteriorly reddish-brown; the rest of the limbs hoary; beneath whitish.

The hair is rather scanty except on the neck, on which there is a thick mane, harsh and rough; the horns are seated posterior to the orbits, but below the crest of the frontals, stout, roundish, ringed more than half way, tapering, much curved backwards, slightly divergent, with the points inclining outwards; average length about 10 inches, but they are said to reach 14 occasionally.

Length of male about 5 feet to 5½; height at shoulder about 3 feet 2 inches. Weight about 200 lbs.

Colonel Markham says that the *Serow* is something in appearance between a jackass and a *Tahir* (*Hemitragus jemlaica*), with long stout legs, and a strong neck. Hodgson states that its back is straight, with the withers higher than the croup, stout rigid limbs, high hoofs and callous knees. By its structure it is well fitted for climbing, but not for leaping.

It inhabits the precipitous wooded mountains of the central ranges of the Himalayas, from Kashmir to Sikim. It is almost always found in the forests from 6,000 to 12,000 feet, and is solitary in its habits, and awkward in its gait. It rushes down the steepest declivities with fearful rapidity, but is not in general speedy, and does not spring well.

Colonel Markham states that it is not very common, keeps to thickly wooded ravines, and forests in steep and rocky ground, and is very tenacious of life. It is very bold and will keep the wild dog at bay, and has been known to kill three or four of them. Its flesh is coarse.

Adams calls it a stupid animal, and says that unless wounded it is sometimes not scared by the report of a rifle.

Those that I have met with were always alone, in thick forest, and when approached unawares, dashed off down hill in a most reckless manner. They are stated to rut in February and March, and the female brings forth one kid in September or October, but Adams says that in the north-west the female has her young in May or June.

Nemorhædus rubida, Blyth, inhabits the mountains of Arrakan. It is "of a red brown color with a black dorsal list, the hair shorter than the others." *N. sumatrensis* is found in Sumatra, and the Malayan peninsula as high as Tenasserim. There is also a species in China, *Nemorhædus Swinhoii*, Gray, figd. P. Z. S. 1862, pl. 35.

Near this group should be placed that very remarkable animal the *Takin*, *Budorcas taxicolor*, Hodgson, from the Mishmi hills at the head of the valley of Assam. It has something of the aspect of the *Gnu* of Africa.

The next animal differs somewhat in appearance, and also in its haunts, and has been placed in a separate genus, *Kemas*, by Ogilby and others; but the points of distinctions are very slight. The previous group is stated to possess small rounded eye-pits, whilst this has none; but I have not been able recently to examine a fresh head of *Serow* to ascertain if they are actually present in that animal.

231. Nemorhœdus goral.

Antilope apud HARDWICKE, Linn. Tr. XIV. 518, with figure.—BLYTH, Cat. 540.—Figd. F. CUVIER, Mamm. 3, 107—*A. Duvaucelei*, H. SMITH. —*Goral*, throughout the hills.—*Pijur*, in Kashmir.—*Sáh* or *Sarr*, of the Sutlej valley.—*Suh-ging*, Lepch.—*Rá-giyu*, Bhot.

THE GOORAL, OR HIMALAYAN CHAMOIS.

Descr.—Color dull rusty-brown, paler beneath; a dark brown line from the vertex to the tail; chest and front of fore-legs deep brown; ears externally rusty-brown; a large patch of pure white on the throat. The female is paler than the male, and the young are said to be redder in tint.

Length of one, head and body about 50 inches; tail 4; height at shoulder about 28 to 30 inches; horn 8.

The horns are situated on the crest of the frontals, and vary from 6 to 9 inches in length, incline backwards and slightly inwards, and have 20 to 25 annuli. The fur is somewhat rough, of two kinds of hair, and there is a short semi-erect mane in the male.

The *Gooral* is very caprine in appearance, the back is somewhat arched and the limbs are stout and moderately long, and it is well adapted both for climbing and jumping. It inhabits the whole range of Himalayas from Bhotan and Sikim to Kashmir, at a range varying from a little above 3,000 to nearly 8,000 feet, though perhaps most common about 5,000 to 6,000 feet. It usually associates in small parties of from four to eight or so, and frequents rugged grassy hills, or rocky ground in the midst of forests. If one *Gooral* is seen, you may be pretty certain that others are not far off, and they rarely or never forsake their own grounds. If cloudy they feed at all hours, otherwise only morning and evening. When alarmed it gives a short hissing snort, which is answered by all within hearing. The female breeds in May and June gestating for six months, and brings forth her young amid crags and rocky recesses.

Being generally found in somewhat broken ground, it is easily stalked; and as it is to be found close to most of our hill sanataria, it is generally the first game obtained by the sportsman on the hills.

Blyth states that those from Assam or Bhotan are very ruddy in tint. Radde has described a species from Siberia, and there is one in Japan, *N. crispus.*

True Goats.

Next come the goats, having the horns distinctly angulated. Generally speaking they are devoid of eye-pits and feet-pits. There are two generic types in this group, amongst the animals occurring in our province. The first is

Gen. HEMITRAGUS, Hodgson.

Char.—Horns trigonal, compressed, knotted in front; a small muffle; no eye-pits nor feet-pits, nor inguinal pores. Teats two or four.

Sclater does not separate it from the true goats, but most systematists have done so, and Blyth has followed Hodgson.

"This," says Hodgson, "is a remarkable type, tending to connect the keeled, compressed hollow-horned and odorous goats with the deer family, of which they possess the muffle and the four mammæ. Its caprine character is clearly indicated as well by general appearance and odour, as by the acute angle of the occipital line of the skull with the frontal, as distinguished from the large rounded angle of the antelope and deer."

One species has four teats, the other only two.

232. Hemitragus jemlaicus.

Capra apud H. SMITH.—BLYTH, Cat. 541.—*Capra jharal* and *H. quadrimammis*, HODGSON.—Figd. by WOLF, Zool. Sketches, pl.—*Téhr*, variously spelled *Tare, Tahir*, by sportsmen.—*Jéhr*, near Simla.—*Jháral*, in Nepal.—*Krás* and *Jaglá*, in Kashmir.—*Kart*, in Kulu.—*Jhúlá*, the male, and *Thar, tharni*, the female, in Kunawur.—*Esbu* and *Esbi*, male and female on the Sutlej above Chini.

THE TEHR, OR HIMALAYAN WILD GOAT.

Descr.—The male is dark-brown, ashy in front, the inner fur being hoary-blue, and the mane ashy-blue, the upper part of the limbs rusty-brown, the front of the legs and belly being dark-brown; head in front dark ashy or blackish-brown, with a darker patch below the gape, and a dark line along the back. Tail short and depressed, nude below; knees and sternum callous; a long mane, and the hair on the cheeks, neck and sides long and copious. The horns touch at the base, are sub-compressed and sub-triangular, uniformly wrinkled except at the tip, short, curve slightly backwards, and diverge somewhat.

Length about 4 feet 8 inches to root of tail; tail 7; 36 to 40 inches high; the horns about 12 inches long, very thick at the base.

The female is much less with much smaller horns, wants the mane, and is of an uniform drab or reddish-brown color above, dirty whitish below. Some of both sexes are occasionally paler, of a "dirty whitish-fawn color. The kids are said to be very pale with a black stripe down the back.

"The *Jhâral*," says Mr. Hodgson, "has a finely formed head, no vestige of a beard, the facial line straight, ears small, narrow and erect, a small moist muffle between the nostrils; limbs long, robust, rigid, with straight pasterns. The back is slightly arched, and the shoulders higher than the croup. The mane is long and sometimes sweeps below the knees. The male has a powerful odour at times."

The *Téhr* is found throughout the whole extent of the Himalayas, only however at great elevations, generally above the limits of forest, and not far from the snow. It frequents rocky valleys, and very steep and precipitous rocky ground, and is often seen perched on what appear to be inaccessible crags. It feeds on the grassy spots among rocks, and though not unfrequently found solitary, is more generally seen in flocks, sometimes as numerous as 20, 30 or even 40 it is said. If alarmed whilst feeding they all go off at speed with a clattering sound, but soon halt to gaze on the intruder. They generally follow the guidance of an old male, and will make their way up almost perpendicular precipices if there be but a few rough edges, or crevices. In the north-west, they are said to be sometimes seen along with *Markhor*. Captain E. Smyth states* that, "the males herd separately from February till October, ascend to a much greater height than the females and very young males, and are very difficult to find. In March and April they chiefly frequent the forests. During the rutting season the males are always fighting, and numbers are killed by falling down the crags.

* Trans. Hist. Soc. Lancashire, Vol. IX. 1856.

Colonel Markham says that, "the *Tahir* in general haunts the rocky faces and grassy slopes of hills free from forest, but occasionally one will be found in a patch of forest. Seen at a distance it looks like a great wild hog, but when near it is a noble beast. One shot fell 80 yards perpendicular without touching, rebounded and fell again 15 yards more; he got up, went off and was lost. The flesh of the female is tolerable; that of the male scarcely eatable at any time."

It is bold and pugnacious but easily tamed. It is living in the Zoological Gardens, in London, and has been beautifully figured by Wolf.

Hodgson relates that a male *Jháral* at Nepal, had intercourse with a female spotted deer, which produced a hybrid of mixed appearance, more like the mother than the father, which lived and grew up a fine animal. The name *Jemlaica* (I may state) is taken from the Júmla valley, north of Nepal.

233. Hemitragus hylocrius.

Kemas apud OGILBY.—BLYTH, Cat. 542.—*Capra warryato*, GRAY.—*Warra-ádú* or *Warri átú*, Tam.—"Ibex" of sportsmen on the Neelgherries.*—Figd. by WOLF, in "My Indian Journal," by Colonel W. Campbell, p. 369.

THE NEELGHERRY WILD GOAT.

Descr.—Adult male dark sepia-brown with a pale reddish-brown saddle, more or less marked, and paler brown on the sides and beneath; legs somewhat grizzled with white, dark brown in front, and paler posteriorly. The head, is dark, grizzled with yellowish-brown, and the eye is surrounded by a pale-fawn colored spot. Horns short, much curved, nearly in contact at the base, gradually diverging; strongly keeled internally, round externally, with numerous close rings, not so prominent as in the last species. There is a large callous spot on the knees surrounded by a fringe of hair, and the male has a short stiff mane on the neck and withers. The hair is short, thick and coarse.

Length of adult to root of tail 4 feet 2 to 4 feet 8; tail 6 or 7; height at shoulder about 32 to 34 inches; horns occasionally 15 inches, rarely more than 12. Colonel W. Campbell gives the length as 6 feet 5 inches† (inclu-

* Colonel W. Campbell states that it is called the "*Chamois*" by Madras sportsmen. This name I never heard applied to it.

† Query 5 feet 6?

sive of tail); height 3 feet 6 inches at the shoulder. These measurements appear to me to be unusually large, and I suspect are erroneous.

The female and young male are of a dusky olive-brown color, paler below; and the very old male appears almost black at a distance, with the pale saddle usually showing conspicuously. The horns of the female are shorter and less stout than those of the male. She has only two teats.

This wild goat was first described by Gray from a drawing and notes of General Hardwicke, and it was said to have been sent from Nepal and from Chittagong. This is of course erroneous. It has hitherto only been found on the Neelgherry and neighbouring hills, extending south along the Western Ghâts nearly to Cape Comorin. The specific name given by Gray is the *Tamul* word for rock or precipice-goat. It is called an Ibex by sportsmen in Madras. It chiefly frequents the northern and western slopes of the Neelgherries, where the hills run down in a succession of steep stony slopes or rocky ridges, to the high table land of Mysore and the Wynaad, both of which districts are themselves hilly. It has also been seen on several rocky hills in the interior of the plateau, especially near the so-called Avalanche hill. It is occasionally seen on the summit of the northern and western faces, but more generally some distance down, at an elevation of 4,000 to 6,000 feet; and, if carefully looked for, the herd may be seen feeding on an open grassy glade at the foot of some precipice. I have seen above twenty individuals in a flock occasionally, but more generally not more than six or seven. With the large herds there is almost always one very large old male, conspicuous by his nearly black color. If alarmed or followed, they rush rapidly down hill, and are lost to sight among the inequalities of the ground, or go straight down to the hilly country at the foot of the slopes. Now and then they have been known to take shelter in woods, through which they will freely pass if followed. They are very wary animals, and from the limited extent of the Neelgherries have been so much hunted there, that it is difficult (I am told) to get a near shot at them at present. The female is said to produce two young at a birth.

Besides the Neelgherries, this wild-goat occurs in the rocky ranges south of these hills, on the Animallies, and along the range of Western Ghâts, nearly, I have been informed, to Cape Comorin. It has not been observed in Ceylon. I have no doubt also of its being the wild-sheep so-called of the highlands of Madura, and of the neighbouring Pulney hills, as I long ago heard of the Neelgherry Ibex having been killed near Madura and Dindigul.

The Rev. Mr. Baker, in sending a fine skull and horns from the Western Ghâts inland from Cochin, to Mr. Blyth, wrote as follows:—"The animal when alive was as large as an ordinary donkey, and so heavy that six men could with difficulty bring him in. They are very numerous, feeding like a flock of sheep on the hill-tops, and only flee to the precipices when alarmed. They will even hide in jungle and grass. There is a solitary Roman Catholic Church on a rock in the jungles, on the borders of Travancore and Cochin, where the wild 'Ibex' are common, and though numbers of people go there on pilgrimage, these 'ibex' walk about among them, and eat the sesammun seed given them, but do not allow themselves to be touched. They are considered holy and belonging to the church." Elsewhere the same observer, writing of the game animals of the Western Ghâts, remarks that, "if the mountains are at all rocky and precipitous you will find the wild-goat or Ibex close to the rocks, often in large herds." As an article of provender, Mr. Baker remarks that, "a quarter of ibex hung, as the country people in the mountains do at home, within a wire or muslin bag, and exposed to the air, is equal to Welsh mutton."

Baikie, in his work on the Neelgherries, stated that the Neelgherry Ibex had very large knotted horns, and a long black or brown beard." Lieut. Beagin also informed Mr. Blyth that, the "Ibex" of the Neelgherries had a considerable beard; and on my first visit to the Neelgherries I was told by more than one good sportsman that the male had a beard. Yet no specimen that I ever saw (though some were very old) had a vestige of a beard; and I imagine that the preconceived idea of the Ibex had involuntarily deceived the observers into believing that those they saw had beards.

There are no other species of this strictly Indian genus.

Gen. CAPRA, Linnæus.

Char.—Horns in both sexes, of moderate or large size, angular, flat in front; no muffle; no eye-pits nor inguinal pits; feet pits in the fore-feet only, or in none; females with two mammæ.

The knees are callous, both sexes are more or less bearded, and the males are odorous. The muzzle is usually concave. Species of this genus are chiefly Palæarctic, but they extend into the North of Africa, and two are found, in our limits, on the Himalayas and the Punjab, one of them a true wild goat of the same type as the domestic goat, the other an Ibex.

234. Capra megaceros.

HUTTON,* Calc. J. N. Hist. 2, 535, pl. XX. (the horns).—BLYTH, Cat. 545.—*C. Falconeri*, HUGEL.—*Markhor*, *i. e.*, snake-eater of Afghans, Kashmir, &c.—*Rá-ché* or *Rá-pho ché*, in Ladak, *i. e.*, the great-goat.

THE MARKHOR.

Descr.—Horns very long, massive, straight, angular, with two to three spiral twists, closely approximate at the base, and diverging outwards and backwards, quite similar in character to those of many domestic goats, but of gigantic size. Color in summer light grayish-brown, in winter dirty yellowish-white with a bluish brown tinge; the adult male with a long black beard, and the neck and breast also clad with long black hair reaching to the knees; the hair generally long and shaggy; the fore-legs chesnut brown. Stands 11½ hands high. The females have a short black beard, but want the long mane.

The horns of a large old male have been seen as long as 52 inches; not uncommonly 4 feet; and the tips distant 34 inches. One recorded by Cunningham, was 3 feet 9 inches long; 11 inches in circumference at the base; 3 feet 2½ inches distant at the greatest interval, and the tips 2 feet 8½ inches apart. The longest horns have three complete spiral twists. Specimens from the hills west of the Indus have the horns rounder, straighter, and with an uniform spiral twist, like that of a cork-screw, but are said not to differ otherwise.

This magnificent wild goat is found on the Pir Panjal range of the Himalayas, to the south of the valley of Kashmir, in the Hazara hills, and the hills on the north of the Jhelum, and in the Wurdwan hills separating the Jhelum from the Chenab river; not extending, it is stated, further east than the sources of the Beas river, and certainly very rare further east than the Wurdwan hills. It is also abundant on all the hills to the west of the Indus, the Sulimani range as far south as the junction of the Sutlej with the Indus, and extending north into Afghanistan. It is also found in Ladak, but not apparently further east.

The *Markhor* associates in small herds, frequenting steep and rocky

* Cunningham, I see, also suggests the same specific name. "Travels in Ladak."

hills above the forest region in summer, but in winter descending to the bare spots in the wooded regions. It is much sought after by sportsmen, and the horns considered a great trophy.

A male *Markhor* is now living in the Zoological Gardens, at London, and has bred with the common goat.

Capra ægagrus, Gmelin, considered by some to be the original of the domestic goat, is a native of Persia and other parts of Central and Western Asia.

The next group is that of the Ibex, which has sometimes been separated generically from the true wild-goats, there being several allied species all with the same character of horn, viz., very long, curved backwards and knotted. One species extends from Northern Asia into the Himalayas.

235. Capra sibirica.

Meyer.—Blyth, Cat. 543.—*C. sakeen* and *Ibex himalayana*, Blyth.—*C. Pallasii*, Schinz.—*Skin*, *Skyin*, *Sakin* or *Iskin*, of the Himalayas, generally, and Tibet; the female *Dan-mo*, in Tibet.—*Búz*, in the upper Sutlej.—*Kyl*, in Kashmir.—*Tangrol*, in Kulu.

The Himalayan Ibex.

Descr.—The horns similar to these of the Ibex of Europe, but longer, more abruptly curved and tapering, diverging less and with more slender tips. Color in summer light brownish with a dark line down the back; in winter dirty yellowish-white, faintly tinged with brown or grayish. The female and young have a tinge of reddish in the brown. The beard is from six to eight inches long, of shaggy black hair. About the size of the *Téhr*, *Hemitragus jemlaicus*. Horns of the male 4 feet long occasionally, and 11 inches in circumference at the base. Those of the female about 1 foot long. A pair are recorded 4¼ feet long.*

The Himalayan Ibex is found throughout the Himalayas from Kashmir to Nepal, at all events. In the west of Kashmir it is rare, and is not found, it is asserted, to the west of the Jhelum river, the *Markhor*, which has its eastern limit in Kashmir, taking its place. It is found, however, in the Pir Panjal range, and a few in the range of hills north of Baramulla; and more numerous in the Wurdwan ranges, east of Kashmir; it is abundant in parts of Kunawur, on some of the ranges on both sides of the Sutlej;

* Proc. Zool. Society, 1840, p. 80.

and also near the source of the Ganges, where however more rare. It occurs in many other localities on the south side of the great Himalayan chain, and is not restricted, as stated, to the Tibetan slopes of the Himalayas; where, however, it is more numerous than in the ranges to the south. It extends through Central Asia to Siberia.

The Himalayan Ibex is "agile and graceful in its movements," says Colonel Markham, "and frequents the highest ground near the snows where food is to be obtained. The sexes live apart generally, often in flocks of one hundred and more. In October the males descend and mix with the females, which have generally twins in June and July. It is an exceedingly wary and timid animal, and can make its way in an almost miraculous manner over the most inaccessible looking ground. No animal excels the Ibex in endurance and agility."

Adams states that many are killed by avalanches, and that they are much preyed on by the panther (*i. e.*, the ounce). He also states that the female has in general only one kid.

I have only seen the Ibex near Chini in the Sutlej valley. In some of the villages high up the valleys there, many are killed every year during the winter, and their horns may be seen hung up on all the temples.

Mr. Vigne states that one or two hundred are killed yearly in Balti, in winter, when forced to descend to the valleys. In Ladak they are snared at night, and shot in the gray dawn of the morning when they venture down to the streams to drink. They are killed for the sake of the soft under fleece which, in Kashmir, is called *Asali tús*. This is used as a lining for shawls, for stockings, gloves, and is woven into the fine cloth called *Túsi*. No wool is so rich, so soft, and so full. The hair itself is manufactured into coarse blanketing for tents, and twisted into ropes.

A skin of an Ibex killed in the Balti valley by Major Strutt, R.A., was much darker than any I have seen. Its general color was a rich hair-brown with a yellowish-white saddle on the middle of the back, and a dark mesial line; the head, neck and limbs were dark rich glossy sepia-brown with a still darker central line on the front of the legs; the belly was brown grizzled with yellowish-white. Others were seen by Major Strutt in the same locality yet darker. The horns did not appear to differ from those of individuals of the ordinary color. Major Strutt, who has shot many in different parts of the hills, never saw any of the dark race except in Balti.

Dr. Adams in his list of animals of India and Kashmir, gives *Capra caucasica*, from Sindh and Beloochistan, but does not state if he procured specimens or not.

Besides the European Ibex, *Capra ibex*, and the Caucasian ibex just alluded to, other species have been recorded, viz., *C. pyrenaica*, from the Pyrennees, *C. walie*, from North Africa, *C. nubiana*, &c.

Domestic goats have feet-pits in the fore-feet, but not in the hind, whilst sheep have them in all four feet, and by this means, as Blyth long ago pointed out, a hind quarter of goat with the foot attached can be at once distinguished from one of sheep, a point of some domestic interest in India, where *goat mutton* is so often substituted for sheep.

Gen. Ovis, Linnæus.

Char.—Horns in both sexes, large, angular, heavily wrinkled, turned downwards almost into a circle, with their flat points directed forwards and outwards. No muffle; no beard; chaffron convex; large but immobile eye-pits in some, wanting in others; small feet-pits in all feet; inguinal glands distinct; two mammæ.

The characteristics of sheep compared with goats are, according to Hodgson as follows:—A feebler structure and more slender limbs, shorter hoofs and small false hoofs; a larger and heavier head; an arched chaffron; longer and more pointed ears; croup higher than the withers; want of hircine odour; paler eyes; shorter and more equal hair, and straighter back. The sheep bears change of climate ill, is incurious, staid and timid; does not bark trees; and, in fighting, runs a tilt, adding the force of impulse to that of weight. Blyth remarks that all the wild races of sheep differ conspicuously from most of the domestic races by their short deer-like tail, but the fine *Húnia* sheep of Tibet has a short tail, 4½ to 5½ inches, and the fighting ram has also a short tail.

Sheep are found in Northern and Central Asia, in the South of Europe and in Northern Africa; and one species in the Nearctic region. Two species are found in our province, and a third, still larger, occurs on the other side of the great snowy range.

236. Ovis cycloceros.

Hutton, Calc. J. N. H., 2. pl. XIX.—Sclater, P. Z. S. 1860, p. 126, with figure of the horns; and the animal figd. Illustrated Proceedings of Zoological Society, pl. LXXX.—Blyth, Cat. 548.—Figured by Wolf, Zool. Sketches.—*O. Vignei*, BLYTH (in part).—*Uriá* or *Uriál* H., in the Punjab.—*Koch* or *Kuch*, of the Sulimani range.

THE OORIAL, OR PUNJAB WILD SHEEP.

Descr.—Male with the horns sub-triangular, much compressed laterally, transversely sulcated. They touch at the base, curve backwards and downwards, then the tip is turned forwards, upwards and inwards towards the orbit. The hair strong and wiry, not woolly. General color rufous-brown or rufous-fawn, the face livid, sides of the mouth, chin, belly, legs below the knee, white; a blotch on the flanks, the outside of the limbs and a lateral line blackish; a profuse black-beard from the throat to the breast, intermixed with some white hairs reaching to the level of the knees. Tail short, white. Eye-pits large. The horns of the male sometimes measure above 2½ feet round the curve, and are nearly 4 inches in diameter at the base. The male measures about 5 feet in length, more or less, and stands nearly 3 feet high.

The female is much smaller of a more uniform and paler fawn-brown, paler beneath with the belly whitish; no beard; horns very short and nearly straight, only 3 or 4 inches long. The group to which this species and *O. Vignei* belong, was formerly separated as a sub-genus, *Caprovis*, Hodgson, distinguished, among other points, by the large beard and mane, and the goat-like character of the hair.

This wild sheep was formerly confounded with an allied species, *Ovis Vignei* of Blyth, found only in highly elevated districts. Living specimens of the Punjab sheep having been presented to the London Zoological Gardens, the distinctions were seen and pointed out by Sclater, who restored the name Hutton had long previously given it, but which I think he evidently applied to both races. The *Oorial* is found over the whole Salt range of the Punjab, on the Sulimani range across the Indus, the hills of the Hazára, and those in the vicinity of Peshawur. In most of these localities it occurs at a very low elevation, from 800 feet to 2,000 feet, and rarely 3,000 feet, and it is therefore capable of enduring great heat, and is fully entitled to be included in the strictly Indian Fauna.

Small flocks of the *Oorial* may be seen not far from Jhelum. They frequent the rocky and stony hills, and are wary and shy, but from the nature of the ground are not very difficult to stalk. The male has a loud shrill whistle which he sounds as an alarm, and their usual call is a sort of bleat. They rut in September, and have generally twins. Seen at a little distance the *Oorial* is a game-looking animal, looking more like an antelope than a sheep, and it is very speedy and active over rocky and stony ground. Hutton remarks that it possesses "a moderate sized lachrymal sinus, which appears to secrete, or at all events contains a thick gummy substance of good consistency and of a dull grayish color. The Afghan and Belooch hunters make use of this gum by spreading it over the pans of their matchlocks to prevent the damp from injuring the priming."

The nearly allied *Ovis Vignei*, Blyth, is the *Sha-poo* or *Shá* of Tibet and Ladak, *Ovis montana* apud Cunningham, and is not found in general below 12,000 feet of elevation in summer. It is found in the Hindoo Koosh, the Pamir range, and west as far as the Caspian sea; also in Ladak. Further east it is replaced by the next species. In this the horns are more strongly wrinkled, curve outwards and backwards with divergent points, and do not tend to form so complete a circle as in *cycloceros*. The color of the sheep is brownish or reddish gray, and its beard is short. The suborbital pits are smaller, deeper, and more rounded in *cycloceros*, the nasal bones are shorter; and the series of molar teeth is also shorter than in *O. Vignei*.

The next sheep was placed by Hodgson as the type of his genus *Pseudois*, with smooth and sub-cylindrical horns that form a bold arc outwards, and have the tip turned backward. They have no eye-pits, and want the mane and beard of the last group.

237. Ovis nahura.

HODGSON.—BLYTH, Cat. 549.—*O. nahoor*, HODGSON.—*O. Burhel*, BLYTH, Ann. Mag. Nat. Hist. VII. 248, with figure.—*Bharal* and *Bharur*, in the Himalayas; the male *Menda*—*Wá* or *Wár*, on the Sutlej.—*Nervati*, in Nepal.—*Ná* or *Sná* of Ladak and Tibet.

THE BURHEL, OR BLUE WILD SHEEP.

Descr.—Horns moderately smooth, with the wrinkles not numerous, rounded, nearly touching at the base, directed upwards, backwards, and outwards with a semi-circular sweep, then the rounded points are recurved forwards and inward. Color of the pelage dull slaty-blue, more or less tinted with fawn-color or pale earthy-brown; beneath yellowish-white; the nose, front of limbs, a band along the flanks, the chest and the tip of the tail black; the edge of the buttocks behind, and the tail pure white.

In summer the coat is overlaid with a distinct rufous tint. In winter the coat is stated by some to be dark-brown in certain localities, thus corresponding with Blyth's account of *O. burhei*, but these were probably young animals.

Length of male to root of tail 4½ to 5 feet; height 30 inches to 36; head 11 inches; tail 7; horns 2 feet and upwards round the curve, and 12 to 13 inches in circumference at base.

The female is smaller, with small, straightish, sub-erect, depressed, slightly recurved horns. The dark marks are smaller, and of less extent, and the chaffron is straighter. The young are darker and browner.

The head of the *Burrel* is somewhat coarse, with the chaffron arched and a heavy muzzle. There is no mane, the knees and sternum are callous; the limbs long and slender, and the false hoofs mere callosities.

Blyth at one time, from the examination of a very dark skin, contended that there were two species confounded under the name of *burrel*, but he has since reduced them to one species. He stated that his *O. burhel* was smaller, and more robust than *O. nahoor*, with a very short tail, and a harsher coat than that species.

The *Burrel*, or blue wild sheep, is found from Sikim, and probably Bhotan to near Simla, but not extending further west than the valley of the Sutlej, its place being taken to the north and west by *Ovis Vignei*. It is found on this side the great snowy range at the head of the Tonse river, in the Buspa valley, near the source of the Ganges, and still more abundant eastward in Kumaon and Gurhwal, in the ranges between the Pindar and Bhagirutty rivers. It is found at great elevations, from the limits of forest to the extreme limits upwards of vegetation, in summer generally keeping to the tops of the hills, and even in winter rarely descending below the forests.

These animals prefer grassy slopes to rocky ground, and associate in flocks of various size, from four or five to fifty or even a hundred. They are timid and watchful, one or more being always on the look out, and giving a sharp shrill whistle on being alarmed, but they do not heed noises much, not even the report of a gun if the shooter is concealed. Early in the spring is the best time to shoot them, as the supply of grass being then small, their ground is more limited, and they are obliged to feed all day; later in the season they only feed morning and evening. The males and females sometimes associate all the year round, but generally large flocks of both sexes are often met with separately, especially in summer. They lamb in June and July, commonly producing two young.

When in rocky ground there are few animals, "which appear to move with more ease and facility. On the faces of almost perpendicular cliffs of the wildest character, it leaps from rock to rock with scarce an apparent effort. In winter, when snowed in, they actually browze the hair off each others bellies, many together having retired under the shelter of some overhanging rock, from which they come out wretchedly poor."*

The same sportsman writing of the supposed difference between the *Ovis nahoor* and *O. burhel*, states that, near Gangootrie, he saw some sheep which appeared to differ slightly from the others, being apparently shorter, more bulky and stouter, particularly about the head and neck, and the horns shorter and more curved: on the same hills he saw females without horns. The shikarees called them *Moossa menda*, to distinguish them from the common *Menda* or *Burrel*.

The Burrel gets very fat in September and October, and is most excellent eating.

Beyond the great central snowy range on the Tibet side a magnificent wild sheep is met with. This is the Ovis AMMON, Linnæus (*O. argali*, Pallas; *O. ammonoides*, of Hodgson; and *O. Hodgsonii*, of Blyth). It is the *Hyan*, or *Nuan*, or *Nyan*, or *Niar*, or *Nyund*, or *Gnow*, as differently spelled by travellers, and pronounced in Tibet.

It has not to my knowledge been killed on the Indian side of the hills, (though one writer states that it has been seen near the source of the Ganges), and therefore cannot be introduced here as a member of the Indian Fauna. One is said to have been killed nearly 13 hands in height, *i. e.*, 4 feet 4 inches; but the more usual height is 3½ feet. One that stood this height measured 6 feet 2 inches in length; tail with the hair 8 inches; ear 6; horns along the curve 3 feet 4 inches, circumference at base 17 inches. Colonel Markham mentions that he has known the horns 24 inches in circumference, and that the skull and horns of one when dry weighed 40 lbs. They are also stated to be sometimes so enormous that the animal cannot feed on level ground, the horns reaching below the level of the mouth. The natives say that foxes occasionally take up their abode in an empty horn! Those of the female do not reach more than 18 inches in length, are nearly straight with only a slight curve. The horns of the male are much wrinkled, massive, trigonal, somewhat compressed, being

* Mountaineer, in "India Sporting Review."

deeper than broad at the base. They run backwards and outwards with a bold circular sweep, and the flattened points again recurve outwards. The forehead is flat and broad, the nose scarcely arched, and the muzzle fine. The limbs are long and the tail very short. The vesture is close and thick, consisting of more or less porrect piles concealing a scanty fleece. The color is a brownish-gray, the sides mixed hoary and slaty gray-brown. There is a well defined dirty white disk on the croup, and a more or less marked dark mesial. tine. The throat, neck and breast are white, with long hair, and the rest of the lower parts are dirty white. In summer the pelage has a dull slaty tint, more or less tinged with rufous, and hoary beneath. The female is paler, and wants the long hair of the neck.

This splendid sheep is never perhaps seen in summer lower than 15,000 feet of elevation, and is often found much higher in the midst of the snows, being often snowed up in winter for many days, and many perish yearly from this cause. It lives in flocks, the males and females generally apart. They run and leap like deer, it is said, but are not adapted for rocky ground, and as climbers are inferior to the *Burrel*. It is the shyest and wildest of all animals, and is very hard to kill. To shoot the *Ovis ammon* is the greatest ambition of the sportsman on the Himalayas.

Cunningham states that the horns along with those of Ibex and the *Sna (O. vignei)*, are placed on the religious piles of stones met with in Ladak and in other Buddhist countries.

Another wild Asiatic sheep is *Ovis Polii*, Blyth, found on the elevated plains of Pamir, east of Bokhara, 16,000 feet high. This magnificent wild sheep has immense horns, less massive but more prolonged than those of the rocky mountain sheep. The horns of one specimen were 4 feet 8 inches in length, round the curvature, and 14¼ inches in circumference at their base. It is the *Rass* or *Roosh*, of Pamir. *O. Gmelini*, Blyth, from Armenia; and *O. nivicola*, Eschscholtz, from Kamtschatka, are also described; and another from the Caucasus is indicated, *O. cylindricornis*, Blyth. *Ovis musimon*, L., the Moufflon sheep, is found wild in Corsica and Sardinia, and the large *O. tragelaphus*, the *Aondad* of the Moors, is found on the Atlas mountains in North Africa. Two species are recorded from North America, *O. montana*, the Rocky mountain sheep, and *O. californiana*.

Hodgson has published a paper on the domestic sheep of the Himalayas, with figures of many.*

* Jour. As. Soc., Calcutta, 1847.

Blyth states that he considers the fighting ram of India to be descended from *O. vignei (cycloceros)*. Hutton argues that the broad-tailed Afghan sheep, the *Dumba*, was most probably the sacrificial ram of the ancient Jews.

Sub-fam. Bovinæ, Cattle.

Horns always in both sexes, usually inclining upwards or forwards; the osseous core cellular; muffle large and broad; tail moderately long; no eye-pits; four mammæ.

Of large size, heavy and massive body, limbs stout; a dewlap often present. The horns are inserted laterally on the apex of the frontal crest. The occipital plane of the skull forms a small angle with the frontal plane.

This sub-family may be further divided into three groups. The Bisontine, the Taurine, and the Bubaline.

The Bisontine group comprise the Bison of Europe and North America, the Musk Ox of Arctic America, and the *Yák* of Central Asia.

The true bison of Europe, *Bison urus*, or the *Aurochs*, has a broad forehead, long limbs and a shaggy mane. It has 14 pairs of ribs. It is very savage, and though formerly spread over most of Europe, is now restricted to the marshy forests of Lithuania and a few other parts. The American bison, *Bison americanus*, is similar to the European animal, but with shorter limbs and has one more rib, *i. e.*, 15 pairs of ribs. It is called the Buffalo in North America. The musk ox, *Ovibos moschatus*, is covered with long hair, stands low on its limbs, and has a very strong musky odour. It inhabits the very coldest parts of Arctic America.

The *Yák*, *Poephagus gruniens*, L., is found wild on the other side of the snowy Himalayas, and has lately been shot by several of our sportsmen. It is called the *Ban-chowr*, H.; or *Brong Dhong*, in Tibet; has the hair long, coarse and shaggy, and the tail thick, shaggy and black. The horns of a wild Yâk measured 2 feet 4½ inches round the curve, 1 foot in circumference, and the tips 1 foot 8 inches apart. Another measured head and body 9½ feet; tail 3 feet 4 inches; height 16½ hands; horns 30 inches; circumference of horns 15. It is found only at considerable elevations, and a wounded bull will occasionally charge his assailant, but in general it will retreat when possible.

The domestic Yâk, (*Chaori gao*, H.,) is much used in all the elevated districts of the Himalayas, both as milch cattle and for burden, and breeds freely with the common cattle. The milk is remarkably rich. It is the best carriage for rugged hill work, as they can ford a rapid stony torrent in a way that no other animal dare attempt, and can scramble up and down rugged hills in a perfectly wonderful manner. The tails of the domestic Yâk, or chowries, are much used in India to keep off flies, &c.

The next group is the Taurine, sub-divided by Blyth into—1, the Zebus, or humped domestic cattle; 2, *Taurus*, the humpless cattle with cylindrical horns; and 3, *Gavæus*, the humpless cattle with flattened horns, peculiar to South-eastern Asia. They have all 13 pairs of ribs.

The common humped cattle of India belong to the Zebus. In many parts of the country small herds of these have run wild. Localities are recorded in Mysore, Oudh, Rohilkund, Shahabad, &c., and I have lately seen and shot one in the Doab near Muzuffurnuggur. These, however, have only been wild for a few years. Near Nellore, in the Carnatic, on the sea-coast, there is a herd of cattle that have been wild for many years. The country they frequent is much covered with jungle and intersected with salt-water creeks and backwaters, and the cattle are as wild and wary as the most feral species. Their horns were very long and upright, and they were of large size. I shot one there in 1843, but had great difficulty in stalking it, and had to follow it across one or two creeks.

The genus *Taurus* contains the cattle of Europe with cylindrical horns, including the feral race of Chillingham.

The next group is that called by Blyth the flat horned Taurines.

Gen. GAVÆUS, H. Smith.

Syn. *Bibos*, Hodgson.

Char.—Head large, massive; horns slightly flattened on one side (the section not cylindrical), thick, remote, spreading; tail short; muffle small; dewlap small or wanting; frontals concave; spinous processes of the dorsal vertebræ greatly developed. Otherwise as in *Taurus*.

This genus comprises three species peculiar to the Indian region or South-eastern Asia, one of which is common in our province.

238. Gavæus gaurus.

Bos apud HAM. SMITH.—BLYTH, Cat. 506.—*Bibos cavifrons*, HODGSON. —ELLIOT, Cat. 58, with figure.—Figd. DELESSERT, Souvenirs d'un Voyage dans L'Inde.—*Bos gour*, TRAILL, Edin. Phil. Journal, and HARDWICKE Zool. Journal, 111-232, pl. VII. 2.—*B. asseel*, HORSFIELD.—*Gaur*, H., or *Gauri-gai*, generally through India; popularly *Jangli khúlgá*, *i. e.*, Jungle buffalo.—*Bod*, at Seonee.—*Ban parrá*, at Mundlah.—*Gaoiya*, Mahr.—*Kar-kona*, Can.—*Vana-go*, quasi *Ban-gau*, Beng.—*Perá-máoo*, of Gonds in the South.—*Katu-yeni*, Tam.—Bison of sportsmen in Madras.*

THE GAUR.

Descr.—Horns pale greenish with black tips, curving outwards, upwards and slightly backwards, and finally inwards. General color dark chesnut-brown or coffee-brown; legs from the knee downwards white.

Length 9½ to 10 feet; height at shoulder 6 feet; tail 34 inches.

This magnificent animal was described by Dr. Traill, in the Ed. Philos. Journal, by General Hardwicke in the Zoological Journal, and by Geoffroy St. Hilaire, in the Mem. Museum d' Hist. Nat., all it appears from the same animal, one killed in Central India, but Hodgson was the first who fully defined its peculiarities, and the following detailed account is chiefly taken from the published observations of Hodgson and Elliot.

The skull is massive, the frontals large, deeply concave, surmounted by a large semi-cylindric crest rising above the base of the horns. There are 13 pairs of ribs. The head is square, proportionally shorter than in the ox, the bony frontal ridge is 5 inches above the frontal plane. The muzzle is large and full, and the eyes small, with a full pupil of a pale blue color. The whole of the head in front of the eyes is covered with a coat of close short hair of a light grayish-brown color, which below the eyes is darker, approaching almost to black. The muzzle is grayish, and the hair is thick and short. The ears are broad and fan-shaped. The neck is sunk between the head and the back, is short, thick and heavy. Behind the neck, and immediately above the shoulder, rises a fleshy gibbosity or hump of the same height as the dorsal ridge. This ridge rises gradually as it goes backwards and terminates suddenly about the middle of the back. The chest is broad, the shoulder deep and muscular, the forelegs short with the joints very short and strong, and the arm exceedingly large and muscular. The hair on the neck and breast and beneath is longer than on the body, and the skin of the throat is somewhat loose giving the appearance of a slight dewlap. The forelegs have a rufous tint behind and latter-

* Colonel W. Campbell states that Madras sportsmen call this animal a wild-bull and not a bison, for which he rebukes them. Now I have always heard it called the bison, but in reality the name wild-bull would be much more correctly applied to it.

ally, above the white. The hind quarters are lighter and lower than the fore, falling suddenly from the termination of the dorsal ridge. The skin on the neck shoulders and thighs is very thick, being about 2 inches and more.

The cow differs from the bull in having a slighter and more graceful head, a slender neck, no hump, and the points of the horns do not turn towards each other at the tip, but bend slightly backwards; and they are much smaller. The legs too are of a purer white. The very young bull has the forehead narrower than the cow, and the bony frontal ridge scarcely perceptible. The horns too turn more upwards. In old individuals the hair on the upper parts is often worn off. The skin of the under parts when uncovered is deep ochrey-yellow.

A few additional measurements are added from Elliot.

Length from nose to root of tail 9 feet 6½ inches; height at shoulder 6 feet 1½ inches; at rump 5 feet 3 inches; tail 2 feet 10½ inches; length of dorsal ridge 3 feet 4 inches; height of dorsal ridge 4½ inches; head from muzzle to top of frontal ridge 2 feet 1¾ inches; breadth of forehead 1 foot 3½ inches; ear 10½ inches; circumference of horn at base 1 foot 7½ inches; distance between the points of the horns 2 feet 1.

The horns are smooth and polished; and in old individuals are generally broken off at both tips. They are slightly flattened at the base.

The Gaur is an inhabitant of all the large forests of India, from near Cape Comorin to the foot of the Himalayas. On the west coast of India it is abundant all along the Syhadree range or Western Ghâts, both in the forests at the foot of the hills, but more especially in the upland forests, and the wooded country beyond the crest of the Ghâts. The Animally hills, the Neelgherries, Wynaad, Coorg, the Bababooden hills, and the Mahableshewur hills, are all favorite haunts of this fine animal. North of this it occurs, to my own knowledge,. in the jungles on the Taptee river, and neighbourhood, and, north of the Nerbudda, a few on the deeper recesses of the Vindhian mountains. On the eastern side of the peninsula it is found in the Pulney and Dindigul hills, the Shandamungalum range, the the Shervaroys, and some of the hill ranges near Vellore and the borders of Mysore. North of this, the forest being too scanty, it does not occur till the Kishna and Godavery rivers, and hence it is to be found in suitable spots all along the range of Eastern Ghâts to near Cuttack and Midnapore, extending west far into Central India, and northwards towards the edge of the great plateau which terminates south of the Gangetic valley.

According to Hodgson it also occurs in the Himalayan Terai, probably however only towards the eastern portion, and here it is rare, for I have spoken to many sportsmen who have hunted in various parts of the Terai, from Sikim to Rohilcund, and none have ever come across the Gaur at the foot of the Himalayas.

It also occurs in the countries to the east of the Bay of Bengal, from Burmah to the Malayan peninsula. Horsfield, in his Catalogue, considered that a distinct race which he named *Bibos asseel*, from the native name *Asseel gayal, i. e.*, the genuine gayal, in contradistinction to the ordinary *Gayal, Gavæus frontalis*. Blyth, however, states that he knows the individual specimen on which this supposed race was founded, and that it is only a female Gaur.

It was also formerly an inhabitant of Ceylon, but has been extinct there for above 50 years.

Hodgson states in the Sub-Himalayan forests it does not ascend the hills, and that it is not a mountain race at all. Sportsmen in Southern India could tell Mr. Hodgson a different account of its habits there, for it undoubtedly prefers hilly and even mountainous countries, and I have seen it killed at above 6,000 feet of elevation.

The Gaur associates in herds of various numbers up to thirty and forty or more, though perhaps generally met in smaller numbers, and a bull is often seen alone. The herd generally consist of from ten to fifteen cows and a bull. They feed mostly at night, or early in the morning, chiefly on grass, but also browzing on the tender shoots of the bamboo, and during the heat of the day retire to some cool and shady spot, the thick bed of a dry nullah, a dense clump of bamboos, or long grass. Hodgson states that they never venture into the open Terai to depredate on the crops as the wild buffaloes constantly do. In southern India, however, they do occasionally at least, according to Mr. Fisher, as quoted by Mr. W. Elliot. "The chief food of the bison seems to be various grasses, the castor oil plant, and a species of *convolvulus*, but they will eat with avidity any species of grain commonly cultivated in the hills or plains, as the ryots find to their cost. The bison is particularly fond of the *Avary cotty* (*Dolichos lablab*) when in blossom; that they will invade and destroy fields of it in open daylight in despite of any resistance the villagers can offer. In other respects it is a very inoffensive animal, rarely attacking any one it encounters, except in the case of a single bull driven from the herd. Such a one has occasionally been known to take up his location in some deep bowery jungle, and deliberately quarter himself on the cultivation of the adjacent villages. The villagers though ready to assist Europeans in the slaughter of bison, will not themselves destroy them, (the inviolability of the cow extending to the bison,) and so bold does this freebooting animal become in consequence that he has been known to drive the ryots from the fields, and deliberately devour the produce. But in general it is a timid animal, and it is difficult to get within gun shot of them."

The same observer also remarks: "The bison ordinarily frequents the hills, seeking the highest and coolest parts, but during the hottest weather, and when the hills are parched by the heat, or the grass consumed by fire, the single families in which they commonly range the hills, congregate into large herds, and strike deep into the great woods and valleys; but after the first showers, and when verdure begins to re-appear, they again disperse and range about freely. In wet and windy weather they again resort to the valleys to escape its inclemency, and also to avoid a species of fly or gnat, which harasses them greatly. In the months of July and August they regularly descend to the plains for the purpose of licking the earth impregnated with natron or soda, which seems as essential to their well doing as common salt is to the domestic animal when kept in hilly tracts."

The breeding season appears to be in the cold weather, and the young are born from June to October, the greatest number in August. The old male drives the others from the herd at the breeding season, and the single ones seen in the jungle are young males of this description, and it is probable the very old bulls are sometimes expelled also by younger and stronger males. The period of gestation is said to be the same as with the cow or buffalo. Hodgson was informed that it was longer.

The Gaur is, in general, one of the most timid and wary of animals, and requires to be stalked most carefully. Where the hills are grassy, with tracts of dense forest, they may be discovered occasionally, early in the morning, feeding outside the forest, or even lying down in pretty close proximity however to the wood, and if very carefully approached against the wind, and perfectly noiselessly, the sportsman may get a favorable shot. Now and then too they are stalked in the depth of the forest, a good tracker following them to their mid-day lair. When disturbed the first who perceives the intruder stamps loudly with his foot to alarm the rest, and the whole rush through the forest breaking down every obstacle, and forcing their way with a terrible crash. When suddenly approached in the night they start off with a loud hissing snort. The Gowlees say that they see great numbers of bison when pasturing their herds in the neighbouring forest. They describe them as very timid and watchful, more so than any other wild animal, always reposing in a circle with their heads turned outside ready to take alarm.

The bison is generally driven towards the sportsman by a line of beaters, he remaining concealed behind a tree. A wounded bison will occasionally charge, and several fatal instances are recorded, but in general he will turn and seek safety in flight. Hodgson says that "in the Tarai, the Gaur will pursue his assailant, and if he climb a tree will watch for a whole day;" but this account is evidently from native shikarees, and such conduct must be perfectly exceptional. Mr. Elliot remarks that, "the persevering ferocity of the bison of the Sub-Himalayan range," described by Mr. Hodgson, "is quite foreign to the character of the animal in southern forests."

Various attempts have been made to rear the young Gaur, but they have all failed, the young animal never living over his third year. Blyth had a young calf at Calcutta procured near Singapore, which he shipped for England, but it died on the voyage. An engraving of a photograph of this calf was published in the "London Illustrated News." "It was tame and tractable," says Blyth, yet full of life and frolic." The natives of Malabar, according to Buchanan Hamilton, MSS., assert that the bison takes up stones with his nostrils, and discharges them at their adversaries with the force of a musket-ball, and the wound is always mortal!

The flesh of the Gaur is excellent if not too old, and the marrow bones and tongue are delicacies always preserved by the successful sportsman.

The *Gayal* or *Mithun*, *Gavæus frontalis*, is found in the hilly tracts to the east of the Burrampooter, and at the head of the valley of Assam, the Mishmi hills and their vicinity, probably extending north and east into the borders of China. It is domesticated extensively and easily, and has bred with the common Indian cattle. It is a heavy, clumsy looking animal compared with the *Gaur*, the wild animal similarly colored and with white legs. It browzes more than the *Gaur*, and, unlike that, it has a small but distinct dewlap. The domesticated race extends south as far as the Tippera and Chittagong hills, and, northwards, has been seen grazing in company with the Yâk, close to the snows. It is better adapted for rocky and precipitous ground than the *Gaur*. *Gayals* have often been taken alive to Calcutta. The *Bos sylhetanus*, figd. by M. F. Cuvier, is a hybrid with the Zebu.

The *Banteng*, or Burmese wild cow, *Gavæus sondaicus*, extends northwards as far as the interior of the Chittagong hills, where all three species meet, according to the testimony of the Rev. M. Barbe. South it extends through Burmah and the Malayan peninsula to the larger islands. The young and the cow are red in this species, which resembles the *Gaur* more than the *Gayal*, and it wants the dewlap. It is the *Tsoing* of the Burmese, the *Gaur* being the *Pyoung*. A young male is now living in the London Zoological Gardens.

Lastly, the Buffaloes,

Gen. BUBALUS, H. Smith.

Char.—Horns large, attached to the highest line of the frontals, inclining backwards and upwards, depressed, angular, more or less horizontal; muffle large and square; no true dorsal ridge or hump; cranium elongated, narrow, with an excess of facial over the frontal and cerebral portion; the frontals form a somewhat obtuse angle with the occipital plane. Thirteen pairs of ribs.

239. Bubalus arni.

Bos apud KERR and SHAW.—*B. buffelus* apud BLYTH, Cat. 508.—*B. bubalus*, Auct. wild var.—*Arna*, the male, *Arni* the female, H.—*Jangli bhyns*, vulgo, H.—*Múng*, of Bhagulpore.—*Géra érumi*, of Gonds.

THE WILD BUFFALO.

Descr.—Forehead convex, rounded; horns large, black; general color dark blackish-slaty; hair scanty, black. Length $10\frac{1}{2}$ feet and upwards from snout to root of tail which is short, not extending lower than the hock; tufts of hair on the forehead, over the eyes, and on the knees. Height at shoulder up to $6\frac{1}{2}$ feet.

The horns are of two kinds—the one very long, nearly straight, well thrown back, var. *Macrocercus* of Hodgson—the other much shorter and well curved, more directed upwards, var. *Spirocerus*, Hodgson.

Individuals with the longest horns are chiefly found in Assam and the countries to the eastward. A single horn in the British Museum, figured Phil. Trans. for 1727, is 6 feet 6 inches long. The head of another also in the British Museum, and killed by Colonel Mathie in Assam, measured as follows:—Round the outside of both horns and over forehead 12 feet

2 inches ; circumference of right horn at the base 1 foot 8½ inches ; width of forehead 11 inches ; skull 2 feet 4 inches long.

The horns of the spiral race are rarely much more than 3 feet long each.

The wild buffalo is found in the swampy Terai at the foot of the hills, from Bhotan to Oude; also, in the plains of lower Bengal as far west as Tirhoot, but increasing in numbers to the eastwards, on the Burrampooter, and in the Bengal Sunderbuns. It also occurs here and there through the eastern portion of the Table land of Central India, from Midnapore to Raepore, and thence extending south nearly to the Godavery. South and west of this it does not, to my knowledge, occur in India, but a few are found in the north and north-east of Ceylon.

"The Arna," says Mr. Hodgson, "inhabits the margins rather than the interior of primæval forests. They never ascend the mountains, and adhere, like the Rhinoceros, to the most swampy sites of the districts they inhabit. It ruts in autumn, the female gestating 10 months, and produces one or two young in summer. It lives in large herds, but in the season of love, the most lusty males lead off and appropriate several females, with which they form small herds for the time. The bull is of such power and vigour, as by his charge frequently to prostrate a well sized elephant. They are uniformly in high condition, so unlike the leanness and angularity of the domestic buffalo even at its best."

Mr. Blyth states it as his opinion that except in the valley of the Ganges and Burrampooter, it has been introduced and become feral. With this view I cannot agree, and had Mr. Blyth seen the huge buffaloes I saw on the Indrawutty river (in 1857), he would, I think, have changed his opinion. They have hitherto not been recorded south of Raepore, but where I saw them is nearly 200 miles south. I doubt if they cross the Godavery river.

I have seen them repeatedly and killed several in the Purneah district. Here they frequent the immense tracts of long grass abounding in dense, swampy thickets, bristling with canes and wild roses ; and in these spots, or in the long elephant grass on the bank of jheels, the buffaloes lie during the heat of the day. They feed chiefly at night or early in the morning, often making sad havoc in the fields, and retire in general before the sun is high. They are by no means shy (unless they have been much hunted), and even on an elephant, without which they could not be successfully hunted, may often be approached within good shooting distance. A wounded one will occasionally charge the elephant, and as I have heard from many sportsmen will sometimes overthrow the elephant. I have been charged by a small herd, but a shot or two as they are advancing will usually scatter them.

Hodgson remarks that, "there is no animal upon which ages of domestication have made so small an impression as upon the buffalo, the tame species being still most clearly referrible to the wild ones." He also states that the tame buffaloes when driven to the forests to be depastured have intercourse with the wild bulls, and the breed is thus improved. In Purneah I was informed, however, that the wild buffalo dislike the presence of tame ones exceedingly, and will even retire from the spot where the tame ones are feeding.

The domestic buffalo is extensively used in India both for draught and as milch cattle, and its milk is richer than that of the cow of India. Some of the hill races, such as those on the Neelgherries, are very fine animals, resembling the wild buffalo; and many along the crests of the Western Ghâts, and elsewhere, are seen with white legs like the *Gaur*.

The Cape buffalo, *B. cafer*, has very large horns which nearly cover the forehead. Another African species is *B. brachyceros*, Gray.

Sub-Ord. SIRENIA. Herbivorous Cetacea.

Nostrils opening in the upper lip. Teeth of two kinds; incisors preceeded by milk-teeth, and molars with flat crowns. Two pectoral mammæ. Body slightly hairy, and bristly moustaches on the lips. No hind limbs. Posterior part of body ending in a horizontal cartilaginous fin; anterior limbs in the form of fins or flappers.

The bones of the skull are dense and massive, and the intermaxillaries large. They are only loosely connected together, and this, with the generally dense nature of the other bones, and their not having medullary cavities, shows a reptile-like condition. There are traces of pelvic bones in all. The bony nostrils open near the summit of the cranium. There is a short but distinct neck. The number of ribs is large—nineteen pairs in some. The stomach is divided into four sacs, of which two are lateral; they possess a large cœcum, and the intestinal canal is long.

The herbivorous *Cetacea* approach in structure perhaps nearest to some of the *Pachydermatous Ungulata*, near which they might have been placed, but I have thought it more adviseable to bring them in here at the conclusion of the order *Ungulata*. They feed entirely on plants, either plucked at the bottom of the sea, or on rocks laid bare by the retreat of the tide, and they do not venture far out to sea, but keep near the shore and the mouths of large rivers.

Their pectoral mammæ, and the peculiar physiognomy of these animals as observed when they raise their bodies partially out of water, has probably led to the fabulous accounts by mariners of Tritons, Sirens and Mermaids.

One species has been observed on the southern coasts of India.

Gen. Halicore, Illiger.

Syn. *Dugongus*, Tiedimann.

Char.—Two large upper incisors in the adult; none in the lower jaw. No canines. Molars $\frac{5-5}{5-5}$ in the young, fewer in the adult, flat; body elongated; pectoral fin without claws; caudal fin lunate, broad.

The incisive teeth assume the form of pointed tusks, but are nearly covered by the thick fleshy lips which are bristled with moustaches.

The milk incisors are stated by Kelaart to be $\frac{4}{8}$, and in the adult the molars are only $\frac{2-2}{2-2}$. The grinding surface has a ring of enamel at the circumference, and a slightly excavated centre of ivory.

The tongue is spiny in front, and has a curious horny process on each side of its base. The stomach is double, the cardiac portion large, the pyloric narrower, with two tubiform cœcal prolongations: it is divided into distinct compartments. The cœcum is simple and cordiform. The heart is deeply cleft, separating the ventricles. The superficial air-vessels of the lungs are large, turtle-like, and the lungs and bronchi generally are like those of the Turtles. The organs of generation resemble those of *Ruminantia.* There is a nyctitating membrane.

240. Halicore dugong.

Trichechus apud ERXLEBEN.—BLYTH, Cat. 472.—Fig. F. CUVIER, Mamm., 2, 120.—*H. cetacea,* ILLIGER.—*H. indica,* DESMAREST, figd. HARDWICKE, Ill. Ind. Zool.

THE DUGONG OR DUYANG.

Descr.—Skin uniform bluish, sometimes blotched with white beneath, or pale fulvous with white under parts; eyes very small; incisors nearly concealed; a few scattered bristles on the body. With eighteen pairs of ribs (Kelaart). Up to 9 or 10 feet in length and upwards; usually 5 to 7 feet.

The Dugong has been taken on the Andaman islands, in Ceylon, and on the west coast of India as high, it is stated, as the Concan, *i. e.*, the coast of Canara. It appears that they are known as Seals, and found along the shore, and in the salt-water inlets of the Concan and south Malabar. It is said to feed on the vegetable matter found about the rocks, and also to bask and sleep in the morning sun.

The Seal of Forbes (Oriental Memoirs) appears to be the Otter. The flesh of the Dugong is highly esteemed. It is tolerably abundant in Ceylon, where called *Talla maha;* and in the Malayan regions at Singapore, &c. The female gives birth to one young only at a time, and it is said to show strong affection for her young. Sir J. Tennent, in his Natural History of Ceylon, figures a Dugong holding her young.

Another species recorded is *Halicore tabernaculi,* Rüppell, from the Red Sea, so named by him because he considers it to be the animal with whose skin the tabernacle was veiled.

Another species is *Halicore australis*, found numerous on the coasts of Australia. It is stated to be bluish on the back, with a white breast and belly. It grows to 18 or 20 feet in length. The oil obtained from the fat is highly prized.

Other herbivorous Cetacea are the Manatis, *Manatus*, Cuvier, with two or three species, from the mouths of rivers in Africa and America. They have vestiges of nails on their swimming paws, and the adults have no incisors.

The Stellerines, *Rytina*, Illiger, are now extinct.

ORD. EDENTATA.

Bruta in part, Linnæus.

No teeth in the front of the jaws in any, and altogether wanting in some. Toes with large, curved, and often compressed, claws.

The *Edentata* are not uniformly toothless, except the Ant-eaters and the Pangolins, but they never have any incisors or teeth in the front of their jaws, and the molars, when present, are mono-phyodont, *i. e.*, are never displaced by a second series, but are without enamel or distinct roots, having a hollow base, and growing continually. Their huge claws are something of the nature of hoofs. Mr. Fry considers that the *Edentata* are in many points of their structure nearly related to Reptiles, in opposition to Owen, who stated that they offered several relations to Birds.*

They are divided into two groups, the *Tardigrada,* or Sloths ; and the *Effodientia* or Burrowers.

The former consists of a single family, the BRADYPODIDÆ, or Sloths. These are peculiar to America, and live entirely on vegetable matter. They have a short face, sharp canines, and cylindrical molars. Their toes are completely joined by the skin, their fore limbs longer than their hind extremities, the pelvis large, and the thighs directed outwards. They have huge claws. They have two pectoral mammæ. They are evidently made for hanging on the branches of trees, and their long arms are of use to gather the leaves on which they browze. They have long and shaggy hair. Some have three claws on their fore-feet, others only two. Their stomach is enormous and divided into four compartments; the intestines are short, and there is no cœcum. They are only found in the forests of the warmer regions of South America.

The *Effodientia* have the muzzle long and narrow. They are divided into the following families :—*Dasypodidæ*, or Armadillos; and *Orycteropodidæ*, or Cape Ant-eaters, both with molar teeth; and the *Myrmecophagidæ* and *Manididæ*, or the Ant-eaters of the new and old world, respectively, without any teeth at all.

The Armadillos (DASYPODIDÆ) are covered with a scaly and bony shell divided more or less into compartments; the muzzle is tolerably long; the molars cylindrical, 7 or 8 on each side in both jaws; large ears, and great claws, 4 or 5 on the fore-feet, always 5 posteriorly. The tongue is but

* Proceedings Zool. Soc., 1846.

little extensile, their stomach is simple, and they have no cœcum. They all inhabit South America, and live chiefly on insects. There are some twenty species, divided into several genera.

The Cape ant-eaters, *Orycteropidæ*, have molars, and flat claws, but otherwise are similar to the true ant-eaters, and have a somewhat extensile tongue. Their teeth are cylindrical and solid, but traversed by numerous little longitudinal canals. The stomach is simple and the cœcum small. They comprise only one genus.

The next two families are totally unprovided with teeth.

Fam. MANIDIDÆ, Pangolins.

No teeth. Body and tail covered with large, imbricate, horny scales; tail long. Tongue round, exsertile. Ears small, mostly indistinct. Two pectoral mammæ. All feet with five toes.

The scales are evidently, from their structure, a congeries of agglutinated hairs. They have the power of rolling themselves into a ball. The stomach is slightly divided in the middle, and they have no cœcum. They are found in India and Africa.

Gen. MANIS, Linnæus.

Char.—Those of the order, of which it is the only genus.

241. Manis pentadactyla.

LINNÆUS.—BLYTH, Cat. 553.—*Manis crassicaudata*, GRIFFITHS apud ELLIOT, Cat. 47.—*M. macroura*, DESMAREST.—*M. brachyura*, ERXLEBEN.—*M. laticaudata*, ILLIGER.—*M. inaurita*, HODGSON.—*Pangolinus typus*, LESSON.—*Bajar-kit*, Sansc. and H.—*Bajra kapta*, in some parts.—*Sillú*, H., in other parts; also *Sukunkhór*.—*Sál*, *Sálú*, H., in the south.—*Shálmá*, of the Bauris.—*Armoi*, of the Coles.—*Kauli mah*, or *Kowli manjra*, and *Kassoli manjur*, Mahr.—*Alawa*, Tel.—*Alangú*, Mal.—Vulgo *Banrohu*, in the Deccan, *i. e.*, the jungle carp.—*Keyot-mach*, in Rungpore, *i. e.*, the fish of the Keyots.—*Kát-pohú*, or timber animal, in other parts of Bengal.

THE INDIAN SCALY ANT-EATER.

Descr.—Tail shorter than the body, very broad at the base, with 16 or

17 scales in each longitudinal line; 16 scales on the dorsal series in 10 or 11 rows; middle nail of the fore-feet much stronger than the others. Scales thick, striated at the base, pale yellowish-brown or horny clay color; the lower side of the head, body and feet nude, brownish-white; nose fleshy; soles of the hind-feet blackish; auricles indistinct.

Length of one head and body 26 inches; tail 18. A female measuring 40 inches, weighed 21 lbs.

The common Pangolin or Scaly Ant-eater, is found throughout the whole of India, most common perhaps in somewhat hilly districts, but nowhere abundant. It appears to extend into the lower Himalayas, for both this and the next species were found by Hodgson in Nepal. It is strictly nocturnal, and feeds almost exclusively on ants, especially the white ants (termites). Its gait in walking is very peculiar, the back arched, the fore-feet with their anterior surface bent over and brought into contact with the ground, on which it progresses very slowly. Tickell has given (Journ. As. Soc., XI. 221) a very good account of this animal, with characteristic figures.

Mr. Elliot says: "The Manis burrows in the ground in a slanting direction to a depth of from 8 to 12 feet from the surface, at the end of which is a large chamber about 6 feet in circumference in which they live in pairs, and where they may be found with one or two young ones about the months of January, February and March. They close up the entrance of the burrow with earth when in it, so that it would be difficult to find them but for the peculiar track they leave. A female I kept alive for some time slept during the day, but was restless all night. It would not eat the termites or white ants put into its box, nor even the large black ants (*Myrmica indefessa*, Sykes), though its excrement was at first full of them. But it would lap the water that was offered to it by rapidly darting out its long, extensile tongue, which it repeated so quickly as to fill the water with froth. When first it came it made a sort of hissing noise if disturbed, and rolled itself up, the head between the forelegs, and the tail round the whole."

The name of *Bajar-kit*, means stone, or hard reptile, from its scales. It is popularly believed to eat stones, and these are sometimes found in its stomach. Dr. Burt, in a paper in the 2nd Vol. of the Asiatic Researches, gravely propounds the question whether it cannot live entirely on mineral substances. Its flesh is considered aphrodisiac by the natives; and it is much infested by a blue tick.

I add a few anatomical observations taken from Tickell and others.

The tongue is 12 inches long, flattish or subcylindric, extensile, generally covered with a slightly viscid saliva. There is a strong opaque, nyctitating membrane. The right or pyloric side of the stomach is immensely muscular, almost cartilaginous in structure, like the gizzard of a bird; the left side is thin and membranous. The cardiac and pyloric orifices are approximate. The gall bladder is very large, as are the kidneys. The penis is not apparent externally; and the fœces are long, black, truncated cylinders.

242. Manis aurita.

HODGSON.—BLYTH, Cat. 554, olim *M. javanica.*

THE SIKIM SCALY ANT-EATER.

Descr.—Tail a little shorter than head and body, not quite so thick at the base as the last, with 5 rows of scales about 20 in number in each row; 15 to 17 rows of scales in a line on the back, most of them with a few whitish hairs or bristles beneath them, especially in young individuals. Muzzle very acute; ears conspicuous, large; all the anterior claws large, especially the middle one, and the next outer; posterior claws small. There is a less marked difference in the size of the scales of the head and neck and body than in *pentadactyla*, in which the scales of the head are very much smaller.

Length of one, head and body 19 inches; tail 15¼.

This species of Manis was described by Hodgson in one of his earliest papers, but it is not enumerated in either edition of the Catalogue of Hodgson's Collections, whilst *M. pentadactyla* is given, a decision which that gentleman appears to accept in the annotated copy of the new edition of his Catalogue, kindly forwarded to me. I suspect that it is rare in Nepal, and that probably he did not procure it latterly, but he evidently had both species before, when he named them respectively *aurita* and *inaurita*, on the more or less prominence of the auricle, which character is very evident in fresh specimens.* Blyth too had considered the few specimens he had seen from other localities than the Himalayas, as the *M. javanica* of authors. I procured one fine specimen near Darjeeling, as well as other smaller ones, on examining which, in company with Mr.

* Probably some at least of Hodgson's specimens at the British Museum, or elsewhere, will turn out to be this species.

Blyth, we perceived that they were Hodgson's species, and identical with Blyth's *Javanica*, and that his *leucura* was true *Javanica*.

This *Manis* appears to be the only species in Sikim, and thence extends through the Indo-Chinese countries to China itself. My specimens were procured about the level of 3,000 feet above the sea. In China it is called *Ling-li*, or the Hill-carp, which I mention to show how similar resemblances appear to strike different races, the common *Manis* being called the jungle carp in the south of India.

Dr. Adams* states that this Pangolin is sold in the markets at Canton, its scales being considered medicinal, and the flesh is said to be excellent. The same observer gives a few anatomical notices of a female procured by him. This had the small intestines 10 feet 10 inches long, the large intestines 10 inches; the uterus two-horned, and the vagina long and muscular. It was furnished with a sac close to the anus, opening by a transverse, linear slit, studded with papillæ, and with the scent of the peculiar odour of the animal, which is alliaceous.

Manis javanica, Desmarest, (*leucura*, Blyth) inhabits Burmah, and the Malayan peninsula and islands. *M. leptura*, Blyth, is probably African, and there are several other species from that continent.

The Ant-eaters of America, *Myrmecophagidæ*, are clad with long hair, and have long tails, with a very elongated, slender muzzle. The largest species, the Maned Ant-eater, *Myrmecophaga jubata*, is terrestrial. The *Tamandua*, *M. tetradactyla*, L., has the tail naked at the tip and prehensile, and it ascends trees, hanging from the branches. *M. didactyla*, L., is only the size of a rat, and is stated to have undoubted affinities for the Sloths.

The only group of Mammals not previously referred to, is that most remarkable tribe, the Marsupials, MARSUPIALIA, which, with some, constitute a class of nearly equal value with the previous orders, viz., the *Implacentals*. In most of these animals the young are expelled from the uterus at a very early period of their development. Incapable of motion and barely exhibiting the rudiments of limbs and other external organs, these minute offspring attach themselves to the teats of their mother, and remain fixed there until they have acquired a degree of development analogous to that in which other animals are born. The skin of the abdomen is almost

* Proceedings Zool. Soc., 1859, p. 132.

always so disposed round the mammæ as to form a pouch, in which these imperfect young are preserved as in a second uterus; and into which, long after they can walk, they retire for shelter on the apprehension of danger. Two peculiar bones attached to the pubis, and interposed between the muscles of the abdomen, support the pouch and prevent inconvenient pressure of the young, when grown, upon the bowels. These bones are also found in the male, and even in those species in which the fold that forms the pouch is scarcely visible. The matrix of the animals of this order does not open by a single orifice into the extremity of the vagina, but communicates with this canal by two bent lateral tubes. The premature birth of the young appears to depend on this singular organization. The scrotum of the male, contrary to what obtains in other quadrupeds, hangs before the penis, which at rest is directed backwards.

The members of this group are lower in their organization than any other mammiferous animals, approximating the oviparous type, and particularly reptiles, in sundry details of their conformation. The hemispheres of the brain, which is small, are not united by a corpus callosum; and they are observed to be very defective in intelligence, as is indicated by their physiognomy; the blood is returned to their heart by two principal veins as in Birds and Reptiles; and the sutures of the skull never become united. In short, they hold an analogous relation towards other Mammalia to that which the *Batrachia* present to all other reptiles. Their incisor teeth frequently exceed six in number, which is the maximum throughout the rest of their class, another indication of their inferiority.*

Although they all show a general resemblance to each other in this peculiar structure and organization, yet they differ so much in the teeth, digestive organs, feet and external form, that they sub-divide into several distinct families, or sub-orders, which by some are ranged parallel to the orders of Placental Mammals; and they are, by a few, looked on as degraded types of these last, or rather, that their inferiority of type is a sign of their earlier introduction, and that Nature has advanced in organization since the earlier types were formed. The earliest fossil Mammals belong to this order. All are from the Australian region except one group, the Opossums, found in South America, and Central America as far north as Virginia.

* Cuvier's Animal Kingdom, English translation.

Many are exceedingly like the *Insectivora* in the structure of their teeth, but possess a much greater number, and the incisors especially are more numerous than in true placental mammals, being in some cases ten above, and eight below. They possess canines also, and sharply tubercled molars. Such are the Opossums, PERAMELIDÆ, *Perameles*, *Didelphis*, *Myrmecobius*, &c. They mostly possess a small cœcum.

Others with fewer and more powerful teeth represent the *Carnivora*, and these want the cœcum. Such are the DASYURIDÆ, *Dasyurus*, *Thylacinus*, *Sarcophilus*, and others, popularly called Wild Cats, Wolves or Hyænas, and native Devils.

Others have two large and long incisors in the lower jaw, with pointed and trenchant edges sloping forwards, and six corresponding teeth in their upper jaw. The upper canines are long and pointed. Their diet is chiefly frugivorous, and their intestines long, with a large cœcum. Such are the Phalangers and Petaurists, PHALANGISTIDÆ, *Phalangista* and *Petaurus*, &c., which, in spite of their numerous teeth, would in many ways, really appear to represent the Rodents. The Wombat indeed, *Phascolomys*, Fam. PHASCOLOMYIDÆ, is a true Rodent as to its teeth. It has a cœcum with a vermiform appendage.

Some of large size, the Kangaroos, MACROPODIDÆ, *Macropus*, *Halmaturus*, and others, have the stomach complicated, formed of two elongated sacs inflated in places, and the cœcum also large and inflated. They want the upper canines, and the middle incisors are short. Their fore-feet are diminutive, but the hind limbs are much developed, and with a nail like a hoof. They are gentle herbivorous animals, living in troops, and making enormous leaps. They would appear to faintly shadow forth the Ruminants.

Lastly, some want teeth altogether, and were included by Cuvier among the *Edentata*, but are now, by universal consent, placed among Marsupials, as they possess the marsupial bones, though without a pouch. Such are the celebrated Duck-bill, *Ornithorhynchus anatinus*, and the curious Spiny *Echidna*, sometimes placed in a distinct sub-class from Marsupials, viz., *Monotremata*, as they possess only one external opening for all their excretions. In this and other points they somewhat resemble birds, and at one time were thought to be Oviparous, but that is of course erroneous.

APPENDIX.

Page 56, No. 74. Sorex Tytleri.—This is a well-marked species. It is the common musk-rat of Deyra, with a very strong musky odour.

Page 69, No. 89. Ursus isabellinus.—I see that Dr. Gray, in a revision of the species of this family in the Proc. Zool. Socy., keeps *isabellinus* of the Himalayas distinct from *U. syriacus*, as well as from *U. arctos*.

Page 83. Gen. Mustela. Dr. Gray, in a late revision of the family classes the Indian species of *Mustela*, under the genera *Vison* and *Gymnopus*. In the former group, he place 97, *M. hemachalana* and *M. Horsfieldii;* and under *Gymnopus*, *M. kathiah* and *M. strigidorsa*. I may mention here that the first named species, *M. hemachalana*, is called *Kran or Gran*, in Kashmir.

Page 88, No. 101. Lutra Vulgaris.—Dr. Gray makes *L. monticola*, Hodgson, distinct from *vulgaris*, but states that the British Museum specimen, on which he founds this opinion, is in a bad state. He has also another species, Barangia nipalensis, founded on a skull sent as that of Hodgson's *L. monticola*. His genus *Barangia* comprises Otters with hairy muzzle, rather long toes, and rudimentary claws, and is founded on *L. barang* of the Malayan isles.

Gray also indicates, but without any description, *Lutra kutab*, Hügel, from Kashmir, which I regret to say I have not been able to procure, and there is no specimen of it in the British Museum.

Page 89, No. 102. Lutra leptonyx is given by Gray as *Aonyx indigitata*, Hodgson; but he allows that the British Museum specimen is very imperfect.

Page 92. The Lion has quite recently been killed as far east as the Allahabad and Jubbulpore road.

Page 102, No. 107. Felis diardi.—Blyth has recently changed his opinion about this leopard, and now states that he considers the Himalayan race distinct from *F. diardi* vel *macrocelis* of Malayana. It will probably stand as F. nebulosa.

Page 104. F. MARMORATA.—Blyth now is inclined to consider the Himalayan and Assamese race as distinct, but "not strongly specialized apart from marmorata;" in this case, I presume, it will stand either as *F. charltoni*, Gray, or *F. ogilbyi*, Hodgson.

Page 112, No. 115. The dimensions of a fine jungle-cat, *F. chaus*, killed lately at Amballa, are—Total length 39 inches; height 18 inches; weight 18 lbs.

Page 113, No. 116. F. CARACAL.—I am assured that the red lynx occurs in the N. W. Provinces and the Punjab, and that it has been killed near Delhi, Lahore, and other places.

Page 125, No. 123. PARADOXURUS MUSANGA.—Dr. Gray has an elaborate synopsis of this genus and its allies, in the Proc. Zool. Society. He makes the Indian race distinct from the Malayan one, and places it *P. hermaphroditus*, Pallas. He even places *P. prehensilis*, Buch. Hamilton, as distinct, though he allows that he has not seen a specimen. Of the other synonyms, he places *P. Pallasii*, and *P. musangoides*, as synonyms of the Malayan race, which, on very slight grounds, he classes as *P. fasciatus*, Desmarest. He considers *P. Crossii*, from India, and *P. dubius*, from Java, as distinct species; and referring to *P. quadriscriptus* of Hodgson, states that is very like *P. musanga.* I am still inclined to keep my nomenclature.

Page 128, No. 125. P. BONDAR.—Gray gives this as a true *Paradoxurus.* He remarks that it may be known from *P. Grayi* by the rigid harshness of the fur, and the dark color of the outside of the limbs.

Page 128, No. 124.—*P. Grayi.*—This is a *Paguma*, and *P. auratus*, Blainville, is a synonym. The genus *Paguma* is stated to differ from *Paradoxurus* in the form of the flesh-tooth, which is short in *Paguma*, elongate in *Paradoxurus.*

The *Herpestinæ* are placed by Gray quite distinct from the *Paradoxuri*, being more digitigrade, and more nearly related to the *Viverridæ.*

He divides them (Proc. Zool. Soc., 1864) into several genera, *Herpestes*—*Calogale*—*Calictis*—*Tæniogale*—and *Onychogale.* HERPESTES has the tail conical, with long hairs throughout, and the false molars $\frac{3-3}{4-4}$. To this group belong No. 127, HERPESTES GRISEUS; No. 129, HERPESTES MONTICOLUS; and No. 132, H. FUSCUS. In this paper, Gray describes my *H. monticolus* as H. JERDONI, and this name will have the priority. He states that it closely resembles *H. ichneumon* of Egypt. The dimensions of one in the British Museum are—Head and body 19 inches; tail 17.

H. fulvescens of Ceylon, with which I had compared it, belongs to another group, *Onychogale*, distinguished by its long curved claws, and stands now as *O. Maccarthiæ*, Gray.

CALOGALE has the tail long, slender and cylindric, with short hair, long only at the tip, and the false molars $\frac{2-2}{3-3}$. To this belong Nos. 128 and 131, *H. malaccensis* and *nipalensis*. Gray places the former of these as CALOGALE NYULA, making it distinct from the Malacca Mungoos; but he states that there is no specimen from Malayana in the British Museum, so the distinction of the species is still doubtful, I think. These two forms, viz., *Herpestes* and *Calogale*, have the flesh tooth long and narrow. The next two forms have the flesh-tooth broad and triangular.

CALICTIS has the false molars as in Herpestes, viz., $\frac{3-3}{4-4}$, and the tail thick and tapering. To this belongs No. 130, CALICTIS SMITHII, which I see is figured in the Illustrated Proceedings of the Zool. Society for 1851, pl. 31.

TÆNIOGALE is described as having the whiskers small and slender; the soles of the hind feet bald; the orbit complete; and 42 teeth. To this belongs No. 133, TÆNIOGALE VITTICOLLIS apud Gray. Should not TÆNIOGALE give place to *Mungos*, previously proposed for this species?

With reference to *H. thysanurus*, Wagner, from Kashmir, I may state that I have recently again procured a mongoos from the valley of Kashmir, which is decidedly *H. nipalensis*.

Page 141. A black wolf is occasionally seen in Tibet by sportsmen, and it is considered by the natives to be a distinct species. Two young ones, male and female, were brought from Tibet last year by Messrs. Kinloch, Rifle Brigade, and Biddulph, 19th Hussars, and are now on their way home to the Zoological gardens. They are called *Hakpo chanko* by the Tibetans, *i. e.*, the Black Wolf.

Page 185, No. 171. GERBILLUS ERYTHROURUS. I forwarded a skin of this rat to Dr. Gray, British Museum, and he writes me that it is most undoubtedly his *G. erythrourus*, and that the skin I forwarded was the facsimile of the type specimen in the British Museum.

Page 199, No. 180. M. RUFESCENS.—This rat is also *M. decumanoides*, T. apud Horsfield.

Page 314, No. 241. MANIS PENDADACTYLA.—This species is classed by Dr. Gray, in a late synopsis of the family, as PHOLIDOTUS INDICUS, Gray. The genus *Pholidotus* is stated to differ from *Manis* in having the upper part of the fore and hind feet covered with scales to the toes, whilst in *Manis*, as restricted, the fore feet are hairy without scales. The scales of the body too are said to be shorter and broader than in *Manis*.

Page 316. *M. aurita* is placed as PHOLIDOTUS DALMANNI, *Manis Dalmanni*, Sundevall, described from China. Gray states that the skull is stouter and more solid than in the last species, and that the nasal bones are more rounded. He also considers that *Le Pangolin*, figured by Buffon, Vol. X., t. 34, is intended to represent this species, and not the common one.

The following species of Cetacea have been described by Owen from collections made by Walter Elliot, on the East coast, mostly near Vizagapatam.

DELPHINUS GODAMA.

D. LENTIGINOSUS.

D. MACULIVENTER.

D. FUSIFORMIS.

D. POMEEGRA.

PHOCÆNA BREVIROSTRIS.

PHYSETER (EUPHYSETES) SIMUS.

I regret not to be able to furnish descriptions of these.

ENGLISH INDEX.

INDEX.

SYNONYMS ARE IN ITALICS.

B.

C.

D.

E.

T

FINIS.